Quality Management
with SAP R/3

Quality Management with SAP R/3

Making it work for your business

Michael Hölzer and Michael Schramm

Addison-Wesley

an imprint of **Pearson Education**

Harlow, England • London • New York • Reading, Massachusetts • San Francisco • Toronto • Don Mills, Ontario •
Sydney • Tokyo • Singapore • Hong Kong • Seoul • Taipei • Cape Town • Madrid • Mexico City • Amsterdam •
Munich • Paris • Milan

PEARSON EDUCATION LIMITED

Head Office:
Edinburgh Gate
Harlow
Essex CM20 2JE
Tel: +44 (0)1279 623623
Fax: +44 (0)1279 431059
Website: www.aw.com/cseng

London Office:
128 Long Acre
London WC2E 9AN
Tel: +44 (0)20 7447 2000
Fax: +44 (0)20 7240 5771

First published in Great Britain in 2001

© Galileo Press GmbH 2001

The rights of Michael Hölzer and Michael Schramm to be identified as Authors of this Work have been
asserted by them in accordance with the Copyright, Designs and Patents Act 1988.

ISBN 0-201-67531-5

British Library Cataloguing in Publication Data
A CIP catalogue record for this book can be obtained from the British Library

Library of Congress Cataloging in Publication Data
Applied for.

The programs in this book have been included for their instructional value. The publisher does not offer any
warranties or representations in respect of their fitness for a particular purpose, nor does the publisher
accept any liability for any loss or damage arising from their use.

Many of the designations used by manufacturers and sellers to distinguish their products are claimed as
trademarks. Pearson Education Limited has made every attempt to supply trademark information about
manufacturers and their products mentioned in this book. A list of trademark designations and their owners
appears on this page.

Trademark Notice
Excel, MS Windows, MS Explorer, MS SQL Server, MS Project, MS Word and MS Internet Explorer are
trademarks of the Microsoft Corporation; UNIX is licensed through X/Open Company Ltd (Collaboration
of Novell, HP and SCO); Oracle is a trademark of the Oracle Corporation; Adobe and Acrobat Reader are
trademarks of Adobe Systems Inc.; Netscape is a trademark of Netscape Communications Corporation;
CorelDraw is a trademark of Corel Corporation; SAP, SAP R/3, ABAP, ASAP and mySAP are trademarks of
SAP AG.

10 9 8 7 6 5 4 3 2 1

Designed by Claire Brodmann, Book Designs.
Typeset by M Rules, London, UK.
Printed and bound in Great Britain by Biddles Ltd.

The Publishers' policy is to use paper manufactured from sustainable forests.

Contents

| **7** | **QUALITY INSPECTION** | **200** |

| **8** | **QUALITY CONTROL** | **242** |

Foreword

This book deals with the functions of Quality Management in SAP R/3 in the core processes of logistics: Purchasing, Production, Sales and Distribution, and Service. As the Quality Management module is embedded in the individual processes, not only the components themselves but also the interfaces and contact points to other components are explained.

Building on the quality-relevant master data of the material and the basic data of the Quality Management module, we describe the processes of inspection planning, inspection lot creation and inspection lot completion. Furthermore, the quality notification, test equipment management and many other topics of significance are discussed in detail. The various functions are clearly described, illustrated with examples, scenarios and screenshots.

The basis of our descriptions and source of the screenshots is the R/3 Release 4.5B, whereby the preceding versions 3.1 and 4.0 are taken into account in the discussion. Most of the examples were created using the IDES training system from SAP, Release 4.5B.

The book is directed at all readers interested in Quality Management with SAP R/3, whether you are already working with R/3 or planning to switch to R/3. It addresses users, implementation project managers, quality managers and staff, consultants for the implementation of R/3 and/or for the Quality Management module of R/3, and all those who wish to further their careers with profound specialist knowledge.

The idea for the book came about during a joint implementation project for the Quality Management module. The successful cooperation and the fact that there has so far been hardly any literature dealing with this subject led to this joint project.

The authors have both been able to gather 10 years of experience in quality management. The practical experience of SAP consulting, the experience in implementation of the Quality Management module in companies, the know-how from operative quality management and as R/3 users form an ideal combination that will be particularly informative and interesting for readers.

Michael Hölzer
Michael Schramm
Ulm, January 2000

Acknowledgements

Schwarz, Professor Spruth & Associates GmbH has provided us with generous technical and expert support in this book project.

We would like to express our special thanks to the Tally Computerdrucker GmbH and SAP AG for their support, for the documents and the technical information provided for our book.

We would also like to thank T. Wehren, S. Ludwig and A. Schramm for proofreading, tips and support for the graphics.

Michael Hölzer
Michael Schramm
Ulm, January 2000

Introduction

This chapter explains how this book is structured and the best way for you to benefit from it. It describes the target group this book is aimed at, provides a brief overview of the other chapters, and explains how the various chapters are related.

TARGET GROUPS

The book is aimed at all those who are interested in how SAP R/3 supports quality management. It is suitable for first-time R/3 users, for those switching from old systems or from R/2, as well as for experienced R/3 users who want to extend their existing system to include the Quality Management (QM) module or want to use it productively. Consultants who deal with other modules can obtain an overview of the functions of the QM module and consultants who deal with the QM module will find that this book contains valuable tips to help them with their work.

It is assumed that the reader is familiar with the basic terms and processes from the general field of quality management and has the usual knowledge of a PC system with menu-guided applications.

TOPICS COVERED

Although the topic of quality management – including quality planning, quality inspection and quality control – is the central focus of the book, the points at which QM interfaces with the other components of the SAP R/3 system and the business processes in which quality management plays an important role are also described in detail. You will receive information on how you can map your quality management system using R/3, as well as how you can structure and describe your business processes. Even though the important functions 'Vendor evaluation' and 'Test equipment monitoring' are part of other R/3 modules, they are closely related to Quality Management and are also explained in detail here.

TIP Information that might, under certain circumstances, be of particular importance to you is indicated in this way. Sometimes, this is a matter of pointing out awkwardly located or hidden menus, giving suggestions for the mapping of your processes or alternative implementation options if no direct solution is provided by R/3. The tips are drawn from the practical experience of the authors, and have helped to solve quite a few problems. The tips are mainly intended for users.

CUSTOMIZING TIP

In contrast to the above target group, these items concern specialists who are able to change the Customizing settings. Otherwise, they have the same aim as mentioned under 'normal' tips: important recommendations from the authors' practical experience have been marked in this way so that the most elegant and fastest implementation option can be applied to your processes.

STRUCTURE OF THE BOOK

The book is structured in such a way that not all the chapters have to be read through in order. It is recommended, of course, to start with this chapter, the introduction.

Those who have so far had little to do with SAP software should certainly read Chapter 3, 'R/3 overview'. However, even those who have already used the software will find some interesting information there.

Chapter 5, 'Quality management in the logistics chain', is intended to provide a taste of Chapters 6, 7 and 8.

The topics covered in Chapters 6, 7 and 8, 'Quality and inspection planning', 'Quality inspection' and 'Quality control', are related. It is therefore recommended that you read these as a group.

Most of the other chapters can be read independently of one another.

CONTENTS OF THE CHAPTERS IN BRIEF

Chapter 1, 'Management systems, standards and SAP R/3': the structuring of a quality management system is usually based on standards. Various standards and developments are explained; the ISO 9001 standard is the basis for detailed explanation of the demands made by the elements of this standard and the possibilities for implementing them in SAP R/3.

Chapter 2, 'Modeling QM business processes using the EPC method': you are provided with information on how you can map your business processes, with special consideration to quality management using the R/3 system. Event-controlled process chains (EPCs) are presented as a suitable tool for modeling and description of processes; their application is illustrated using examples.

Chapter 3, 'R/3 overview': this chapter provides you with an overview of the company SAP AG. The R/3 system and its modules are described insofar as this is required to explain the interplay with the Quality Management module. The structure of typical SAP workstations is mentioned, as is the organization of the implementation project, the transfer of data from legacy systems, or the interfaces to external systems.

Chapter 4, 'Operation of R/3': this chapter contains a basic introduction to the operation of the R/3 interface. It is mainly aimed at less experienced users and first-time users in R/3. The explanations are of a general nature and they concern all the modules, but the examples and screenshots have mostly been taken from the QM module.

Chapter 5, 'Quality management in the logistics chain': this chapter represents a kind of introduction to the central chapters 'Quality planning', 'Quality inspection' and 'Quality control'. It shows how quality management is present in each step of the logistics processes and is, so to speak, the thread that passes through the logistics chain. Study of this chapter makes it easier to understand the overall content of the next three chapters.

Chapter 6, 'Quality and inspection planning': this is the first of the three central chapters on quality management using R/3. It contains explanations of the required base and master data, the various plan types – routing, inspection plan and reference operation set – and the relevant catalogs. The creation and function of sampling procedures, sample plans and the dynamic modification rules are explained. Control cards and batch inspections are included here. The applications in Materials Management, in Production, and in Sales and Distribution provide you with a clear link to practical use.

Chapter 7, 'Quality inspection': this chapter describes how you can create inspection lots and perform planned (but also unplanned) inspections. You will find out how you can implement your inspection strategy using the QM module. Based on practical examples, the quality inspections are run and the special features of Materials Management, Production, and Sales and Distribution are emphasized.

Chapter 8, 'Quality control': this chapter shows various possibilities for initiating and tracing management and improvement measures using the Quality Management module. First, the usage decision, which functions not only as the conclusion of the quality inspection but also involves the short-term management measures such as sorting or reworking, is described in detail. A central topic in this chapter is vendor evaluation. It can be used to form ranking lists of vendors, which have been evaluated according to various criteria, or to plan tasks for quality improvement, or to evaluate their success retrospectively. In addition, the tools 'Quality level', 'Dynamic modification' and 'Statistical process control', as well as the recording of quality costs, are explained in detail.

Chapter 9, 'Quality notification': this chapter provides you with a precise description of how this excellent tool can be best used in your company. With quality notifications, not only can information be transferred or archived, but also activities and measures can be planned and monitored. Convenient evaluation options can be applied to use the data from quality notifications in the long term.

Chapter 10, 'Information systems and evaluations': one strength of the R/3 system is the wide variety of evaluation options using the various information systems. This chapter provides you with an overview and a small introduction into the comprehensive options for calling up and processing data.

Chapter 11, 'Test equipment management': test equipment is of great importance for the planning and performance of inspections as well as for compliance with the requirements of the quality standard. Thus the possible solutions for the management of test equipment as well as planning and documenting calibration using the R/3 system are presented here.

Chapter 12, 'Internet scenarios with SAP R/3 QM': this chapter is devoted to the increasing significance of the 'network of all networks', namely the internet. Today, the internet is already a tool that many companies cannot afford to ignore. The possibilities for using the internet provided by the R/3 system, and how quality management in particular can profit from it, are described in this chapter.

Chapter 13, 'Customizing': Customizing is the menu-guided adaptation of the R/3 system to your company. Although this chapter is not to be viewed as a course in Customizing, it nonetheless provides you with some insight into how you make the desired settings when adapting your R/3 system. Knowledge of this topic is not strictly essential, but the content provided here will help you towards a better understanding of the R/3 system and its customizing options.

Chapter 14, 'Migration concepts': if another IT system was used prior to implementation of the R/3 system, or if an existing CAQ (Computer Aided Quality Assurance) system is being replaced by the Quality Management component of the R/3 system, the question of consistent data transfer arises. This is also termed migration. This chapter provides you with valuable information on how to plan data transfer of this kind and what to bear in mind in the process.

Chapter 15, 'ASAP (AcceleratedSAP)': due to the time pressures and high costs generated by a long implementation phase, SAP AG has developed and compiled processes and methods that you can use to reduce the overhead involved in an implementation. This chapter describes what you can expect from this accelerated implementation and how your company can achieve the target of a productive start on the 'ASAP Roadmap'.

Appendix A, 'Glossary': a comprehensive glossary explains terms and expressions from quality management in general, from the R/3 system, and the Quality Management module in particular.

Appendix B, 'Abbreviations': a detailed list of abbreviations provides rapid assistance in understanding the abbreviations used in this book and in the R/3 help texts. The abbreviations for the modules can be found in Chapter 3, 'R/3 Overview'.

Appendix C, 'Bibliography': here you can see the sources we have used, or you can get hold of literature that will provide more information on the individual topics covered.

CHAPTER 1

Management systems, standards and SAP R/3

Until a few years ago, only a small number of industrial companies, mainly in the automobile industry, had introduced and documented a quality management system and applied for the appropriate certification. This has now become standard practice: the number of companies that use a quality management system has grown considerably. The example set by industry was followed by construction companies, the retail and wholesale trade, service companies, hospitals and other care institutions, the trades and finally state authorities who obtained certification in accordance with ISO 9001–9003.

Nowadays most people refer to management systems, as quality management was just the beginning. An increasing number of companies have obtained certification for their environment management in accordance with the Eco Audit directive (EU) No. 1836/93 or ISO 14001. These are supplemented by standards covering work safety that are integrated into a joint management system.

The development of ISO 9001 into ISO 9001:2000 is opening the path towards process management, in which all the business processes are described. An important aim of the revision of the standard is to replace the twenty elements used to date with a process-oriented management model that can be used practically in companies. Consistent process organization supports the development of an organization and improves its competitiveness (cf. Taucher 1999, p. 1197). Recommendations from ISO 9004 are being adopted into ISO 9001:2000. The strong orientation towards processes

The Process Model

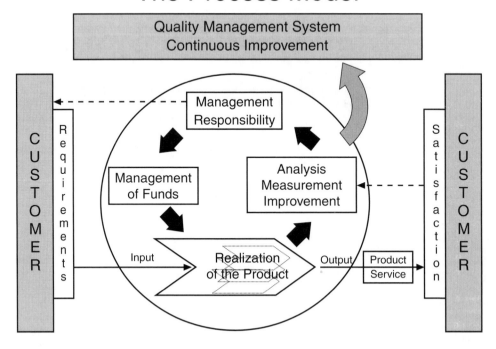

FIGURE 1.1 The process model of ISO 9001:2000 (draft, May 1999)

relevant to quality is to a certain extent making way for a holistic view of process flows and business processes (Fig. 1.1). This favours implementation of SAP R/3 to a great degree, as its quality management is tightly integrated in the core logistic processes.

1.1 BASIC PRINCIPLES

A quality management system (QM system) itself cannot be standardized, as the demands placed on companies and products vary from one case to the next; only a model for mapping a quality management system has been standardized. This is supplemented by less binding guidelines for setting up a QM system and also by minimum requirements for such a system.

As early as the 1950s, initially in the USA, the need was recognized to create a set of rules for quality management. This development was driven by the high quality standards in the military field and the construction of nuclear power stations. These rules took concrete shape when the MIL Q 9858 standard appeared in 1963; this was then developed in the early 1970s into a set of NATO rules: AQAP (Allied Quality Assurance Publications). In the automobile industry, the best known was the Q101 guideline for quality assurance systems published by Ford in 1990.

In the 1980s, an increasing variety of country-specific and industry-specific sets of rules came about, which motivated the ISO committee (International Standardization Organization) to develop a uniform and globally applicable standard. This appeared in 1987 and was adopted by most ISO member countries. In the meantime, this standard, comprising the series of standards ISO 9000–9004, has become known everywhere; following European harmonization and its implementation as a national standard, it is called DIN EN ISO 9000–9004.

In spite of the harmonizing and still dominant influence of the ISO 9000ff series of standards, specific sets of rules have survived and developed. The military standard AQAP still exists, but the requirements of the ISO 9000ff series of standards have been integrated into it. Using Q 101 as a starting point and incorporating ISO 9000ff, the American automobile industry has developed the QS 9000 set of rules which goes beyond the requirements of the ISO 9000 series. The German automobile industry has developed a comparable standard in the form of the updated VDA (Verband der deutschen Automobilindustrie – Association of the German Automobile Industry) set of rules. The new quality standard ISO TS 16949 attempts to group multiple certification in accordance with QS 9000 and VDA 6.1 into a joint standard (cf. Hake et al. 1999, pp. 1244 ff). This would make things considerably easier for suppliers. The future will show whether it will succeed or whether an additional standard will simply add to the complexity of the situation.

In order to prove to third parties that you adhere to one of these sets of rules, you can obtain certification from an accredited association. This is possible, for example, in accordance with the standards ISO 9001, 9002 or 9003, VDA 6 or QS 9000.

One thing that all the sets of rules have in common is verification of the existence of certain elements and the documentation of procedures and processes. This is where the advantage in using the SAP R/3 system comes into play. It supports your QM system in the entire logistics chain. It helps you in setting up and maintaining a QM system in your company, and it takes on numerous tasks in mapping the QM system in accordance with the relevant standards. As SAP R/3 is an integrated system, it is highly suitable for supporting the entire QM system with its various business processes.

The management system is not the sole preserve of the quality department: the entire management works on maintaining and improving the system. The support of the management system provided by SAP R/3 is thus not restricted to the Quality Management module of R/3 but rather is fully integrated into the overall R/3 system, in the same way as the QM system is integrated in the overall company process (Fig. 1.2).

No matter whether you have already introduced a quality management system or are only planning to do so, you will certainly profit from implementing your processes with R/3. If you have already set up a QM system in your company, it will be easier for

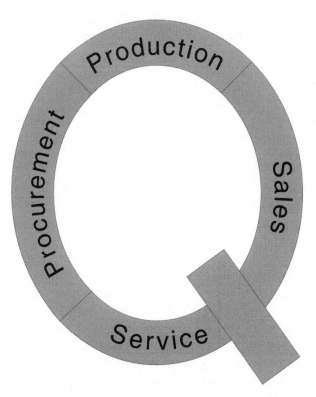

FIGURE 1.2   Integration of the QM system in the logistics chain (© SAP AG)

you to describe the business processes for the SAP implementation, as you can fall back on the existing QM manual and process instructions. Interfaces are already defined and described there, which means that your SAP consultant will find a better initial basis than if he or she first has to 'tease out' all the information. However, after the SAP implementation, do not forget to work in the changes that have become necessary to your processes (which will come about automatically) into the QM manual and the process instructions.

If you are planning to set up a quality management system only after the SAP implementation, the SAP system provides you with various support options. This is not intended to create the impression that the implementation of the SAP system is a substitute for setting up a QM system, though it does supplement and facilitate it. If the requirements to be met by a QM system are taken into account during the implementation of SAP, a great deal of additional work can be avoided later. For example, the flow of your business processes (and their mapping, for example with the EPC method) can be adopted without further ado into your QM manual or your process instructions (see also Chapter 2, 'Modeling QM business processes using the EPC method').

TABLE 1.1   Relationship between elements and R/3 modules

Elements	Modules								
	QM	PM	SD	HR	MM	PP	PS	CO	CA
4.1	X	X		X				X	X
4.2	X					X	X		X
4.3			X		X				X
4.4						X	X		X
4.5									X
4.6	X					X	X		
4.7	X	X			X				
4.8	X				X				
4.9		X				X			X
4.10	X								
4.11	X	X				X			
4.12	X								X
4.13	X								
4.14	X	X							
4.15			X		X				
4.16	X				X				
4.17	X								X
4.18				X				X	
4.19	X	X							
4.20	X								X

1.2   QUALITY ELEMENTS

In illustrating the possibilities for implementing the ISO elements by means of the SAP R/3 system, we will limit ourselves to the quality elements of the ISO 9001 standard. Corresponding implementation possibilities can be found for the QS 9000 and VDA 6 sets of rules.

Table 1.1 provides an overview of the relationship between the ISO elements and the modules in the SAP R/3 system. Table 1.2 shows in more detail how you can implement the appropriate element and where several modules might be affected.

The element numbers specified in Table 1.1 are given in Table 1.2 with their full description. The abbreviations of the R/3 modules can be found in Chapter 3; the descriptions are not repeated here.

| TABLE 1.2 | Elements of ISO 9001 and implementation options with SAP R/3 |

Element	Standard requirement (abbreviated)	Implementation option with R/3
4.1	**Management responsibility** Organization: responsibility and authority must be specified and documented – Funds must be provided – QM evaluation must be performed.	The implementation of SAP R/3, the deployment of the required modules, the responsibilities for the processes within the modules and the user authorizations concept mean that many requirements are met directly. The information systems of R/3 provide access to virtually all facts you require for a QM evaluation.
4.2	**Quality system** Implementation and documentation of the QMS – Creation of QM process instructions – Quality planning for the QM system with QM plans.	With the implementation of a complete SAP R/3 system, and the QM module in particular, you have introduced most of the QM system. The documentation of your R/3 implementation, which is required one way or another, can be done in such a way that it is also the documentation of your QM system, or can be used in part to create this documentation. If you use the EPC method to document your R/3 implementation (see Chapter 2), these process descriptions can be adopted directly into the process instructions and QM plans.
4.3	**Contract review** Checking the requirements and the capability to meet them – Administration of contract changes – Records.	This element is supported by your R/3 system in various modules. The documentation management can be used to manage contracts; the material master data allows checks of part of the requirements; production planning and warehouse management are used to check capability; the change management with the change master record (date, edited by, etc.) enables administration of contract changes and the overall system records all administration data. In addition, you can use the 'comments' fields in various transactions and the 'Notification' tool to create or supplement records.
4.4	**Design control** Design and development planning – Specifying organizational and technical interfaces – Establishing and documenting design specifications – Verifying the design result and validating with planned inspections and documented results – Documenting design changes.	Although there is no module that deals specifically with design or development, the requirements can still be covered to a great extent by other components. The Project System (PS) module can be used to plan a development project. The organizational and technical interfaces are located at different points in R/3 and have to be specified and described there. In a company that both develops and produces, important interfaces include Purchasing (MM) and Production (PP). Design specifications affect the material master data (e.g. the purchasing order text), the requirements for vendor selection and the goods receipt inspection. The QM module is very well suited to verification, inspection planning and inspection documentation. Changes that affect the interfaces of the design department (e.g. in the material master data, bills of material) are fully documented by the R/3 system (engineering change management, information systems, document management system).

TABLE 1.2	*continued*

Element	Standard requirement (abbreviated)	Implementation option with R/3
4.5	**Document and data control** Approval, inspection and release of and changes to documents and data by authorized personnel and with suitable verification.	The entire R/3 system is configured in such a way that this requirement is met. Every time a document or data is created or changed (if handled using R/3), it is recorded with the user name, date and time. This makes suitable verification possible at any time. The release following the inspection is implemented by means of a status concept and the suitable personnel are defined using the user authorizations concept and the responsibility given for certain processes. Special user authorizations are implemented using the digital signature.
4.6	**Purchasing** The subcontractor must be assessed – Type and scope of monitoring must be specified dependent on the product type – Quality-related records must be created – Purchasing data must be accurate.	R/3 also provides full support here. The vendor evaluation can be used to gain information on the status of your subcontractors at any time. Suggested criteria enable not only a quality assessment but also the assessment of adherence to quantities and deadlines – for all supplied materials or only for specific materials. You can define regulations for each vendor as regards their QM system or manage the existence of that system. The purchasing information is all available in the system (e.g. material master data, purchasing information record, vendor information record, Q information record, etc.) and it can be used for the order, for goods receipt or the goods receipt inspection.
4.7	**Control of customer-supplied product** Verification and storage of the products.	Verification can be achieved using R/3, e.g. by means of a goods receipt inspection or certificate query. Warehouse management from R/3 can be used for storage.
4.8	**Product identification and traceability** Identification of the product during all phases of production, delivery and assembly. Also, identification of an individual product or a batch if required.	As regards identification, R/3 allows you to be very flexible and to meet standard requirements. In every phase, you can print out the corresponding papers for identification and enclose them with the goods, e.g. the goods receipt on arrival, the manufacturing order in production or the delivery note and the inspection certificate on delivery. You have the possibility of printing labels, where required with bar code. R/3 also supports the administration of physical samples and batches. A serial number administration also enables tracing of individual products.
4.9	**Process control** Production, assembly and maintenance processes must be identified and planned.	Routings provide you with the best way of planning your production and assembly processes. You can specify the methods of production and maintenance, including the associated production resources or consumables. The Service Module (SM) and the module for preventative Plant Maintenance (PM) enable you to plan the maintenance of your products and manufacturing facilities.

TABLE 1.2	*continued*

Element	Standard requirement (abbreviated)	Implementation option with R/3
4.10	**Inspection and testing** Goods receipt inspection – Intermediate inspection – Final inspection, corresponding to the specified quality requirements. Inspection records must be created.	The functions 'Inspection planning', 'Inspection with results recording' and 'Quality control' from the R/3 QM module can be used to meet all requirements. Goods receipt inspections can be triggered automatically or manually, enclosed inspection certificates can be managed, intermediate and final inspections in production can be specified or, if required, inspections can be initiated automatically prior to delivery. All inspection results are saved in the database, which provides numerous evaluation options.
4.11	**Control of inspection measuring and test equipment** Test equipment must be released and monitored at regular intervals if required to meet the quality requirements. Records of this monitoring must be kept.	The combined possibilities of the PM and QM modules of your R/3 system enable complete test equipment monitoring. This comprises the master records of each item of test equipment, the status (blocked, free, etc.), the administration (who has which item of test equipment where) and the calibration monitoring, which ensures that each item of test equipment subject to monitoring is regularly recalibrated on the basis of a maintenance plan. As usual, all the data on test equipment monitoring is kept in the system database and is available as information or for further evaluation. However, the integration of an existing subsystem for test equipment monitoring is possible; this then communicates with the R/3 system across a specified interface.
4.12	**Inspection and test status** The inspection status of a product must be identified and preserved everywhere in assembly, production and maintenance.	In the R/3 system, the inspection status can be seen at any time from the status of the material or feedback on the procedure. The identification at the product itself can, where required, be supported by printouts of the relevant work papers. The system can also be set in such a way that no product can be shipped without previous feedback of the prescribed inspection results and before a usage decision has been made.
4.13	**Control of nonconforming product** Authority must be specified – Evaluation for reworking, special release, scrapping must take place – Defect description must be recorded – Re-inspection after rework.	You will find the tools to meet these requirements mainly in the QM module. Authority is handled in the user authorizations concept. Here, too, the digital signature provides ways of ensuring authority. The evaluation takes place at the same time as the assessment of the inspection results and the usage decision. For defect description, you have the inspection comment, the defect code, various long texts and finally the quality notification – re-inspection can be ensured via the automatic inspection lot generation.

TABLE 1.2	*continued*

Element	Standard requirement (abbreviated)	Implementation option with R/3
4.14	**Corrective and preventive action** Corrective measures must include: Customer complaints – Analysis and recording – Specification and monitoring. Preventive measures must include: Sources of information on processes, quality records – Specification of steps – Monitoring – Presentation of information for QM evaluation.	The QM and PP modules in particular contain direct implementation of these requirements. The defect recording for inspection results and the usage decision can be used to set up and monitor corrective and preventive measures directly. You can work with your own catalogs for these measures or use free texts and quality notifications to initiate, time and monitor individual measures or actions. Intermediate and final inspections in the production process provide you with all the required information and Q records. Customer complaints can be recorded using the quality notification; they can be assigned measures and pursued further. Your R/3 system can inform you at any time about all measures, steps and their processing status, and provide information for a QM evaluation.
4.15	**Handling, storage, packaging, preservation and delivery** Suitable methods and processes for the handling, storage, preservation and shipping must be applied.	You can use the components Materials Management, Warehouse Management and Sales and Distribution to configure your system to these requirements of the standard. You can also describe in detail in the long text at any time the methods and processes that need special attention at certain stages in the manufacturing process, for example in routings or inspection plans.
4.16	**Control of quality records** Q records must be created and stored; they must also be in a readable form that can be evaluated.	The input of inspection results and usage decisions in the R/3 system meets the requirements for this element. The periods of preservation can be specified in the rules for data backup. The standard system provides a broad selection of evaluations (e.g. the quality information system). You can generate individually tailored reports or import the data into, for example, a spreadsheet program and evaluate it there.
4.17	**Internal quality audits** There must be a check as to whether the quality-related activities meet the specifications – Internal Q audits must be laid down in a plan – The results must be recorded.	This element is supported indirectly by SAP R/3 in that it is easy to call up the required information on quality-related activities. The internal quality notification is ideal for documenting and monitoring measures arising from the internal audits.
4.18	**Training** The training requirement must be determined, necessary qualifications obtained and records on the status of training must be kept.	The requirement for recording the status of training can be met using the HR module (Human Resources Management). There, you can manage the corresponding information on each employee.
4.19	**Servicing** Where this is a requirement, performance and inspection must be proven.	The Service module can be used to map the process of maintenance and specify how it is to be performed. The required inspections are ensured and evidenced by the corresponding inspection plans.

TABLE 1.2	*continued*	
Element	**Standard requirement (abbreviated)**	**Implementation option with R/3**
4.20	**Statistical techniques** The requirement for statistical methods for monitoring process efficiency and product characteristics must be determined and the application must be preserved.	The QM module of R/3 provides the most common statistical evaluation options; these should normally be adequate. You can determine the process efficiency, mean value and standard deviation, analyse them in graphic form, create control charts and control processes with SPC. If you wish to apply special statistical methods, you can exchange the relevant data across an interface with an external system and process it there.

We have only selected a few of the most important standard requirements. A complete analysis of the text of the standard with all requirements would go far beyond the scope of this discussion.

1.3 DOCUMENTATION OF THE QM SYSTEM

The SAP R/3 document management system (DMS) provides you with a suitable means of documenting your QM system.

The DMS can be adapted to your requirements when customizing. You can save the original documents in the R/3 system or file them on your PC systems and only manage them in R/3. For each document, you can record the following data, for example:

- Document number (various options possible).
- Changes (freely definable).
- Storage location (also in external computer systems).
- Processing status.
- Other administration data.

You can therefore use this tool to manage and store your QM manual, process instructions, work instructions, quality assurance agreements, as well as all other documents related to your QM system. A user authorizations facility enables you to set who can view documents and who is allowed to edit them. In this way, each authorized user can obtain information on the current status of the documentation of your QM system. This also eliminates the problem of informing all those concerned about, for example, a new process instruction, as each current status can be found on the system.

Furthermore, you can link various documents with bills of material, define documents as production resources and thus assign them to routings or inspection plans, and link documents with other SAP objects, e.g. the material master record etc. With integration into the SAP workflow, you are provided with other possibilities to trigger follow-on actions.

You reach the document management system by the path:

LOGISTICS | CENTRAL FUNCTIONS | DOCUMENT MANAGEMENT

1.4   THE QM INFORMATION SYSTEM

As shown in item 4.2, Quality System, in Table 1.2, the standard frequently requires the recording and documentation of inspections and inspection results. Everything you enter in or confirm to the R/3 system is available to you for this verification. The R/3 information systems enable you to find this data quickly and analyse it further. These are described in Chapter 10, 'Information systems and evaluations'. One of these information systems is the Quality Management Information System (Fig. 1.3), which can be reached by the path:

LOGISTICS | QUALITY MANAGEMENT | INFORMATION SYSTEM

There you will find numerous analyses and evaluation options that will help you with quality planning and the evaluation of your quality management system.

1.5   ENVIRONMENT MANAGEMENT

The increased sensitivity of companies and customers regarding environmental problems has meant that environment management has gained in importance. In modern companies, environmental protection has become a strategic objective that can be pursued by introducing environment management systems.

The directive (EU) No. 1836/93 and ISO 14001:1996 created a joint system for environment management and for an environment audit that companies can take part in on a voluntary basis.

As already mentioned at the beginning of this chapter, the various management systems are increasingly merging; this development can be seen very clearly from the

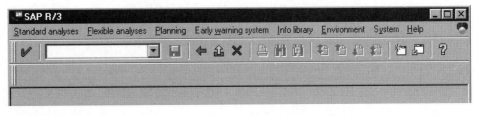

FIGURE 1.3   Menu of the Quality Management Information System (© SAP AG)

example of environment management systems. Many companies create a separate environment management manual for certification in accordance with the Eco directive; this has to be maintained parallel to the QM manual. These days, a joint management manual is preferred. The stronger orientation towards processes, as is envisaged by the revision of the quality management standard ISO 9001:2000, further promotes this development.

ISO 14001 in particular refers expressly to the joint principles of the standard series ISO 9000ff as regards management systems. Any existing system that complies with the ISO 9000 series can be extended to include environment management, with the application of the various elements being adapted in each case.

This means that the statements made in the previous sections on quality management also apply to environment management. A great deal of information regarding the implementation of the elements in Tables 1.1 and 1.2 applies accordingly to the elements of ISO 14001. In part, the elements even have the same or similar descriptions, for example 'Management of the documents' or 'Corrective and preventive measures'. A more precise correspondence of the ISO 14001 elements to those of ISO 9001 can be found in Table 1.3. With this as a starting point, you can use Table 1.2 to relate this information to the modules of the R/3 system. As you can see, you are well supported by SAP R/3 in the implementation of your environment management system.

Over and above the general support for the 150 elements, the R/3 system provides concrete components for environment management, which can be found by the path LOGISTICS | MATERIALS MANAGEMENT | ENVIRONMENT MANAGEMENT. It covers the area of Environment, Health & Safety (or EH&S). There are also two submenus: PRODUCT SAFETY and DANGEROUS GOODS MANAGEMENT.

SAP has integrated environmental protection in the R/3 system by means of its environment management (Fig. 1.4): this link enables a view of the entire life cycle of products, materials, wastes and residual substances in a company. The aspects of

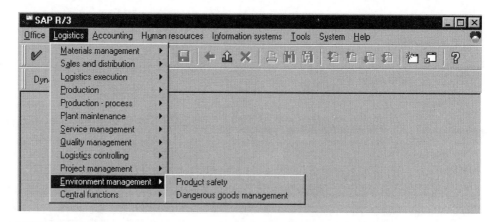

FIGURE 1.4 Menu structure for environment management (© SAP AG)

| TABLE 1.3 | Corresponding features of ISO 14001 and ISO 9001 |

ISO 14001:1996		ISO 9001:1994	
General requirements	4.1	4.2.1	General
Environmental policy	4.2	4.1.1	Quality policy
Planning			
Environmental aspects	4.3.1	–	
Legal and other requirements	4.3.2	–	
Objectives and targets	4.3.3	4.1.1	Quality policy – Objectives
Environment management programme(s)	4.3.4	–	
	–	4.2.3	Quality planning (for QM system)
Implementation and operation			
Structure and responsibility	4.4.1	4.1.2	Organization
Training, awareness and competence	4.4.2	4.18	Training
Communication	4.4.3	–	
Environment management system documentation	4.4.4	4.2.1	General
Documentation control	4.4.5	4.5	Documentation and data control
Operational control	4.4.6	4.2.2	Quality system procedures
	4.4.6	4.3	Contract review
	4.4.6	4.4	Design control
	4.4.6	4.6	Purchasing
	4.4.6	4.7	Control of customer-supplied product
	4.4.6	4.9	Process control
	4.4.6	4.15	Handling, storage, packaging, preservation and delivery
	4.4.6	4.19	Servicing
	–	4.8	Product identification and traceability
Emergency preparedness and response	4.4.7	–	
Checking and corrective action			
Monitoring and measurement	4.5.1	4.10	Inspection and testing
	–	4.12	Inspection and test status
	–	4.20	Statistical techniques
Monitoring and measurement	4.5.1	4.11	Control of inspection, measurement and test equipment
Nonconformance and corrective and preventive action	4.5.2	4.13	Control of nonconforming product
	4.5.2	4.14	Corrective and preventive action
Records	4.5.3	4.16	Control of quality records
Environment management system audit	4.5.4	4.17	Internal quality audits
Management review	4.6	4.1.3	Management review

product safety, waste and emissions management as well as work safety are integrated in the processes of the overall logistic chain.

Product safety

The R/3 part component 'Product safety' provides you with an environmental data system that you can use to manage all the environmentally relevant information regarding pure substances, preparations, mixes and residual substances. These are listed under the general term 'substances' (Fig. 1.5).

The system provides the following functions for the management of substance data:

- Substance database
  The data for the substances is managed here. This includes substance identifications, material assignments, compositions, substance lists and substance characteristics.

- Literature source management
  This ensures low recording and maintenance overhead of literature sources and enables you to define these at a central point.

- Phrase management
  Standard texts can be managed in catalogs and adopted into reports with a minimum of effort.

Another function of the environmental data system is the substance report. This is generated from report templates and data from the substance database and can then be managed and shipped automatically. When a substance report is created in shipping management, shipping data can be added to it.

Examples of substance reports are safety data sheets, accident information sheets, labels and product descriptions.

Dangerous goods management

The part component 'Dangerous goods management' can perform the following tasks for you:

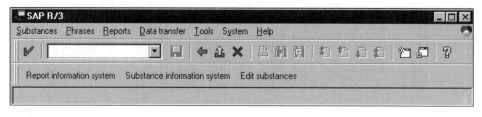

| FIGURE 1.5 | Submenu Product Safety (© SAP AG)

- Record material data relevant to dangerous goods (dangerous goods material master record).

- Define dangerous goods inspections and run them in distribution.

- Define dangerous goods transport papers and output them automatically or manually.

As these part components work in conjunction with the other components Sales and Distribution (SD), Materials Management (MM) and SAPscript, they should naturally also be used on your system.

1.6   A VIEW TO THE FUTURE

Management systems will continue to develop. In the case of the EFQM (European Foundation for Quality Management) model (Fig. 1.6) and ISO 9001:2000, the ideas behind business processes and integrated processes now dominate more than ever before. As the R/3 is a process-oriented system, support for these advanced systems should not be a problem in the future.

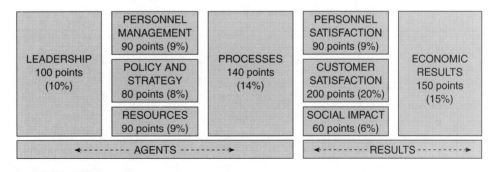

FIGURE 1.6   EFQM model (© SAP AG)

CHAPTER 2

Modeling QM business processes using the EPC method

BASIC PRINCIPLES

At the start of an SAP R/3 QM project, there are not only a virtually unmanageable variety of functions but also recurring core questions on each business event. Where is the organizational delineation? Who performs which tasks with what system support? How are the various R/3 components used? How are forms structured? The immediate result of these many questions is a new question: how can business processes be described, structured and made visible in the simplest possible way? With a view to adequate project stability, all these questions require precise answers. As a rule, the pure text form, if it is to be meaningful, is too complicated and consumes too much time. Moreover, a written description of the various relationships appears confusing, is frequently difficult to read and thus is liable to sink in the remaining profusion of project documentation.

The solution, which has surely occurred to you by now, seems at first glance to be quite simple – we map our business events not in written form but in graphical form. Looked at a little more closely, however, this supposedly simple approach really does present some difficulty: everyone involved has his or her own idea of what constitutes a clearly laid-out diagram. We need only to think of the countless flipchart diagrams with equally countless ways of presenting the same topic and the frequently varying results produced by identical content!

So what would be ideal? A systematic form of display that can be understood quickly and is suitable for simple definition of complex relationships – and one which above all stands up to critical scientific analysis. Non-existent? Then let's have a closer look at the EPC method (event-controlled process chain), and perhaps by the end of the chapter you will be just as much a convinced supporter of this method as many others involved in projects in the SAP environment now are.

2.1 DEFINITION OF TERMS

The business process

The standards publications frequently used in quality management such as ISO 9000ff, QS 9000 or VDA do not provide a clear definition of the expression 'process' or 'business process', although they do use both expressions frequently. However, as we do not need a standard for every expression, let us approach the business process from both the business management and the technical angle. From the point of view of business management, a process is a consecutive sequence of actions with determinable results. A good example of this is quality planning (see Fig. 2.1).

From a technical point of view, a process is an operation that runs according to the principles of chemistry and/or physics based on the law of cause and effect. In industry, the term 'process manufacturing' is used when continuous processes are involved. Otherwise in production, the expression 'process' is identical to the business management definition, which says that a process consists of several successive activities resulting in value-creation. The linguistic usage within a project with the aim of implementing an improvement in a company could therefore be covered by the following definition of the term (cf. Keller 1999; p. 154):

- A process/business process is a chain of commercial activities with individual results.

- Various business processes influence each other and trigger other processes.

- In most cases, several people or organizational units are involved in a business process.

- Business processes have a defined beginning and a defined end.

- A successful business process must be planned and geared to the resources of the company.

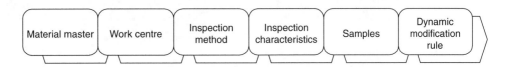

FIGURE 2.1 The quality planning business process (© SAP AG)

Modeling business processes

Techniques for modeling company processes with the purpose of optimizing them have been used since the start of industrialization. The formal description and discussion with those involved in the process means that continuous improvements can be made during business process modeling. Measurable variables can be used to indicate the success or lack of success of chains of action. Here, there is also a nice parallel to the philosophy of quality assurance systems: the requirement for continuous improvement, which would not be possible without continuously recurring process modeling (Fig. 2.2).

Particularly in the case where standard software is implemented in quality management, the modeling of existing processes will play a central role. As the degree of integration of quality management into the logistics chain continues to grow, the operations relevant to quality must be woven in with an even greater level of precision and geared to the neighbouring processes. This is the only way to ensure the required acceptance of total quality management involving R/3 QM.

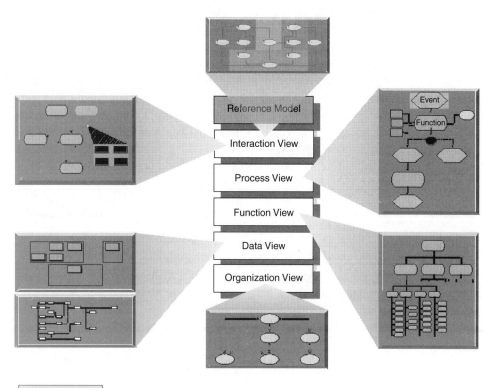

FIGURE 2.2 Process views

Business processes and reference models in R/3

Standard business management software relies on the representation of generally valid business processes. In these processes and process chains, the manufacturer interprets the requirements of the market – with knowledge acquired and developed from a wide variety of customer projects. In order to provide the user with this experience and the conception of a company procedure, the R/3 system offers the so-called 'reference models' as the basis of knowledge. We strongly recommend that everyone responsible for projects makes use of the reference models stored in the system as the basis for business process modeling. To do so, select TOOLS | BUSINESS ENGINEER | BUSINESS NAVIGATOR | PROCESS FLOW VIEW from the main menu (see Fig. 2.3).

All reference models in the R/3 system have been designed using the EPC method, which will be discussed in more detail shortly. When setting up your system, the reference models should be used as an initial solution, whereby it is certainly possible to add or omit process components. As regards process diagrams, many other functions can be started in R/3 by double-clicking or unfolding selection menus, such as:

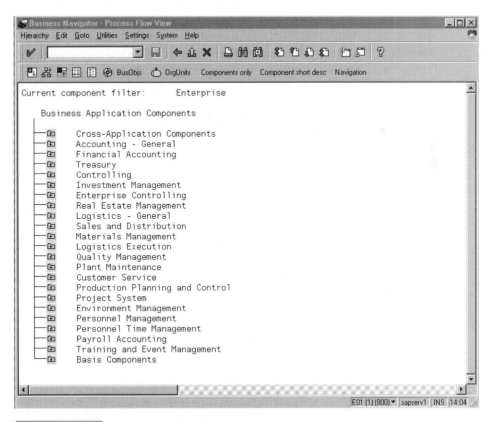

FIGURE 2.3 Process flow view of the sap reference model (© SAP AG)

■ The relevant transaction.

■ Customizing tables.

■ Data models.

■ Explanatory texts.

The use of reference models therefore has the following benefits for a QM project in particular:

■ The standard sequence of the closely related processes can be viewed directly.

■ The options of the QM component are displayed graphically and logically.

■ The integration character of QM is clearly highlighted and easy to read.

■ Non-critical processes can be adopted immediately, as it is possible to obtain a faster overview.

■ Specifying a unified scheme promotes communication between subprojects.

This method of mapping business processes and the R/3 reference model with an event-controlled process chain was in fact developed by SAP AG (cf. Keller 1999 pp. 158–174). However, the process itself is not a patented or otherwise legally protected application, which means that nothing prevents us from using the EPC method in modeling our business processes. All the reference models in the R/3 system are of course copyrighted.

2.3 STRUCTURE OF THE EVENT-CONTROLLED PROCESS CHAIN (EPC)

The event-controlled process chain enables us to structure the process models for the desired company processes in a simple way. The reduction to as few symbols as possible, as well as clear semantics, mean that the method can be learned quickly and it does not present the uninitiated user with any great problem. The modeling of processes using the event-controlled process chain is also an excellent option for use in a team meeting. Especially in what are frequently very lively integration meetings, the focus on the components relevant to the study leads to accelerated, result-oriented work. In work sessions using the EPC method, the following questions are considered in particular:

■ When should something be done?

■ What should be done?

■ Who should do something?

■ What information is required to achieve this?

2.3.1 Elements of the event-controlled process chain

The elements of the EPC method are used to map the temporal and logical sequence of a process. Here, the essential elements, events and functions (actions, tasks), always follow one another in a temporal sequence, which means that an event is always followed by a function, never by another event (see Fig. 2.4). The six basic elements of an event-controlled process chain are easy to describe (see also Table 2.1):

▨ *Event (hexagon)* which describes when a state is to occur. The event is the business state that exists after an operation. This means that the event is the central control element within a process. The description of events follows fixed syntactic rules – a preceding noun is always followed by the perfect participle of the verb chosen, for example:

 – Results recorded.

 – Q information record created.

 – Inspection plan created.

 – Usage decision made.

▨ *Function (rounded rectangle)* describes what is to be done. The term function describes the operative task of an employee in the company. For the user of a computerized system such as SAP R/3, the function frequently means the same as a 'transaction' in the system.

▨ *Organizational unit (ellipse)* which describes who does something. The organizational unit stands for offices and departments in the company. These can be units sorted according to tasks, objects (market segments, product groups) or processes.

▨ *Information objects (rectangle)* which describe which information is necessary to perform the task. Information forms the basis for the execution of business functions. It is generated in an information system on the basis of certain rules or imported into the system from outside.

▨ The links between the elements are mapped by lines, arrows and operators:

 – *Control flow (dotted arrow pointing downwards)* which maps the temporal-logical procedure and links the events to the functions.

 – *Information flow (unbroken arrow)* which specifies whether a function reads, changes or writes; it can also be used for the assignment of materials.

 – *Organization assignment (unbroken line)* which specifies which organizational unit (ellipse) is responsible for a function; it can be used for the assignment of resources.

 – *Link operator (circle)* uses 'and', 'or' and 'exclusive or' to describe the logic between functions and tasks. If several arrows exit from a link operator, only one arrow can enter it (distributor); if several arrows enter it, only one arrow can exit (linker).

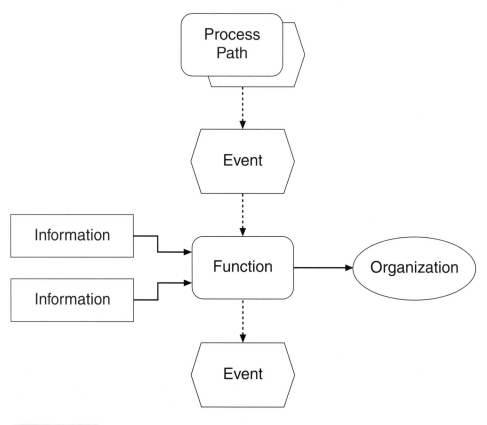

FIGURE 2.4   Basic structure of an EPC

 Process path (combined function and event symbol), whereby the function symbol is in
 the foreground and the event symbol in the background, summarizes a process and
 links different processes.

2.3.2 Structure of the event-controlled process chain

The elements of the EPC can be used to describe complex models on different hierarchy
levels. An EPC on the lower level is referred to as a process module and it contains functions, events, the information flow and the organizational unit. The EPC always begins
with an event and/or a process path and ends with an event and/or a process path. A
process path can contain one or more process modules and thus forms the upper level.
EPCs that only consist of process paths, and thus individual process modules, are
described as scenarios; the term 'scenario EPC' is also used. The process can be detailed
in each of the hierarchy levels. A fully structured EPC then contains all the elements
occurring in the syntax.

TABLE 2.1	Symbols of the EPC	

Description	Symbol	Definition
Event		The event describes the occurrence of a business state that can trigger a function or can be the result of a function, as the case may be.
Function		The function describes the business task for transformation of an initial state into a target state.
Link operators	XOR ∧ ∨	The link operator describes the logical connections between events and functions.
Control flow		The control flow describes the temporal-logical dependencies of events and functions.
Process path		The process path shows the connection to one or another process (navigation aid).
System organization unit type		A system organization unit describes an organizational unit of the R/3 system that enables the mapping of organizational units and structures of the company in the R/3 system.
Information object		An information object is an illustration of an object from the real world (e.g. a business object, entity).
Information flow		Information flows show the data flow between two functions.
Assignment of system organization units		This assignment describes which organizational unit of the R/3 system is required to execute a process/function.

However, the term 'lean EPC' is also used in connection with EPCs. Here, you can initially do without the information flow and the organizational unit: the 'lean EPC' consists only of functions and events to which the control flow arrows and link operators have been applied. In an even simpler form, even the link operators can be omitted from the first step. This form is especially suitable for sketching models during a workshop or for consistency checks of an operation in the R/3 system during the prototype stage.

The formal structure corresponds to a graph-based model made of nodes and edges. Operative methods such as graph grammars or declarative methods with specification languages for graphs are suitable for the scientific description of the syntax (cf. Keller 1999). However, a detailed description of these goes beyond the scope of this book. For our purposes, the description of the procedure for creating an EPC on the basis of examples will be sufficient. To do so, we will set up step by step an EPC for a process module from the area of inspection parallel to production.

2.3.3 Scenario

The example covers simple inspection lot processing in production with discrete manufacturing. Goods are produced in lots for individual job orders. Lot-based inspection at the end of a manufacturing step is intended to assure the quality of the goods. The inspection plan is fully integrated in the routing and already contains all the required information (inspection characteristics, process control) for results recording. If a defect is detected, a quality notification is generated from results recording. The inspection lot processing ends with the usage decision (inspection lot completion). The quantity feedback of production takes place via the feedback transaction in the PP component.

Step 1

Initially it makes sense to look at the process modules involved in inspection lot processing in the R/3 reference model (Fig. 2.5).

There are now two possible methods for creating the EPC. Method 1 requires a tool with changeable reference models (ARIS Toolset® from the IDS Professor Scheer GmbH, or IPW® from Intellicorp) and involves simply using the existing reference model and changing it to suit your requirements. In Method 2, you use a normal drawing program (VISIO, CorelDraw, etc.) and create the required symbols on your own. For the sake of simplicity, we will assume that you start with Method 2.

We also specify that only a certain area of the EPC, the 'usage decision' function, is to receive special detail with the elements information flow and organizational unit.

Step 2

Let us now restrict the scope of the process module to be mapped. We place the incoming process path at the start of the EPC; the process paths that complete the process module are placed at the end of the EPC. A glance at the reference process module in the R/3 system now shows us the potential of the individual functions (Fig. 2.6).

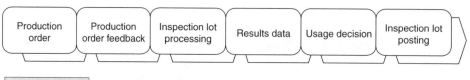

FIGURE 2.5   Process modules for inspection lot processing

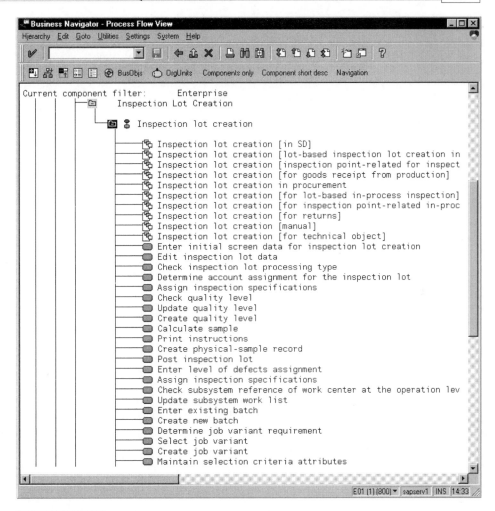

FIGURE 2.6 Reference model for inspection lot creation (© SAP AG)

Step 3

We start the modeling at the incoming process path and set an event (Fig. 2.7). The first applicable event is 'Results of the sample to be recorded'. The rule of the EPC 'an event is always followed by a function' is observed and the function 'Selection type to be entered' is edited. The process path is linked to the function by means of a control flow arrow towards the function. In principle, this function produces three options for the selection of the inspection lot: you can enter the inspection lot directly, select it from a selection list, or work with the report 'Worklist for results recording'. The EPC is now to be developed in such a way that both functions 'Enter inspection lot' and 'Enter additional selection criterion' can be performed as parallel tasks. The link is effected by

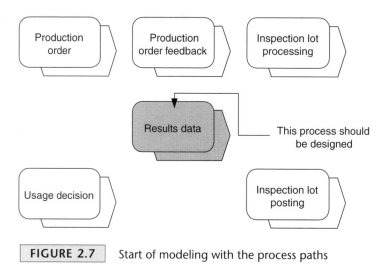

FIGURE 2.7   Start of modeling with the process paths

means of the function operator 'AND'. As the inspection lot can be selected via the 'Worklist to results recording' as an alternative, this path is again to be linked using 'XOR'(or) (see Fig. 2.8).

Step 4

In the next step, we model the process up to the next process path 'Inspection lot completion', whereby we have shown the individual steps of results recording in a slightly simplified form (Fig. 2.9).

Step 5

Let us have a brief look at defect recording. This variant of results recording refers to a special version of the QM module in inspection planning. In the event of a defect (with the characteristic evaluation 'Reject'), a defect data record in the form of a quality notification is created automatically. You can then edit the quality notification and use another function to send it as e-mail.

With the subsequent defect recording, the process around 'Results recorded' can also be mapped as shown in Fig. 2.10.

Step 6

The process is now structured and contains the necessary process modules for the description of the inspection lot selection with subsequent results recording. All that is missing now are IT-related and organizational assignments of the functions. This will be shown using the defect recording function as an example. There, you can see both the

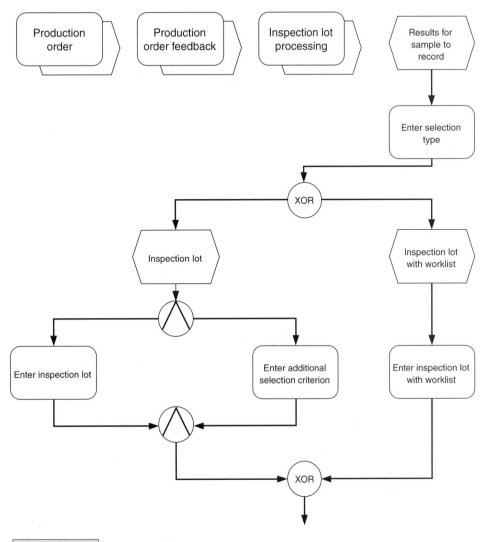

FIGURE 2.8   Selecting inspection lots

data flow for the automatic functions 'Create quality notification' and 'Send e-mail' and the organizational assignment to the 'Quality Management' department.

Organizational units

When an R/3 system is used, the organizational unit must be given special attention. The forms, documents and other information object data media used in their actual state can frequently be omitted. Information can be replaced by the corresponding data structures of the SAP system and can be edited consistently across process borders. By

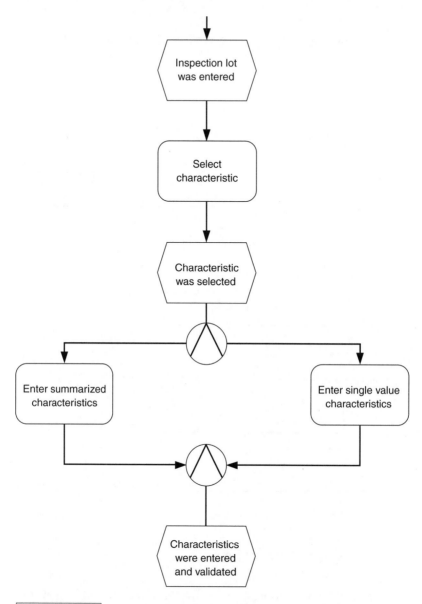

FIGURE 2.9   Selecting characteristics and recording results

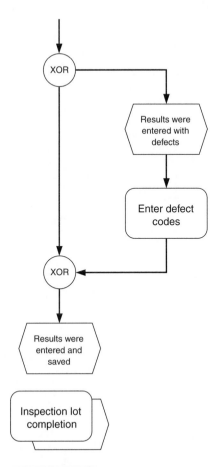

FIGURE 2.10   Recording defects for the result

mapping functions and their organizational assignment together (Fig. 2.11), you also create the basis for the user rights concept in the R/3 system.

We always conclude the event-controlled process chain (EPC) with an event, 'Results recorded' in this case. In doing so, we have reached a state that allows connection to another process module. With the EPC, we now have a 'schedule' for process prototyping in the R/3 system.

Depending on the detail provided, an EPC of this type can almost completely replace a verbal description of the business process, the data flows involved and the organizational assignment. The EPC also has extensive multiple uses in the areas:

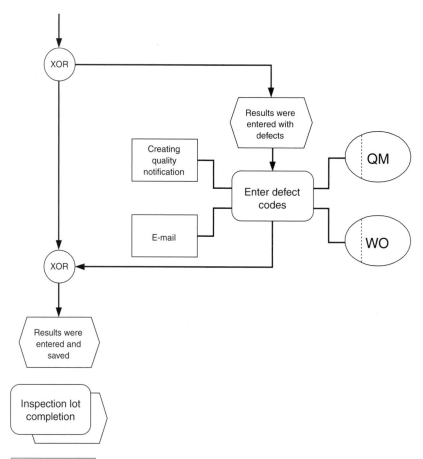

FIGURE 2.11   Organizational assignment of the function 'defect recording'

- Project documentation.
- Process visualization.
- Process instructions.
- Maintenance of interfaces of subprojects.

Advantages at a glance

- The EPC method of mapping for business processes is easy to learn.
- Difficult technical content can be shown in a clear manner.
- Changes are possible.
- The EPC method is equally beneficial to users and consultants.

- EPC mapping in an implementation project promotes interdepartmental communication.

- Working with the EPC is the best precondition for an implementation by means of AcceleratedSAP (ASAP).

- The step from business process to Customizing is made much easier when the reference model is used.

CHAPTER 3

R/3 overview

3.1 SAP

SAP GmbH 'Systeme, Anwendungen und Produkte in der Datenverarbeitung' (Systems, Applications and Products in Data processing) was founded in 1976. It replaced the partnership 'Systemanalyse Programmentwicklung' (System Analysis Program Development) formed in 1972. This was the foundation stone of today's corporate software group, and it was laid by the former IBM employees Dietmar Hopp, Hans-Werner Hector, Hasso Plattner, Klaus Tschira and Claus Wellenreuther. In 1988, SAP went public as SAP AG. Since 1998, it has been one of the 30 shares that is used to calculate the important German stock market index DAX.

In 1999, SAP AG achieved sales revenues of approximately 5 billion Euro with approximately 21,000 employees worldwide.

3.2 DEVELOPMENT OF THE R/3 SYSTEM

The first standard software developed by SAP in 1973 was the 'System R'. R stands for realtime and it means that the input data can be processed immediately, that is, in real time. With this, SAP rose above the batch processing programs that had existed until then, by which data had first to be entered and then processed, usually overnight, in batches. Frequently, the results were only available the next day in the form of computer lists.

The next software was the R/2 system, developed from 1978 onwards, which is still in use today and is still being updated. It is used mostly by very large companies and corporate groups. The essential difference to the R/3 program package (developed from 1987 onwards) is that the R/2 system was conceived for use on a central computer with terminals, whereas the R/3 system uses so-called client-server technology. Here, although the main part of the software also runs on a central computer (server), certain dialog functions, above all the graphical user interface, are placed on intelligent workstations (clients, personal computers). From around 1992 onwards, the R/3 system provided the company's breakthrough on to the world market.

3.3   THE R/3 SYSTEM

The R/3 system is conceived as a kind of module kit. The central database and the Basis Components (BC) are surrounded by the so-called components (also referred to as modules). The purchasers of R/3 can choose one of several databases (Oracle, DB/2, MS SQL Server, etc.) and the modules (or components) they wish to use. Many companies start out with Financial Accounting (FI) and Controlling (CO), and later expand the system to include, for example, Materials Management (MM) and Quality Management (QM). However, if the entire data processing of a company is to be changed, there is no other way but to implement most of the modules from the outset.

In addition to this, you have difficult decisions to make when implementing the R/3 system as regards the different operating systems. There is a choice between, for example, different UNIX derivates, Windows versions or OS/400.

TIP SAP software has always made full use of all available hardware potential. This is why the planning of the IT structure in your company is of particular importance. It is no coincidence that there are many jokes made regarding the interpretation of the abbreviation SAP, for example 'Search, Activate, Pause' or 'Slow Application Program'. Choose state-of-the-art hardware with good performance specifications, otherwise any savings you might be anticipating could turn out to be very expensive!

3.4   MODULES OF THE R/3 SYSTEM

Although we are going to deal 'only' with the Quality Management (QM) module, it is an advantage to know at least the names of the other modules. The abbreviations of the modules (or components, in SAP-speak) are derived from the English names (see Table 3.1). The R/2 counterparts (where applicable) can also be found in this table.

TABLE 3.1	Names of the modules (components)	
R/3 module	**Name in English**	**R/2 module**
AA	Assets Accounting	RA
BC	Basis Components	RS
CA	Cross Applications	–
CO	Controlling	RK
EC	Enterprise Controlling	–
FI	Financial Accounting	RF
HR	Human Resources	RP
IM	Capital Investment Management	–
MM	Materials Management	RM-MAT
PM	Plant Maintenance	RM-INST
PP	Production Planning and Control	RM-PPS
PS	Project System	RM-PM
		RK-P
QM	Quality Management	RM-QSS
SD	Sales and Distribution	RV
SM	Service Management	–
TR	Treasury	–
WF	Business Workflow	–

As you can see from the structure of the chapters, the Quality Management module does not lead an isolated existence. It is closely integrated with other modules, which means that it cannot entirely be viewed as an independent module. We talk of Quality Management in Materials Management, of Quality Management in Production and of Quality Management in Sales and Distribution, referring to the applications and close links to the modules Materials Management (MM), Production Planning and Control (PP) and Sales and Distribution (SD). This is supplemented by links to Controlling (CO) and involvement in Plant Maintenance (PM). Naturally, the shared functions of the Basis Components (BC), the different Information Systems (IS) and, where applicable, of the SAP Business Workflows (WF) are also used.

To improve your understanding, the next section contains brief explanations of the basic functions of the three modules that are particularly closely related to Quality Management.

Materials Management (MM)

This module forms the core of the logistics functions. It represents the business process 'Materials Management', from requirements planning through procurement to warehousing and storage of goods.

The material master data is saved in a database and it can be supplemented after the base data has been created by various items of additional information (Views for material). One of these supplementary information items is the view for Quality

Management, which is used to specify whether a material is, for example, relevant to quality as regards procurement or inspection. The entire procurement process with vendor data and terms of delivery is as much a part of Materials Management as Goods Receipt and Warehouse Management. Every material movement takes place as a certain defined type of movement, to which subsequent functions or conditions can be linked. Particularly in the area of movement types and stock types (free stock, quality stock, blocked stock), the interplay with Quality Management is very close. The quality-relevant elements such as vendor selection, vendor evaluation, delivery release or requirements for the Quality Management system of the vendor are assigned to Quality Management in Materials Management; the two modules are closely interlinked as regards this aspect.

Production Planning and Control (PP)

The R/3 Production Planning and Control (PP), in the same way as Materials Management, is assigned to the application area 'Logistics'. It provides comprehensive functions for quantity and capacity planning and control of production in various branches of industry. These include:

- Master data management.
- Production planning.
- Manufacturing control.
- Special production methods.

The special production methods include job lot, series and Kanban manufacturing.

The component PP–PI (Production Planning – Processing Industry) has been specially tailored to the needs of the processing industry (chemicals, pharmaceuticals, food). It can be used to manage, for example, substances, samples, batches, recipes and resources.

Quality Management is also closely related to this module. Inspection planning is based on routings, inspection lots can be triggered using the manufacturing order and test equipment can be assigned to individual work steps as production resources. Quality Management in Production is the planning and performance of in-process inspections and inspections at the end of production, using elements and functions from the Quality Management module.

Sales and Distribution (SD)

In the R/3 Sales and Distribution module (SD), there is the master data, which is available to virtually every module, and there are also the functions 'Sales', 'Delivery', 'Invoicing' and 'Export Sales'.

The Sales function covers the processing of inquiries, the creation of offers and order confirmations with the usual commercial details of pricing. Its other tasks include specifying the partners involved (not only the selling company but primarily the customer), the recording of product and service features, specifying the price and delivery date, and the creation of forms (confirmation of offer or order).

Delivery is covered by a comprehensive instrument for monitoring of deadlines for the existing orders. Product availability and the creation of the usual delivery forms such as stock notes and delivery notes are taken into account when setting up and handling deliveries. Quality Management plays a role here: it can create inspection lots with the outgoing goods and is responsible for drawing up inspection certificates. When delivery has been completed, the material stocks are updated as regards value and quantity.

Order handling is concluded with invoicing. Invoices are drawn up here and the information is passed on to accounts receivable accounting. Credit and debit notes can be processed and delivery invoices grouped or split.

For export sales, the Sales and Distribution module also offers various useful functions that are required for international trade. These include suitably maintained master data for import and export handling and support of appropriate documents, for example freight papers, customs invoices or the MITI trade document for Japan.

Thus, Quality Management in Sales and Distribution regulates the outgoing goods inspections as well as inspection certificates related to a delivery. It also supports the processing of customer complaints by means of a special type of quality notification.

3.5   PREVIOUS VERSIONS (RELEASES) OF R/3

As is the case for all software, the R/3 system is also subject to continuous development. In SAP jargon, the various versions are referred to as releases. The explanations in this book are largely based on Release 4.5, whereby the examples and screendumps were created using the IDES test system. Nevertheless, all the information will be just as useful for users of the older versions 3.1 and 4.0, as a great many of the functions and options described are available either precisely as described or in a very similar form in all versions. The only exception is Chapter 11, 'Test equipment management'; in the scenario described in that chapter there is improved integration of test equipment management in the Quality Management module from Release 4.0 onwards.

If a new version is installed within an R/3 system, this is referred to as a release change. As a rule, customized settings can be applied to the new release. Where appropriate, new, supplementary settings have to be configured. Difficulties might occur where special customer programs have been created or special adaptations have been performed that were not intended in the standard version of the system. In many cases, these must be revised for a release change.

TIP   In order to eliminate as many difficulties as possible during a release change, special customer adaptations that are not intended in the standard version should be omitted where possible. In the long term, it is better to use suitable methods such as business process re-engineering to restructure processes in such a way that they can be set up with the R/3 standard.

The HELP | RELEASE NOTES menu item allows you to see the changes to your R/3 version. Some innovations of Version 4.0 in the area of quality management are:

- Digital signatures.
- A distinction between manufacturer and vendor (important for procurement via distributors).
- Quality inspection for external processing under the manufacturing order (important in the case of extended workbench or job processing).
- Mass change of inspection data.
- Improvement for certificate receipt and certificate creation.
- New functions for sample management.
- Changes to sample due to new inspection specifications.
- Histogram and value chart for results recording and characteristic evaluation.
- New quality control charts (np-, p-, c-chart, etc.).
- Interface to external statistical systems (QM-STI).
- Improvements to links with the Quality Management Information System (QMIS).
- Test equipment management with calibration planning, orders, inspections and usage decisions.

With Release 4.5, the following functions (among others) have been improved or added:

- Manual inspection lot for physical sample.
- Inspection specifications on the basis of batch determination.
- Batch input for inspection characteristics.
- Defect recording via data interface (QM-IDI).
- Specification of preferred inspection type.
- Evaluation or deletion of quality situation.
- Quality control charts and results history for test equipment management.

Users of the R/3 versions prior to 4.5 are sure to recognize the variations in the display and find their way around very quickly, as the changes to the interface are not too extensive and the menu paths have remained largely the same.

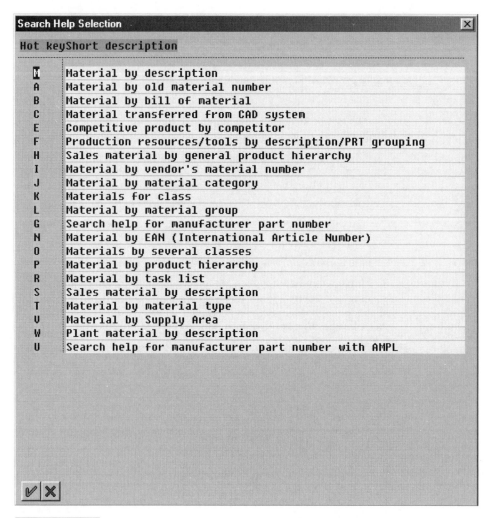

FIGURE 3.1   Search help selection in Release 4.0 (© SAP AG)

The differences between Release 4.0 and 4.5 should become clear from the following examples. Figures 3.1 and 3.2 show the search help for a material number in version 4.0. First, the type of search (here MATERIAL BY DESCRIPTION) is selected and the short description is entered in the input window that follows.

In 4.5 on the other hand, a kind of card index with tabs appears (see Fig. 3.3). Each type of search corresponds to a tab. The search then takes place in the same window as the selection of the tab.

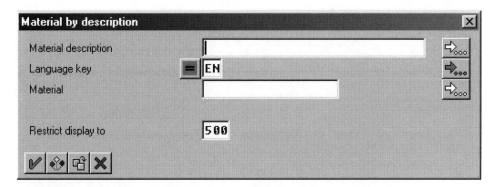

FIGURE 3.2   Search with 'Material by description' in Release 4.0 (© SAP AG)

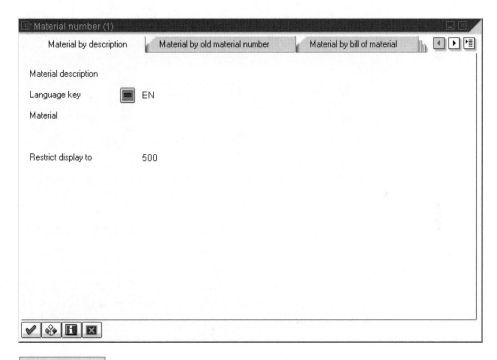

FIGURE 3.3   Search with 'Material by description' in Release 4.5 (© SAP AG)

Another variation can be seen in Figures 3.4 and 3.5. In the RECORD USAGE DECISION screen, toggling the partial views CHARACTERISTICS and STOCKS was implemented in Release 4.0 by means of a button in the display. In Release 4.5, tabs have been used for the display. The DEFECTS tab can be seen immediately in Release 4.5, whereas the DEFECTS button in 4.0 only appears after defects have been recorded.

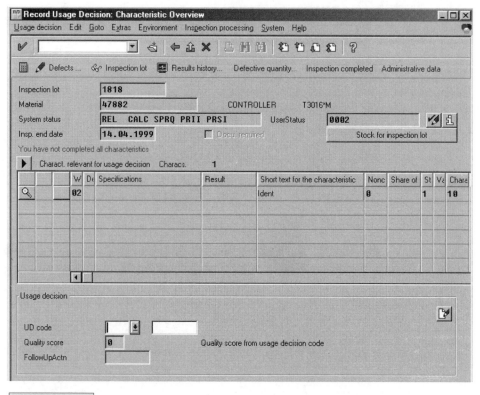

FIGURE 3.4   RECORD USAGE DECISION screen in Release 4.0 (© SAP AG)

3.6   PROJECT MANAGEMENT FOR IMPLEMENTATION

This section does not contain a fully comprehensive description of project management and is not intended to replace the usually necessary support of an external consulting firm. It is only intended to provide a rough overview of what has to be considered when managing an R/3 implementation project and what has already proved effective in practice. In this context, specific features of the implementation of the Quality Management module will be mentioned. There are, of course, many ways to skin a cat, which means that other approaches can also succeed.

Independent of whether you are implementing the R/3 system with all or only a few of its modules, or the Quality Management module is implemented retrospectively, well-planned and thoroughly organized project management is always required. The scope of such an implementation and the effort required should not be underestimated. Depending on the branch of industry and the company itself, the implementation of R/3 is one of the largest projects the company has to deal with. In this connection, the internal and external deployment of personnel, know-how and the commitment of all

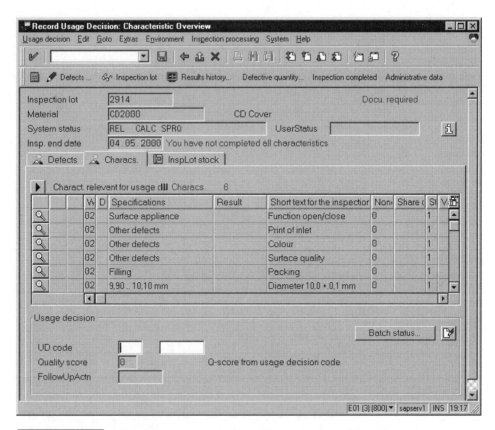

FIGURE 3.5   RECORD USAGE DECISION screen in Release 4.5 (© SAP AG)

those involved are just as important as strong financial support. Depending on the starting conditions, the implementation of the new software involves a more or less extensive change to the entire IT structure, e.g. networks (LAN and WAN), repeaters, workstations, operating systems, including larger monitors and new workstations.

At the start of the project, one of the first questions to ask is whether the implementation is to take place with or without external support. The authors' view is that external support is absolutely necessary, independent of the type and number of modules to be implemented. Although the internal IT or organization departments may well possess a great deal of know-how, a fully independent implementation by internal personnel is unlikely to succeed in most cases.

If you share the view that external support is essential, the question as to the choice of partner arises. Currently there are a great many companies that offer consulting services relating to SAP R/3; this makes the choice even more difficult. If you are planning an implementation of the entire R/3 system with all modules, it is recommended that you use the services of a company that provides consulting for all modules. If, however, the Quality Management module is to be implemented retrospectively, i.e. after other modules are already working productively, an option would be to use a consulting firm that specializes in this module. Consulting services are also available from SAP AG itself. Moreover, SAP AG also offers the so-called SAP Partner Consulting, which comprises 20,000 consultants worldwide. There are also a great many freelance consultants, many of whom possess extensive know-how. The choice, however, has to be made by your company itself. The possible range of fundamental questions relates to all consulting services offered:

- Is the desired scope of consulting services provided?
- What experience and reference projects are available? Who are the contact persons there?
- Which consultants are available for which modules?
- Are the consultants available for the entire duration of the project?
- How many times a week are the consultants available?
- Are the consultants in the surrounding area (travel time)?
- How qualified are the consultants?
- What costs are involved?

Placing the costs at the end of the list was deliberate. A low-cost offer for consulting services is of little use when the consultants are unavailable, change continuously, and have to travel so far so that they are already tired when they reach the company!

The quality of a consulting firm stands and falls with the qualification of its staff. The Quality Management module alone is so complex that no single consultant will be able to know all the fine points and possible uses. There are also the interfaces to the other modules, which require a certain knowledge of the entire R/3 system. Every project and subproject will therefore involve ups and downs, whereby the 'downs' will not depend alone on the service provided by the consultants. There will also be less experienced consultants who inhibit progress in the project. One way of covering yourself is to request evidence of suitable qualifications in the form of résumés, training certificates, practical experience in the relevant module, years of service in the consulting firm, or reference projects. In addition, SAP AG offers qualification and training programmes for consultants which conclude with a certificate as an SAP R/3 'Certified Application Consultant'. However, this certification is not yet offered for all modules.

Parallel to the search for a consulting firm, the project must be structured and a rough project plan worked out, whereby the milestones have to be specified from the start of the search. A project team structure as shown in Figure 3.6 has proved effective in practice.

The core team with the project manager within the company coordinates the progress of the project and the deployment of consultants together with the project manager of the consulting firm. For an overall project involving several modules, the following project management tools have proved effective:

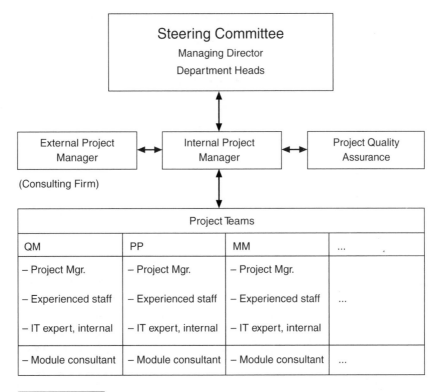

FIGURE 3.6   Project structure for the implementation of R/3 (© SAP AG)

- Project manual (description of the project, aims, interfaces, basic principles, etc.).
- Project plan (schedule).
- Regulation of information interchange (intranet, e-mail, documentation server).
- Regular project meetings with the module project managers.

This list could of course be much longer. The last item on the list has proven to be particularly important. Regular project meetings for all subprojects are the only way to recognize interface problems at an early stage and to initiate measures for solutions. The closer the links between the modules, the more important this collaboration. Where necessary, these points should be covered in more detail in integration meetings among the individual project teams and dealt with appropriately. The Quality Management module is particularly susceptible to interface problems, as it interacts with very many other modules in R/3. This is frequently underestimated in the implementation.

It has been shown that – parallel to the work of the core team for the overall project – work in small project teams is particularly effective for the implementation of the individual modules. A project team consists of:

- A module project manager from the specialist department.
- Key users from the specialist department.
- Members of staff from the company IT department.
- Module consultants of the consulting firm.

This module project team also works according to the rules of project management. These include, for example:

- A project description (project manual) with objectives and definition of interfaces.
- Schedule.
- Logging of decisions, agreements, etc.
- Logging of the project status at fixed intervals (e.g. monthly).
- Concluding report with a description of the scope implemented.

Depending on the topics covered in the individual project meetings, the module project team meetings involve all or only some team members. The intervals between the team meetings are based on the requirements and aims, on the progress of the project and the dependency on other module project teams.

When work is started in the project team, the entire IT structure should be ready so that from the first day onwards it is possible to work and demonstrate on the R/3 system. Ideal for the demonstration is an additional demonstration system, for example IDES from SAP AG. When the IT structure is set and the basic implementation in R/3 has taken place, the actual work in the module project teams can begin.

Essentially, the following phases are required:

- Concept phase.
- Customizing.
- Test and correction phase.
- Training and documentation for the users.
- Master data transfer.
- Productive phase.

It is very important at the start, i.e. at the beginning of the concept phase, to coordinate terminology and language. After only a very short time, you will notice that there is a separate terminology in the R/3 system and especially in the Quality Management module. As a rule, the consultant will have adopted the vocabulary of R/3, whereas you use the standard descriptions in your company. This is why a mutual understanding is required to define these expressions from the outset and specify what they mean. Under certain circumstances, this can lead to the production of what amounts to a proper dictionary, listing the company terms against the R/3 expressions.

The next step after definition of a uniform language is to run an implementation workshop over one to three days. The aim of this workshop is to provide an opportunity for the consultant to explain the possibilities provided by each module, and for the module project manager and future users to formulate their requirements and wishes. During this early period, the scope, aims and several details can be agreed on. The results of the workshop are documented in the form of a project manual, so that all those directly and indirectly involved can check this information at any time (ideally, the project manual is located in the intranet).

An existing Quality Management system is a great help at this stage. The process descriptions from the Quality Management manual and the process instructions provide a good basis for discussion as to how these can be implemented by R/3 and the QM module. To support this, the relevant processes with flow charts or EPC methods described elsewhere can be documented during the workshops and in other team meetings.

It is important from the point of view of user acceptance, and thus for successful productive deployment of R/3, to structure the transition from the old to the new system as simply as possible. Frequently, small matters such as old codes or number ranges can be used to create familiarity with the R/3 system. So-called 'talking numbers' that are composed logically are usually easier to understand than consecutive numbering. It is normally easy to change captions and descriptions or adopt them from the old system, which means that the user finds familiar items in the new system. In part, this must be considered as early as the concept phase (e.g. number ranges, internal and external number assignment), whereby further adjustments in the context of the user test should not be excluded.

For the Quality Management module, individual integration discussions must definitely take place with the other module project teams in the planning phase. For example, if Quality Management is planned for purchasing, coordination with Purchasing and Warehouse Management is required. If Quality Management in Production is the central topic, the module project team must get together with Production Planning.

The sequence of the phases 'Concept' – 'Customizing' – 'Test' must not be viewed as a simple linear process: they form a control loop with an increasing level of detail. During the test, it is not only a matter of checking the correctness of the settings, but also of checking the concept. If the method chosen has turned out to be correct, fine tuning is often required in Customizing to improve the performance of the system. However, it can turn out that the concept does not adequately reflect the processes in the company or has not taken them sufficiently into account. In this case, the concept must be corrected and adjusted, and this must then be tested until the team has reached the set target.

Caution is required when repeating procedures insofar as the increasing familiarity with the possibilities of R/3 in general, and the Quality Management module in particular, stimulates new desires. However, too many 'nice-to-have' functions can endanger the project schedule.

One danger to the implementation within the framework of the Quality Management module is that too many of the possible functions are to be used in the first step. Under certain circumstances, this can jeopardize both the implementation itself and the acceptance on the part of the subsequent users. The complexity of the QM module is easily underestimated. The division into:

- Quality Management in Purchasing.
- Quality Management in Production.
- Quality Management in Sales and Distribution.

indicates that the module is tightly interwoven with each of the other modules that have to be coordinated, implemented and used in the day-to-day work of the company. It is therefore recommended to start with a lower level of complexity (key word: lean implementation) and to extend the functionality later, step by step. The improvements and extensions can thus be defined, set and tested continuously and then adopted into the productive system. Under certain circumstances, re-engineering of the business processes or part processes might be required in the company beforehand. On account of the clear and comprehensible process flow in Purchasing, Quality Management in Purchasing is the ideal starting point for implementation.

A continuous test of all customized functions, with a separate concluding and approval test at the end, is an essential requirement for a successful productive start. Here, not only should the consultants test the functions they have customized but so should the key users. Faults and errors discovered in the test phase can thus be remedied prior to the productive start. The basic settings of catalogs, sampling procedures and dynamic modification rules are also checked in the test with regard to their suitability for use in day-to-day operations. Once disadvantageous settings have been used in the productive system and saved in the database system, it is practically impossible to change or delete them.

Users from the specialized departments should be involved in the test phase to the greatest possible extent. This cooperation means that errors can be detected at an early stage and proposals for improvement made and considered. The level of acceptance for the system change will grow with the involvement of the users. This is very important, as the business process must continue without disruption after the productive start. A good choice of test data is also a requirement for a valid and informative test result. Do not forget that although a 'lean implementation' is the goal, it must remain possible to process special cases and special materials without high overhead, even if these are only one per cent of cases. Bear in mind that, in productive operation, several thousand cases per day may have to be processed and it is no use if 99 per cent of these can be processed without a problem but one per cent still requires a great deal of effort and overhead!

The training of all users is of course an essential requirement for a smooth productive start. Training can be provided by specialized service companies, by the consultants, or by the key users. At any rate, preference should be given to training on the customized R/3 system of the company, as this is the only way to learn the processes as they will later occur in day-to-day work. If key users are willing to provide training, their internal knowledge of the company can optimize SAP training. Training documents tailored to the company and the customizing should be created and made available.

Before the productive start, the master data has to be transferred. As most companies would already have been working with a computer system before R/3 came along, the old master data must be adopted into the new system. The same applies to the Quality Management module. The overhead involved in data transfer increases in relation to the extent to which Quality Management was implemented in the old system. This is referred to as data migration or a migration from the old (or legacy) system to R/3. The material master data has to be transferred into the R/3 system for the other modules anyway, or it is already there. If inspection plans were already in use in the legacy system, these must be transferred into the QM module. As of Release 4.5, there are transactions for the batch input of inspection plans. This data transfer must be precisely defined and described beforehand (migration description) and performed on a specified date, shortly before the productive start. The overhead involved in the description, provision and migration of the data is quite considerable and this factor must not be overlooked during project planning and implementation.

Before the data transfer into the productive system, basic data must have been provided in the Quality Management module. These include sample rules, sampling procedures, dynamic modification rules and catalogs, as otherwise, for example during the batch input of inspection plans that access sample procedures, error messages would occur.

Reward for the careful preparation can be seen at the productive start. In the first few days, all test cases on the productive system should be observed again and logged. Here, it is not possible to run just any test, as real business transactions are now started and processed in the productive system. This means that checks can only be performed on real processes. However, after good preliminary tests, errors in the productive system should be the exception.

SAP supports project management with its own methods. These include in particular the procedural model in Customizing (see Chapter 13) and ASAP (AcceleratedSAP, see Chapter 15).

| 3.7 | **CUSTOMIZING** |

Every R/3 system is first installed with the shipped client 000 (standard version). Unfortunately, this standard cannot be used directly. First of all, the software must be set up and adapted to your company. This process is referred to as Customizing. Depending on the size of the company, number of modules used and the number of employees involved, this Customizing phase can take several weeks or even months for each module. However, to provide you with a clearer picture of realistic periods, a company with approximately 500 employees was able to start productive work with all modules of the R/3 system after 12 months. Those involved in the project included seven employees from the IT department, an external consultant for each module, as well as one or two competent employees from each specialized department.

For the Quality Management module, depending on the scope of the implementation, 20–60 consultant days should be assumed. These are shared across concept design, customizing, instruction and training, test, troubleshooting, and other tasks. From specialized departments, an additional one or two employees will require anything from the same period to three times the period (depending on the scope and aim of the project).

More information on customizing can be found in Chapter 13, 'Customizing'; more information on master data transfer can be found in Chapter 14, 'Migration concepts'.

3.8   CLIENT CONCEPT

Companies that are managed using SAP software are referred to as clients and they each have a client number. The client represents the top level of the R/3 organization structure. Each client number implies a complete system with separate master and movement

| TABLE 3.2 | Simple client concept |

Client number	Description	Comments
100	Customizing client	Here, all settings are made with the standard system (shipped client 000) as the starting point. Even after the productive start, all the changes are made here and then transferred by transport order to the other clients.
200	Test client	All changes to customizing are transferred by transport orders to this client, which means that it is a mirror-image of the first client. The business transactions are then imported and systematically tested using master data that is entered manually or automatically. All errors detected in the process can *only* be corrected in the customizing client. The corrections are then passed on again to the test client by means of transport orders. Even when the productive system has started, this client is used to test all changes and developments.
300	Productive client	Following a successful test with the test client and the transfer of all customizing settings per transport order, the required master data is transferred into the productive client on the key day. From the productive start onwards, this is the client with which you will work.

data, and possibly different customizing or server hardware. It is standard procedure that a separate client is set up for each subsidiary (e.g. private corporation) or foreign subsidiary of a large company. As a rule, a company only requires one single client (productive client). However, at least two more clients are added to set up the software, as described in Table 3.2.

This should make it clear to you why it is so important to specify the correct client number when you log on to the R/3 system (see also Chapter 4, 'Operation of R/3').

3.9 ORGANIZATION STRUCTURE

As mentioned in the previous section, the client represents the top element of the R/3 organization structure.

The company code is an expression used in the Accounting modules. It is subordinate to the client and forms an independent and closed accounting area. A client can comprise several company codes. The company code can be further subdivided into cost accounting codes and profit centres.

Within Logistics, the 'plant' is the most important organization element. It is subordinate to the company code and represents the place of production. The company code can contain several plants. Production planning and control takes place mainly at plant level, but it can also be implemented across several plants.

The purchasing organization is an organizational unit and always assigned to a company code. It can procure materials or services for one or more plants. Vendor evaluation refers to the purchasing organization. If the purchasing organization is responsible for several plants, vendor evaluation is also cross-plant.

The storage locations are assigned to plants and enable stock management at plant level.

3.10 THE R/3 WORKSTATION

A typical R/3 workstation consists of a networked personal computer (client) with a sufficiently large monitor (at least 17-inch). Although virtually all functions can also be accessed via the keyboard, a mouse is essential as an input device. You have various options when choosing the operating system for the workstations. Windows NT or Windows 98 are chosen in many cases, but Macintosh or UNIX are also supported.

The SAP client installed on each personal computer has the same properties as a typical Windows program and it has a graphical user interface that corresponds to the SAA (System Application Architecture) standard, across which the user can communicate with the R/3 system. SAP also refers to this client as the SAPGUI (SAP Graphical User Interface). In addition, it is recommended that you install MS EXCEL™ on the PC, as at various positions R/3 provides the possibility to transfer lists by download and to import them into spreadsheets. Further processing and evaluations can then be performed there without difficulty.

A printer is required for printouts; this can be either connected locally at the workstation or can be a shared network printer, which should be located nearby for convenience. A local printer can also be used by other workstations, provided the PC is switched on and the print data reception program (SAPlpd) is enabled. Where several users are to access a printer, a network printer is recommended, as this is on standby independent of the status of the PC. In principle, any type of printer is suitable, i.e. pin, inkjet or laser, each type of printer technology having its strengths and weaknesses. Before a printer can be activated, the system administrator has to set up the printer in the SAP Basis Components (BC) with its name and driver. A setup that is only local, for example, with Windows and Windows print drivers, does not enable output with SAP R/3!

3.11 SAPSCRIPT

The SAPscript editor can be used to design the appearance of forms and printed texts. It is a type of page description language which you can use to create virtually any type of form, depending on the output options provided by the installed printer. For example, work papers, inspection plans or certificate forms can be adapted to your company's corporate identity.

3.12 REPORTS

A report is an R/3 program that outputs a list in table form on your screen or on the printer. This list is the result of the report and contains selected data from your database. The data for the report is selected in a selection screen in which you can specify the selection criteria, for example, a material number range. The selection is started by means of RUN and not with ENTER, which makes it clear that a program is involved here.

The list or report can be viewed on the screen or printed. Frequently (unfortunately not always), a so-called download is possible. This can be used to download the list onto your personal computer and continue work on it using a spreadsheet program.

Usually, the standard reports can be found in the relevant modules, sometimes at the ENVIRONMENT menu item and sometimes at Other. Unfortunately, this is not a uniform function in the R/3 system. Your own reports have a program name and they are accessed from the main menu using SYSTEM | SERVICES | REPORTING with your name. An example can be found in Chapter 11, 'Test equipment management'; here, the maintenance plan overview is started as a report in this way.

TIP   Plan the customization of your forms and reports at an early stage, and reserve sufficient programming capacity for the task!

The best way is to proceed as follows:

1 Make a list of all printouts, forms and lists that you currently receive from or create with your computer system and that you need for your work.

2 Try to work on the list with this question in mind: Which of these reports do you still need and which can be eliminated? Can reports be grouped?

3 Find out (possibly with the help of a consultant) whether there are similar reports in your R/3 system or if you can create them; make test printouts.

4 Define the adjustments that have to be made to the existing reports and which reports have to be reprogrammed, then commission this work.

For Quality Management, do not forget, for example, quality notifications to vendors and the 'internal quality notification', printouts of inspection plans, inspection instructions, inspection results, statistics on the number of inspections, percentage evaluations or vendor evaluation.

It is important that this preliminary work is completed at an early stage: experience has shown that a great deal of requests for report adjustments are made shortly before the productive start.

3.13   ABAP/4 PROGRAMS

ABAP/4 is SAP's own fourth-generation programming language. ABAP stands for Advanced Business Application Programming. The applications in the R/3 system themselves and the above-mentioned reports have been programmed in ABAP/4. The IT specialists in your firm also have access to ABAP/4 programming. The ABAP/4 Development Workbench can be found in the TOOLS I ABAPWORKBENCH menu. From there, you have access to numerous utilities for the development and testing of ABAP/4 programs. In particular, you will use these options to create individual reports.

3.14   R/3 QM AS A CAQ SYSTEM

CAQ systems are being used to an increasing extent, especially in the automobile industry. CAQ stands for Computer Aided Quality Assurance. This involves support for the tasks of Quality Management by electronic data processing. The necessity for this results on the one hand from the demands of ISO 9000 standards for systematic inspections and 'controlled' quality records and, on the other hand, from the increasingly urgent desire on the part of management to obtain quality data and analyses of quality costs, as these are required as a starting point for increases in efficiency and growth in productivity. It is only with the aid of an electronic CAQ system that the quantities of data from inspection and quality control can be processed, evaluated, prepared and archived at adequate speed.

The typical demands made on CAQ systems are:

- Quality planning.
- Quality inspection.
- Inspection order management.
- Quality data recording.
- Quality data evaluation and reporting.
- Quality control.
- SPC.
- Test equipment management.

Frequently, CAQ systems only specialize in a few of the above-mentioned requirements. Some specialized systems, for example for SPC processing, have been extended by the manufacturers so that the essential requirements of the customer can be met. CAQ systems that satisfy all the wishes listed above are often expensive and complex.

Insofar as companies already have a CAQ system, these are single PCs or PC networks. The advantage of the single PC solution is that it is possible to make a start with relatively low expenditure and overhead. In many cases, this is an SPC workstation in the quality laboratory which, for example, already contains functions for planning and evaluation. Depending on the size of the company, decentralized inspection locations will make it necessary sooner or later to network several PC workstations and to move on to a file server solution. The disadvantage of the single PC or network solution is the inadequate integration of such a CAQ system in the logistics chain of the company.

The R/3 Quality Management module is nothing less than a CAQ system that meets a wide range of requirements. You can benefit from all the advantages that CAQ systems offer. The complete integration of Quality Management in the overall system turns the disadvantage of external CAQ systems into an advantage of R/3. With Quality Management in Materials Management, in Production and in Sales and Distribution, the interfaces to these modules become seams. Smooth data interchange between Purchasing, Goods Receipt, Manufacturing Orders or Deliveries enable effective work and optimized data consistency: multiple input in different systems is eliminated. The system integration also affects quality costs is such a way that is hardly possible with external CAQ systems. For example, the connection to Human Resources Management (HR module) means that training costs that are posted to defect prevention costs can be called up easily, as can the inspection or defect costs from Controlling (CO module).

If for whatever reason you do not wish to forgo your external CAQ system after the implementation of R/3, this is not a problem. SAP AG has developed a defined interface (QM IDI) that you can use to link external systems to the R/3 QM module. More detailed information on this can be found in Chapter 7, 'Quality inspection'.

CHAPTER 4

Operation of R/3

This chapter teaches you the basics of operating the R/3 system. It is mainly intended for first-time users, but the practised user will also find one or two useful items of information. The screenshots were created using an IDES training system with Release 4.5B, and care has been taken to ensure that the examples match the displays in the Quality Management module. At the end of the chapter, you will also find important display options from other components (from Materials Management in particular) which will be very useful in day-to-day work in Quality Management.

4.1   LOGGING ON AND LOGGING OFF

Logging on

You start your client and open the SAP Login window by double-clicking on the SAP icon (here: IDES45, see Fig. 4.1). If there are several icons on your desktop, each of them refers to a particular client.

Two to three inputs are usually required for the logon (Fig. 4.2):

▓ The client number: in many cases, this has already been entered, but it must be checked and, where appropriate, overwritten.

▓ Enter the user name you have been assigned.

FIGURE 4.1   SAP logon (© SAP AG)

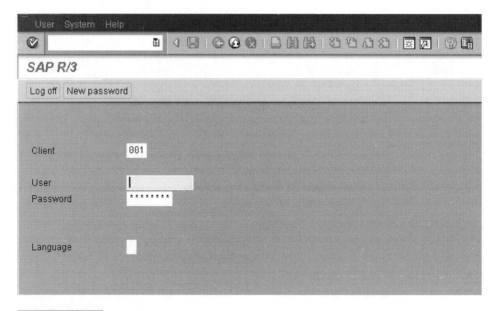

FIGURE 4.2   The logon window (© SAP AG)

▨ Enter your password. This is your personal key to the system and you should protect it against unauthorized access.

▨ The language has normally been preset and only has to be entered if you want to have a different language to that which has been set.

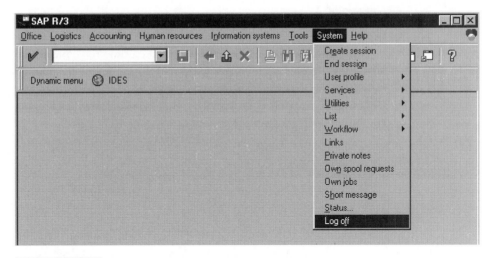

FIGURE 4.3 Logging off from the main menu (© SAP AG)

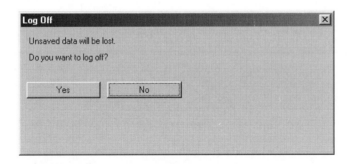

FIGURE 4.4 Fig. 4.4: Safety query at log off (© SAP AG)

At the same time as the logon, your personal settings and access rights for the entire user session take effect. For example, at logon your standard printer is already defined. The system administrator can use the user settings or user profile to specify for each user the extent to which he or she can move around the system, that is, which data can be seen and which can be edited. For example, it is usually not possible for the quality manager to view personnel and salary data.

If the 'System Messages' and/or 'Copyright' windows appear, confirm them both with ENTER until you reach the SAP main window (entry menu).

Logging off

You log off on the path SYSTEM | LOG OFF (Fig. 4.3).

The fastest way of logging off is the usual method for Windows applications: a click on the top right corner of the window ('×'). This closes each opened R/3 window (session) individually.

At log off, the query shown in Fig. 4.4 always appears. If you are not sure whether you have saved all of your transactions, click on NO.

4.2 USER INTERFACE SAP R/3

Main window

After logon, the main window of SAP R/3 appears. The basic structure with the various menu and icon bars is the same for all windows in the R/3 system (Fig. 4.5).

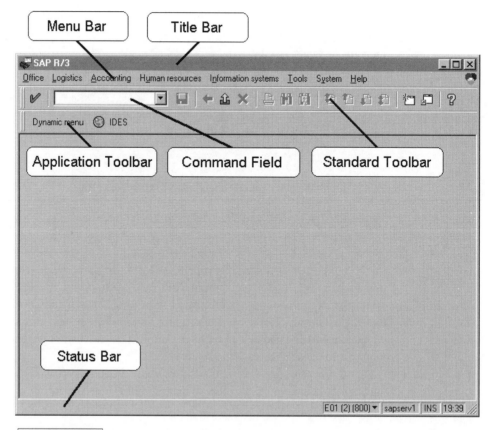

FIGURE 4.5 Main window with names of the menu and icon bars (© SAP AG)

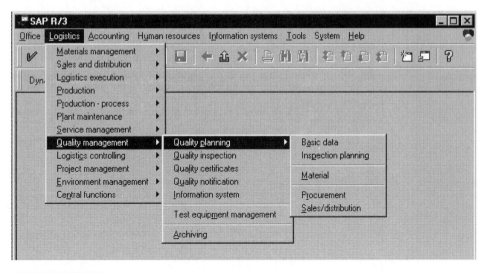

FIGURE 4.6   Selection using the menu bar (© SAP AG)

FIGURE 4.7   Application toolbar (© SAP AG)

The title bar

The title bar contains the name of the window. The title in the main window SAP R/3 in the menu for inspection planning, for example, is DISPLAY INSPECTION PLAN or CREATE INSPECTION PLAN.

The menu bar

The menu bar shows all the currently available menus (Fig. 4.6). The SYSTEM and HELP menus are displayed in every window of the SAP R/3 system. Selections are made in the same way as in Windows applications: using the mouse or keyboard with F10 and the cursor keys ($\leftarrow$, $\uparrow$, $\rightarrow$, $\downarrow$).

The application bar

The application toolbar contains icons for frequently used functions, as shown in Figure 4.7. The icons that are currently available are shown in colour, whereas the disabled icons are only shown as grey shadows.

The icons available and their meaning can be found in Table 4.1.

TABLE 4.1	Icons and their meanings

Icons	Meaning
	ENTER (data input) – keyboard input: ENTER
	Command field (for input of transaction codes)
	SAVE (File) – keyboard input: F11
	Back – keyboard input: F3
	EXIT – keyboard input: Shift + F3
	CANCEL – keyboard input: F12
	PRINT – keyboard input: Ctrl + P
	FIND – keyboard input: Ctrl + F
	FIND NEXT – keyboard input: Ctrl + G
	4 browse keys – keyboard input: Shift + F9, Shift + F10, Shift + F11, Shift + F12
	Create session or shortcut
	HELP – keyboard input: F1

FIGURE 4.8	Function buttons (© SAP AG)

The toolbar

The toolbar is located below the application toolbar. It contains some of the functions available in the relevant menu as buttons (Fig. 4.8). This means the appearance of the toolbar changes depending on which menu is currently open. Frequently used buttons can be found in Table 4.2.

The function of an unknown button is displayed as soon as you hold the cursor for approximately one second over this button without clicking.

An overview of the currently available functions is provided if you click the right-hand mouse button (Fig. 4.9) or use the key combination CTRL+F.

TABLE 4.2	Button icons and their meanings

Button Icons	Meaning
	Run – F8
	Delete – Shift + F2
	Plan inspection – Ctrl + Shift + F1
	Edit long text – Shift + F4
	Help for selection screen – Shift + F6
	Detail or selection – F2
	'Hat' indicates header data – F5
	Display document – F2 or Select – F2

Help	F1
Back	F3
Possible entries	F4
Task list overview	F5
Operation overview	F7
Save	Ctrl+S
Cancel	F12
Exit	Shift+F3
Long text	Shift+F4
First task list	Shift+F5
Previous task list	Shift+F6
Next task list	Shift+F7
Last task list	Shift+F8
Mat-T List assignment	Ctrl+F7

FIGURE 4.9	Overview using the right-hand mouse button (© SAP AG)

The functions can also be selected using the menus from the menu bar of the current window. The icons and buttons available, as well as the functions that appear when the right-hand mouse button is clicked, are a selection and can sometimes offer more, sometimes fewer, functions than the menu bar.

The status bar

The status bar at the bottom edge of the screen consists of an output field (unfortunately rather small), in which the R/3 system outputs messages – unless it opens a separate window for this purpose. A distinction is made between three types of status messages:

- Information
- Warnings
- Errors

The message type can be seen from the first letter (bold) of each message (Fig. 4.10). This is followed by other information regarding the status of the system (client, session, server, Insert/Overwrite, time).

If a question mark appears in the status bar at a message, a double-click on the status bar opens Help.

| **FIGURE 4.10** | The status message (© SAP AG) |

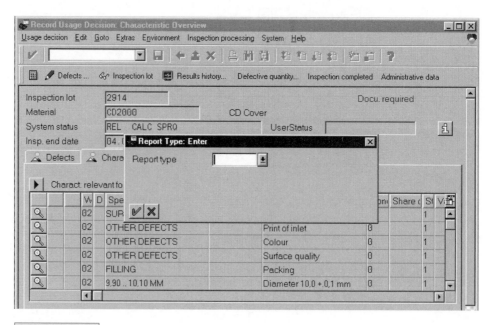

| **FIGURE 4.11** | Dialog window (© SAP AG) |

Dialog windows, checkboxes and radio buttons

Another window element is the dialog window (Fig. 4.11). This appears superimposed on the active window and requires an input or a selection.

When the dialog window is opened, it is often the case that a message is displayed in the status bar.

You are likely to encounter the message box shown in Figure 4.12 quite often. In some cases, an appropriate message appears in the status bar instead of the window. You can use ENTER to close the window and then provide the missing input. As a rule, required fields contain a question mark '?', which tells you that an entry must be made there.

There are also checkboxes (several options) and radio buttons (precisely *one* option). An example is shown in Figure 4.13.

Matchcode search

Whenever the F4 help (input options for a field) contains a list that is too long, it makes sense to use the matchcode search.

Wildcards used are '+' for precisely one character and '*' for one or more unknown characters. These characters can be omitted at the end. For example, if the input *book* is made in the MATERIAL DESCRIPTION field in Figure 4.14, all materials containing the word component 'book', whether at the beginning, in the middle or at the end of the

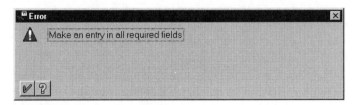

FIGURE 4.12   Message box – error (© SAP AG)

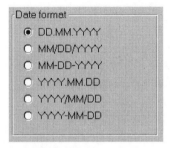

FIGURE 4.13   Window with radio buttons (© SAP AG)

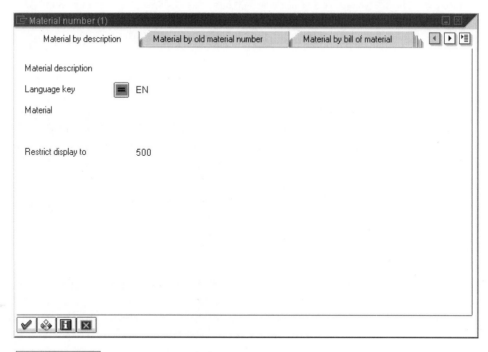

description, are displayed.

Instead of this direct search, F4 (input options) starts search help (for example when searching for material, creditor, etc.).

For searches for a material, search help, as shown in Figure 4.14, is offered. Select a search method by clicking on one of the tabs. For example, if the search is to run using the material description, click on the corresponding tab. A dialog window appears as shown in Figure 4.14. There, you enter the search term (e.g. material description).

If, for example, you want to search for material numbers from our book example, CD covers, you could enter 'CD' in the MATERIAL DESCRIPTION field. The result would be a display of all material descriptions that start with 'CD', with the associated material number.

The selected search (tab), as here via 'Material by description', is displayed immediately when the search help is opened again later, i.e. this setting remains until it is changed. By clicking the multiple selection icon, a search can be run for several values or within a specified value range.

| 4.3 | **PRINT** |

Output of an inspection plan

Using the inspection plan as an example, this section shows you how you can print the plan or view it in a print preview.

Open the INSPECTION PLANNING window (path: LOGISTICS | QUALITY MANAGEMENT | QUALITY PLANNING | INSPECTION PLANNING) and from there select the menu path: PRINT | PLANS | GENERAL INSPECTION TASK LISTS. The PRINT LISTS FOR TASK LIST window opens (see Fig. 4.15).

Enter the material number and tick off the desired checkboxes. The RUN icon or the keyboard input F8 takes you to the print preview of the inspection plan (Fig. 4.16).

By clicking the print icon or using the LIST | PRINT command, you obtain the desired printout on the assigned output printer. The set OUTPUT DEVICE is displayed beforehand. If you want to output to another printer, you still have a chance to specify another OUTPUT DEVICE.

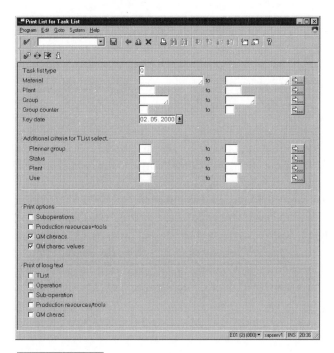

| FIGURE 4.15 | Print list for task list (© SAP AG)

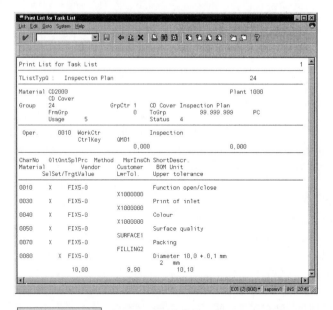

FIGURE 4.16 Print preview for task list (© SAP AG)

4.4 USER SETTINGS

User profile

You can use the menu path SYSTEM | USER SETTINGS | HOLD DATA to keep user profiles during a session (connection with the system) and thus avoid a considerable amount of additional input. If, however, you want to specify a permanent, personal user profile for any particular input field, proceed as follows.

Position the cursor on the input field and press F1 for Help. The Help window appears. Select TECHNICAL INFORMATION and note the PARAMETER ID. In the example shown in Fig. 4.17 for the 'Purchaser group' field, the PARAMETER ID is 'EKG'.

Exit from Help and select the menu path SYSTEM | USER SETTINGS | OWN DATA. In the menu MAINTENANCE (of own user settings), you have access to three tabs:

- ADDRESS
- DEFAULTS
- PARAMETERS

The ADDRESS view contains entries regarding the PERSON, such as address, title, department, or regarding COMMUNICATION by telephone and fax or e-mail. These values are used, for example, in the quality notification if the coordinator name (clerk) is to be supplemented by the telephone or fax number.

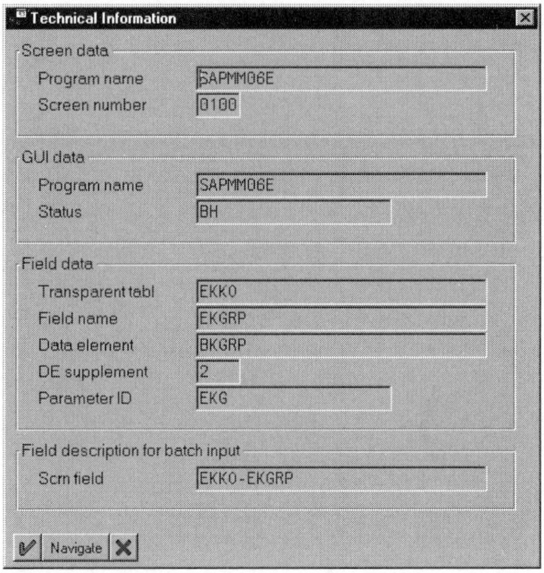

FIGURE 4.17   Technical information (© SAP AG)

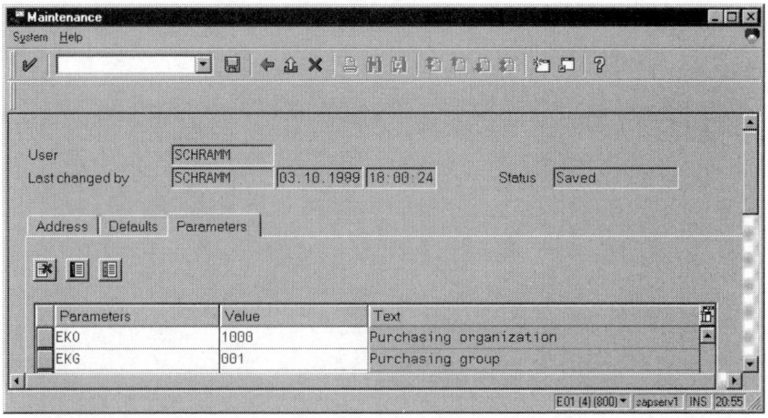

FIGURE 4.18   User parameters (© SAP AG)

The DEFAULTS view contains, among other things, the name of your output printer or the date format for this user.

Finally, in the PARAMETERS view, the PARAMETER ID we obtained previously from the TECHNICAL INFORMATION can be assigned a user profile value. A list that might already be there can, for example, now be given the parameter EKG and the desired user profile value (Fig. 4.18). To conclude, SAVE the altered inputs!

WORKING WITH TRANSACTION CODES AND MULTIPLE SESSIONS

During the familiarization period in the operation of R/3, it is recommended that you click on all the menus across the menu paths with the mouse. Working in this way helps you to learn the descriptions and, over time, you gain an overview of the existing menus, even if you do not know them all and do not use them at the beginning.

After a few weeks, you can also use the transaction codes. These are a kind of short description for each processing menu (the transaction). Over time, you will be so familiar with the transaction codes that you will use them to jump from one menu to the next instantly without having to waste several seconds using the mouse to select path names.

First of all, it is important to find out the transaction code for a desired menu. You have two possibilities:

1 *Display of system status*

Use the menu paths to select the desired application. From here, the SYSTEM | STATUS menu provides you with the status display. For the application CREATE INSPECTION PLAN, for example, a display as shown in Figure 4.19 appears. You can read off the transaction code (here: QP01) in the TRANSACTION field.

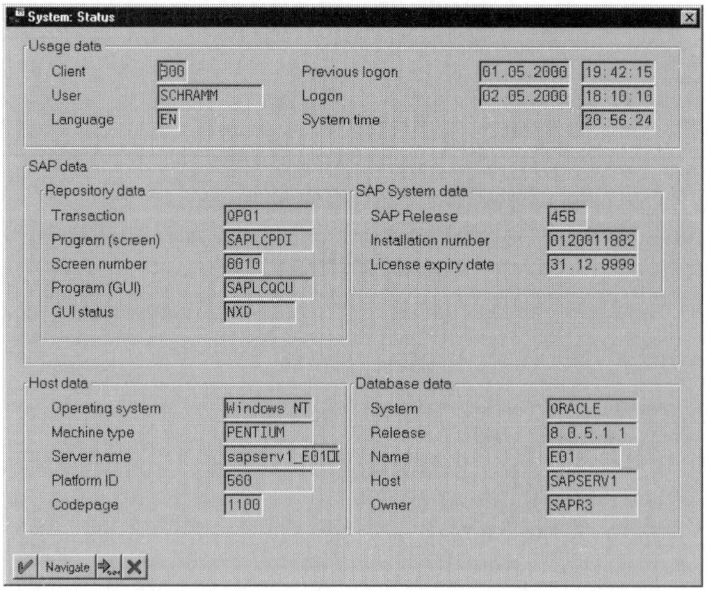

| **FIGURE 4.19** | System: Status with the transaction code (© SAP AG) |

FIGURE 4.20 Dynamic menu (© SAP AG)

2 *The dynamic menu*

If you want to have an overview of several transaction codes in one work area, begin at the start screen and select the DYNAMIC MENU button or press F5.

The relevant submenus open when you click on the branch on the menu tree. If you also click on the magnifier icon in the toolbar (TECHNICAL NAME), the transaction codes appear on the side branches of the menu tree.

Figure 4.20 shows, for example, the transaction codes for CREATE INSPECTION PLAN (QP01), CHANGE INSPECTION PLAN (QP02) and DISPLAY INSPECTION PLAN (QP03).

As in R/2, there is the possibility of working in several sessions (i.e. display windows) at the same time. The switch between sessions takes place as normal between windows (e.g. with the key combination ALT+TAB). The combination of various sessions and transaction codes enables rapid and efficient work. A maximum of six sessions can be opened at one time, whereby each session uses a certain portion of system power.

Using the transaction codes found in this way and the command field located in the toolbar, it is possible to jump quickly from transaction to transaction. With the key combination CTRL+TAB, the cursor jumps into the command field of the toolbar:

In this command field, you can enter the following commands and start them with ENTER:

▓ Starting a transaction
  – In the same session (window)
    enter: /nxxxx (xxxx = transaction code).
  – In an additional session
    enter: /oxxxx (xxxx = transaction code).

▓ To terminate the transaction
  enter: /n (unsaved changes are lost without warning).

▓ If you want to delete a session
  enter: /i

▓ To create a session list
  enter: /o

It is not important at this point whether you use upper or lower case letters for the commands and transaction codes.

If you are switching from the SAP R/2 system to R/3, you already know a great many transaction codes. Most of these have been retained, or those in R/3 are at least very similar to those in the R/2 system. For example, the transaction code for REQUISITION DISPLAY in R/2 is 'te53' and 'me53' in R/3. The input of /nme53 in the command window, followed by ENTER, opens the entry menu for the transaction DISPLAY REQUISITION directly.

TIP You can, for example, use a session to view an inspection plan in the INSPECTION PLANNING menu and at the same time use a second session to view the associated data in the MATERIAL MASTER DATA.

In addition to placing /o in front of the transaction code, you can also open a new window (session) from the menu bar via the path SYSTEM | CREATE SESSION or using the icon 🗐 in the toolbar.

4.6 **HELP IN THE R/3 SYSTEM**

The SAP R/3 system provides you with a variety of help options. These possibilities will be explained briefly below.

Direct help (F1 help)

In most cases, the help you require will be direct help relating to an input field. Mark the text of the input field with the left mouse button (the text is framed with a broken line) or place the cursor in the input field and press the F1 key. A short help text regarding this field appears (Fig. 4.21).

If this help text is not sufficient, you can click APPLICATION HELP (in Version 4.0 called EXTENDED HELP). However, a requirement is that, when working with the MS Windows™ operating system, you have also installed the MS Explorer™, as the APPLICATION HELP needs to use this browser as an interface. Instead of the F1 key, you can also use the HELP menu, called DIRECT HELP in Version 4.0, by clicking the question mark in the toolbar. The third possibility is the so-called 'context menu', which you can reach by clicking with the right-hand mouse button. The first menu item of this context menu is also direct HELP.

From direct HELP, you can select not only APPLICATION HELP but also TECHNICAL INFORMATION. As already explained in the section 'Working with transaction codes and multiple sessions', this provides you with a variety of information such as the transaction code or field and table name which, for example, could be important when searching for errors.

Possible entries (F4 help)

Another help option provided by the system is the so-called 'Possible entries'. This is always useful when you have to enter a value or code in an input field but do not know the precise value or code. Position the cursor on the relevant field and click on the arrow symbol to the right of the field, or press F4.

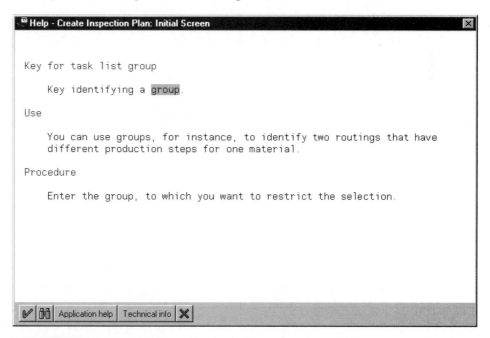

FIGURE 4.21   Help window called with F1 (© SAP AG)

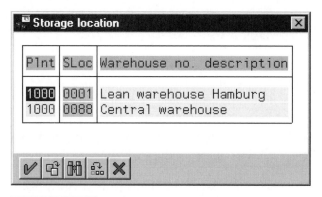

FIGURE 4.22 Options for storage location (© SAP AG)

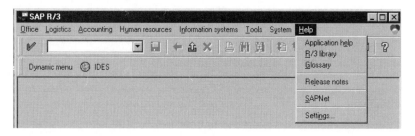

FIGURE 4.23 Help menu (© SAP AG)

For the STORAGE LOCATION field, the display as shown in Figure 4.22 appears.

Double-clicking on the relevant line makes the selection. For all date input fields, F4 calls up a calendar. The quickest way to make a selection is with a double-click.

If the field offers a large number of input options, pressing F4 opens a dialog window for restriction of the options (see the section on 'Matchcode search' in this chapter).

The Help menu

The HELP menu from the menu bar provides you with various options (Fig. 4.23).

Application help (formerly: Extended help)

The path HELP | APPLICATION HELP takes you to the R/3 library (Fig. 4.24). On selection, the browser is opened and a menu structure appears in the left-hand section and the relevant help text in the right-hand section. You can move around the tree structure and select help topics from there. This is how you can find a detailed explanation of each module and each function.

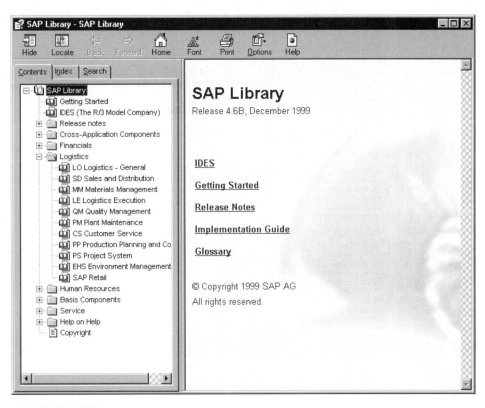

FIGURE 4.24   R/3 online help (© SAP AG)

For example, via LO – LOGISTICS, you can select the QUALITY MANAGEMENT area.

If you are already in an application (and not in the start menu), for example in 'Inspection planning', the APPLICATION HELP shows the application-related topic right away. If this displayed topic is already too specialized or does not contain the desired information, you should go back a few menus before starting the help function.

TIP   Beginners sometimes have difficulty using the online help effectively. However, the authors can give the assurance based on their own experience that the online help is very useful. One requirement is that the user is already familiar with the terminology and language used in the R/3 environment. Knowledge of the structure of the modules also makes it easier to find the desired information quickly. This is precisely what this book is trying to help you achieve, but without making the online help completely superfluous.

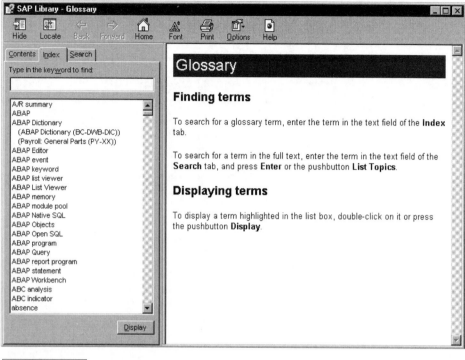

R/3 Library

On this path, you come to the same help window as with APPLICATION HELP.

Glossary

Definitions of specific SAP expressions can be found not only in this book, but also online under the menu path HELP | GLOSSARY (Fig. 4.25).

Release notes

In this submenu of HELP, you will find information on what has changed from one R/3 release to the next. The information is once again structured according to application components. This information is mainly of interest when you have switched to a new release and want to know what changes are important to you.

Introduction to R/3

The submenu INTRODUCTION TO R/3 has been eliminated since Release 4.5. It contained basic explanations of the R/3 system; these are available either through EXTENDED HELP or APPLICATION HELP, as the case may be.

Help settings

At the HELP | SETTINGS menu item, you can choose whether the F1 HELP is to appear in a normal R/3 window (modal window) or, as is the case for the APPLICATION HELP, an external viewer or browser (amodal window) is to be started. However, this option is only available to you in a Windows environment and as of Release 3.1G.

Help on Help

The menu path HELP | HELP ON HELP has been omitted from Release 4.5 onwards, as it led into the same help system as APPLICATION HELP.

4.7   DISPLAY FUNCTIONS AND LIST DISPLAY

The following pages are intended to illustrate the practical application of some important display functions from the logistics process; these are very useful for your work in quality management. You can find more information on the topic of displays and evaluations in Chapter 10, 'Information systems and evaluations', as well as in the relevant sections of a few other chapters.

Vendor data

Contact to vendors is important for quality management. To ensure this, you need addresses and other contact information. This can be found in the PURCHASING menu, which you reach at the path LOGISTICS | MATERIALS MANAGEMENT | PURCHASING. From there, select MASTER DATA | VENDOR | PURCHASING | DISPLAYS (CURRENT) (Fig. 4.26).

After you have entered the vendor number and the purchasing organization, and have placed a check mark in the 'Address' field, the address and communication data is displayed.

List display: goods received from vendors

It is often the case that you want to know not only the current worklist of inspection lots but also the development of the last goods receipts from a certain vendor. The list display function is very suitable for this task; it can be found at many different points in the R/3 system. The starting point is the PURCHASING menu. There, select ORDER |

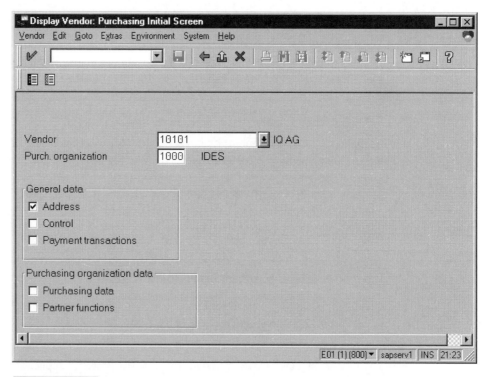

FIGURE 4.26   Display vendor address (© SAP AG)

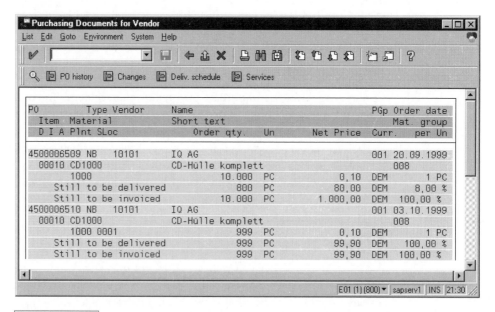

FIGURE 4.27   List display: Purchasing documents for vendor (© SAP AG)

LIST DISPLAYS | FOR VENDORS and then move into a selection screen with the title PURCHASING DOCUMENTS FOR VENDOR. Selection screens are easy to recognize: in addition to the many input fields, which usually allow a value range from/to, the icon for RUN stands out. You can enter various selection parameters, for example the

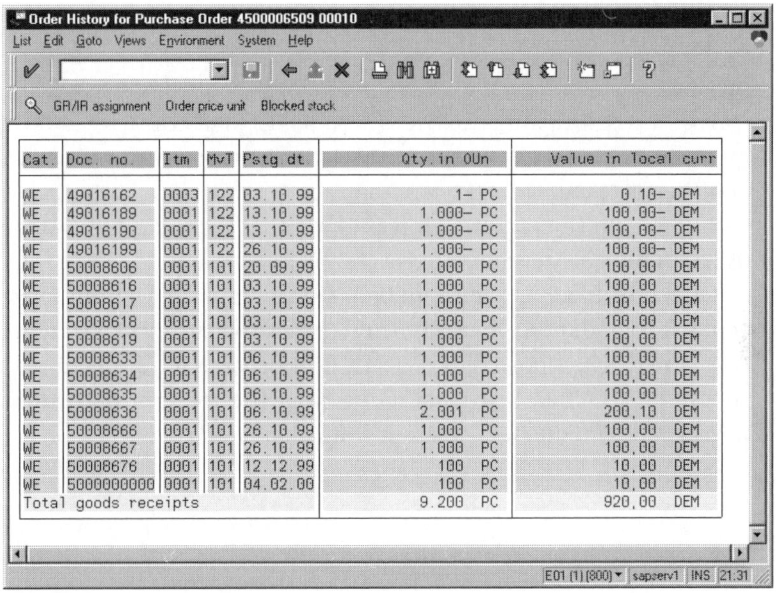

Cat.	Doc. no.	Itm	MvT	Pstg dt	Qty.in OUn	Value in local curr
WE	49016162	0003	122	03.10.99	1- PC	0,10- DEM
WE	49016189	0001	122	13.10.99	1.000- PC	100,00- DEM
WE	49016190	0001	122	13.10.99	1.000- PC	100,00- DEM
WE	49016199	0001	122	26.10.99	1.000- PC	100,00- DEM
WE	50008606	0001	101	20.09.99	1.000 PC	100,00 DEM
WE	50008616	0001	101	03.10.99	1.000 PC	100,00 DEM
WE	50008617	0001	101	03.10.99	1.000 PC	100,00 DEM
WE	50008618	0001	101	03.10.99	1.000 PC	100,00 DEM
WE	50008619	0001	101	03.10.99	1.000 PC	100,00 DEM
WE	50008633	0001	101	06.10.99	1.000 PC	100,00 DEM
WE	50008634	0001	101	06.10.99	1.000 PC	100,00 DEM
WE	50008635	0001	101	06.10.99	1.000 PC	100,00 DEM
WE	50008636	0001	101	06.10.99	2.001 PC	200,10 DEM
WE	50008666	0001	101	26.10.99	1.000 PC	100,00 DEM
WE	50008667	0001	101	26.10.99	1.000 PC	100,00 DEM
WE	50008676	0001	101	12.12.99	100 PC	10,00 DEM
WE	5000000000	0001	101	04.02.00	100 PC	10,00 DEM
Total goods receipts					9.200 PC	920,00 DEM

FIGURE 4.28 Order history (© SAP AG)

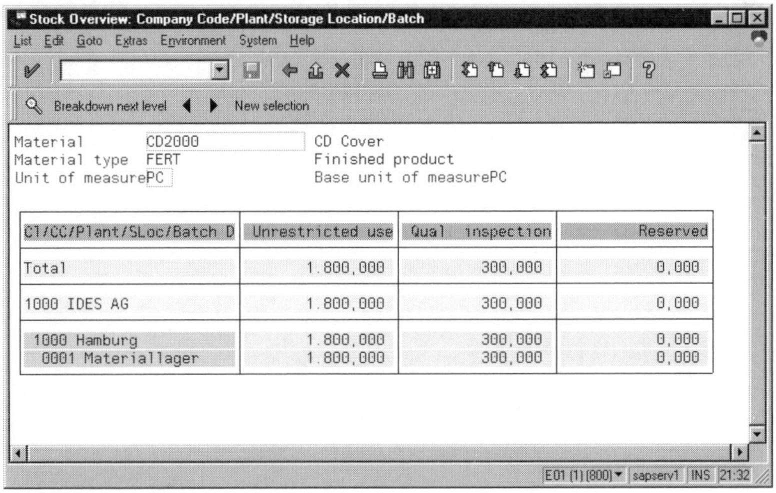

Cl/CC/Plant/SLoc/Batch D	Unrestricted use	Qual. inspection	Reserved
Total	1.800,000	300,000	0,000
1000 IDES AG	1.800,000	300,000	0,000
1000 Hamburg	1.800,000	300,000	0,000
0001 Materiallager	1.800,000	300,000	0,000

FIGURE 4.29 Stock overview (© SAP AG)

vendor number, in the input fields. If you do not know the selection value precisely, you can use the matchcode search explained earlier (function key F4). After clicking RUN, a display similar to that in Figure 4.27 appears.

By selecting the order item and clicking the PO HISTORY button, you are given a display that shows you the date you received which delivery quantity (see Fig. 4.28).

Stock overview

Another item of information that is frequently required is the stock of a certain material.

First, select the path LOGISTICS | MATERIALS MANAGEMENT | MATERIAL and then the menu OTHER | STOCK OVERVIEW. A selection list appears in which we enter the PLANT and the MATERIAL NUMBER and then receive a display of the stocks with a specified storage location and information as to whether the goods are available for unrestricted use or in the quality stock (see Fig. 4.29).

Of course there are any number of possible displays from logistic processes that could be important to your company. The examples shown above are intended to illustrate a few of the possibilities. The list displays that you require for your own tasks should be specified in collaboration with the relevant departments – Purchasing, Logistics and Production – in your company.

CHAPTER 5

Quality management in the logistics chain

5.1 BASIC PRINCIPLES

This chapter is aimed especially at quality managers, the head of IT, and at the project managers of SAP R/3 logistics projects. First, you are given an overview of the most important flanking and integrated R/3 QM functions in the logistics chain (see Fig. 5.1); then you can move on to the more detailed descriptions of the individual modules. It is important to understand quality management as a productive unit in the value creation chain of a company in order to be able to recognize both the basic requirements and the potential for process improvements. As soon as the work of quality management is viewed as 'genuine' operational output, the question as to the whole point of computerization no longer applies.

Within the logistics chain, activities relevant to quality take place in the spheres of both internal and external relations. With a homogeneous process design from the point of view of quality management, combined with the deployment of integrated software, these activities can be brought up to the required level. Another positive effect that results from a consistently implemented R/3 QM system is the excellent transparency in the quality-relevant aspects of logistics. In general, the properties of the QM component are based on the conceptional models of the quality control cycle and the quality pyramid (cf. Masing 1988).

Procurement	Production	Sales	Delivery	Service

Quality Planning

Quality Inspection

Quality Notification

Quality Control

Batch Management

Controlling

Measurement Management

Certificates

FIGURE 5.1 QM elements in the logistics chain

The quality cycle (Fig. 5.2) is a result of the demands and expectations of the customer. Here, the customer assesses not only the product quality but also the overall concept. As suppliers usually audit their customers nowadays, an overall QM concept structured in relation to the process chain has a significantly more positive effect on a quality assessment than a concept with island CAQ (Computerized Quality Assurance) solutions.

5.2 SUPPLY CHAIN MANAGEMENT (SCM)

Cooperation with vendors

Increasing competitive and technological pressures force many companies to concentrate on their core skills; this is confirmed by the continuous reduction in manufacturing depth. This development leads to a permanent rise not only in the number of sourced materials or components, but also in services. Efficient vendors are thus important – important to survival! In addition to the internal logistics value creation chain, the interfaces between vendors and purchasers contain a great deal of potential for optimization. The strategy of 'supply chain management' is based on this (see Table 5.1). Purchasing, which is frequently run as a pure 'vendor rating' function, becomes a strategic corporate function.

TABLE 5.1	Comparison between traditional purchasing and supply chain management
Traditional purchasing	**Supply chain management**
Short-term view, opportunistic cooperation	Long-term partnership
Price-oriented	Total costs
Broad base of vendors	Single sourcing, module sourcing
Frequent vendor changes	Infrequent vendor changes
Unreliable delivery	Synchronized delivery
Functional separation	Functional integration
Separate development	Joint development
Uncoordinated capacities	Coordinated capacities
Interrupted information flow	Consistent information flow

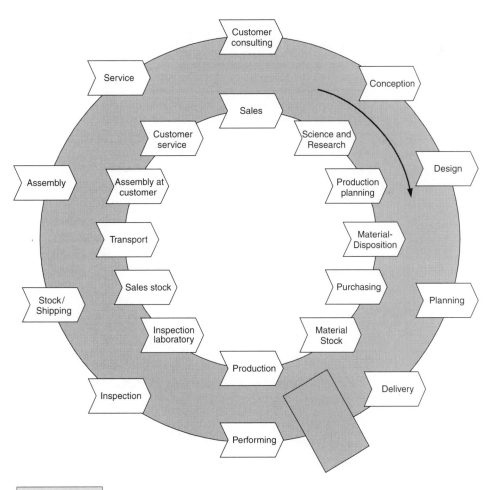

FIGURE 5.2   Quality control cycle

TABLE 5.2	The development towards partnership-based supply chain management	
Factor	Low intensity of partnership	Full partnership
Vendor relationship	Mistrust, broad vendor base, frequent change of vendors	Full trust, single sourcing, partnership, vendor support
Management	Focus on direct production costs, no commitment to partnerships, purchasing as a 'necessary evil'	Focus on supply chain, concentration on quality, costs, cycle times, early involvement of vendors, share of savings
Organization	Functional, decentralized purchasing	Horizontal, cross-departmental teams, central corporate sourcing and decentralized purchasing
Controlling	Price	Total costs (price, costs of inadequate quality as well as poor delivery service)
Quality	No clear specifications, incoming goods inspection, no SPC (Statistical Process Control)	Target quality, specified QM system, planned dynamic goods receipt inspection, SPC
Costs	'The vendor with the lowest price offer gets today's order', growing range of parts	Target costing, reduction of the range of parts, concentration of business volume
Cycle times	High safety stocks, long throughput times, no forecasts	Pull system (Kanban), just-in-time, short throughput times, rolling forecasts

Setting up a value-creation partnership requires a mutual willingness to improve the efficiency of the cooperation. The basis of every partnership is trust, without which a close collaboration will never succeed. For the assessment of the cooperation between vendors and customers in supply management, various determining factors are evaluated, some of which are of essential significance to quality management (Table 5.2).

Supply chain management will also continue to gain in importance for quality management in the logistics chain. The system functions and processes in the SAP R/3 system support you in this development towards partnership-based customer–vendor relationships.

5.3   MATERIALS MANAGEMENT

The business processes of Materials Management are flanked by the activities of quality management that take place in the following areas:

- Purchasing
- Production
- Sales and Distribution
- Service

5.3.1 Purchasing

Release of supply relationships

With the functions of the *Q information record*, you control the release of material/ vendor relationships. The release can take place in relation to time or quantity, or based on other criteria, for example the existence of certain documents (acceptance of technical terms of delivery, specifications, etc.). Depending on how the quality standards are weighted, the inquiry, order or goods receipt is blocked.

Vendor selection

The activities involved in vendor selection for new and existing products are organized across departments and meet in Materials Management and vendor evaluation. In vendor evaluation, you can illustrate the criteria from delivery, price and quality in scores, weighting and grouping as you wish. When you audit your vendors, the audit result is also included in the calculation of the quality scores.

A comparison of the required and actual configuration of a quality management system (ISO 9000ff, QS 9000, VDA, etc.) ensures that only companies with the appropriate certification are considered as vendors.

Inquiry and order

Release of the supply relationship includes the QM agreements with the vendor. If these are not yet available at the time of the inquiry/order, Quality Control can warn Purchasing automatically prior to placement of the order or, if appropriate, slow down the procedure.

Status of the supply relationship

In the case of delivery of industrial products, the actual delivery is usually preceded by a sampling procedure with initial samples, and for series deliveries with initial samples, a pre-series and series delivery. Different inspections are required for the delivery stages. Depending on the delivery status, the system is able to provide the correct inspection plans.

Approval

Especially in the case of mechanical and plant engineering, approval of the products for delivery by the vendor itself is advisable. You can use the QM component to manage the approval dates and open inspection lots with the approval criteria.

Stock management with QM

So that the properties of the material in a delivery are documented, a material inspection certificate is often a direct component of the delivery process. If a certificate of this kind is missing, it should be found without fail. The system provides possibilities to query whether a certificate has been delivered at goods receipt and to ensure that the correct certificates are received. In critical cases, you can block the acceptance of goods or post the delivery into blocked stock. If document management is to be included in your project, you have the possibility to archive the certificates visually and assign them to deliveries.

At the Materials Management (MM) level, you can post a delivery through goods receipt to various stock categories such as RELEASED, USABLE, BLOCKED or to the QUALITY INSPECTION STOCK. In the event of a planned goods receipt inspection, the system places the goods in the QUALITY INSPECTION STOCK. The material is thus protected against unwanted posting to the released stock. Quantity postings or stock movements are only possible from here via the usage decision. Entries in the material master data regarding the overall goods receipt duration and the duration of the inspection provide stock planning with another important form of support. In the R/3 system, the functions for stock management and for the QM component are integrated. In their shipped condition, the processes of QM stock posting and inspection lot creation are capable of functioning and are available after the business transaction modeling. For inspection lot creation, there is a choice of processes with which only the first goods receipt, an individual delivery or one batch per order are to be inspected.

In order to reduce the inspection overhead in the case of high delivered quality, there are so-called 'skip-lot' processes for inspection waivers. To achieve this, the system creates inspection lots that automatically trigger a usage decision ACCEPTANCE at a skip level; this posts the goods into released stock.

Inspection and release of received goods

The inspection lot, together with the inspection plan provided via the planned usage, contains all the details of the flow of documents, the inspection instructions/specifications as well as quantities and sampling instructions. For the handling of the inspection, the inspection lot is the core of all the activities that now follow. You enter the course of the inspection via the inspection lot number or the structure list in the WORKLIST STOCK FOR RESULTS RECORDING. For the inspection, there are quantitative and qualitative characteristics in various types of recording.

On the basis of inspection results, the USAGE DECISION is made. You record the quantities of the delivery following acceptance and reject criteria, specify the usage and post the desired stock from this location.

When the usage decision is concluded using an evaluation code, the quality score is incremented. The quality situation for the next inspection can be updated after the usage decision or on lot creation.

Manufacturer inspection

If the vendor of the goods is not the actual manufacturer, but you want to assess the manufacturer, record the delivered quality at manufacturer level. A relation to the manufacturer is therefore possible in most QM functions. In the areas of inspection planning, vendor approval/assessment and quality notifications are considered separately.

Complaints regarding delivered goods

Defects can be discovered at the goods receipt inspection or in the further processing of delivered products. In order to remedy the defects, measures directed at the vendor and the internal organization are required. An important task when making complaints to vendors is to inform the vendors and request rapid removal of the defects or faults. The complaint must contain a description of the problem, the defect analysis and all measures related to the event. The vendor receives this in writing with printed forms enclosed. A direct relationship to the delivery, order and return handling can be seen from the complaint. The functions of the complaint have the character of a workflow and can be processed by several departments.

Warehouse management

The Warehouse Management (WM) system is a separate component within the R/3 logistics package. The stocks at storage locations are distributed to storage bays. Frequently, the assignment to the storage bay must take place before the delivery is subjected to the goods receipt inspection, or an inspection waiver posts the goods directly there. The administration of QM assigns the goods at the storage bay the stock code 'Q'. The comprehensible flow of documents of the goods movements gives you exact information regarding which goods at the individual storage bays are already available for unrestricted use or which goods have withdrawal blocked.

As early on as the inspection planning, you can specify that the random sample proportion of the inspection lot is sent to the inspection department; the remaining quantity is moved immediately from the goods receipt zone to the storage bay. Alternatively, it is also possible to keep the delivery in the goods receipt zone until it is released with the usage decision and then post it manually to the storage bay later. For the lot quantities, the system creates the transport orders that precede storage and, depending on the usage decision, qualifies the stocks at the storage bays.

Batches

The interplay of the MM and QM components means that a batch-based quality strategy can be used. If batch management has been enabled on the MM side, the inspection lot receives a batch relationship for incoming goods inspections and recurring inspections. The usage decision defines the batch status on inspection lot completion. You can divide the various batches with recurring inspections into released and non-released stocks. Another function within the recurring inspection is the monitoring of the sell-by date of a batch. As soon as the latest possible sell-by date has been reached, the system transfers the batch into the blocked stock and changes the batch status into NOT RELEASED.

5.3.2 Production

With the PP (Production Planning and Control) component, the R/3 system contains a complete system for the processes of production with different production strategies such as:

- Batch production in chemicals and foods processing (PP-PI).
- Single part and lot manufacturing in mechanical engineering.
- Series production, for example in the automotive field.

With QM, SAP provides a uniform approach to all activities relevant to quality for the various forms of production.

Integrated planning

In principle, in-process inspection operations are just as much value-creating activities as other work operations required to manufacture a product. Inspection planning in production is thus fully integrated in the routing. Inspection planning and work planning have the same design and the same operation. The inspection characteristics and production resources/tools are each assigned to one or more operations in the routing. As the operation with inspection characteristics is no different from other operations, capacity and schedule planning are also possible.

Inspections in production

The automatic inspection lot creation for inspections parallel to manufacturing is triggered in production with the release of the manufacturing order. Other forms of automatic inspection lot creation are also provided by goods movements, e.g. on outgoing goods or goods withdrawal from production on the basis of separate inspection plans. Batch-based production is supported with inspections for individual batches or for the entire production order.

Inspection points

The alternative to lot-based inspection is random sample inspection at regular intervals or when specified events occur. This inspection control can be used to monitor production processes with series/process manufacturing or large lot sizes more accurately. For SPC inspections, an interval-controlled inspection sequence is essential. In the QM component, repeated inspections parallel to production for a production order are referred to as *inspection points*.

Process control

The functions of SPC control chart technology mean that QM provides a complete tool for statistical process control. The plant self-inspection is supported by the visual control chart in the form of graphical processes. The flanking statistical techniques help on the basis of the measured values entered to analyse the process and determine optimum intervention limits.

In simple words, the SPC is a method that not only checks the process as regards adherence to specification limits, but also uses the distribution form and statistical variables to optimize the process. Proceeding in this way means that the process flow can be relieved of unnecessary fluctuations and influences that lead to losses of quality. The error rate in SPC-stabilized processes is also significantly lower.

Process management

If production processes cannot be set using SPC, or this is very difficult, graphical representations of measured values can provide important information on the stability of production. These representations of results are not interrupted even if characteristics are modified during production. If changes to the inspection plan are necessary in the process that is running, you can create a new inspection lot with the updated inspection plan for the same order after inspection lot completion.

Batches

QM supports batch-based production processes by connecting the inspection results with the batch number and the batch evaluation.

Feedback

Feedback from a manufacturing order is normally provided using the functions of the PP component. The feedback contains the quantity produced, the scrap, and the proportion of units that require reworking. If you are working with inspection points, the feedback is integrated in the results recording for the inspection point.

A work step that is used exclusively for an inspection is suitable for connecting the feedback with the quality notification. By means of a simple extension, the feedback triggers the quality notification directly, or the quality notification is created during the results recording for the inspection. In later analyses, this makes it easy to establish a link between the manufacturing orders and procedures and the main defects.

5.3.3 Sales and Distribution

Quality documents for the supply relationship

The technical terms of delivery and specifications for products can be managed with information records in the same way as the procedures in purchasing. Here, the system-integrated document management can also provide support for fast access to documents.

Outgoing goods inspection

If a special qualification of the products is required, events during the delivery process create inspection lots. The control of when an inspection is performed and which usage decision allows delivery can be set depending on the customer, sales organization and material.

Inspections for configuration variants

Variants of products with the same material numbers can be produced and sold. The system supports this procedure with the so-called 'variant configuration'. Naturally, characteristics that refer to variable attributes must also be configured variably. In the system, it is therefore possible to lay down that the specifications defined in the customer order are also assigned the suitable characteristic for inspections.

Batch tracing

The system provides supporting functions for all processes where you or your customers require batch management/tracing. In this connection, knowledge of the relationship between delivery and the batches used is of central importance. Batch tracing in the logistics chain also indicates the raw material batches from which the later product is composed. All inspection results, the usage decision, as well as the inspection lots, contain the batch number as supplementary information and can be analysed accordingly.

If various batches come together in one product, the product can be inspected as regards its component batches. The reverse path – which batches were used to produce which products – can also be shown.

Practical evidence provides the required information for a quality certificate with the inspection results from the preceding or included batches. All results can then be placed together on a certificate and printed out as a form.

Customer complaints

The system supports comprehensive customer complaints management with integrated functions. The complaints process can be documented from the initial recording of a complaint through the defect analysis to measures monitoring. Customer complaints management is a component of the R/3 notification system, with uniform and typical function characteristics. Quality management can use the notification system to structure all the business events relevant to the notification, and use the system to create a workflow for Service Management.

Certificates

The documentation of the materials contained in the product and other inspection results are often part of the delivery and must be compiled with the same care and attention as the delivery itself. Complete documentation includes so-called 'plant inspection certificates', the form of which is specified in international standards, but freely defined certificates can also be involved.

The creation of certificates is a matter of individual customer preference as regards form and content of the documents. The system provides the possibility to use SAPscript to design customer-oriented forms on the basis of suitable templates.

For deliveries, you can set the desired certificate in advance. When the certificate is created, the recipient, form and content, as well as the method of shipping, are taken into account. In compiling the data for the certificate and preparing the report, the program accesses the master and movement data and merges them in the printout of the certificate. The report provides access to all the relevant data from Materials Management, Quality Management and Sales and Distribution, e.g. batch values, characteristic values, inspection results and order information. The quality documents created in this way can then be filed in the integrated document management using SAP ArchiveLink.

Internet

Your customer can gain direct access to information on the contents of quality certificates across the internet. The special advantage here lies in the ability to access certificate data immediately. Complicated shipping processes and creation of the certificate in paper form are eliminated completely. The customer can assess the information in the certificate even before the actual delivery and make the necessary decisions.

5.3.4 Service

The operations within the service management (SM) component are frequently initiated by quality-related influences. Here, customer problems are recorded and documented in notifications that describe the problem and initiate further processing through to solution of the problem. In addition to other SM functions, the service notification, along with customer complaints, is part of the R/3 notification system (see Fig. 5.3). In using these components, Quality Management and Service speak more or less the same language.

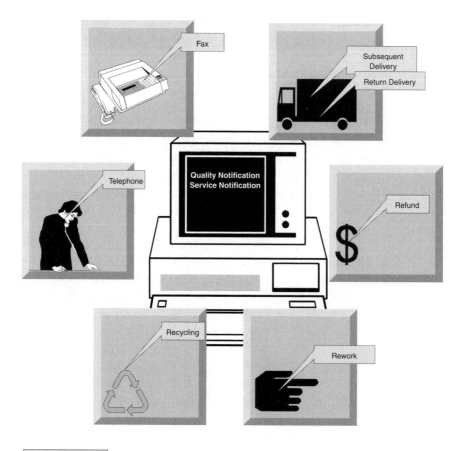

FIGURE 5.3   Customer service

Starting from the recording of the notification, SM enables handing of measures, service and customer orders as well as the connecting processes of feedback, recording of output/costs, delivery and invoicing.

Returns

Service management is not a separate component; it is composed of numerous functions from Materials Management, Production, and Sales and Distribution. Service management is then put together with the selected system functions. The basis can also be a customer complaint in the form of a quality notification. Starting from the notification, the departments involved place, for example, a rework order, make stock postings, record complaint costs and initiate special inspections. The core processes of service management are stored in the system as a reference model and you can use them as the basis for business process modeling.

Service management (repairs)

In precisely the same way as for service management, a process spanning several components is responsible for service management (repairs). The repair of a product runs through different organizational and technical phases. The most important object here is the repair order, which can be started either from the quality notification or the service notification. In most cases, the material to be repaired arrives in a delivery. The goods movement to incoming goods can now open an inspection lot and this initiates an immediate defect analysis. At the same time, a posting to the quality inspection stock prevents confusion of the material.

The rework order created from the repair order is similar to a manufacturing order and contains the required procedures for remedying the defect. After the repair has been completed, the inspection department makes a usage decision and can then release the stock for delivery. From the repair order, the process is concluded with a goods delivery and invoice to the customer.

Maintenance

'Preventive maintenance' is of fundamental importance to functioning quality management systems. This includes, in particular, internal and external maintenance tasks on production systems and production resources/tools. To support maintenance tasks that are relevant to quality and of a general nature, the system provides a separate application component Plant Maintenance (PM). All work processes in maintenance are linked to one another via data and functions without interfaces. The integration of PM in the logistics chain spans virtually all the application components of the SAP R/3 system – in much the same way as QM.

Test equipment management in particular, as part of the maintenance of production resources/tools, is an integrated process through the QM and PM components. In this context, test equipment management draws on, for example, the objects equipment, technical bays, maintenance plans from PM as well as inspection plans, characteristics, calibration regulations and inspection lots from QM. The calibration check is triggered by the maintenance order, which also contains details of the intervals for periodically recurring inspections.

What do you have to bear in mind for the QM implementation along the logistics chain?

- Most of the QM functions can also be implemented individually; a general QM implementation is not absolutely essential.
- The implementation of QM requires profound knowledge of logistics and all related aspects of business management.
- Optimized process design prior to the implementation is the only way to exploit the powerful functions of QM.

- QM is integrated into logistics business processes to an extent unmatched by any other application component.

- Considerable benefits and savings potentials can be gained through QM. The functions listed are usually perceived in companies as obligatory, but often not computerized.

CHAPTER 6

Quality and inspection planning

BASIC PRINCIPLES

Quality planning is a function which spans various specialist areas and is used for the general quality improvement of products and processes, combining this with the desire to reduce total quality costs. Its task is to use the data acquired from quality-relevant events and processes to:

- Refer demands arising from individual tasks to the quality department
- Set up a quality assurance system
- Develop methods for the quality inspections
- Incorporate quality costs in the result improvement strategy

The next sections of this chapter are primarily concerned with the tasks and overall handling of inspection planning as an element of quality planning. Various preconditions must be met before it is possible to plan the quality of products.

- *Evidence of producibility must be provided*

  On the basis of the customer's specifications, all departments involved determine a concept for the implementation of the customer requirements.

▓ *Design and process FMEAs must be prepared*

The early recognition of problems in the production process minimizes the risk of unexpected quality costs.

▓ *An inspection plan must be prepared*

Inspection planning adapted to the realities of the production process, in conjunction with the critical selection of the characteristics to be tested, is a prerequisite for effective defect prevention. Inspection characteristics and frequency are not rigid specifications for the life cycle of the product. Continuous adaptation is an important task – also from the point of view of appraisal costs.

▓ *Vendor assessments must be prepared*

The choice of vendor determines overall quality just as much as the quality of your own performance.

▓ *Machine and process capability must be established*

Examinations of machine and process capability, which have the aim of defect prevention, play a very important role.

▓ *Prototype inspections must be carried out*

The prototype inspection, together with the presentation to the customer and documentation, reflects the effectiveness of the adopted measures and successful quality planning.

Nowadays, quality planning in companies has a high status similar to that of production planning and controlling; this is because it represents the most important link for a customer-oriented process. In the quality assurance systems as per ISO 9000ff and QS 9000, quality planning is among the most important elements of the company business plan.

The preparatory activities for quality control constitute a further element of quality planning. In this respect, extremely accurate definitions from various catalogs on the subject of problem description and defect analysis are required in order to produce meaningful results during later evaluations.

Inspection planning

The aim of careful planning is to organize the tasks of the inspection process so that they are easy to handle at a later time and so that the related work steps can be completed as smoothly as possible. Furthermore, the total inspection overhead involved in the logistics chain is usually considerably reduced if inspection planning is carefully directed. Inspection planning itself is formally defined as 'planning of the quality inspection' (cf. DGQ, 'Concepts in the field of quality assurance', 1987 p. 3) and is also implemented as such in R/3–QM. The term 'inspection planning' refers to the planning of the quality inspection for the entire production sequence from goods receipt to goods issue. It is used to apply quality-promoting measures to products and processes and, at the same time, must adapt to conditions specific to the company (cf. VDI/VDE/DGQ 2619).

Inspection planning, while bearing aspects of economic efficiency in mind, stipulates inspection activities and operations according to type, place, frequency, time and production process, including the type and scope of the quality inspection. All company operations must be incorporated in the planning to produce comprehensive quality assurance (cf. VDI/VDE/DGQ 2619).

A selective and methodical procedure is the key to effective and successful inspection planning. As far as economic efficiency is concerned, the time and expenditure involved in inspection planning and the inspection itself should be kept to a minimum, but the quality improvement attained should be as high as possible. Due to the antithetical nature of these demands, it would appear that a certain potential for conflict is pre-programmed. A polished system of inspection usually results in significantly improved product quality; the increased time and effort involved in quality planning, however, must not place a greater burden than planned on company costing.

Inspection planning terms (from VDI/VDE/DGQ 2619)

For the remainder of this chapter, we will mainly be using SAP-internal terms for the area of inspection planning (not only where unequivocal definitions of terms exist, but also in most other cases where there is general agreement about the meanings of the terms). However, it is also important to consider company-specific terms, as well as those familiar from the relevant specialist literature, in order to establish a homogenous language framework for the project work. The most important terms and definitions are:

- *Attribute inspection*

  Quality inspection based on qualitative characteristics. SAP correctly describes the attributive characteristics as qualitative characteristics.

- *Receipt inspection*

  Quality inspection of a delivered product.

- *Final inspection*

  Last of the quality inspections before delivery to buyer.

- *Defect weighting*

  Classification of all possible defects in one unit into defect weighting classes on the basis of a defect assessment. The aim of this is to establish an economically feasible level of inspection time and expenditure.

- *Production inspection*

  Quality inspections of production processes.

■ *Characteristic*

A characteristic that makes differentiation within a totality possible – either quali-tatively (qualitative characteristic) or quantitatively (quantitative characteristic).

■ *Process inspection*

Quality inspection of a process on the basis of characteristics of the process itself or process results.

■ *Inspection sequence plan*

Specified sequence of quality inspections.

■ *Inspection instruction*

Instruction on performance of quality inspections.

■ *Inspection data*

Inspection result details; individual statistical results, measurement results and data on the peripheral conditions influencing the measuring result.

■ *Inspection dimension*

Dimensions (as per DIN 406, Part 2) that should be given particular attention when defining the inspection scope, e.g. to ensure the functioning of the inspection item. In a technical drawing, a frame round the dimension highlights the inspection dimension.

■ *Inspection level*

Specified characteristic of a sampling scheme based on random samples and scope of lot, and the selectivity (inspection severity) of the plan.

■ *Inspection plan*

The inspection plan contains:

– Inspection specification
  Stipulation of inspection characteristics and, if necessary, the inspection methods for a quality inspection.

– Statistical quality inspection
  Quality inspection with the help of statistical methods, particularly random samples.

– Sampling instruction
  Instructions on the scope of the samples to be drawn, the sampling itself, and the criteria for establishing the acceptance of the inspection lot.

– Sampling scheme
  Compilation of sampling instructions based on higher priority perspectives drawn from the sampling system. Examples of these higher-order perspectives are the acceptable quality limits and the inspection level.

– Random sample inspection
  Quality inspection on the basis of a sampling instruction for the evaluation of an

inspection lot.

– Sampling system
Compilation of sampling schemes with rules for their application.

– Inspection by variable
Quality inspection on the basis of quantitative characteristics (measuring inspection).

6.2 OVERVIEW OF QUALITY AND INSPECTION PLANNING

The quality planning in the R/3 system contains an extensive modular system consisting of a variety of master data and functions for all preparatory activities in inspection planning and inspection lot processing.

In this section, we would like to draw your attention to the objects and interconnections involved in quality planning, and use practical examples to implement the knowledge gained. The section contains information on the following:

- General master data.
- Basic data for inspection planning.
- Elements of inspection planning and administration.
- Practical application of the inspection plan in the logistics chain.

A current requirement, especially in the automobile industry, is the fulfilment of the QS 9000 requirements, including the element 'QM Control Plan'. Although R/3 still does not contain a special modular unit for the QM Control Plan, the requirements of the QS 9000, however, are easy to implement using the individual elements of the component QM (inspection plan, routing, reference operation set). In this respect, the quality planning dialogue between vendor and customer becomes an obligatory element of the services that have to be performed by the vendor. At this point, the customer becomes a partner in the preparation of all quality-relevant planning.

Before we return to the R/3 system, here are a few brief, general explanations on the nature of inspection planning. The main elements of inspection planning in the R/3 system are the inspection plan/routing and the inspection sequence control. The following must be specified in the inspection plan:

- Material purchasing.
- Inspection characteristic with inspection instruction.
- Inspection scope.
- Inspection frequency (dynamic modification).
- Inspection data processing.

The inspection sequence control stipulates the interaction between the activities in Purchasing and Production Management with the following input:

- Necessity for inspection.
- Inspection sequence.
- Inspection method.
- Test equipment.
- Inspection lot processing.

Ideally, before either of the above are carried out, an FMEA (failure mode and effect analysis – or, more simply, an analysis of possible errors and effects) should be conducted and its results incorporated in the planning for quality assurance and production.

Quality inspections are usually carried out using inspection characteristics that are determined in coordination with the specialist departments involved: Engineering/Design, Production and Purchasing. It follows that quality planning is another important integrating element as far as the process is concerned. Through the system integration of quality planning, the problem of the CAQ (Computer Aided Quality Assurance) interface to master and process data is almost completely eliminated. Online access to all necessary data simplifies the preparation of an inspection plan without a system and media change.

6.3   BASIC DATA FOR QUALITY AND INSPECTION PLANNING

Particularly in the case of inspection planning, you will use a large amount of intramodular master data from Materials Management, from Production, and from other logistics components. Before accessing this data, it is certainly advisable to enter into a dialog with the user responsible regarding future use. These discussions usually uncover new aspects of system use and further synergy potential for the QM integration. Table 6.1 offers you an introductory overview of the master data; we will then explore the master data most relevant to quality management in greater detail.

6.3.1 General master data

Material master data

The *material master record* in the R/3 system is a complex construction used for controlling commercial and logistic processes. For clarity purposes, the material master data is divided into different VIEWS which, as of Release 4.5, are represented on the screen in the form of tab registers. A further view is one from the Quality Management perspective. If this VIEW of the material is not yet available, the material master data administrator can create it any time without this having any effect on business logistics, for example in Stock Management. The functions for inspection lot creation, the stock posting and, especially, the controls for the QM in Purchasing are not activated until

TABLE 6.1	Master data in the R/3 system	
General master data	**Module**	**QM usage**
Material master data	PP	Inspection plan
Change master record	MM	Material master data, inspection plan, Q-info record
Vendor master data	MM	Inspection plan
Customer master record	SD	Inspection plan
Batch master record	MM/PP	Results recording
Routing, reference operation set, line plan, and recipe	PP	Inspection plan, Q notification
Work centre	PP	Inspection plan, Q notification
Production resources/tools	MM/PP	Inspection plan, Q notification
User master data	BC	Inspection plan, Q notification
Quality documents	CA	Inspection plan, material specification
Basic data on quality/inspection planning		
Catalogs (defects, attribute, usage, etc.)	QM	Inspection plan, Q notification
Sampling control (sampling scheme, sampling procedure, dynamic modification, SPC)	QM	Inspection plan, routing
Master inspection characteristic	QM	Inspection plan
Reference operation set (referencing in inspection plan)	QM/PP	Inspection plan
Inspection plan/routing	QM/PP	Purchasing, Production, Sales and Distribution
Material specification	QM/MM	Material master record
Q information record, Purchasing	QM/MM	Purchasing
Q information record, Sales and Distribution	QM/SD	Sales and Distribution

the *Q view* has been further updated (see Fig. 6.1). For mass updating of the inspection data, a function is available under MATERIAL MASTER DATA | ENVIRONMENT | QM UPDATE FUNCTIONS for entering, activating and deactivating inspection data.

The control mechanisms for opening an inspection lot must first be entered with the use of an inspection type in the submenu INSPECTION DATA. Please also remember to activate the inspection type you want to use later to inspect; otherwise, an inspection lot will not be created.

TIP   When updating the inspection data control indicators, it is advisable to make use of the predefined settings in Customizing for each individual inspection type; otherwise, deviating entries on different materials with the same inspection type could easily cause difficulties during inspection lot creation. If a special inspection lot control at material level for the same inspection type is required, this must be documented exactly for each individual case.

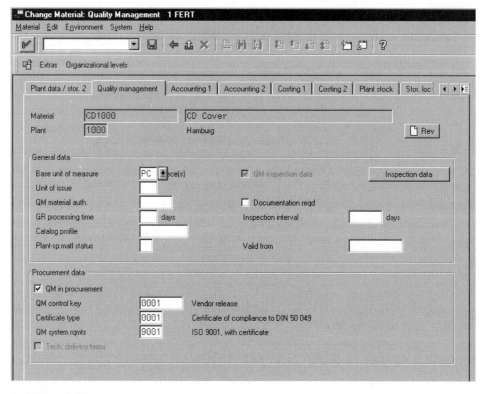

The inspection types

The following list contains examples of the various inspection types that you can assign in the material master data, and which you really describe yourself with your own text:

- 01 Goods receipt inspection.
- 02 Goods receipt inspection, prototype.
- 03 Goods receipt inspection, revised sample.
- 04 Goods issue inspection.
- 05 Inspection in Production.
- 06 Goods receipt inspection from Production.
- 07 Goods receipt inspection of preliminary series.
- 08 Inspection of other goods received.
- 09 Inspection of goods returned from customer.
- 10 Audit inspection.
- 11 Inspection due to storage relocation.

- 12 Recurring inspection.
- 13 Inspection on delivery to customer with order.
- 14 Inspection on delivery to customer without order.
- 15 Inspection on delivery to customer, general.
- 16 Inspection of series orders.
- 89 Other inspection.

The above-listed inspection types are available to you as soon as you receive client 001 or 000 from SAP and can be found in your test, consolidation and productive client. The scope and short description may change depending on which Release version you have. In any case, it is advisable to use the inspection types of the shipped client.

Controls of the inspection type in the material master data

Each inspection type, even in its delivered condition, consists of different combinations of control indicators and a connection to an inspection lot origin. The connection between inspection type and inspection lot origin is set in Customizing (see Fig. 6.2).

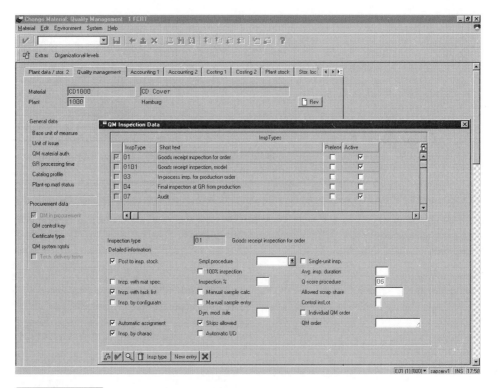

FIGURE 6.2   Inspection type in material master data (© SAP AG)

For certain inspection types, the inspection lot origin is linked to the automatic inspection lot creation (e.g. by goods movements or order start).

The control elements for the respective inspection types have a considerable influence on the running of the inspection; in implementation projects, a false interpretation quickly leads to sluggish processes. Hence we provide in Table 6.2 a list of the associated effects: these are the original SAP explanations taken from the context-sensitive Help system. At this point, we believe it is important to show the entire contents in one overview to enable you to make the correct decision when choosing a control indicator.

TIP Practical experience in project work has shown that it pays to create a separate column for each inspection type with the corresponding control indicators. This model is then used in Customizing to define the proposed values. By doing this, you can ensure that identical control indicators exist – at least within the same inspection type.

TABLE 6.2 **Control indicators of the inspection types** (© SAP AG)

Control indicator	Effects
Making entries in in Q stock	A goods movement entry is made in the quality inspection stock for the material. Posting out from the quality inspection stock can only be carried out by QM if a usage decision has been made. This function is not supported by all movement types in Materials Management. In some exceptional cases, therefore, the movement type itself determines whether the quantity is entered into the quality inspection stock.
Inspection with specification	If you set this indicator, you can carry out an inspection on the basis of a material specification. An inspection based on a material specification can supplement, or even replace, a plan-based inspection. When the indicator has been set, the material specification for the material must be updated in order to carry out an inspection.
Inspection with plan	This means that a plan is required for inspection with this inspection lot. *Procedure:* The indicator is set by the system if a plan is necessary. Whether a plan is necessary or not is decided during the update of the inspection data in the material master data. The scope of sampling can only be determined when a plan has been allocated to the inspection lot.
Inspection by configuration	With this indicator, configurations from the customer and/or production order are taken into consideration during the inspection lot creation to the effect that the inspection specifications from the plan or the material specification are supplemented or changed.
Automatic assignment of specifications	This means that the system attempts to automatically assign a plan or a material specification.
Inspection by characteristics	This means that the system attempts to automatically assign a plan or a material specification. Mark this indicator if characteristic-based results recording is to be carried out.

TABLE 6.2	*continued*

Control indicator   **Effects**

	Dependent variables: If you wish to record results on the basis of certain characteristics, you must test with plan or material specification. Characteristic-based results recording is a prerequisite for characteristic-based dynamic modification. You can select a dynamic modification level in plans.
Sampling procedure	Process by which the sampling scope is determined for an inspection. The sampling procedure also defines the type of valuation used for results recording (attributive, variable, manual etc.). *Application:* This field only applies to inspections not based on a plan or a material specification. If you enter a sampling procedure here, the total sampling scope will then be calculated on the basis of the lot scope. Select a sampling procedure that is intended for a valuation mode without valuation parameters. *Note:* In the case of an inspection without a plan or material specification, you can stipulate the inspection scope for a certain material with one of the following options: ▪ You select the indicator 100% inspection. ▪ You stipulate an inspection percentage. ▪ You enter a sampling procedure without valuation parameters.
Dyn. mod. rule	Dynamic modification rule. Contains the definition of the inspection stages and the conditions that lead to inspection stage changes. *Application:* This field only applies to inspections not based on a plan or a material specification. If you enter a dynamic modification rule here, a quality situation in relation to material, plant and inspection type is created, whereby the dynamic modification criteria of the inspection lot origin are determined during the automatic creation of the quality level. *Dependent variables:* If you also activate the sampling scope via a sampling procedure, the system checks whether the combination of dynamic modification rule and sampling procedure is permitted (permissible relationships).
100% inspection	If you set this indicator, you must differentiate between two cases: ▪ Inspection without plan or specification The total sampling scope of the lot created corresponds to the lot scope. ▪ Inspection with plan or specification The total sampling scope of the lot created corresponds to the lot scope. The sampling procedures entered in the inspection plan or the specification are not taken into consideration during the sample determination for the inspection characteristics. Instead, the system uses rules specified in Customizing for sample determination. The sampling scope of the created characteristics depends on whether the base unit of measure has decimal places or not: If the base unit of measure has decimal places, the sampling scope of the characteristic is always 1; if the base unit of measure does not have any decimal places, 100% of the lot scope must be inspected for the characteristic in sample measure units (rounded up). *Dependent variables:* If, in addition to the indicators '100% inspection', 'Inspection with Plan' or 'Inspection with Specification', you set the indicator 'Skips allowed', this does not affect the sample calculation. However, the system also checks to see if the characteristic is to be inspected or not. It draws on the following criteria when doing this:

TABLE 6.2	*continued*

Control indicator   Effects

	■ Current quality level (if available).
	■ Indicator 'Stage change permitted' in the sampling procedure.
Skips allowed	This means that inspection characteristic skips are allowed during the calculation of the sampling scope.
	Dependent variables: The indicator takes effect in the inspection lot once it has been set in the QM inspection data of the material for the relevant inspection type. If the indicator is not set, during dynamic modification the system selects, instead of a skip stage, the next inspection stage which is not a skip stage. When all characteristics that have to be inspected in an inspection lot are in 'Skip' status, a skip lot is created. If both skips and automatic usage decision are allowed, in the case of a skip lot this leads to inspection lot processing without direct intervention on the part of the user. For this purpose, a time delay can be set in Customizing. In the case of goods receipt, this results in a ship to stock, since the lot quantity is immediately entered in the released stock.
	Note: In the QM control system in Purchasing (Q information record), you can stipulate a waiver of goods receipt inspections. Furthermore, you can stipulate in the inspection data of the material that an inspection be carried out only after the first goods receipt per purchase order and/or production order. You can prevent skips of individual inspection characteristics in the following way:
	■ Assign weighting to the characteristics which prohibit skips.
	■ Assign sampling procedures which prohibit stage changes to the characteristics.
Manual sample calc.	This means that the sample calculation in the inspection lot must be initiated manually. A distinction must be made between the following cases:
	■ In the case of an inspection with plan or specification, the sample is calculated on the basis of the sampling procedures that have been entered in plan or specification on the characteristics level.
	■ In the case of an inspection without plan, either a 100% inspection is carried out or the sampling scope is calculated on the basis of an inspection percentage. To do this, you have to set the indicator for the 100% inspection in the QM inspection data or else enter an inspection percentage.
Manual sample	If this indicator has been set, the sampling scope must be entered manually during the inspection for this inspection lot. The indicator is taken into consideration only in inspections not based on a plan or a material specification.
Inspection percentage	This field is only relevant for inspections not based on a plan or specification. In this case, the total sampling scope is calculated on the basis of this percentage from the lot scope.
Relev. for autom. UD	If this indicator is set, the system can make automatic usage decisions on inspection lots. The inspection lots must fulfill the following preconditions:
	■ All characteristics are completed.
	■ No characteristics were rejected.
	■ No defects and/or quality notifications were recorded.
	■ The lead time set in Customizing must have elapsed. Inspection lots in 'skip lot' status can also be taken into consideration.

TABLE 6.2	*continued*

Control indicator   **Effects**

The indicator takes effect in the inspection lot once it has been set in the inspection data of the material for the relevant inspection type. Activation is via job administration. You can plan and start the jobs from the worklist in the Quality Inspection main menu. You can find further details on planning the automatic usage decision in the introductory guide.
Note: If an automatic usage decision cannot be made, you have to do it manually. The system makes a note of the automatic usage decision in the long text on the usage decision.

Single-unit insp. possible

This means that it is possible to work through the inspection lot on the basis of single units.

Application: The single-unit operation is on the basis of serial numbers, with the prerequisite that the material has a compulsory serial number and is marked as such by a serial number profile.

Average inspection duration

States the average duration of an inspection in days for each inspection type.

Application: If the starting date of the inspection is entered on inspection lot creation, the system calculates the final date of the inspection on the basis of the average inspection duration which is entered in this field. If the final deadline of the inspection is entered on inspection lot creation, the system calculates the starting date of the inspection using the average inspection duration entered in this field.

Quality-score procedure

Reference code of the process which is used to calculate the quality score.

Procedure: For each inspection type, a quality score procedure can be stored in the material master data. At inspection lot creation, this field is incorporated in the inspection lot record.

Example: In the simplest process, the quality score is derived from the usage decision code. A further process calculates the quality score on the basis of the scrap shares in the inspected characteristics. The actual calculation of the quality score takes place in a functional module with a permanently defined interface assigned to the quality score procedure in a table (TQ06). In this way, users can define their own process in the form of functional modules.

Allowed scrap share

In order to calculate the quality score, certain quality score procedures require an allowed scrap share.

Procedure: Usually a scrap share is selected so that it equals half of the AQL value.

Control inspLot

The indicator comes into effect with receipt of goods. It is used for inspection origins 01, 04, 05, 08. The following settings are possible:

'<Blank>': One inspection lot per goods receipt document item. An inspection lot is opened for every goods receipt document item.

'X': One inspection lot per ordering or job item and batch. If you set this value, the system creates an inspection lot only for the first goods receipt per order item or production order or, if the material is being processed in batches, only for the first goods receipt per order item or production order and batch. This setting is limited to the inspection lot origins 'For purchase order (inspection lot origin 01)' or ' For production order (inspection lot origin 04)'.

'1': One inspection lot per material document, material and batch. If you set this value, the system creates for a material document (i.e. within a goods receipt transaction) only one inspection lot per material and batch (where batch is compulsory). This may occur if several purchase orders or partial deliveries of the same material are processed within one goods receipt transaction.

TABLE 6.2	continued

Control indicator	Effects
	'2': One inspection lot per material and batch. If you set this value, the system creates only one inspection lot per material and batch (where batch is compulsory). This setting is only practical for materials with compulsory batch processing. In cases 'X', '1' or '2', the stock of the inspection lot created with the first goods receipt is not yet fully discharged with the receipt of further partial deliveries but is increased by the respective goods receipt quantities. In cases '1' or '2' with skip lot, a direct change of stock type from 'in quality inspection' to 'unrestricted use' does not take place. Reposting in this case is within the framework of the automatic usage decision with delay.
Individual QM order	This indicator specifies that an individual QM order with allocation to account should be opened when the inspection lot for this inspection type is created.
	Application: If you set this indicator, you specify that an individual QM order should be opened for this combination of material and inspection type.
	Dependent variables: If, in addition to the indicator for the individual QM order, the field for the QM order is filled in, this field will only be taken into consideration if, due to a missing allocation to account in the inspection lot, an individual QM order could not be created. A precondition for the preparation of an individual QM order is that the inspection lot contains an allocation provision such as sales order, cost unit or plant.
QM order	Number which clearly identifies the QM order upon which costs are to be recorded. The QM order stipulated in the material master record in the inspection data is adopted as a model for the preparation of inspection lots, insofar as an individual QM order for the inspection lot has not been created.

Change master record

In order to administer the different versions of a drawing, for example, to material master data, it may be beneficial to assign each material a version as well. For this purpose, each version of the material master data is linked to a change master record. Via the path LOGISTICS | CENTRAL FUNCTIONS | ENGINEERING CHANGE MANAGEMENT, we reach the menu for CHANGE CHANGE MASTER (Fig. 6.3). If you wish to enter inspection plans in the change service in addition to the material master data, the appropriate *objects*, in this case the inspection plan, must also be entered. Before working with the change master record in Quality Management (see Fig. 6.3), a few things must first be taken into consideration. Is a version-dependent update of the following types of master records always appropriate?

- Material master data (Q view).
- Q information record.
- Inspection plan.
- Routing.

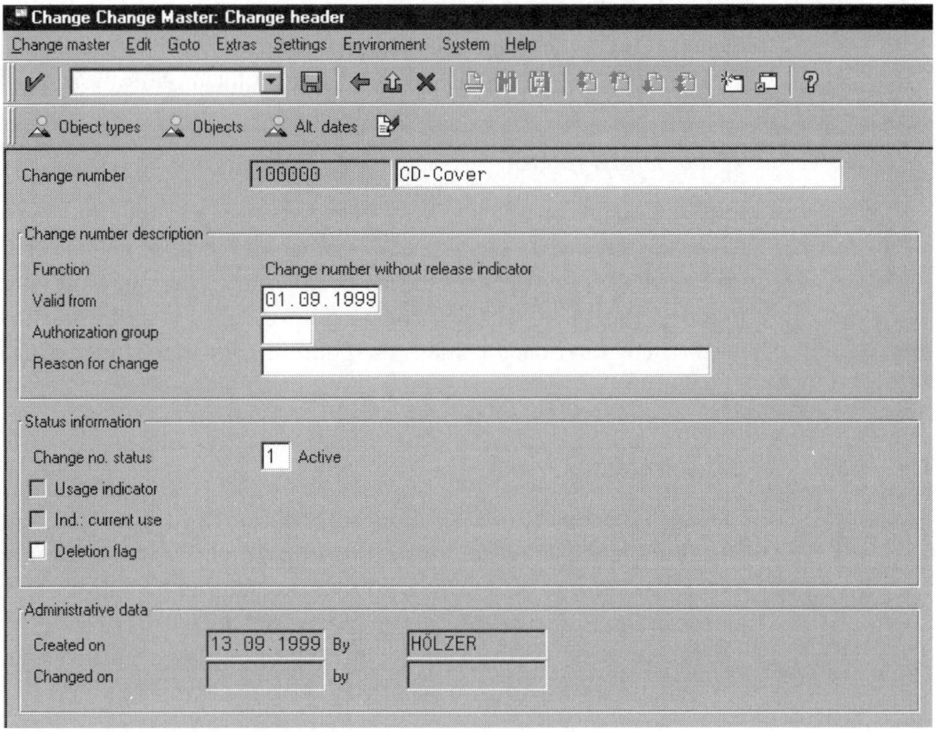

FIGURE 6.3   Change master record (© SAP AG)

If so, which elements of the respective master record are subject to version-dependent processing. In this respect, it is particularly important to consider the extra effort and expenditure involved, which is sometimes quite considerable, in the project work and later updating of data.

EXAMPLE In a production plant there are three versions of material master data available for one material. Material planning stipulates that version status 2 was valid until the end of 1999, after which (as of 01.01.2000) version status 3 applies to production and deliveries. Quality management now has the task of allocating appropriate inspection plans to the versions/change master records allocated to the material. This is shown in more detail in the section 'Inspection planning'. If the material is designated for a goods receipt inspection and the supply relationship is controlled via the Q information record, the relationship version/change master record must be set up here as well.

It is not possible for all areas of the component QM, however, to refer to change master records. This applies especially to the inspection data in the material master data and to the quality level in the inspection lot dynamic modification.

Vendor master record

In this master record, all necessary information on a vendor required by Purchasing and Financial Accounting is updated. The purchaser can also set a block for quality reasons under BLOCKED DATA: the blocked data contains the same list entries that are to be found in the quality information record for delivery control on the material-vendor level. The partner data includes the point of contact for purchasing and quality management.

Customer master record

In this master record, all necessary information on a customer required by Sales and Distribution and Financial Accounting is updated. The salesperson can also set a block for quality reasons. You will also find more 'partner data', for example, your contact person at the customer. Here, it can also be very beneficial to enter your contact person for quality matters. This contact will also be displayed in the customer complaint as customer contact person and printed out on the complaint form.

Batch master record

If a delivered material or a company-manufactured material is to be subject to a batch operation, a batch master record is created via LOGISTICS | MATERIALS MANAGEMENT | MATERIAL MASTER DATA | BATCH. The assignment of the batch number can be carried out automatically or manually, during the goods movements or production orders or at any other time. If batch operation for a material is active, the input of a batch number is requested during inspections and the data for the inspection lot is assigned to the batches.

An important aspect for the processing industry is the separation of batches of a material on the basis of their different characteristics. For this purpose, batches are assigned to different classes, which must be stipulated beforehand in the batch characteristics. If, during the inspection, a batch fulfils the specification of a *batch characteristic*, it is allocated to the corresponding *batch class*. If a material with the desired properties is to be used for follow-up processing or for a sales order, the BATCH CLASSIFICATION finds the suitable material.

You also need the batch master record (Fig. 6.4) for order processing in the PP-PI module (Production Planning – Processing Industry).

Through the influence of batch operation, stocks in Materials Management allocated to batch are administered separately, and directed individually to the storage bay stocks of warehouse management. This then guarantees that inspection results can be traced

| FIGURE 6.4 | Batch master record (© SAP AG) |

back via batch selection. Batch classification makes it possible for Sales and Distribution to allocate appropriate batches to meet varying customer requirements. To this end, the batches are assigned general characteristics from the basic data of Quality Management. The batch products with special properties from general characteristics can now be added to the sales order delivery.

Routing

In this type of plan, the work preparation department records all elements from the field of work planning and Quality Management collects all data for the inspection planning. Here, the production steps and capacities are linked to work centres and the necessary control functions for the production order are stipulated. The elements of inspection planning, inspection characteristics, sampling procedures etc. are fully integrated into the routing. For more details, see the paragraphs 'Types of plan' and 'Inspection planning in Production'.

Reference operation set

The reference operation set almost all objects and functions of the routing. It serves primarily as a plan model for variations of a production process, or as a general model. For this purpose, the individual operations in the reference operation set are referenced in the routing or inspection plan (permanently integrated, each change to the reference operation set also affects the inspection and routing). The reference operation set, routing and inspection plan are similar as regards their structure and central functions. This facilitates navigation in the different types of plan for the inspection planner who has to update quality-relevant data in all plan types. The subject of referencing reference operation sets in inspection plans and reference operation sets will be covered in more detail in the section 'Inspection plan operations', as this is an essential module for effective inspection plan preparation.

Work centre

The work centre is a master record of importance mainly for production planning and control, and is usually also managed and updated by this specialist department. Within Production, the work centre is the core organization element which illustrates the work centre hierarchy in the system. Since capacity planning and scheduling are also relevant to quality inspections, it is advisable, particularly for special inspection processes, to create your own work centres. The fact that each work centre is assigned to a cost unit allows Accounting to assess quality costs. Each cost unit has associated cost rates which the system uses to calculate the cost of the output produced at the work centre.

Production resources/tools

All resources/tools necessary for production such as documents, auxiliary and working materials, test equipment, tools etc. are compiled under the term PRT (production resources/tools). You assign operations and inspection characteristics of a plan to the production resources/tools. Whether the master record is a material, a document, a PRT master record or an equipment master record depends on which type of PRT are being used. The functions of test equipment management are described in Chapter 11, 'Test equipment management'.

To accomplish this task, considerable extensions have been introduced to the system as of version 4.0, including elements of quality planning, maintenance and repair (calibration check) and their master records (equipment) which overlap into different subject areas. In the meantime, computerized test equipment management has become such an important element of Quality Management that we have dedicated an entire chapter to this subject.

User master data

The master data records are created for every SAP user and contain numerous control functions and the assigned authorization profile. Users play a significant role for Quality Management in many areas as people authorized to make inputs, for example, for tracing changes to inspection plans and stipulating participants in workflow tasks from the quality notification. The user can also select worklists for inspection lot and complaint processing at any time. Users' rights are entered in so-called 'Profiles'. It is advisable to contact the system administrator responsible, in good time and before the productive start, to discuss the options of the standard profile for the QM component and establish any possible changes and extensions.

Material specification

After navigating through LOGISTICS | QUALITY MANAGEMENT | QUALITY PLANNING | MATERIAL | QUALITY PLANNING FOR MATERIAL, you will find the material specification (Fig. 6.5), although it is somewhat hidden. This alternative to the general inspection plan (with operations and characteristics) in the R/3 system offers, on the one hand, a simple alternative form of inspection plan organization, without the need for operations. A lot more important than this, however, is its application within batch classification. In the material specification, in simple terms, a work specification for quality inspections is prepared with the use of completely updated master inspection characteristics or general characteristics. The completed inspection characteristics automatically transfer the inspection results to the batches.

Before you can update the material specification for a material with a linkup between general characteristics and master inspection characteristics, you have to assign the appropriate batch class to the material when updating the material master data on the 'Classification' screen. In this way, you set up the connection to the general characteristics of this batch class. The assignment of the 'referenced master inspection characteristics' is almost identical to the procedure for inspection plan characteristics and is described in the section 'Inspection characteristics'.

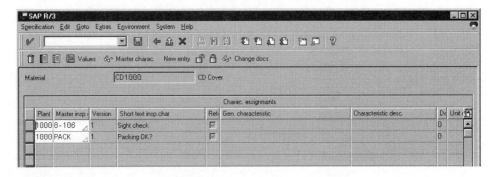

FIGURE 6.5   Material specification (© SAP AG)

For a material without a batch class, you can only use the material specification on the basis of master inspection characteristics without a linkup to general characteristics. Furthermore, in contrast to the plant-specific inspection plan, the material specification applies to all the clients in the system.

Quality documents

The document management system (CA module) of the R/3 system offers a variety of administration functions for documents, which may be found both within (R/3 records) as well as outside (e.g. documents from your office environment) the R/3 system. Documents may be drawings from external CAD systems, but they may also be written specifications. These documents, however, cannot simply be called up to the screen but rather require special extensions, so-called 'Viewers'. For quality planning, the documents are defined as production resources/tools. Inspection instructions and work specifications are examples. However, the R/3 document management is also perfectly suitable for administering a Quality Management handbook.

With the help of document management, it is possible to make documents available company-wide, and to link them to SAP objects from various company areas such as material master record, change master record and the production resources/tools listed above.

6.3.2 Basic data for quality and inspection planning

Catalogs

Due to its central importance for inspection planning, the subject of catalogs will be dealt with at a later point in a bit more detail in a section devoted to the process of catalog creation as a whole. We will then examine the implementation of the R/3 system, viewed from a general perspective.

General

The term catalog, in connection with quality planning and inspection, involves a compilation of unique codes (keys) for describing both negative and positive aspects of an actual situation. The catalogs contain defect descriptions, measures and special attributes of an object or output.

In the project work, the organization of defect and other catalogs often takes up a lot of unplanned time, since the catalog structures already existing in the company have to be imported into a scheme compatible with R/3 QM. For this reason, the problems that frequently occur have nothing to do with missing catalogs, but are rather due to the large number of catalogs that often deal with the same problem descriptions. Also, with regard to the traditional categorization of catalogs for problem descriptions into defect location, defect type and cause, uncertainty often exists when allocating the corresponding codes. Let us first break down the above catalogs according to their importance, using a CD with packaging as an example:

1 *Defect location – where did the defect occur?*
The main reference point of an inspection or a complaint is usually either an individual material item or an assembly. If a single material is involved, the next level of defect location determination is at the position of the material itself.

Defect locations: the CD cover is a simple assembly with the main elements CD cover, CD pick up, CD inlet, CD etc. The individual parts, in turn, consist of various components. There are various defect locations on the main elements as well as on the smaller components. Organize the structure so that the same defect locations always have identical codes in the catalog. Carry this out disregarding process progress, whether this be during the production, goods receipt or issue inspections.

Defect locations in the CD example: CD cover, CD pick up, CD inlet, CD.

TIP You can also define the place where the defect was caused as defect location, e.g. a certain place of assembly or production. It is not particularly advisable, however, to use terms from both definition types in the same catalog type.

2 *Defect type – how is the object defective?*
Each OK definition must have a corresponding not-OK definition. The not-OK definition refers to the type of defect, i.e. the actual defect. This is a simple aid used in catalog creation to prevent causes from being directly encoded with the defect types. It is advisable to arrange assemblies according to their function and individual materials on the basis of their properties.

Types of defect in the CD example:

– Function: OK – lid should close securely, not OK – lid does not close.

– Property: OK – engaging points present, not OK – no engaging points.

3 *Cause of defect – how did the defect arise?*
In the case of the problem description, determining the cause of the defect is usually the level that demands the best technical knowledge in defect analysis. For this reason, always start by stipulating the level of the cause structure, for example:

– caused during previous or accompanying process step: faulty tool.

– caused by a vendor defect: vendor XY.

– caused by environmental influences: assembly temperature too high.

Catalogs in R/3 QM

As of Release 4.0, the catalogs under LOGISTICS | QUALITY MANAGEMENT | BASIC DATA | CATALOGS belong completely to the so-called user data and have now been provided with more comprehensible updating functions. Any amount of code groups can be assigned to any catalog type, and all code groups can be assigned any number of codes. Figure 6.6 gives you an example. The code groups (8–digit) and codes (4–digit) have explanatory texts in the brief description which can also be edited in several foreign languages if necessary. You can have your consultant create new catalog types under the codes P–Z, although this will only be necessary in exceptional cases.

This means that functions, such as creating, updating and structuring the catalogs are carried out directly by the user. Special settings, however, such as the creation of a new catalog type or a special report scheme (in our context, the assignment of certain catalogs to an inspection type or report type) are entered in Customizing by the consultant responsible. Upon delivery of a system, the catalog types are defined as follows:

- *Catalog type 1: Characteristic attributes*

  This catalog type is intended for results recording and the definition of attributive (qualitative) characteristics.

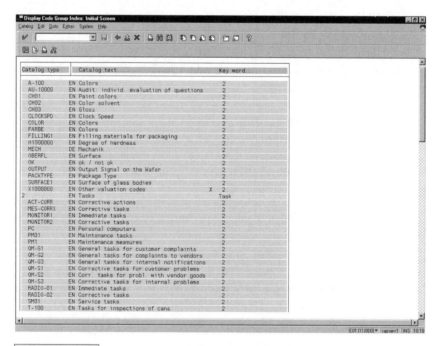

FIGURE 6.6 Catalog type: Defect types with code groups and codes (© SAP AG)

This catalog type has a special status within the catalog system: on the one hand, because both OK definitions and not-OK definitions are to be entered here and, on the other hand, because access to the catalog entries is only possible via selected quantities (see 'Catalog structure' in the following section). If you use a rejecting defect class for vendor evaluation, you must enter a defect class (main defect, secondary defect, etc.). The nature of rejecting defects actually corresponds to the defect types (defects) and, because of this, they should also be organized in the same way. If a qualitative characteristic is entered in the inspection plan, valuation is always carried out using a code from the selected quantity of characteristic attributes.

Catalog type 2: Measures

In this catalog, you enter measures that have arisen within the framework of the quality notifications. Typical measures include, for example:

– Vendor visit

– Measurement tools calibration

– Design modification

– Process capability analysis.

The functions of the 'automatic follow-on action' can be activated.

Catalog type 3: Usage decisions

This special catalog type is only used at the inspection lot completion. Access is only possible via selected quantities. For each selected quantity code, further control functions are possible in the event of acceptance or rejection:

– Valuation (lot decision)

– Quality score

– Follow-on action.

Catalog type 4: Events (PM)

Events affecting the PM (Plant Maintenance) component

Catalog type 5: Causes

This catalog type is also used in the quality notification. Typical causes of defects include:

– Tool breakage

– Improper storage

– Transport damage

– Incorrect delivery specifications.

▓ *Catalog type 6: Consequences of (PM)*

Consequences of defects affecting the PM (Plant Maintenance) component.

▓ *Catalog type 8: Actions*

Here you define actions which follow measures. In the first stage we recommend that you work in the quality notification with measures alone, since it is not usually possible to make a clear, logical distinction between measures and actions.

▓ *Catalog type 9: Types of defect*

You can assign defect classes to this catalog type, just as with the characteristic attributes. The catalog structure complies with our general definition.

▓ *Catalog type A: Activities (PM)*

Catalog for the PM (Plant Maintenance) component.

▓ *Catalog type B: Object parts (PM)*

Catalog for the PM (Plant Maintenance) component.

▓ *Catalog type C: Types of damage (PM)*

Catalog for the PM (Plant Maintenance) component.

▓ *Catalog type D: Codes*

This catalog type contains the global description in the form of a title or subject of notifications (defect notification, problem notification, complaint etc.). Entries made at this point also double up as headers for the textual defect description.

▓ *Catalog type E: Defect locations*

The catalog structure complies with our general definition from the previous section.

TIP The display of catalog entries in the results recording or the Q notifications only shows the description of the code with its short text and code. If the associated code group is also to be displayed, this is done by entering the special character '&' in the code group text. The text of the code is inserted at the position in the code group where the symbol was placed.

Catalog structure

The catalog hierarchy is basically three-stage, but catalogs using selected quantities have four stages (see Fig. 6.7).

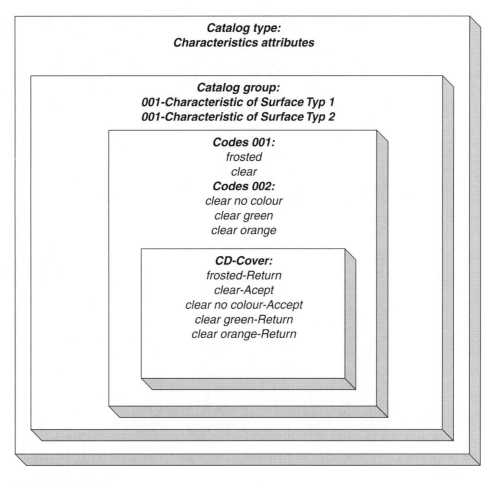

FIGURE 6.7 Catalog structure

Selected quantity

A further hierarchy level is a special feature with the designation 'Selected quantity' for catalog types 1, characteristic attributes, and 3, usage decisions. Here you can compile subsets of a code group based on higher-order factors. In addition, each code in a selection quantity is assigned the valuation 'Accept' or 'Reject' (see Fig. 6.8). You can also assign a follow-on action to the individual codes. In our CD cover example, you can concentrate all terms (codes) for a characteristic attribute that belong to a partial process in one code group. The selected quantities receive only the appropriate codes which correspond to the inspection step, no matter which type of inspection (goods receipt, production or assembly inspection) is being carried out.

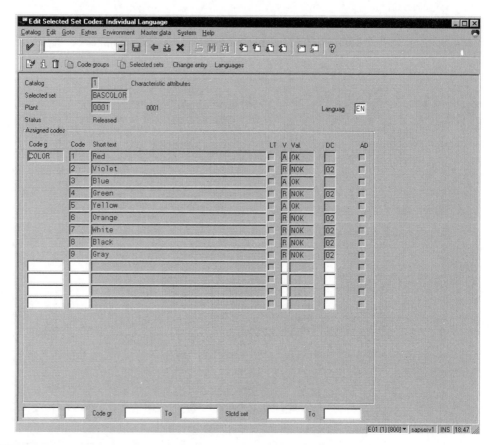

FIGURE 6.8 Example of a selected quantity (© SAP AG)

EXAMPLE CATALOG TYPE 1: CHARACTERISTIC ATTRIBUTES FOR INJECTION-MOULDING PARTS

You receive the same component, in this case the CD cover, from a vendor or, alternatively, from your own production.

Defect classes and quality score

The catalog types

- 1 – Characteristic attributes
- 3 – Usage decisions
- 9 – Defect types

TABLE 6.3		Selected quantities				
Characteristic		**Code group**	**Valuation**			
	100	Attributes of CD covers		Selected quantity for external delivery	Selected quantity for production	Selected quantity quantity for assembly
Shape	001	Shape OK	Acceptance	X	X	
	002	Shape not OK	Rejection	X	X	
Dimensions	003	Dimensions OK	Acceptance	X	X	
	004	Dimensions not OK	Rejection			
Fits	005	Fits OK	Acceptance	X	X	
	006	Fits not OK	Rejection	X	X	
Surface	007	Irregular	Rejection	X	X	
	008	Scratches	Rejection	X	X	
	009	Burrs	Rejection	X	X	
	010	Colour	Rejection	X		
	011	Cracks	Rejection	X	X	
	012	Everything free of defects	Acceptance	X	X	X
Function	013	Mechanics/function not OK	Rejection	X	X	X
	014	Wrong component	Rejection	X		X

as well as the defect classes (catalog types 1 and 9) and acceptance codes (catalog 3) can also be provided with proposed values for quality scores. They require these for the vendor evaluation process as per VDA (German Motor Industry Federation).

During the inspection, the system then determines the quality score on the basis of the defect classes if an assessment is to be carried out of the quality score on the characteristics level with catalogs 1 and 9 or with usage decision with catalog 3. The selection of the respective quality score procedure is defined in the material master data for the inspection type.

During results recording, the quality score is determined from the characteristics as follows:

▨ Inspection characteristic with defect type

– Quality score derived from defect class.

▨ Inspection characteristic without defect type

– Inspection characteristic, quantitative – quality score from proposed values for Accept/Reject at plant level.

– Inspection characteristic, qualitative – quality score from characteristic attribute.

During results recording, users can also decide whether they want to adopt the proposed values or modify them manually. Table 6.4 offers you a typical example of the assignment of defect classes to quality scores.

TABLE 6.4	Defect classes	
Defect classes	Short text	Quality score
01	Serious defects	1
02	Main defect A	20
03	Main defect B	40
04	Secondary defect A	60
05	Secondary defect B	80

Sampling control

This section introduces you to the basic data elements:

- Sampling scheme.
- Sampling procedure.
- Dynamic modification rule.
- Control chart.

The shipped client 000/001 version contains the standard sampling schemes as per DIN ISO 2859–1 for the attribute inspection and for the inspection by variables with the S-method as per DIN-ISO 3951. Together with the sampling schemes, the valuation and dynamic modification rules, the most important international standardized sampling procedures can be depicted:

- ISO 3951, S-method, attributive (SAP: qualitative).
- ISO 2859, Part 1, variable (SAP: quantitative), valuation based on number of defects or number of defective units, without multiple samples and limit values.
- ISO 2859, Part 3; variable, skip lot with definable inspection frequencies.

You can define any other sampling procedure yourself as this data can be updated via the user transactions. Since not all combinations of the various sampling schemes and rules are permissible, a corresponding system error message will appear if this fails to be observed when making assignments.

Sampling schemes

The sampling scheme descriptions contain the codes shown in Table 6.5.

The inspection level is therefore not defined as a function or table assignment within the sampling scheme but must be depicted in several sampling schemes. It is advisable not to change the levels with the assigned inspection severity levels. Literature available on this subject also points out that the standardized use of Level II can be selected for regular cases.

The inspection severity and the AQL are the input variables for the sampling scheme (Fig. 6.9). For one sampling scheme master record, it is possible to enter sampling instructions for several levels of inspection severity and AQLs.

The way the sample determination runs depends on whether or not a dynamic modification rule was selected.

TABLE 6.5   **Description of sampling schemes**

A	B	C
Standard code 1= ISO 3951, 2= ISO 2859	Method code 1 = s-Method	Level code 1, 2, 3, 4, or S=1, S=2 …

Example: 112 – ISO 3951/Level II

1	1	2

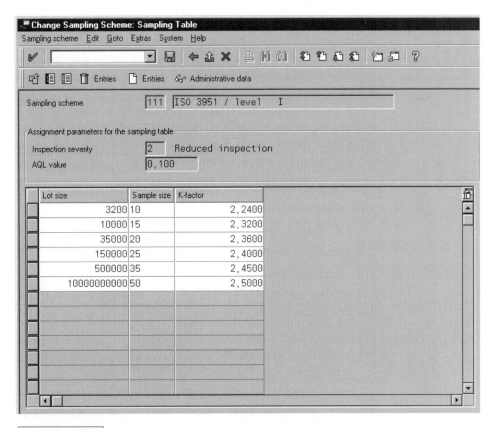

FIGURE 6.9   Sampling scheme (© SAP AG)

▓ *With dynamic modification:* only the AQL is entered in the sampling procedure. The sampling procedure determines the required inspection severity from the current quality level.

▓ *Without dynamic modification:* inspection severity and sampling scheme are entered in the sampling procedure.

Sampling procedure

In a sampling procedure, explained simply, you stipulate the requirements of the sampling scope and valuation rules of the inspection characteristics.

It is not possible to stipulate generally applicable rules governing the selection of sampling procedures. However, it is advisable to use sampling procedures based on AQL and ISO-2851/3951 sampling schemes for lot-based inspections; for inspections in production, on the other hand, fixed samples and SPC-based sampling procedures should be used. The sampling procedures should be selected so that the results are suitable for an ongoing record in the form of quality control charts or quality histories (cf. Franskowski in Masing, 1988, p. 141).

The supplied sampling procedures are usually adequate for this purpose and should not be changed. If required, however, you can create your own sampling procedures from the combination of the following definition attributes and use them for special inspection tasks.

With the sampling procedure functions in the R/3 system, processes typical in the automobile industry in particular, such as Q101, QS9000 and VDA, can be set.

The definable sampling procedures in the R/3 system contain, as part of their definition, a compilation consisting of:

▓ Sampling scheme.

▓ Valuation mode.

▓ Sample type.

▓ Sample determination.

Further indicators in the sampling procedure include the suppressible stage change for the dynamic modification of the inspection scope and the indicator for an independent multiple sample (see Fig. 6.10).

Independent multiple samples

Independent multiple samples should be used when several results for a characteristic of a part, or results from several samples for a characteristic, are to be recorded.

An example of an independent multiple sample is when the diameter of a shaft is measured several times at various points. In this case, the inspection results should be assigned to only one inspection unit. An arithmetical average for the measurements can

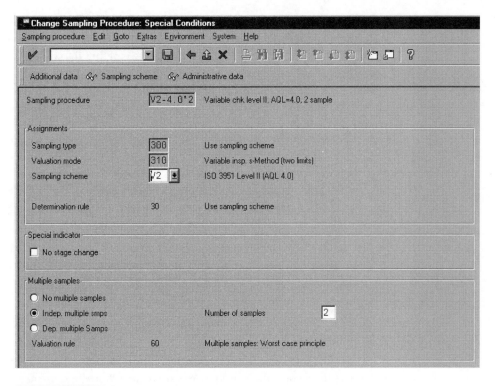

FIGURE 6.10   Sampling procedure (© SAP AG)

then be calculated in a subsequent formula characteristic. The valuation (Accept or Reject) of the characteristic is controlled, in the case of a multiple sample, via a functional module, e.g. according to the 'worst-case principle'. This functional module, implemented as a small ABAP program, is assigned in Customizing and can be modified or extended to meet requirements. An explanation of the method of operation of the functional module is available only in the Customizing table.

Dynamic modification rule

Occasionally it proves beneficial as regards inspection costs analysis and rationalizing the number of inspections performed, while taking the quality level into account, to increase or reduce the inspection scope or inspection severity for a material purchased from a certain vendor. The respective quality level is depicted in its own screen, and you can also influence this yourself at a later time. Instructions on inspection frequency and sample determination are entered in the dynamic modification rule in the form of inspection stages. Conditions are assigned to each inspection stage after a stage change; the criterion for the stage change is the OK or not-OK case. Figure 6.11 illustrates a dynamic modification process.

Via the menu path LOGISTICS | QUALITY MANAGEMENT | INSPECTION PLANNING | BASIC DATA | DYNAMIC MODIFICATION, you arrive at the screen for updating the dynamic modification rule. Here, you stipulate whether dynamic modification should take place after the usage decision or on lot creation. The inspection stages are set up in table form. Here, you define the initial inspection stage, skip (inspection waiver), the short text, the inspection stage, and set the condition for stage change by selecting the icon from the menu bar (see Fig. 6.12).

A dynamic modification rule can be assigned to three different objects:

- To the inspection type in the material master data

  If this choice is made, the indicators set for dynamic modification on the lot or characteristics level are overridden by the settings of the inspection type in the material master data.

- To the inspection plan at header level

  The decision to use a lot reference or a characteristic reference for dynamic modification is made by selecting the appropriate control indicator in the inspection plan header.

- To the characteristic in the inspection plan at characteristic-based dynamic modification

  To do this, the indicator for characteristic-based dynamic modification must be set in the inspection plan header. You then carry out the dynamic modification rule assignment via the update function in the inspection plan DYNAMIC MODIFICATION of the inspection characteristic.

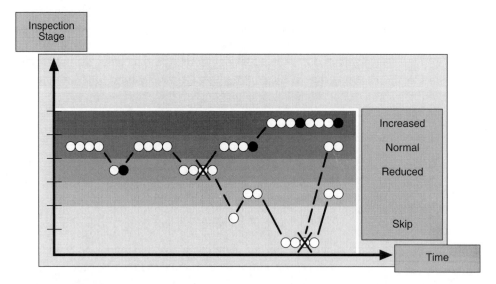

FIGURE 6.11   Dynamic modification process (© SAP AG)

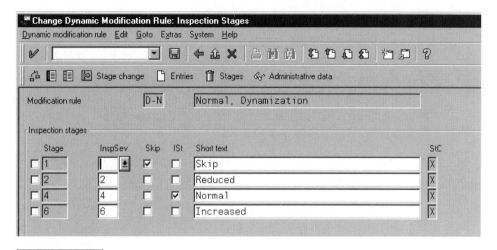

FIGURE 6.12 Dynamic modification table for basic data (© SAP AG)

Inspection severity

A further characteristic of an inspection stage is the inspection severity, which can be used to flexibly control the probability of acceptance and inspection time and overhead. ISO 2859 defines the following inspection severities:

■ Normal

■ Reduced

■ Increased

TIP 1   To update the stage change, the dynamic modification level in the box on the left beside the table must first be marked. Then click on the Stage change icon and the screen with the detailed settings appears.

TIP 2   You will not necessarily find a lot with inspection waiver, skip on lot level and the setting automatic usage decision in the worklist for results recording. Although the inspection lot will be created, because characteristics do not have to be recorded in the case of a complete inspection waiver by skip, the automatic usage decision can accept the inspection lot. It is only in the period between inspection lot creation and acceptance by the automatic usage decision that you can see the inspection lot in the worklist. For further details on this, refer to the section covering usage decisions in Chapter 8.

Of course it is not necessary to assign inspection severity levels to the skip stages for inspection waiver.

When updating the dynamic modification rules, the system demands the input of an inspection severity level for all inspection stages that are not skip stages, even when you are actually working with sampling procedures without a sampling scheme. It makes sense in this case – inspection without sampling scheme – to establish one or several levels of inspection severity.

Quality level

In order to view the current and future quality level, the system also provides you with an overview and update function under LOGISTICS | QUALITY MANAGEMENT | QUALITY INSPECTION | QUALITY LEVEL. You can also carry out a manual inspection stage change here, which then remains documented in the system. The quality level allows you to follow the respective dynamic modification level so that you can intervene manually if required (Fig. 6.13).

For further information on the above, take a closer look at Chapter 8, 'Quality control', and especially the section on 'Usage decisions'. If the usage decision 'Accept' is made, the change in the quality level may well necessitate increased inspection time and expenditure; this will always happen when a single characteristic has been assigned the valuation 'Reject'. This is where the *worst case principle*, set in Customizing under PLANT-DEPENDENT SETTINGS, comes into effect and which describes, by means of a functional module, the behaviour of the quality level in the event of defects in the lot. If you remove the assignment of this functional module, dynamic modification is carried out solely on the basis of the usage decision code.

Control charts and SPC

Control charts are probably most frequently used in production, which is why in this section we will only discuss the most basic setting parameters within the sampling procedure. At a later point in this section we will look more closely at a procedural model for the control chart technique. When your system is delivered, you receive some preset sampling procedures for SPC inspection planning (see Fig. 6.14).

To make your own definition of an SPC sampling procedure in the R/3, proceed in the same manner as with the lot inspection. You will find an additional attribute in the input screen for sampling procedures: the indicator for the inspection point. The control object INSPECTION POINT is used primarily to determine the inspection interval, i.e. whether you wish to inspect on a container basis, in time intervals or event-controlled. First define:

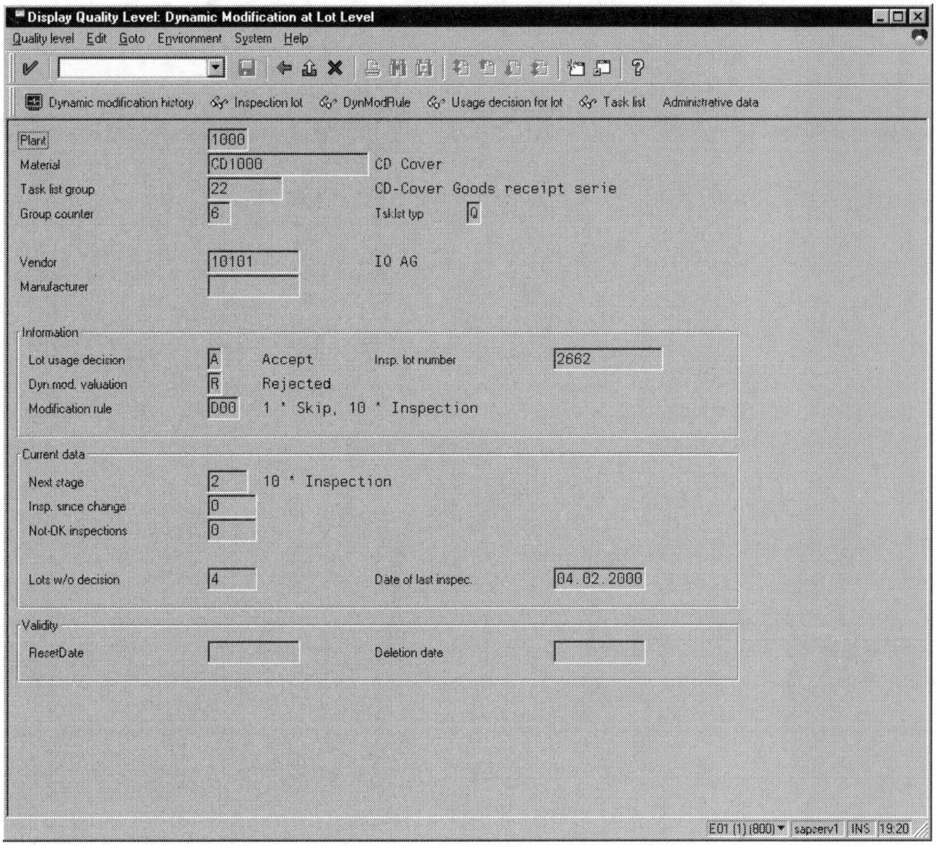

FIGURE 6.13   Quality level (© SAP AG)

■ Sampling type

Only the fixed sample is permitted.

■ Valuation mode

Select the special valuation mode SPC inspection, where the valuation of sample or characteristic is carried out according to the intervention limits of the quality control chart. Here, the violation of an intervention limit leads to rejection. If there are still not enough measured values available to calculate an intervention limit, a switch is made to the manual calculation process until the number is sufficient.

■ Control chart type

For SPC sampling procedures, you have to assign a control chart type, then, the system checks whether the sampling procedure requires inspection points or independent multiple samples. In the case of independent multiple samples, control

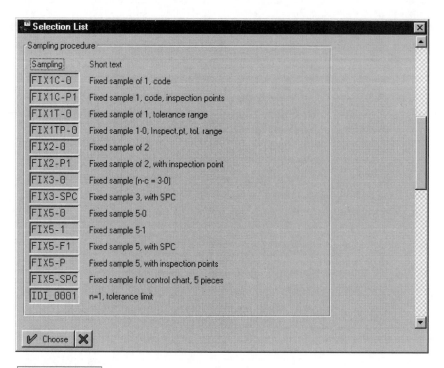

FIGURE 6.14 Sampling procedure for SPC (© SAP AG)

chart types with samples are permissible, otherwise only control charts without samples are permissible.

In the case of control chart tracks with a memory (sliding mean value chart, mean value chart, sliding range chart), the controlled variable refers not only to the current sample. The valuation mode SPC inspection is not supported in these control chart tracks.

Sampling scope

When defining the scope of the sampling, you have to observe certain technical, quality-related peripheral conditions. If you wish to use sampling scope $n=1$, you should ensure that:

- The control chart used does not contain an s-track.
- During the calculation of intervention limits, the process scatter is determined on the basis of the total scatter and not the inner scatter.

The reason for this is that samples with scope $n=1$ always have a standard deviation with a value 0.

With SPC inspections using measured value recording, sampling scopes are usually between 3 and 10; the most commonly used value is *n*=5.

For quantitative characteristics whose initial values have an abnormal distribution, you can make use of the central limit value set of the statistics by selecting a large sampling scope; the mean values will then approach normal distribution. If the parent population is abnormally distributed, you can use Shewhart charts for the mean value. Select your sampling scope to match the distribution of values: the greater the deviation from normal distribution, the larger the scope.

CUSTOMIZING TIP

The SPC criteria control the continuous updating of the control chart and are controlled via functional modules. Before a new control chart is created (during results recording), this functional module checks whether a suitable chart is already available. The functional modules are well documented and can be very easily adapted to suit your requirements. It is therefore no problem at all, for example, to set up a control chart for characteristic/vendor only. This would result in an update as follows: 'The same characteristic via different vendors and different material numbers, written on the same track in one control chart.' (This requirement arose in a project due to the fact that materials that were basically identical but had vendor-dependent keys in the material led to different material numbers.) The following functional modules are already incorporated in the standard:

- QRKS_CHARACTERISTIC – control chart for characteristic.
- QRKS_INSPECTION_LOT – control chart for characteristic/inspection lot.
- QRKS_MATERIAL – control chart for characteristic/material.
- QRKS_MATERIAL_CUSTOMER – control chart for characteristic/material/customer.
- QRKS_MATERIAL_MANUFACTURER – control chart for characteristic/material/manufacturer.
- QRKS_MATERIAL_SOLD_TO_PARTY – control chart for characteristic/material/sold-to party.
- QRKS_MATERIAL_VENDOR – control chart for characteristic/material/vendor.
- QRKS_MATERIAL_WORK_CENTER – control chart for characteristic/material/work center.
- QRKS_PURCHASING_DOCUMENT – control chart for characteristic/purchasing document.
- QRKS_SALES_ORDER – control chart for characteristic/sales order.

Implementation concept for sampling control

Before implementing your SAP R/3 QM concept for sampling control, you will have to take some fundamental issues into consideration. Proceed with your activities in the following sequence:

1 Make a list of the systems available for sample determination and describe the rules of your sampling procedure in a matrix.

2 Which of the available processes do you wish to keep? Assign a process or a rule in the R/3 system to your company process.

3 Analyse your inspection processes with regard to attributive (qualitative) or measuring (quantitative) inspections.

4 Are you using sampling schemes as per ISO? If not, what are your own sampling schemes like? Define your future process.

5 At what points in your inspection activities can the inspection scope be optimized by dynamic modification? Make a list of all inspection types and assign dynamic modification rules to them.

CUSTOMIZING TIP

When you have made all your definitions, set the basic data in the following sequence:

1 Sampling types – Customizing.

2 Valuation modes – Customizing.

3 Sampling schemes – User data.

4 Dynamic modification rules – User data.

5 Permissible combinations of sampling procedures and dynamic modification rule – User data.

Master inspection characteristic

Master inspection characteristics (see Fig. 6.15) are used as a model for copying when you organize your plans or for referencing (integration) in the inspection plan. The individual objects and control functions are the same as those of the characteristic in the inspection plan; they are also described there in detail. For organizational purposes, the master inspection characteristics and the inspection plans are allocated to the plant.

If the master inspection characteristic changes significantly, a new version of this data record is created automatically. The reason for this is obvious: once inspections have been started with defined tolerances, e.g. for SPC inspections, you cannot change the tolerance limits within an updating control chart. The reference in the plan always points to a certain version of the master inspection characteristic. For this reason, it is important to plan the characteristic carefully before it is referenced.

If the master inspection characteristic for quantitative inspections is being used, there is an additional *incomplete update* option. This means that the nominal dimension, tolerance specifications, etc. do not yet have to stipulated when updating the

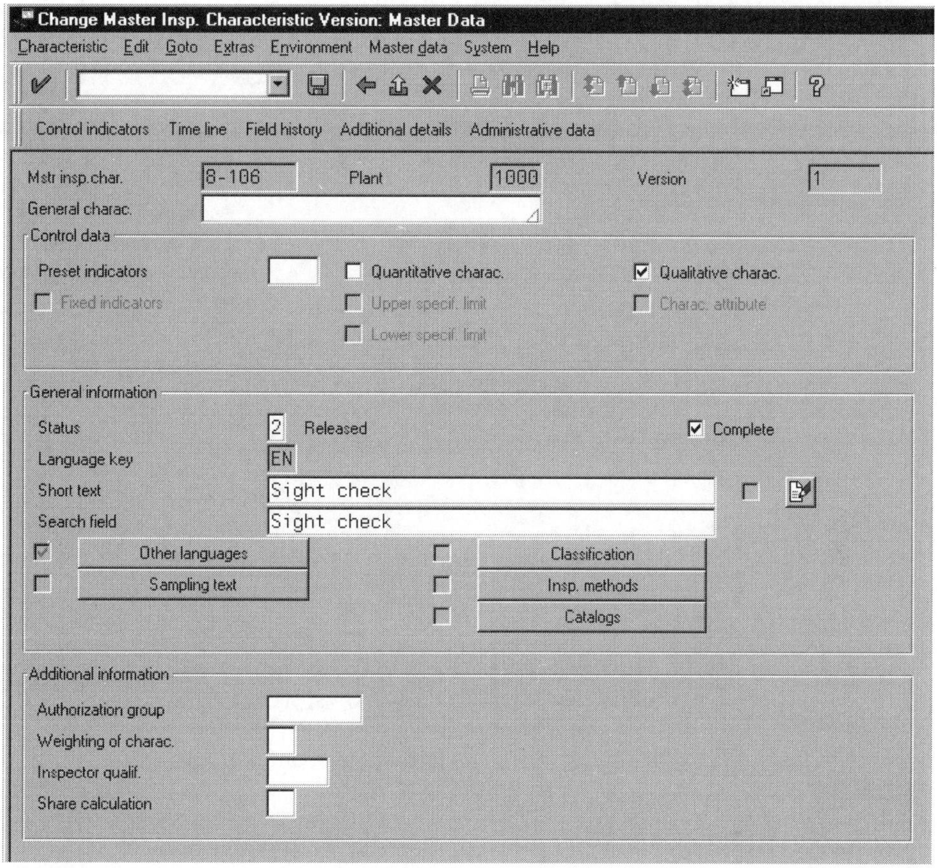

FIGURE 6.15 Master inspection characteristic (© SAP AG)

master inspection characteristic. It is only when the characteristic is used in an inspection plan that you have to make complete entries. An incomplete characteristic like this, in contrast to a complete characteristic, cannot be permanently referenced in an inspection plan and can only be used as a copy model.

Master inspection characteristics are also used for the material specifications into which normal inspection characteristics cannot be entered. Furthermore, master inspection characteristics themselves refer to inspection methods and catalogs.

Quality information record, Purchasing

This information record contains information and controls for the vendor in connection with the delivered material. For every vendor–material combination, there are blocking and control mechanisms for delivery regarding delivered quantity, quality, audit results, time periods and further agreements with the vendor (Fig. 6.16).

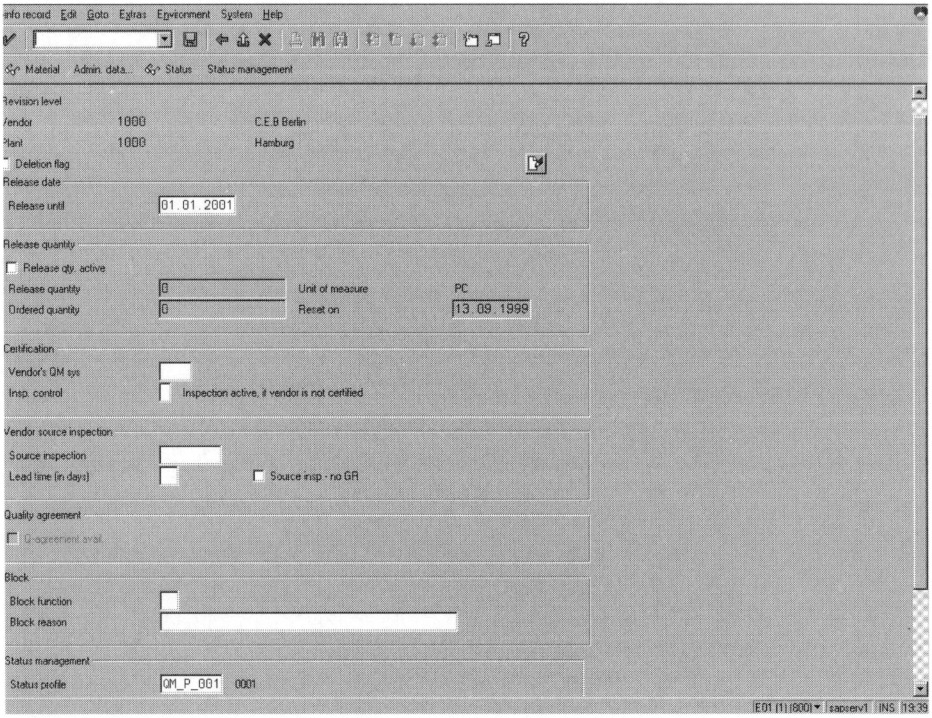

FIGURE 6.16   Quality information record (© SAP AG)

Status sequence

The STATUS PROFILE is a decisive function of quality planning which is used to control the order in which the various inspection types are carried out, e.g. with the launch of a product. The status profile in the Q information record integrates the elements quality planning and inspection planning into one control unit. A status sequence could define a sequence for:

- Prototype inspection.
- Inspection of series delivery.
- Extra model check.

One of the possible settings is designed to determine the sequence of the inspection types according to usage decision. In such an example, the initial status would be the prototype inspection. When this is successfully completed with 'Accept', the system switches automatically to inspection of the series delivery. If the valuation of the usage decision is 'Reject', or if the usage decision has not yet been made, the prototype inspection status remains as it was. The switch to extra model check is carried out manually if the specification is changed, and if this inspection has a positive outcome, the process jumps back to the inspection of the series delivery. The status change and the current status situation can be seen in the Q information record. Here, you can also place the manual control in whatever status you wish.

Unfortunately, the status sequence cannot be set via the user data; updating these tables in Customizing also requires a certain level of experience in this application area. We have therefore prepared a functioning setting in the following illustration. You will find it under 'Defining the status sequence of supply relationships' in the area 'Inspection planning' in the Customizing tables (see Fig. 6.17).

TIP

Always remember that an initial status 'Supply relationship open' without inspection type assignment must be available. The first goods receipt in the example shown in Fig. 6.17 simultaneously initiates a status change to 'Prototype' and creates an inspection lot corresponding to the stored inspection type.

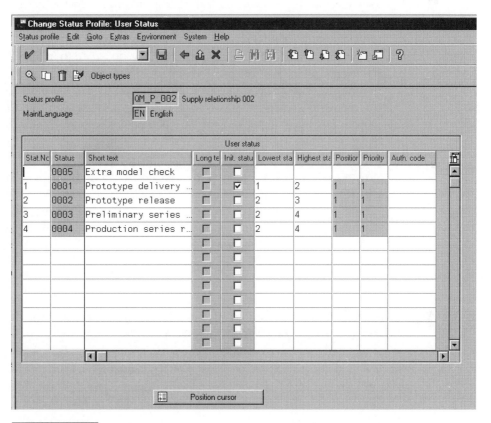

FIGURE 6.17   Customizing table for status sequence for inspection control (© SAP AG)

Quality information record, Sales and Distribution

The Q information record for Sales and Distribution controls the type and scope of the inspections on material level after production for each customer. Depending on delivery status (series, prototype, subsequent delivery), in certain circumstances it may be necessary to carry out further inspections or to comply with special specifications of the customer. It is possible to store documents such as customer specifications for every material. The use of the material in the goods issue inspection is determined via the usage decision of the inspection lot and depends on the customer requirements that have been kept here.

6.4 THE INSPECTION PLAN IN R/3 QM

6.4.1 General

As is usually the case with the other CAQ systems (systems for computerized quality assurance) on the market, the actual inspection plan in the R/3 system is similar in structure to computerized work planning. In the R/3 system, you will find these product-specific plan types in the areas of production planning (PP) and production planning for the processing industry (PP-PI). With regard to its application in QM, this has the advantage that the inspection plan is organized in exactly the same way as the routing and thus already has practical and reliable plan instruments. The basic structure, consisting of operations (work operations, inspection operations), is the same in all plan types (Fig. 6.18). In addition, each plan type then receives its own structures based on its own specific application.

The inspection plan is completely integrated in the logistics chain of the R/3 system and, furthermore, contains the external functions of work planning with regard to capacity and cost analysis. We would like to introduce you to one of the most important aspects in project work with QM in the following section: integrated inspection planning and work planning. It will become clear to you that an understanding of these relationships forms the basis for the positive development of your QM project.

TIP With regard to inspection planning, arrange integration meetings in good time with the project groups from Purchasing, Production Planning, and Sales and Distribution. At these meetings, you should present the main elements of inspection planning and the integration of the various departments; at the same time, you can address the organizational aspects and areas of responsibility which are important for joint work on the inspection plan/routing.

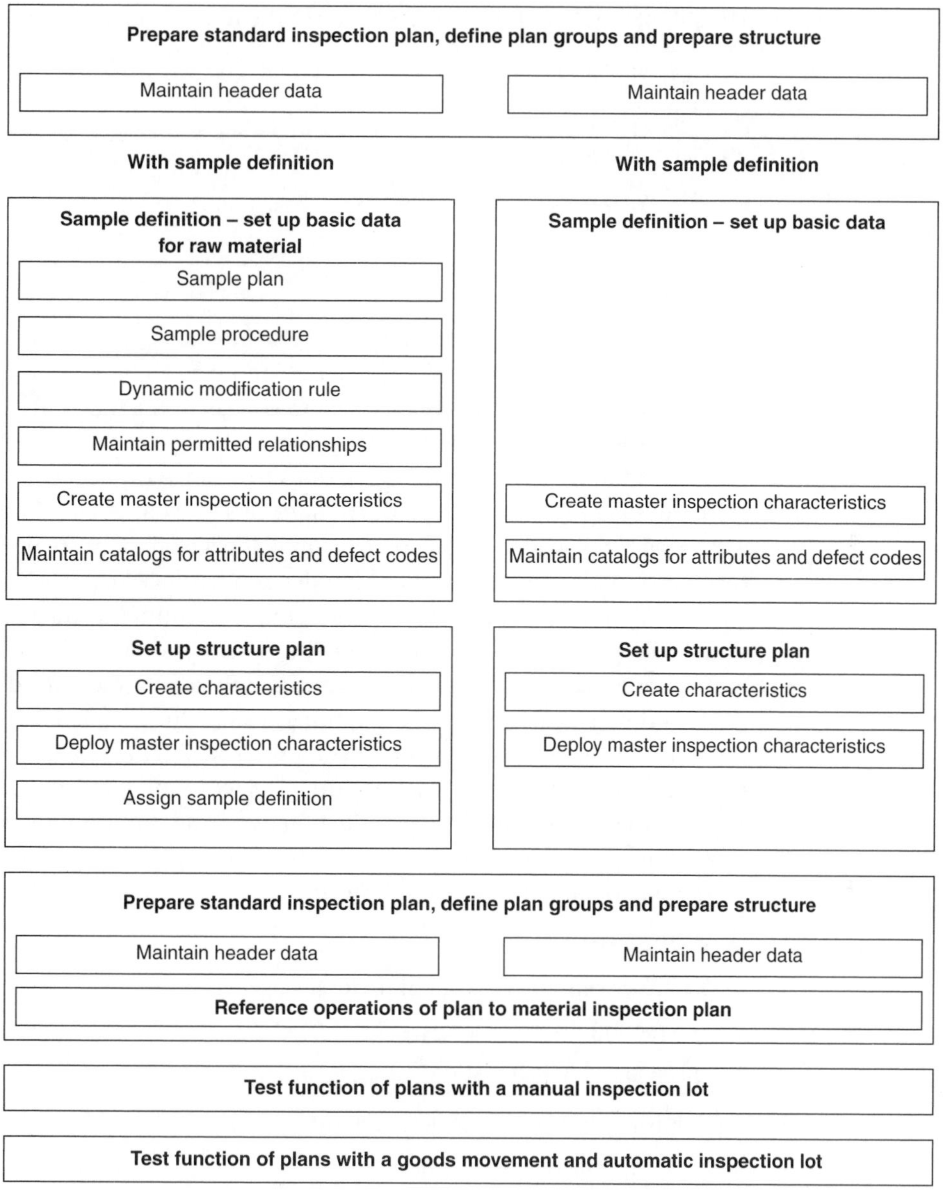

Prepare standard inspection plan, define plan groups and prepare structure

Maintain header data	Maintain header data

With sample definition   **With sample definition**

Sample definition – set up basic data for raw material

Sample plan

Sample procedure

Dynamic modification rule

Maintain permitted relationships

Create master inspection characteristics

Maintain catalogs for attributes and defect codes

Sample definition – set up basic data

Create master inspection characteristics

Maintain catalogs for attributes and defect codes

Set up structure plan

Create characteristics

Deploy master inspection characteristics

Assign sample definition

Set up structure plan

Create characteristics

Deploy master inspection characteristics

Prepare standard inspection plan, define plan groups and prepare structure

Maintain header data	Maintain header data

Reference operations of plan to material inspection plan

Test function of plans with a manual inspection lot

Test function of plans with a goods movement and automatic inspection lot

FIGURE 6.18   Structure and test of an inspection plan with reference operation set

The shipped system differentiates between the following plan types:

- Plan type: Routing.
- Plan type: Recipe (PP-PI).
- Plan type: Inspection plan.
- Plan type: Reference operation set.

Plan type: Routing

The routing contains, apart from its own basic functions, all other inspection plan functions. We will describe the routing in a little more detail in order to make the multiple uses of the integrated plan variants clear to you; all of the functions listed here are also at your disposal for inspection planning.

In the routing, you use work operations to arrange the sequence of the individual work steps in order to plan a production process for your goods. To this end, the routing contains the work centres where the individual work steps are performed, as well as the necessary tools and equipment (production resources/tools) (Fig. 6.19). The material is the main reference object of the routing and initially, therefore, the routing is order-neutral and is not copied into the production order until order release. In the production order, operations can be subsequently removed or added.

With the specified values of the routing, you define the planned times for the performance of the individual work operations. The specified values, in turn, form the basis of the continuous scheduling, the product costing and the capacity planning. They are the plan values for the production order and can be subsequently changed, as can the operations themselves.

The functional objects of a routing are:

- Operations.
- Material components (bill of materials).
- Production resources/tools.
- Inspection characteristics.

The routings are used in the R/3 system:

- In the production order.
- For scheduling.
- For capacity planning.
- In company costing.

These functions bring us directly into the world of Production Planning and Control (PP) and Cost Accounting (CO). The quality order from the QM quality notification, for example, uses the same accounting system as the production order.

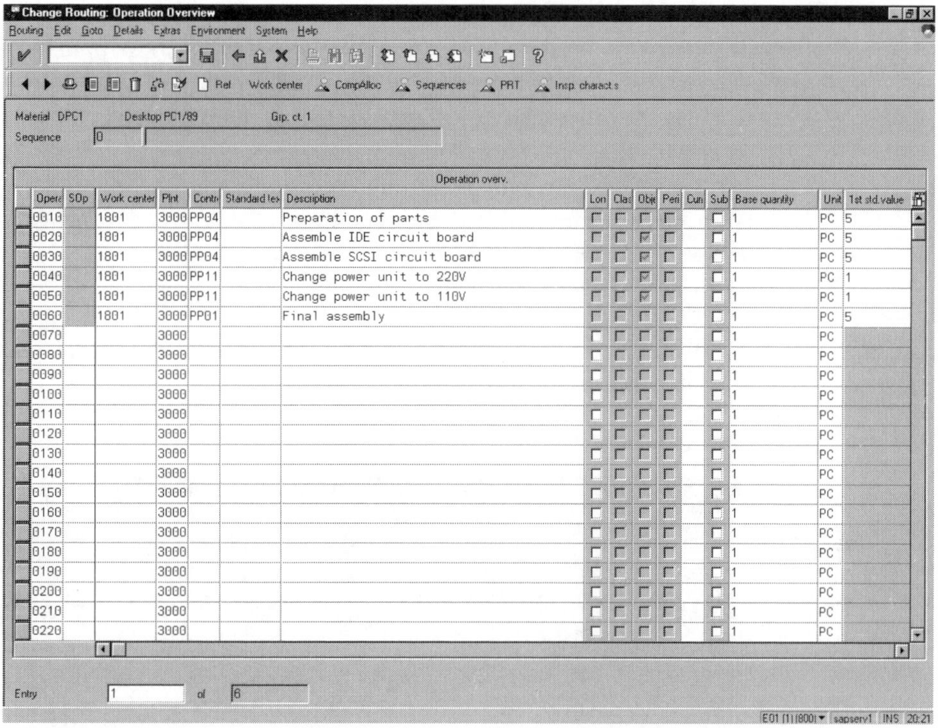

FIGURE 6.19 Routing with operation 'Quality inspection' (© SAP AG)

The line plan is a variant of the routing and is used mainly in series production. The most important functions of this plan type have already been described in connection with the routing.

Plan type: Recipe (PP-PI)

Besides the functions and objects of the routing, the recipe also contains the further attributes derived from the requirements of the processing industry. The recipe is particularly suitable for the handling of batch-controlled production processes and is applied, for example, in the food processing industry, in the manufacture of chemical and pharmaceutical products, as well as in special continuous processes such as in the paper industry – to name but a few of the variants. The recipe is the plan type of the autonomous R/3 component PP-PI (Production Planning – Processing Industry). The attributes necessary to finish the product or to perform a service are brought together here. You will find the recipe, as shown in Fig. 6.20, under the menu path LOGISTICS | PRODUCTION PROCESS | MASTER DATA | RECIPES | CHANGE RECIPE.

It is precisely in the industry-specific solution PP-PI that quality aspects and quality planning are of great significance. Unlike discrete production, many processes run extremely fast, have extremely low defect tolerance and only very rarely permit reworking. For this reason, a selective, integrated inspection planning with inspection characteristics contributes to increased efficiency and quality improvement. Figure 6.21 clarifies once again the various integration options in quality planning and assurance with the application component QM.

You will also find the most important functions of the routing, including Quality Management functions, in the recipe. Furthermore, you can use other objects and master records to plan:

- All resources/tools required for production of a batch.

- All materials that are to be used in the process; secondary products can also be incorporated in the planning.

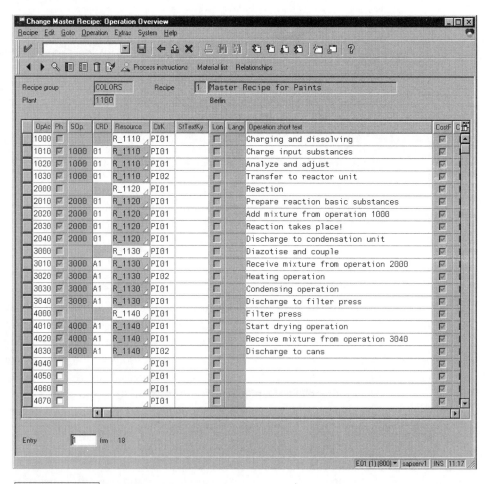

FIGURE 6.20   Recipe (© SAP AG)

■   The operations and phases required to carry out the process.

From a process control perspective, you can stipulate process and control provisions in the form of process specifications and warning instructions in accordance with health and safety regulations.

Since the functions of the inspection planning of the PP-PI do not deviate a great deal from the PP solution, section 6.6, 'Application of quality planning in Production (PP)', gives more information on this subject.

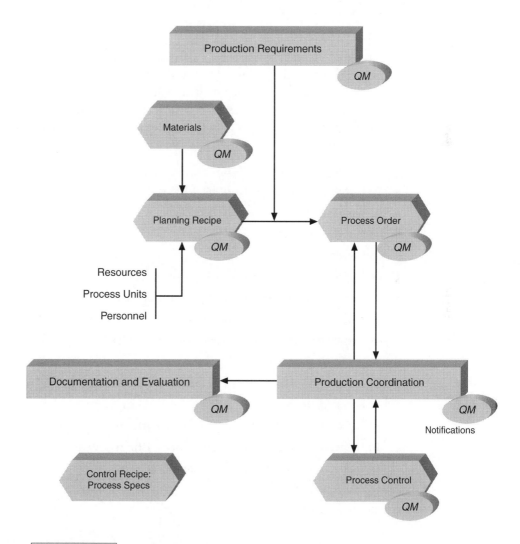

FIGURE 6.21   Overview of PP-PI with QM integration

Plan type: Inspection plan

The plan type inspection plan is used in the QM module for handling quality inspections in Purchasing. Typical uses are in prototype inspections, goods receipt and goods issue inspections, and the incoming goods from production. The essential functions are identical to those of the routing. In contrast to the routing, however, the inspection plan recognizes only a master sequence of operations, no alternatives, and not only the allocation to material but also to:

- Material and vendor.
- Material and customer.

Both the routing and the inspection plan can incorporate the reference operation set in their operations, and can work in this direction with a modular system consisting of operations and inspection characteristics. The inspection types allocated via MATERIAL MASTER DATA | QM VIEW | INSPECTION DATA and those that use the plan type inspection plan, are printed bold in the list; the ones that are not printed bold use the plan type routing:

- **01 Goods receipt inspection.**
- **02 Goods receipt inspection, prototype.**
- **03 Goods receipt inspection, prototype.**
- **04 Goods issue inspection.**
- 05 Inspection in production.
- **06 Goods receipt inspection from production.**
- **07 Goods receipt inspection of preliminary series.**
- **08 Inspection of other goods received.**
- **09 Inspection of goods returned from customer.**
- **10 Audit inspection.**
- **11 Inspection due to storage relocation.**
- 12 Recurring inspection.
- **13 Inspection on delivery to customer with order.**
- **14 Inspection on delivery to customer without order.**
- **15 Inspection on delivery to customer, general.**
- 16 Inspection of series orders.
- 89 Other inspection.

Frequently during project discussions, demands are made for further, alternative inspection types, for example, to make it possible to depict different strategies for the goods receipt inspection for fundamentally different materials as well. Unfortunately, this function of material-dependent inspection types (up to and including Release 4.0B) cannot be supported. Even Customizing with additional inspection types cannot lift this restriction. There is no other choice, therefore, but to individually modify the appropriate control indicators in the Q view of the material under INSPECTION DATA. This means that Customizing really only has the task of adjusting the short code of the inspection type and adjusting the global control indicators for each inspection type being used. It is not advisable, therefore, to create new inspection types for the above purpose.

Plan type: Reference operation set

Reference operation sets are plan types that are not drawn on directly for inspection planning and work planning. For this reason, they are usually not allocated to a material (although this is also possible), and therefore receive an independent number and description. The reference operation set, however, should be regarded as a building block for other plan types; it is used both in PP as well as QM (referenced). In the reference operation set, you describe frequently used operation and characteristic sequences with the full inspection planning functionality. By means of the referencing (integration of the reference operation sets) on operation level, the reference operation set retains a constant link to the routings and inspection plans. This means that all modifications to the reference operation set have a direct effect on the plans which contain the corresponding referencing. You can easily determine in which inspection plans the reference is located by having the system display this in the form of a report. This report contains not only the display itself but also further updating functions.

It should also be noted that the dynamic modification rules at header level in the reference operation set cannot be updated. You will have to do this at a later point in the header data of the 'real' plan. This is because only the operations are used for the reference, and an inspection plan can contain references from various reference operation sets.

6.4.2 Administration of the inspection plans

Plan usage

To promote better understanding, in this section we take a look not only at the user data but also at the Customizing options. In the material master data, you have already become acquainted with the inspection type. When an inspection type is active, an inspection lot is created after a relevant event such as a goods movement 'Goods receipt for purchase order', even if an inspection plan is still not available. Via the associated Customizing setting for updating the inspection types and the plan usage entry in the inspection plan, the relationship of plan usage to inspection type is now set up. This means that the inspection lot creation function finds the correct inspection plan by way of the plan usage and the material. Figure 6.22 clarifies the connection.

Cancelling an inspection type is subject to an economically relevant restriction. If there are outstanding purchase orders for a material, the inspection type can no longer be disabled. All incoming goods must first be posted. This prevents delivery lots, for which a certain inspection has been specified, from being transferred uninspected to the warehouse for unrestricted use.

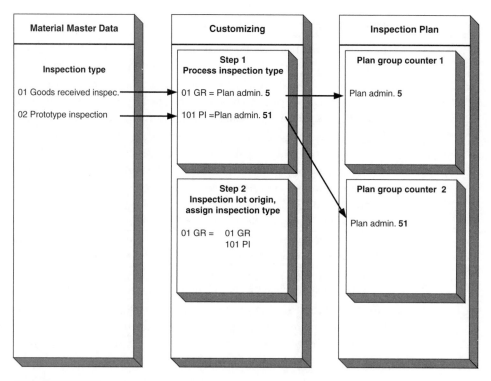

FIGURE 6.22 Relationship between inspection type and plan usage

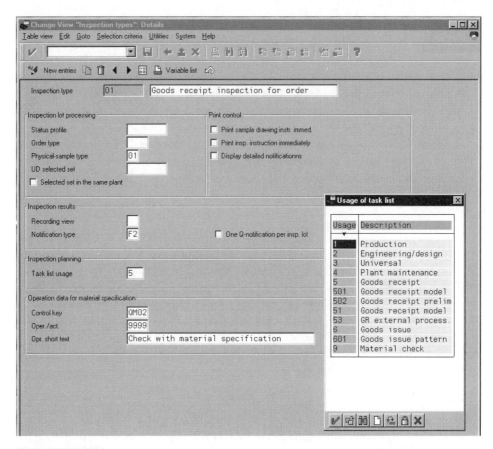

FIGURE 6.23   Customizing the inspection type with input of plan usage (© SAP AG)

EXAMPLE   Here is an example of the manual control of consecutive inspection types: Within an inspection plan, you want to create for the same plan group of a material an inspection plan for the prototype inspection and an inspection plan for the goods receipt inspection respectively; the prototype inspection is to be carried out first. You create the inspection types 01 Goods receipt inspection and 02 Goods receipt inspection, prototype in inspection lot control in the material master data, but enable only inspection type 02 at the start. You identify the plans at the header level using the plan usages with similar relationships (in this case, goods receipt inspection). The system creates an inspection lot upon the first delivery of goods and offers you a selection of the inspection plans defined by the plan usage (Fig. 6.23). Depending on which inspection stage you are at, select a suitable inspection plan. If you are working without a status sequence as in the section in this chapter on 'Master data', once the inspection and acceptance evaluation are completed, you can simply deactivate the inspection type which is not relevant for the next inspection (prototype inspection) and switch to series delivery with inspection type 01.

NOTE   If you have enabled both inspection types for the same material and allocated an identical plan usage (without the use of a status profile) to several plan group counters (inspection plans), the system cannot completely prepare the inspection lot for inspection. The problem is that the sample calculation cannot be carried out because our system cannot decide which plan should be used for the calculation. In this case, although an inspection lot is created, you will have to retrospectively allocate the desired plan manually, as in the above example.

The usage also plays a part in dynamic modification. Depending on the usage, the system determines the criteria for the quality levels e.g. for the combination of material and customer or material and vendor.

Inspection lot origin

In order that the system knows to which event (goods receipt, production order, goods issue) the desired inspection type and correct plan usage belong, you can change more Customizing settings. As a rule, however, you should be able to come to terms with the default settings in the delivered system. Figure 6.24 shows you how the following inspection types are allocated to the inspection lot origin 01 Goods receipt:

- 01 Goods receipt inspection for purchase order.
- 0101 Prototype.
- 0102 Receipt inspection, prototype.

In this example, the inspection lot origin is responsible for the automatic inspection lot creation through a goods receipt with the movement type 101, Goods receipt for purchase order. Since stock management in conjunction with inspection lot creation/inspection planning is an important element of quality planning, a section is devoted to this subject in Chapter 7 'Quality inspection', where you will also find important details on quality inspection stock.

It is still important, however, that you are able to allocate several inspection types to one inspection lot origin, but not different inspection lot origins to a single inspection type. The settings that refer goods movements to a certain inspection lot origin can be found in Customizing under QUALITY MANAGEMENT | QUALITY INSPECTION | INSPECTION LOT CREATION | INSPECTION AFTER GOODS MOVEMENT. Unlike inspection types and plan usages, it is also important that no new inspection lot origins are added, as these tables are in the SAP name space.

Plan allocation and plan groups

To provide you with a proper understanding of the inspection plan administration, we will take a look at the inspection plan structure and its individual components. The first step with the selection QUALITY MANAGEMENT | QUALITY PLANNING | INSPECTION

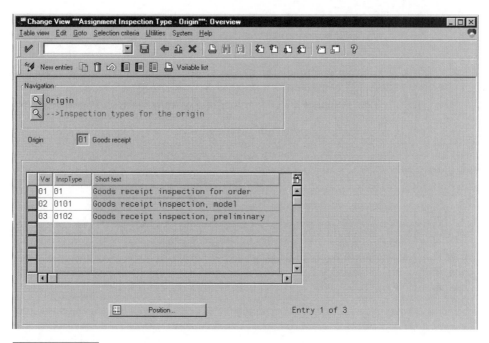

FIGURE 6.24 Customizing of the inspection lot origin for inspection type (© SAP AG)

PLANNING | PLANS | CREATE INSPECTION PLAN leads us to the second level of the administration structure: to 'Material'. (We shall explain soon why we refer to this as the 'second level'.) Then you stipulate the plant to which this inspection plan is to apply. This is especially important because the system uses the plant to call up a further, higher-order hierarchy level.

TIP

In the following hierarchy tables, for the sake of clarity we have assumed that the scenarios are all acted out in a single plant. In this regard, however, you must note the following: if you carry out different inspections for the same material number in plants A and B, from the perspective of Quality Management the material must be entered for both plants. If this is not the case, there will be problems with the inspection plan allocation.

If you do not make any input in the field 'Plan group' and 'Plan group counter', the system creates, by means of an internal number assignment, a plan group and a plan group counter 1; however, the user is also able to assign numbers for the plan group. When you run this function, two specifications are made at the same time:

■ The material is allocated to the plan group.

▨   All other plan group counters for this material (e.g. prototype, goods receipt and extra model check plans), even if they are reactivated with CREATE INSPECTION PLAN, will be allocated to this first plan group with a continuous plan group counter. The hierarchy shown in Table 6.6 is the initial result of this process.

TABLE 6.6   **Plan structure 1 – all vendors of a material with the same inspection plan**

	Plan group 1000	
	Material A	
Plan group counter 1	Plan group counter 2	Plan group counter 3
Prototype inspection plan	Goods receipt inspection plan	Extra model check plan

TABLE 6.7   **Plan structure 2 – different inspection plans for each vendor but identical material**

	Plan group 1000	
	Material A	
Vendor A	Vendor A	Vendor A
Plan group counter 1	Plan group counter 2	Plan group counter 3
Prototype inspection plan	Goods receipt inspection plan	Extra model check plan
Vendor B	Vendor B	Vendor B
Plan group counter 4	Plan group counter 5	Plan group counter 6
Prototype inspection plan	Goods receipt inspection plan	Extra model check plan

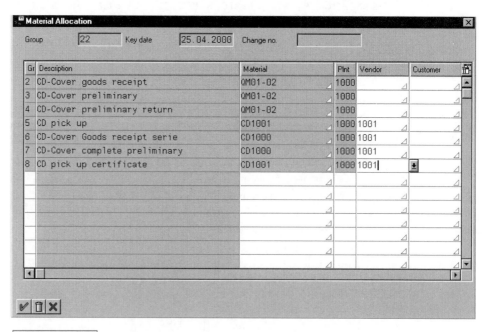

FIGURE 6.25   Material-plan allocation (© SAP AG)

If we are dealing with an inspection plan with the same material but you wish to allocate different inspection plans to the various vendors, the plan allocation will give you the hierarchy shown in Table 6.7.

You will only need this procedure, however, if the inspection plans (equated here with the *plan group counter*) for the various vendors differ from one another. If the same plan applies to all vendors, then the allocation of the vendor can be completely dispensed with. Once again, the hierarchy has the same structure as in Table 6.6, 'Plan structure 1'. The system automatically determines the relationships required for vendor evaluation and for further analyses on the basis of the relationships of the purchase order and the corresponding goods movement.

In the next hierarchy, we see a variant in which the same inspection plan is used for different materials. The materials A, B and C are in the same plan group. Through the application of the MAT-PLAN ALLOCATION (Fig. 6.25), the existing plan group counter remains in the list (Table 6.8).

An allocation of the vendor, as described in the previous paragraph, is not required here either. The last example we will use is one which applies to several of the above alternatives. Plan group counter will be abbreviated to PGC (Table 6.9).

In the various examples, we obviously have not been able to cover all combination possibilities; the following, however, is important:

▓ The top hierarchy is formed by the plan group, not the material.

▓ Different materials can share an inspection plan.

▓ Different vendors/customers can share an inspection plan.

▓ Within a plan group, various alternative inspection plans may be allocated to a material.

▓ Alternative inspection plans may also receive an additional vendor/customer reference, although this is not imperative.

▓ The function Material-plan allocation should really be called Material-plan-vendor allocation!

TABLE 6.8	Identical plan for several materials

Plan group 1000		
Material A	Material B	Material C
Plan group counter 1	Plan group counter 1	Plan group counter 1

TABLE 6.9	Different plans for each material, dependent on vendor (or customer)

Plan group 1000					
Material A		Material B		Material C	
PGC 1	PGC 2	PGC 3	PGC 4	PGC 5	PGC 6
Vendor A	Vendor B	Vendor A	Vendor B	Vendor A	Vendor B

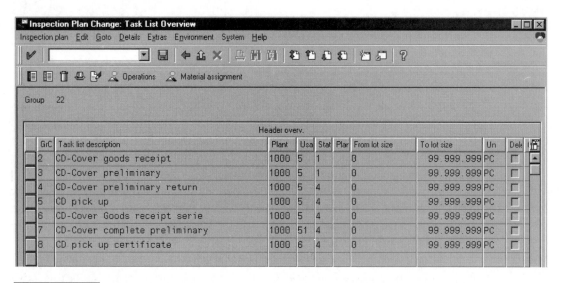

FIGURE 6.26   Plan group counter (inspection plans) of a plan group for different inspection types (© SAP AG)

Take time to analyse your hierarchies and plan allocations that have been valid up to now, and consider the option of a migration (data import) into the R/3 system. Now design a suitable model for your plan administration along the lines of the method described. In some circumstances, you may be able to considerably reduce the original diversity of the plan and save on future time and effort when you are updating it.

Creating an inspection plan for change status

In the section in this chapter on basic data, you will have already become acquainted with the change master record. A constant theme in inspection plan administration is the tracking of plan changes parallel to specification and drawing changes of the material. The system gives you the option, therefore, of recording various change statuses of an inspection plan as individual inspection plans within one plan group by means of the central change service. Modifying by means of the CHANGE MASTER RECORD is of course an option but is only of practical use for major changes. You will probably carry out less incisive modifications without the change master record; the change is also documented here in a change record, and this allows its origin to be traced. You stipulate the time the change comes into effect via the field KEY DATE. In order to link inspection planning to the change system, the object usage still has to be extended to include PLAN, as shown in Fig. 6.27.

TIP

If you are updating inspection plans with change statuses and then you refer to reference operation sets, you must always ensure that the validity period of the reference operation set is permissible. If the validity period of the reference operation set is not within the validity period of the inspection plan, the system indicates this with an error message. Important!: the error message text ('The plan has no original sequence') is not unambiguous.

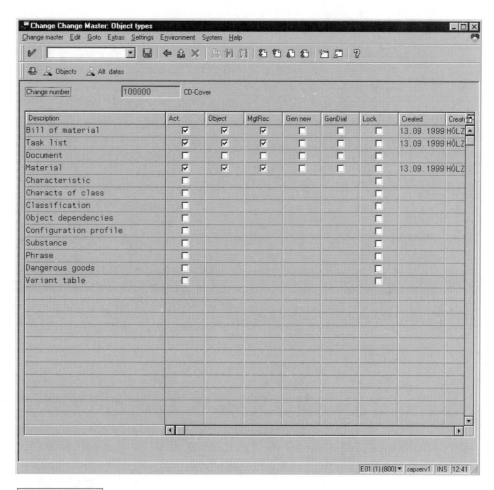

FIGURE 6.27 Extending the object types in the change master record (© SAP AG)

In the course of business operations, we often come across the example of the new drawing index (SAP: version) which, as soon as inspection plan modifications are required, demands an adjustment of the inspection plan parallel to the drawing index. Just as with the inspection plans, you can enter these version statuses for the drawing index of the material as new master records and, at the same time, create a new version status of the inspection plan. You also determine the validity of the version status here by entering a key date. This means that the modifications you have made, which are stored with a change number in the relevant data record in the database, only come into effect on the key date. All previous change statuses are saved in the database. Unlike plan modification without data record, you can reactivate your earlier plans at any time.

6.4.3 Structure of the inspection plan (plan structure)

At the beginning of this chapter, you became briefly acquainted with the theoretical principles of inspection planning and inspection sequence control. We can now incorporate the elements introduced to us into the structure of the R/3 inspection plan (see Fig. 6.28). Inspection planning in R/3 QM is divided into the main elements:

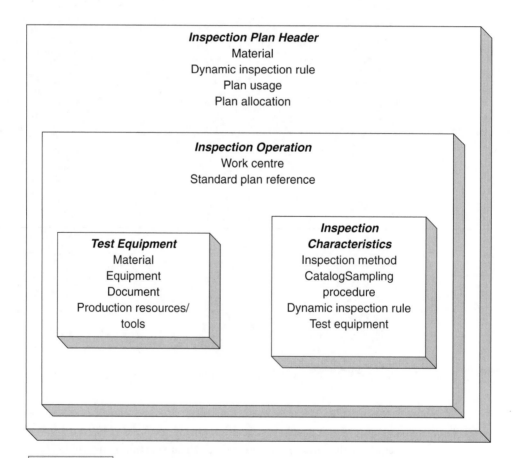

| FIGURE 6.28 | Inspection plan structure

- Inspection plan header.
- Inspection operation.
- Inspection characteristic.
- Test equipment.

Again, the descriptions here apply to both the inspection plan in QM as well as the routing in PP, which only consists of a few more routing-specific objects such as the alternative operation sequence and the bill of materials function (material components).

General functions

Like most R/3 master data objects, the inspection plan also has create, change and copy functions, copy with model, and a variety of other utilities at its disposal. For a very frequently used transaction, you can also work directly with a transaction code (e.g. PP01 for entering an inspection plan). For reasons of clarity, we are consciously dispensing with a detailed description of all options, some of which follow from the functions provided by the routing. In the following paragraphs, you will receive an explanation of all elements that are important from a QM perspective. The practical examples will then be described in sections 6.5, 'Application of quality planning in Purchasing (MM)', 6.6, 'Application of quality planning in Production (PP)' and 6.7, 'Application of quality planning in Sales and Distribution (SD)'.

Inspection plan header

Once you have made the necessary entries in CREATE or CHANGE mode, a screen appears as shown in Fig. 6.29.

To enter new inspection plans, you can also use the function CREATE INSPECTION PLAN AND COPY MODEL. The system then guides you with a selective dialog through the individual steps to plan selection. Following this, the contents of your selected plan model are then copied into your newly created plan. At this point, you should consider one exception: if the model contains reference operation sets that have already been referenced, the copy function is not available!

The number of the plan group is usually set to internal assignment (the system automatically assigns a number). If you wish to have an external assignment, the number range interval should be set accordingly in Customizing. The options available in material/plan/vendor allocation were described in section 6.4.2 in the paragraph 'Plan allocation and plan groups'.

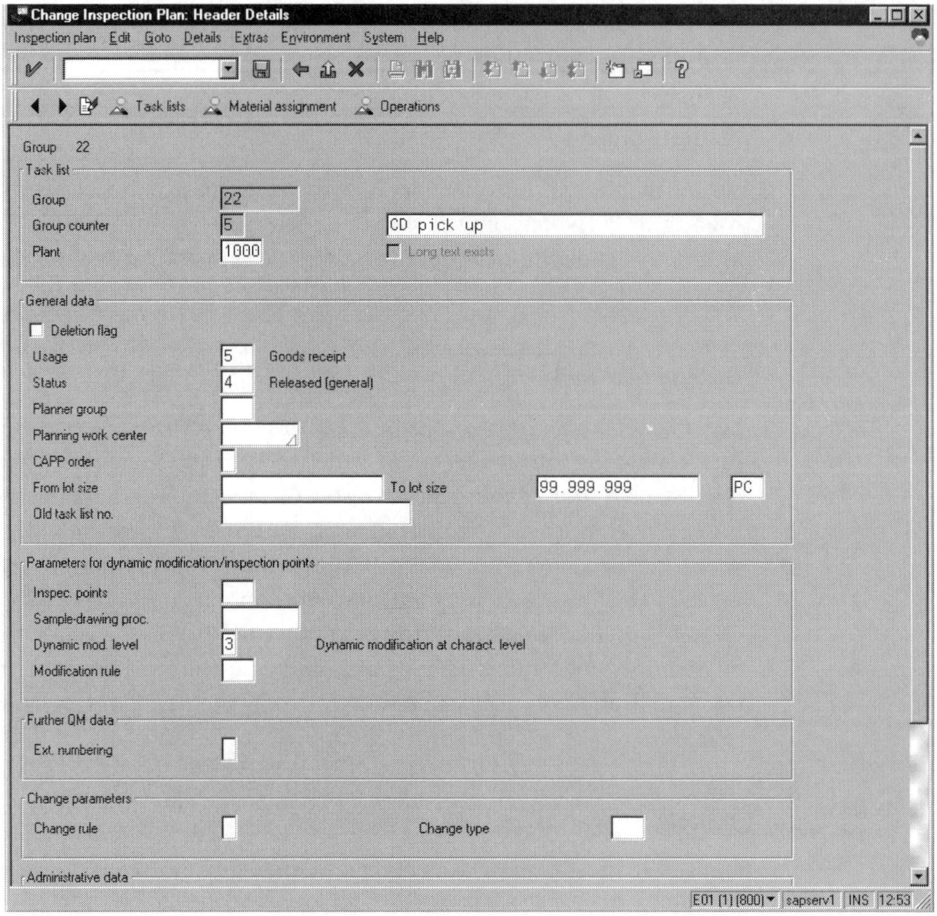

FIGURE 6.29   Inspection plan header (© SAP AG)

Plan group counter

The plan group counter is usually automatically suggested by the system. Manual allocation of the plan group counter is possible in the function MAT-PLAN ALLOCATION.

Deletion flag

The indicator indicates that a plan is to be deleted. During the next reorganization run, the inspection plan with all change statuses and plan objects will be deleted. It is also possible to directly delete a created plan.

Planner group

Not to be confused with plan group. The planner group is simply an independent ordering criterion. You can use the planner group for selecting a choice of plans.

Status

Here, among other things, you assign the plan release. A plan that has not been released can be blocked with status.

Plan unit of measure

Unit of material that has to be manufactured and which is used throughout the entire plan. It must be possible to convert this unit from the material master record into the base unit of measure of the material that has to be manufactured. If the conversion is not updated, an error message will appear during the plan check.

With the unit of measure of the first plan, the plan unit of measure is also stipulated for all other plans of the plan group and can no longer be changed!

Lot sizes

Stipulates the permissible lot size for this plan group counter.

Legacy system

Inspection plan number from the legacy system

Inspection points

This function will be discussed in a bit more detail in section 6.6, 'Application of quality inspection in Production (PP)'; for the time being, suffice to say: the inspection point is an SAP term for the sample in Production for statistical process control or, more simply, for recording continuous inspection data. You can only use the inspection points, therefore, in the routing or in a recipe. If the indicator is set, this excludes the dynamic modification function; such a dynamic modification, after all, is only practical for lot-based inspection. The dynamic modification of the inspection points is now carried out on the basis of the sampling procedure which was assigned on the characteristics level.

Once you have set the INSPEC POINTS checkbox, the FIELD COMBINATION an PL ALLOCATION fields appear.

Field combination

The user fields indicate the quantities assigned to the inspection points. If, for example, you have defined the inspection points as a quantity, you can use such key terms as 'container', 'barrel' or 'pallet'. If this plan is used to perform an inspection, the selected field combination is displayed on the entry screen for results recording.

PL allocation (partial lot allocation)

You stipulate whether the material quantities assigned to the inspection points also apply to partial lots. Depending on which demands are made on the production process, you can:

- Assign the finished quantities to inspection points only (no partial lots).
- Assign the quantities that have been produced for one or several inspection points to partial lots.
- Assign one or several partial lots to batches (provided that the material is produced in batches).

Dynamic modification level

This indicates the level in the plan where the dynamic modification rule is defined (e.g. on the header level or characteristics level of the inspection plan).

Dynamic modification rule

Here you enter the inspection stages and the conditions that lead to an inspection stage change. You were introduced to this process in section 6.3.2, 'Basic data for quality and inspection planning'.

Inspection operation

The OPERATIONS screen with the overview list contains the central control elements of the inspection plan (see Fig. 6.30). At this point, important information required for the work planning such as company costing and scheduling data is assigned to the operation.

In the case of the routing, you assign inspection characteristics to the operation (production operation) in exactly the same way as in the inspection plan. If the plan type inspection plan is being used, the operations subdivide the inspection plan into individual inspection stages. The further assignments affect the master data of the production resources/tools and work centres. Always start planning operations in the overview list. A double-click will give you a detailed illustration of the operation.

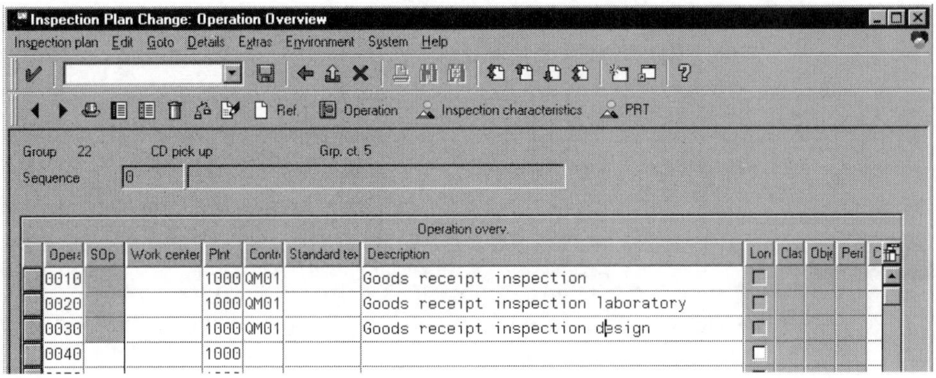

FIGURE 6.30   Operation overview for an inspection plan for goods receipt inspection
(© SAP AG)

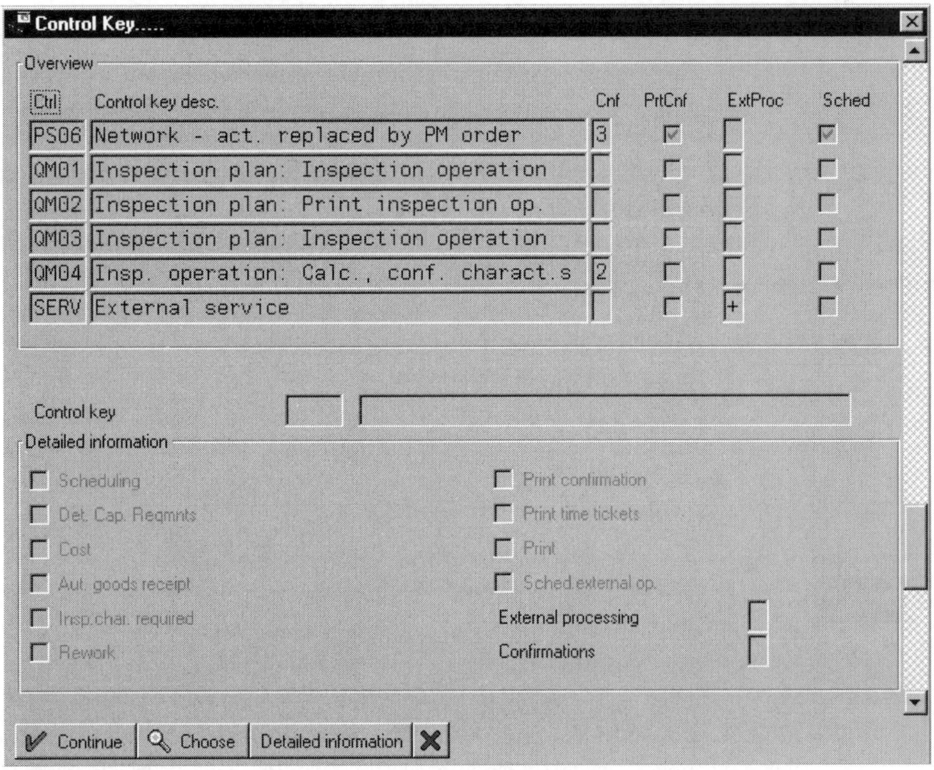

FIGURE 6.31   Control key QM01 with detailed view (© SAP AG)

The procedure for the plan type inspection plan is very simply organized: you stipulate the control key and edit a short text. Now you have completed all mandatory entries for the next step – creating the inspection characteristics.

Inspection characteristics

The control key with the control indicator INSPECTION CHARACTERISTICS (e.g. QM01 as in Fig. 6.31) is not a mandatory input. In the function PLAN CHECK, this simply generates a message if a characteristic is missing. You can also use control indicators from Production without a loss of function.

If, on the other hand, you are working with the plan type routing, then this is another story. The minimum input is also permissible here, although it is not usually in the interests of work planning. In coordination with the work planner, you should now define more accurately the following entries in the operation overview, which we will not, however, describe in detail at this point:

- Work centre assignment.
- Plant number assignment for the operation.
- Standard text key assignment.

In the detailed view of the operation (symbol 'Jig-saw'), you can also enter controlling elements:

- Operation number.
- Standard values.
- Standard value calculation.
- General information.
- Required qualification.
- External processing.
- Quality management: general.

A factor which casts a small shadow on all releases up to and including 4.5 is the simultaneous activation of all inspection operations of an inspection plan or routing when a production order is started. Only one inspection lot can be activated per production order. This feature turns out to be a problem when the order quantity decreases in the course of production or when several inspections, independent of each other, have to be handled in the one production order. SAP is already planning further development in this area. However, as we go to print, the implementation date has still not been announced. You can still create further inspection lots for a production order once you have completed the last inspection lot in each case (Status ICCO: 'Inspection close completed').

Appraisal costs in the operation

Incorporating the appraisal costs requires a completely updated operation with a work centre. With the cost unit defined at the work centre and the output type it uses, the appraisal costs can be determined via the confirmed output times. If you wish to record and evaluate appraisal costs, it is essential to coordinate this point in advance with the Production Planning (PP) and Controlling (CO) teams, as most settings and evaluations on this subject are only possible if you have profound knowledge of the application areas PP and CO and if selective Customizing is carried out. Further information on the subject of appraisal costs is available in Chapter 8, 'Quality control'.

From the operation overview, you navigate first to the INSPECTION CHARACTERISTIC or PRODUCTION RESOURCES/TOOLS in order to complete the inspection plan.

Creating an operation with a reference operation set

If you have already created a reference operation set with all the necessary entries, the alternative to the manual input of the operation would be to reference a reference operation set. This function uses the modular principle for inspection planning for fast and standardized production of your individual inspection plans. Simply move your cursor onto any place in the operation overview, select an operation and click on the symbol REFERENCE in the menu bar. The dialog REFERENCE OPERATION SET will appear. The system then requests that you make the following entries:

- Number of the operation that you wish to create with the help of a reference operation set
- Group of the reference operation set
- Group counter of the reference operation set

When you have selected a reference operation set, confirm with ENTER. The system now creates a reference to the reference operation set and returns to the OPERATION OVERVIEW screen. The new fields in the OPERATION OVERVIEW screen are shaded grey; data from this operation, therefore, can no longer be altered here. Changes made in the referenced reference operation set (to all objects) have a direct effect on all inspection plans and routings that have a corresponding plan reference. In this way, the plan reference can be used for the rational, mass updating of inspection plans without the time-consuming editing of each individual plan.

Test equipment

You set up the link to the test equipment on the operation overview either via the symbol PRT on the application toolbar or via the pull-down menu DETAILS | PRODUCTION RESOURCES/TOOLS. For each operation, it is possible to enter test equipment and tools from the following categories:

▓ Material

▓ Equipment

▓ Document

▓ Production resources/tools

Once you have entered the first item, you can also insert the test equipment of the operation in an overview list per operation and continue processing. As the assignment for test equipment and resources/tools on operation level is often too inaccurate, the system also offers you the possibility of continuing to use the individual PRT items on characteristics level and to link up here specifically with the characteristic. This presupposes, however, that the test equipment has previously been assigned to the operation and the corresponding control indicator has been set in the characteristic (Fig. 6.32).

Due to the increased importance of test equipment management and resource management in R/3 implementation projects, we have dedicated an entire chapter (11) to this subject, to which you can refer for more detailed information.

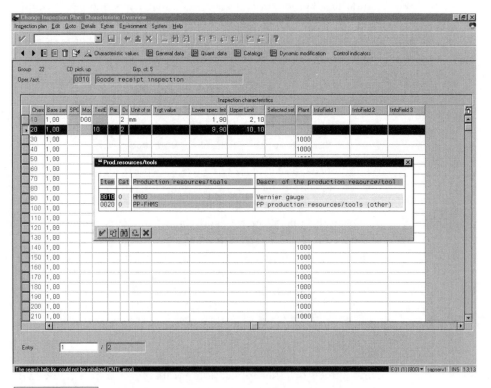

FIGURE 6.32 Test equipment assignment to characteristic (© SAP AG)

Inspection characteristic

From the operation overview, you navigate via icons or menu selection to the CHARACTERISTIC OVERVIEW. Here we find ourselves in an area belonging to SAP R/3–QM which is maintained and updated mainly by the Quality Management department. In all of the previous models of inspection planning, there were integration elements that had to be taken into account. The characteristic overview, constitutes, as it were, the core element of the inspection plan.

Creating a characteristic

Before you start creating a characteristic, an important decision must be made as to the characteristic type. Here we differentiate between two types:

▓ Quantitative characteristic (QN, for measuring inspection).

▓ Qualitative characteristic (QL, for attributive inspection).

This distinction is of course based on the data that you wish to enter in the system, but not on the data that is measured on the workpiece or evaluated by other inspections. Once you have selected QN or QL and made further mandatory entries, you will receive, in any case, another screen for the characteristic type with the control indicators set in Customizing. In the case of characteristics with sampling procedures, a dialog will request that you enter a sampling procedure. You then write a mandatory description in the short text line and now you can either edit another characteristic or switch back to the operation overview.

If you would like to re-edit the control indicator for the characteristic every time, the standard text key is suitable for this purpose. The individual control indicators are predefined in Customizing, where they receive an appropriate short code, e.g. QN01 for quantitative inspections.

TIP In both of these cases, you have still not saved the characteristic. The data is not written into the database until you leave the inspection plan (this also applies to the operations and all other elements of the inspection plan). Take the system dialog seriously that appears at the end of your inspection plan activities: 'Save changes – yes'! On many occasions, we have experienced users who, after a painstaking work session on the inspection plan, have inadvertently confirmed with 'no' and then, with a great deal of frustration, have to repeat their entire input.

The control indicators of the characteristic

The available control indicators of the characteristic are a source of many interactions with other planning elements from the area of inspection planning and the settings in the material master data. To list all possible combinations at this point would lead to complications and confusion. Table 6.10 gives an overview of the functions of the control indicators. For further possible combinations we would refer you at this point to the sections covering the quality planning applications (6.5, 6.6 and 6.7), where a few examples from business operations are described.

| | **TABLE 6.10** | **Description and effects of the control indicators** (© SAP AG) |

	Description	Effects
Lower limit	This means that a lower limit value must be updated in the inspection characteristic in the plan.	
Standard value	Means that you have to enter a standard value for this characteristic.	If you set this indicator and one or both tolerance indicators, the system checks whether the standard value is within the tolerance range.
Upper limit	Means that an upper limit value must be updated in the inspection characteristic in the plan.	
Characteristic attribute	Results in the characteristic becoming attributive and refers to a selected quantity of catalog type 1.	
Sampling procedure	Means that a sampling procedure has to be assigned to the characteristic in the plan.	Process by which the sampling scope is determined during an inspection. The sampling procedure also defines the type of valuation used for results recording (attributive, variable, manual etc.).
SPC characteristic	If this indicator is set, a quality control chart runs for this characteristic.	If you set this indicator, you must also set the indicator for the sampling procedure. Then you have to enter in the plan an SPC criterion and a sampling procedure with control chart type for the SPC characteristic.
Confirmation no. of defects	Means in the results recording that you can confirm the number of defects.	If you do not set this indicator, you can confirm the number of defective units in results recording.
Additive sample	Means that the sampling scope to be drawn is increased by the amount required by this characteristic.	If a sample is to be used for several characteristics, the sample drawing instruction contains only the total sample quantity to be drawn. The indicator can be set, for example, if the inspection is destructive for this characteristic. In such a case, the indicator allows the sample quantity to be increased by the amount required for the inspection of this characteristic.

TABLE 6.10	*continued*

	Description	**Effects**

		Sample quantity:

			I Additive	**II** Additive	**III** Additive
		Characteristic 2	30	X	X
		Characteristic 3	20	X	
		Total	65	30	50

	Description	**Effects**
Destructive inspection	Identifies characteristics which, when inspected, destroy the sample. For the usage decision, the system calculates the destroyed quantity and provides a proposal for the stock posting 'Acc. sample'. During the calculation, all characteristics marked as destructive, and for which inspection results were recorded up to the time of the calculation, are taken into consideration in relation to the actual sampling scope.	These may be optional characteristic, in inspection waiver (skip), long-term characteristics and unplanned characteristics. Physical samples, deviating sample measure units, partial samples and the indicator 'Additive sample' are processed in the same way as in the sample calculation. For the stock posting, the system proposes only that part of the destroyed quantity that exceeds the sample quantity already entered.
Summarized recording	Means that after the inspection only summarized values are confirmed for the inspection results of a characteristic.	
Single result	Means that after the inspection single values (measured values, codes etc.) are recorded for the inspection results of a characteristic.	
No characteristic recording	Means that after the inspection no results can be recorded for the characteristic.	
Classed recording	Allows the inspection results of a characteristic to be recorded as classed values.	
Defects recording	When this indicator is set, defects recording for the characteristic is automatically started if a characteristic is rejected at results recording.	A prerequisite for defect generation in the background is that you enter defect codes in the plan characteristic or master inspection characteristic. In the case of a quantitative characteristic, you can enter three defect codes: ■ Defect code for rejection, general ■ Defect code for rejection at upper tolerance ■ Defect code for rejection at lower tolerance In the case of a qualitative characteristic, enter the defect code for rejection, general.
Required characteristic	Means that the inspection of a characteristic must be completed with confirmation. Inspection results for the characteristic must be confirmed before the usage decision can be made.	If you want a characteristic-based dynamic modification, then you have to identify all characteristics to which dynamic modification is to apply as required characteristics.

TABLE 6.10	continued	
	Description	**Effects**
Optional characteristic	Allows the inspection of an optional characteristic also to be concluded without confirmation. Inspection results for the characteristic do not have to be confirmed before the usage decision can be made.	If you want a characteristic-based dynamic modification, then you have to identify all characteristics to which dynamic modification is to apply as required characteristics.
After acceptance	Means that this conditional characteristic must be inspected when the last preceding required characteristic received the valuation 'A' (Accept) in the same operation.	
After rejection	Means that this conditional characteristic must be inspected when the last preceding required characteristic received the valuation 'R' (Reject) in the same operation.	
Scope not fixed	Means that the inspection scope during results recording is not checked against the inspection scope calculated in advance.	
Fixed scope	Means that the inspection scope must be exactly observed during results recording. Deviation is not possible.	
Smaller scope	Permits the inspection scope during results recording to be smaller than the inspection scope calculated in advance.	
Larger scope	Permits the inspection scope during results recording to be bigger than the inspection scope calculated in advance.	
No documentation	Means that during results recording no additional text for this characteristic needs to be recorded as documentation.	
Docu. if rejected	Means that during results recording an additional text for this characteristic needs to be recorded as documentation only if the characteristic is rejected.	
Docu. required	Means that during results recording an additional text for this characteristic needs to be recorded in all cases as documentation of the inspection results.	

TABLE 6.10	*continued*	

	Description	Effects
Long-term inspection	Means that the inspection for this characteristic can be carried out over a long period.	If you set this indicator for a characteristic, you can make a usage decision for the characteristic or set the status 'Short-term insp. completed'. You can use the inspected material during the long-term inspection, and this eases strain on the inspection lot as far as stock is concerned; this also allows you to record results for the long-term inspection retrospectively.
Scrap share/ q-score	Means that the proportion of defective units of this characteristic is taken into consideration during the calculation of the scrap share in the inspection lot.	If, for the usage decision, you are using a quality score procedure which refers to the scrap share in the inspection lot or in the characteristic, the characteristic will only be used for calculating the quality score if this indicator has been set.
RR change docs	If you set this indicator, change records will be written during the characteristic-based results recording for this characteristic.	The change records are not written until the characteristic processing is completed (status 5) and the data is already available in the database.
Test equipment assignment	If this indicator is set, you have the option of assigning test equipment to the characteristic in the plan. If you do not make an assignment, the system brings this to your attention by means of a warning message.	
Confirm values	Means that for this quantitative characteristic measured values have to be checked and confirmed.	
Calculated charac.	Means that the characteristic is a calculated (formula) characteristic.	The results of a calculated characteristic are not determined through inspection of the characteristic but through calculating from the results of other characteristics within the same operation.
Print	If you set this indicator, the inspection characteristic will be printed on the inspection instruction.	
Do not print	If you set this indicator, the inspection characteristic will not be printed on the inspection instruction.	
Do not print at skip	If you set this indicator, the inspection characteristic will only be printed on the inspection instruction if there is no skip present for the characteristic.	

Assigning the sampling procedures

In the section on sampling procedure, you have already become acquainted with the definition of the sampling procedures. If you have selected SAMPLING PROCEDURE in the control indicators when determining the characteristic type, you will automatically receive the system dialog for entering your sample rules. You can reach this screen later via the DYNAMIC MODIFICATION icon in the application toolbar or by selecting from the pull-down menu.

TIP The selection of the sampling procedures only displays processes that are permitted for this characteristic definition. In the worst case, this selection option is not available at all. Then you will need to check the rules which you created for the sampling procedure. It may be, for example, that you have selected SCOPE NOT FIXED in the control indicators and attempt to assign a sampling procedure for a control chart. Result: the sampling procedure does not appear in the selection because the sampling scope must be fixed if you are using a control chart. You should therefore set FIXED SCOPE.

Attributive (qualitative) characteristics with code groups or selected quantities

To describe a qualitative characteristic, besides assigning the summarizing analysis of a characteristic after acceptance (OK) or rejection (not OK), you can also allocate more exact attributes with codes. When doing this, it is advisable to work with the characteristic control indicator CHARACTERISTIC ATTRIBUTES since this allows you access to the so-called selected quantities.

TIP The characteristic attributes contain not only the 'not OK' criteria of an inspection, but also the 'OK' criteria, and are therefore suitable for a description of good (OK) characteristic results.

Quantitative characteristics with formulas

The calculated (formula) characteristic is a necessary tool for quantitative recording of measurement results. This attribute is assigned via the control indicator of the characteristic (see Fig. 6.33). With the formula interpreters contained in the scope of delivery, you can use the mathematical standard functions for calculation with values from other characteristics, the so-called auxiliary characteristics. The following functions are available in the formula characteristic for input:

- Numerical constants.
- Formula parameters that take values and results from auxiliary characteristics (auxiliary and formula characteristics must be contained in the same operation!).
- Formula parameters for external functional modules (see following Tip).

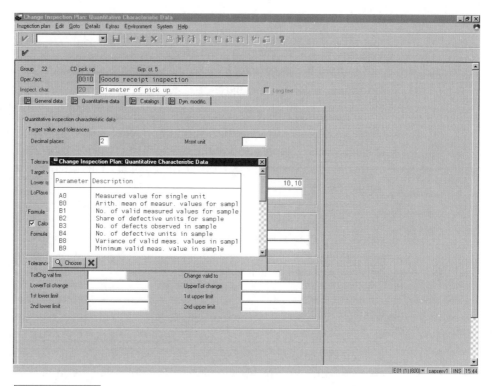

FIGURE 6.33   Formula in detailed view for quantitative data (© SAP AG)

TIP   If the available formula parameters and operands are insufficient for the task, you can introduce extensions via Customizing. As is the case with most extensions, this presupposes profound knowledge of ABAP (the programming language of the SAP R/3 system). Ensure that your system requirements are placed in good time on the agenda in the project discussions, since the programming resources become scarcer with each successive stage in the project.

When constructing your formula characteristic, you should also take note of the element *leading and dependent characteristics*. The auxiliary characteristics used should be identical with regard to their dynamic modification and the sampling procedure. To exclude the possibility of errors, it is advisable to work with leading and dependent characteristics (see the next paragraph). In this example, the formula characteristic would be leading and the auxiliary characteristic(s) would be dependent.

Leading and dependent characteristics

First we will look at the initial prerequisites for leading and dependent characteristics:

- Control indicator DYNAMIC MODIFICATION ON CHARACTERISTICS LEVEL.

- Control indicator REQUIRED CHARACTERISTIC.

If you have used this combination for your characteristics in an operation, inconsistencies may of course occur in the inspection sequence, which means that for different dynamic modification stages of the characteristic, the formula characteristic described in the last section may not work if the auxiliary characteristics are in a skip stage (inspection waiver).

Setting up the leading/dependent characteristic is relatively simple: In the DYNAMIC MODIFICATION screen, you enter a dynamic modification rule for the leading characteristic. In the next step in the equivalent screen for dependent characteristics, you make a reference to the characteristic number. Note that each operation can contain only one leading characteristic.

Using master inspection characteristics

In the section on reference operation sets and section 6.3.2, 'Basic data for quality and inspection planning', we discussed the basic theory of the use of master inspection characteristics, to create standardized modules for ergonomic application in the inspection plan.

The reference operation set and master inspection characteristic are also similar with regard to the method of referencing (permanent connection). Changes to the master inspection characteristic have an effect on the inspection plans they are in – with one minor exception: if you change core attributes of the master inspection characteristic, the system forces you to create a new version. You can then activate this new version for all relevant inspection plans using a function provided specifically for this purpose.

When using master inspection characteristics, we differentiate between two versions:

- The completely updated master inspection characteristic with a fixed reference

- The incompletely updated master inspection characteristic which copies its attributes only into the selected characteristic.

Test equipment assignments for the characteristic

You can assign the characteristic its own test equipment or select an item from the list of test equipment in the operation (see the section covering 'test equipment' and Chapter 11, 'Test equipment management').

TIP Test the functionality of the characteristic first in the inspection plan without referencing, as a simple model for copying. You can create manual or automatic inspection lots in your test system for this purpose. If you use the reference right from the start, in some circumstances a few versions of the master inspection characteristic must be entered if changes are made. This process can easily lead to incomprehensible master data records. If your characteristic displays the desired level of maturity, then you change the master inspection characteristic that is not yet embedded in an inspection plan, and create the fixed reference only after this has been done.

Just as with the referencing of the reference operation set, a further step is now necessary. When you use the control indicator SAMPLING PROCEDURE, you receive a window in the master inspection characteristic for entering the sampling procedure and the dynamic modification rule; these can only be updated on the actual inspection plan level. If you are using updated master inspection characteristics that are still to be completed by further input, such as the formula or tolerance specifications, the system requests that you do this and provides further input screens.

Using inspection methods

In contrast to the qualitative and quantitative attributes of inspection characteristics, the inspection method contains the description of the inspection sequences and further information on overall inspection activities. You use the inspection method therefore primarily for the textual presentation of complex inspection sequences or when supplementary information has to be added to an inspection characteristic or an inspection plan. In this respect, the inspection method also provides you with a universal information medium for inspection planning. The nature of the master data also makes central updating of this module possible and gives you an overview of this procedure. You navigate to the inspection method via the QM basic data menu bar to the inspection methods, where they can be created, changed or deleted. The most important functions within the inspection method are:

- Long text processing.
- Multilingual text creation.
- Classification.
- Administrative data.
- Additional details.

As soon as you have used a data record for an inspection plan or an inspection characteristic, the system sets a usage indicator which serves, among other things, to present the relationships that have been created in the form of a report and, in this way, to make them more lucid. There are some further preconditions that must be met before deleting an inspection method:

- Before setting a usage indicator, all references must be removed.
- The status indicator must be set to '4 blocked'.

Assigning defect codes to characteristics

In many cases, the valuation of a qualitative characteristic with OK/not OK or the assessment of a quantitative characteristic with a measured value is not specific enough. To ensure a more exact defect description, you can provide the characteristic in the event of a rejection with a special catalog of catalog type 9, 'Defect types'. During results recording, this catalog then appears automatically with a rejection and asks you to enter a defect code.

A further important characteristic of this function is the automatic generation of a defect record during defects recording in the form of a quality notification. If you want to use this function, set the checkbox DEFECTS RECORDING in the control indicator of the characteristic to active. You will then be able to completely process the notifications of notification type Q2, INTERNAL QUALITY NOTIFICATIONS.

Updating further allocation values

This function is of significance for you if additional or various criteria are to apply to an inspection in a dependent relationship to vendor, material or customer on characteristics level. You can extend each individual characteristic by the special qualitative and quantitative attributes in MAT-PLAN ALLOCATION. This does not apply, however, to characteristics in reference operation sets or to the master inspection characteristics. Since this function is associated with a relatively 'nondescript' expression, here is a small navigation aid and guide:

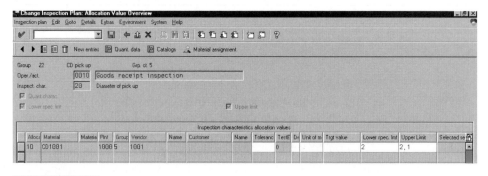

FIGURE 6.34 Allocation values screen (© SAP AG)

1 Mark the desired characteristic.

2 Then select GOTO | CHARACTERISTIC VALUE OVERVIEW in the menu bar; the ALLOCATION VALUE OVERVIEW then appears on the screen, which offers you a view of the existing allocation values.

3 Now you can add further values via EDIT | NEW ENTRIES | ENTER ALLOCATION VALUES. (Pay particular attention to the columns VENDOR, TOLERANCE and TARGET VALUE, see Fig. 6.34.)

6.5   APPLICATION OF QUALITY PLANNING IN PURCHASING (MM)

In the example presented here, we will look at a manufacturer of electronic components for PCs and communication devices with an extensive range of parts. This branch of industry is characterized by rapid product development and is therefore dependent on perfect interaction between all vendors involved in the product. We will look at quality planning in Purchasing for a component which, in the logistics chain and by means of various production processes, is to be subject to further value-creation. The

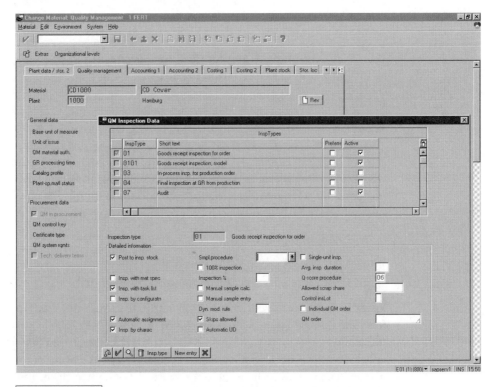

FIGURE 6.35   Material master data with 'QM in Purchasing' (© SAP AG)

materials are purchased from different manufacturers, as no single manufacturer has sufficient production capacity to provide us with all supplies and, moreover, dependency on one vendor does not appear to be beneficial. In this example, the assembly group is once again the CD cover for the software components of an ISDN board. Our material is subject to a simple release process, including prototypes and subsequent series delivery. The follow-up models in the case of component modification are processed separately and lead to a new inspection status of the material. Of central significance to us is the stability of shape and certain special attributive characteristics of critical importance.

We will now follow the quality planning process in the case of a new vendor for the interior part of the CD cover, referred to as the 'CD pick up'. Our previous vendor, 'Duff and Sons Ltd.', on account of a quality score of 35, no longer enjoys our unqualified confidence; the sourcing team, consisting of Purchasing and Quality Management, decided to accept the offer tendered for the same material from IQ plc. The important thing here is that the material number remains identical for our system, no matter from which vendor we acquire the material. Once IQ plc has been recorded in our system with a vendor master record, the purchasing process can begin straight away. However, the new vendor must still fulfil our conditions regarding the release process before series delivery begins. We will now elucidate and control this process with the R/3 QM system.

6.5.1 Quality/inspection planning for Purchasing in the material master data and Q information record

Material master data

We will begin with a look at the material master data in which 'Quality Management in Purchasing' is activated with the key '0001' (Fig. 6.35). The consequence of this is that IQ plc first has to be released for purchase orders and deliveries in the quality information record. By selecting and activating the following inspection types, we can certainly guarantee inspection lot creation for each goods receipt for this material via the movement of goods '101, Goods receipt for purchase order':

- 01 Goods receipt inspection for purchase order.
- 02 Goods receipt inspection, prototype.
- 03 Goods receipt inspection, extra model (as required).

With the inspection type activated, the attribute QUALITY INSPECTION now disappears from the Q view! There is a special reason for this. With activated inspection type and the inspection type definition POST TO Q STOCK, the stock code 'Q' is set for each delivery lot. The stock which has just been entered is therefore not released for further usage. If you set the attribute QUALITY INSPECTION right at the beginning without specifying inspection type usage, this has the same initial effect as far as the stock is concerned and makes an entry in the Quality inspection stock in the event of goods receipt. The special difference is that you can manually book the Quality inspection stock, created in the above manner, back to 'released' without a usage decision.

TIP   Strangely enough, you will also find the attribute QUALITY INSPECTION with exactly the same properties in the Purchasing view in the material master data. Please make sure that you explain this situation to the specialist department responsible during an integration meeting and establish who is permitted to activate this function.

The relevant input on release control is then made in the Q information record, which we already created for the new material-vendor combination (see Fig. 6.36). The release of all vendors must be worked through in accordance with the respective internal departmental process instruction. Beforehand, and in the same way, we used the Customizing variants to generate a *status profile* for the deliveries and selected this for the current Q information record. This is absolutely necessary because otherwise it

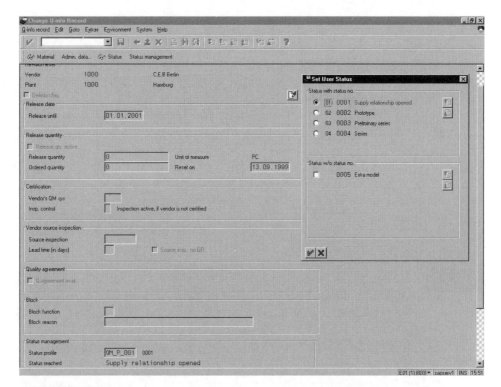

FIGURE 6.36   Q information record with release control and status information (© SAP AG)

would not be possible to generate a complete inspection lot. If the necessary documents have been received (e.g. proof of a QS 9000 certification etc.), and if the vendor had a favourable first audit, the *status of supply relationships* comes into effect and the first delivery generates an inspection lot for prototypes.

TIP 1

If you adopt prototype parts at a later point, this does not necessarily require a purchase order. In the case of deliveries without a purchase order, however, targeted monitoring of the delivery dates is often impossible. It is advisable, therefore, to enter purchase orders even at the prototypes stage.

Only the inspection type 01, Goods receipt for purchase order is relevant for the vendor evaluation. For this reason, we set the control indicator for the quality score procedure 06, Quality score from usage decision, in the Q view of the material master data under the inspection type.

TIP 2

It is possible that the system forces you to enter a quality score procedure in all inspection types. In order to exclude or lessen the influence (if you so desire) of the prototype and extra model on the quality score, there are three options available:

■ Enter the usage decision codes in a code group for prototype and extra models with deviating quality score assignment.

■ Evaluate using the same usage decision codes as usual and define the quality score manually.

■ Define in Customizing a separate quality score procedure which has no influence on the update of the quality score.

6.5.2 Quality and inspection planning for the goods receipt inspection

As we have already been purchasing the above-mentioned material for a long time from Duff and Sons Ltd, the associated inspection plans for the prototypes, series delivery and follow-up models are also available, each with its own *plan group counter*. Each

TIP

Important! The Material/plan allocation offers us special time-saving system support: we don't even have to do anything! As mentioned above, an activated inspection type in the material master data generates the inspection lot; for this reason, if the existing inspection plan for material remains identical, we do not have to enter any further allocations for the vendor in question in the inspection plan. Later in the inspection lot itself, with the movement of goods, the vendor is combined with the material. The calculations of the quality level, the quality score and the status sequence are all system-controlled and are made automatically on the basis of the data from the purchase order and the goods movement for this order.

inspection type has its own plan usage which is set in Customizing. The plan usage is entered in the header data of the plan according to the character of the inspection plan. Via the various plan usages, the appropriate status later adopts the correct inspection plan from the status profile.

The prototype inspection plan

Our actual prototype inspection plan consists of approximately 50 characteristics that are compiled according to specification. For the sake of simplicity, at this point we will only create two characteristics: one for the inspection of all quantitative characteristics and one for the inspection of all qualitative characteristics (Fig. 6.37). The header data does not contain any entries for the dynamic modification level and the sampling procedure, as the delivered quantities are not yet relevant and a dynamic modification is not suitable for prototypes.

The inspection plan for series delivery

This inspection plan, similar to the principles of inspection planning described at the beginning of the chapter, is constructed with the following planning objects:

▦ *Material purchasing*

   The assignment of a vendor is not required. The Material-plan allocation is not extended!

▦ *Inspection characteristic overview with inspection instruction*

   Various quantitative and qualitative characteristics are assigned to the operation GR inspection for series delivery. The inspection characteristics are entered in a reference operation set and referenced in the operation, since this material is being managed in different variants with its own material number and own plan groups. The qualitative characteristics can also be updated as master inspection characteristics and employed in the reference operation set.

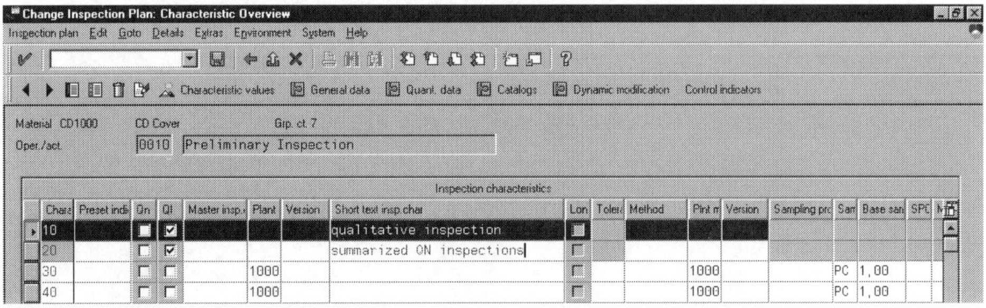

FIGURE 6.37 Prototype inspection plan, characteristics (© SAP AG)

- *Inspection scope*

  The qualitative (QL01) and quantitative characteristics (QL02) have one sampling procedure of their own respectively. Calculation of the sampling scope without sampling scheme for the qualitative and quantitative inspection.

- *Inspection frequency (dynamic modification)*

  Dynamic modification rule with skip stage (DYN01).

- *Inspection data processing*

  Results recording in the characteristic is enabled (see control indicator of the inspection characteristic, Fig. 6.38).

- *Necessity of inspection*

  Is set by activating the inspection type in the material master data.

- *Inspection sequence*

  Inspecting with plan in the inspection type is active; results recording in the characteristic is active; defects recording in the characteristic is active (generates Q notification with defect data record).

- *Inspection method*

  Inspection method assigned, see follow-up model.

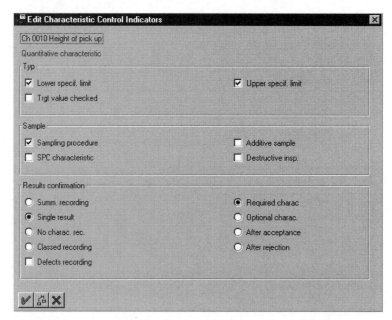

FIGURE 6.38 Control indicator quantitative characteristic from the proposal (© SAP AG)

■ *Test equipment*

Can be assigned to the operation and characteristic as an option.

■ *Inspection lot processing/creation*

The control is via the input of the header data for the inspection plan (dynamic modification level 1, lot level):

– Dynamic modification rule: D00, dynamic modification XY.

– Plan usage: 5, Goods receipt.

– Inspection type: 01, Goods receipt inspection in material master data (see Fig. 6.39).

The inspection lot itself is generated by a goods movement 101, Goods receipt for purchase order.

Quality planning of inspection lot processing with quality level

Once the inspection of the prototype has been completed via the usage decision with the valuation Acceptance, the system switches to the inspection plan for the series

| FIGURE 6.39 | Example of a characteristic overview for the goods receipt inspection of the complete CD cover (© SAP AG) |

delivery. Assuming approximately 20 deliveries of material with delivery lots of approximately 1000 units, we have decided on an inspection dynamic modification on lot level with skip lot function. To do this, we select a suitable entry from the dynamic modification processes we entered ourselves. Our dynamic modification rule specifies an initial stage Inspection; otherwise it is similar to the example in Fig. 6.12 in the section in this chapter on 'Dynamic modification'. In Chapter 8, 'Quality control', in the section 'Quality level', you will find more detailed information on this subject. Here the following also applies: if this inspection plan is to be valid for different vendors, the entries in the header data and characteristics data affect all vendors that deliver the material and therefore draw on the same plan group. If deviating characteristic attributes are necessary in spite of this, the characteristic allocations with vendor-specific inspection plans, as listed in the section 'Inspection planning', can also be used.

To complete the picture, we will now check the characteristics in order to examine the correct assignment of sampling procedures and dynamic modification rules. (Important: when the control indicator 'Sampling scheme' is set in the characteristic, this step must always be carried out on the characteristics level of the inspection plan.) In the case of characteristic-based dynamic modification, the dynamic modification rule is entered on the characteristics level, and with lot-based dynamic modification on the header level of the inspection plan.

TIP Remember that you can manually change the quality level for each material-vendor combination at any time. It is only very rarely necessary, therefore, to enter individual inspection plans (with another plan group counter)! Strictly speaking, this rule really applies to all inspection plan activities. With a little bit of extra thought, you can thus move from many 'vendor inspection plans' to one 'material inspection plan' and save yourself a lot of wasted time and effort in inspection planning maintenance and updating.

Planning of characteristic-based dynamic modification

In the event of a characteristic-based dynamic modification (Fig. 6.40), the intended dynamic modification rule is also added to the characteristic in the menu SAMPLING PROCEDURE. The attribute characteristic-based dynamic modification is set in the header data of the plan group counter.

TIP Basically, characteristic-based dynamic modification is not much more complex than lot-based dynamic modification. Since the functions are supported by the system, this results in a further reduction of inspection time and expenditure. Not only do you have to observe the connections between leading and dependent characteristics, but also the fact that the inspection of series parts, where the characteristics are reduced to the necessary dimension anyway, is usually performed according to a certain scheme.

In the case of characteristic-based dynamic modification, the inspector must answer the following question in every inspection: 'Which material do I have to inspect and which can I leave out?' Such an inspection routine could, in certain circumstances, be more complicated for the member of staff responsible than it would be if they were simply to record all characteristics of the inspection plan and document them in the system. For this reason, the decision on characteristic- or lot-based dynamic modification is ideally preceded by an overhead analysis of both processes.

Inspection plan for extra or follow-up model

Since the inspection operation for the extra or follow-up model is related to that of the prototypes and we are working here with a separate inspection plan anyway, for the sake of simplicity the extra model check plan was created using the prototype inspection plan as a profile. We have also assigned an inspection method to this inspection plan, which describes the exact inspection sequence.

The purchasing procedure with inspection lot creation

Once we have completed all the necessary inspection plan preparation, it is time that we worked our way through a complete business event in Purchasing (see Fig. 6.41). To do this, of course, we have to operate the required transactions. On a practical level

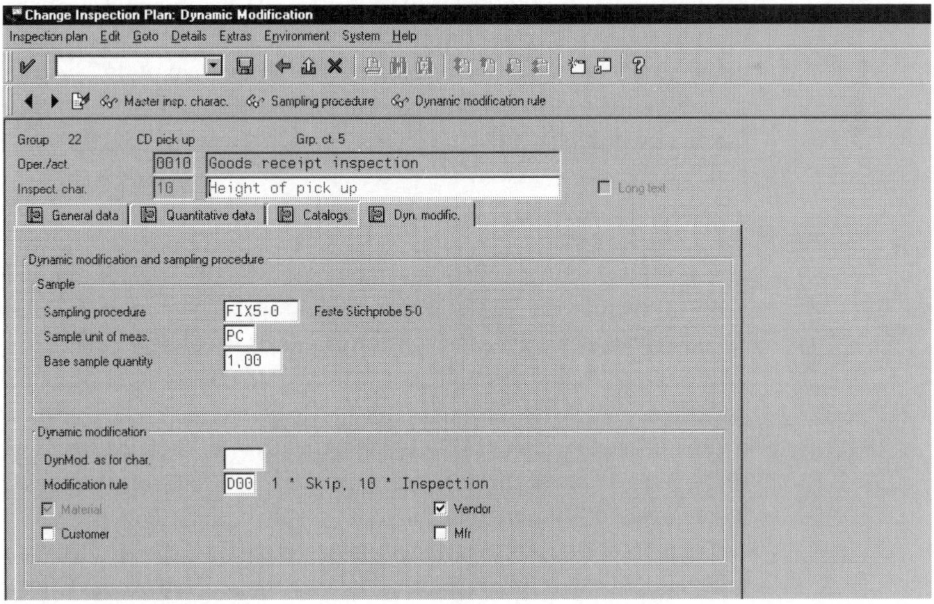

FIGURE 6.40   Sampling procedure and dynamic modification rule in the characteristic details with characteristic-based dynamic modification (© SAP AG)

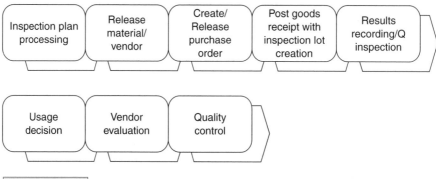

FIGURE 6.41 Purchasing process with the process paths of quality planning

with implementation projects, it is usually the case that the persons responsible for the Quality Management module at least have a command of the basic principles of the transactions involved in ordering and goods movements, so that they are able to test the different versions themselves. In the following section, and using our example, we will introduce you to the most important functions in these areas using a few screen-shots and navigation aids. Initial reservations about this 'new world' are usually very quickly overcome when you realize that things here are not as complicated as they seem.

All tests are also carried out within a development system and therefore, initially, do not have any effect on the business process in the productive system. The best thing to do is to ask a colleague from Purchasing to name a suitable material that permits the desired orders and goods movements. You should then notify the part project managers in Purchasing who are involved and your consultant of this 'QM material' by mail (ideally by means of *SAPoffice* as an express document).

A purchase order is created

The prerequisites for ordering a material naturally include the completely updated views of the material master data for Purchasing. The material CD1000 we have used is already created and provided with the PURCHASING view.

We navigate first through LOGISTICS | MATERIALS MANAGEMENT | PURCHASING and then on via PURCHASING ORDER | CREATE | VENDOR KNOWN and enter the required elements via CREATE PURCHASE ORDER. In the next step, we move with ENTER to the header data of the purchase order and then to ITEM OVERVIEW (Fig. 6.42). This is where we enter the actual items of the purchase order (Fig. 6.43).

From the ITEM OVERVIEW, we navigate back to the header data of the purchase order and release it (menu icon 'green man/flag'). Now we save this quite simply with ENTER, which enables the purchase order to be posted. The purchase order has now been saved under a number which, as usual, appears in the status bar at the bottom

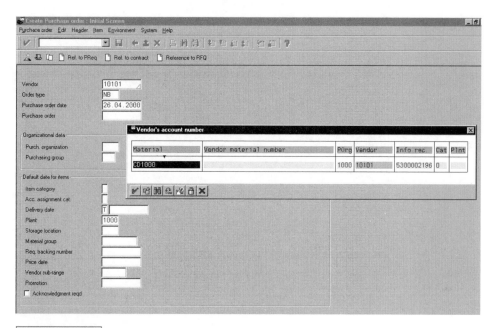

FIGURE 6.42   Create purchase order (© SAP AG)

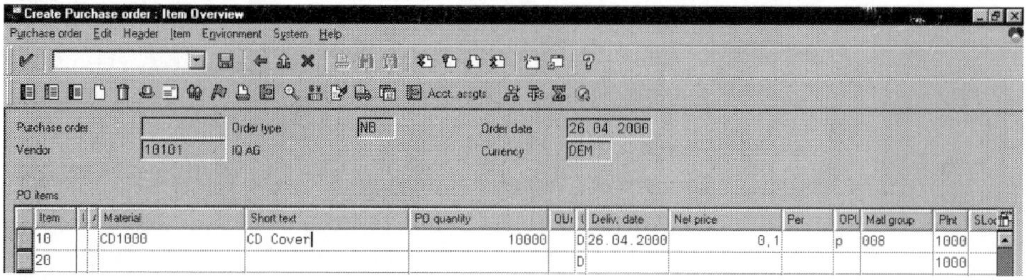

FIGURE 6.43   Item overview (© SAP AG)

edge of the screen. This number, which is internally assigned by the system (purchase document number), can be used later to identify and locate your inspection lot.

Goods receipt for purchase order with inspection lot creation

The goods movement for the purchase order is generally linked to the movement type 101, Goods receipt for order. We follow the menu path LOGISTICS | MATERIALS MANAGEMENT | STOCK MANAGEMENT and then select GOODS MOVEMENT | GOODS RECEIPT FOR PURCHASE ORDER | PURCHASE ORDER NO. UNKNOWN. Once the fields are filled with the appropriate data (Fig. 6.44), press ENTER to reach the PURCHASING DOCUMENTS screen, where we select the relevant document and the item.

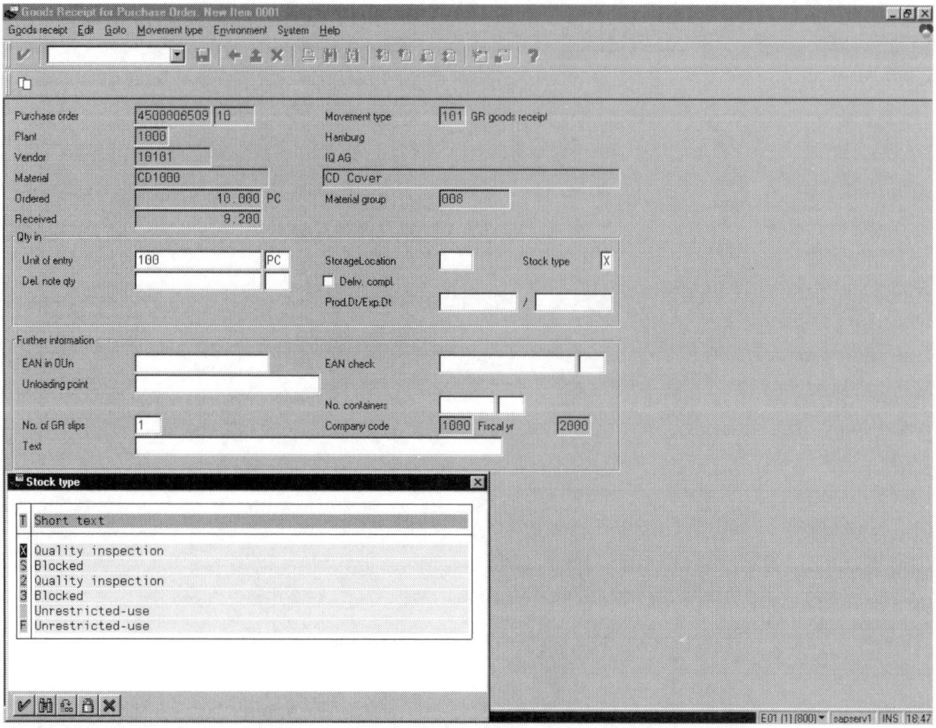

FIGURE 6.44 Goods receipt posting in the quality inspection stock (© SAP AG)

In the next step, we enter the delivered quantity, which may well deviate from the ordered quantity, at the appropriate item in the same screen and post the document with ENTER. Assuming that we are working with the enabled 'QM in Purchasing' and certificate control, the system now opens a dialog window with the question 'Have we received a certificate of the required type?' After answering with *yes* or *no* (in the case of *no*, a status is set in the inspection lot which prevents a concluding usage decision) and pressing ENTER once again, the document is now finally posted and an inspection lot is created. The number internally assigned by the system is now stored as a material document (goods receipt document number) and can be used to search for the inspection lot.

Effects of quality planning on inspection lot processing

We will now carry out the further processing of the inspection lot up to the usage decision (inspection lot completion) and the quantity postings which will be described in Chapter 7, 'Quality inspection', and Chapter 8, 'Quality control'.

Once the usage decision has been made, there are various process routes available with regard to our planned status sequence:

TIP

During the posting procedure in the initial tests, always pay close attention to the status bar at the bottom edge of the screen. If, during a goods receipt posting, the info 'Preparing quality inspection' does not appear, the worklist definitely does not contain an inspection lot for results recording. An incomplete inspection lot, however, may have been created. In this case, search for the inspection lot via QUALITY INSPECTION | INSPECTION LOT PROCESSING | DISPLAY INSPECTION LOT. The inspection lot can usually be found if you follow this route. If you have identified the inspection lot, work step by step through the INSPECTION SPECIFICATION and INSPECTION LOT QUANTITY screens. Both screens must be filled with valid data before you can record results. If this is not the case, recheck your compilation/assignment of the inspection plan and the inspection data in the Q view for material.

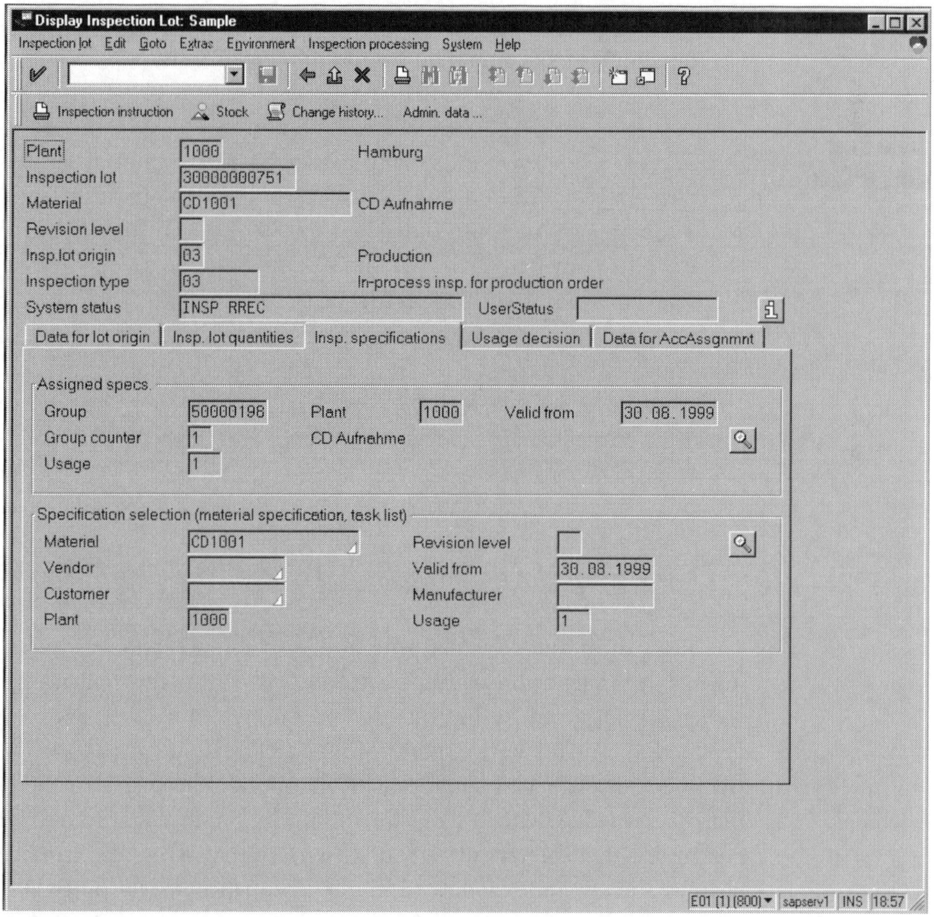

FIGURE 6.45 Plan allocation for inspection lot (© SAP AG)

▓ If the delivery was a prototype and received the valuation 'Accepted' in the usage decision, the status sequence switches at the next goods movement for this material–vendor combination (as defined by us in Customizing) to 'Series delivery'.

▓ If the delivery was a prototype and received the valuation 'Reject' in the usage decision, the status sequence remains at 'Prototype'. During the next movement of goods, another inspection lot with reference to the prototype inspection plan will be created. This is repeated, of course, until we arrive at a usage decision with 'Acceptance'.

▓ If the delivery was a series delivery assigned the usage decision 'Acceptance', the status sequence remains at 'Series delivery' provided it is not overridden manually.

If the situation makes it necessary, we can create an intermediate status by means of an additional status sequence 'Follow-up model' and block the purchase orders/deliveries in the Q information record until the follow-up model has a positive outcome, i.e. the usage decision valuation is 'Acceptance'. An obvious prerequisite here is that our Customizing permits a manual status change.

TIP The status sequence, however, has a minor drawback: it is not possible for the purchase order nor the movement of goods to define a reference to the existing status sequences, so that by assigning a code to the purchase order/movement of goods the system could be notified whether we are dealing with a prototype, etc. The system simply assumes that the sequence of goods received corresponds to the logic of the status sequence. This situation proves to be a problem whenever we have several parallel goods receipts of the same part, since the individual delivery is not identifiable as a prototype, series delivery or follow-up model. At this point, you only really have recourse to an organizational solution, whereby the goods are appropriately identified and then included in the correct sequence and inspected.

6.6 APPLICATION OF QUALITY PLANNING IN PRODUCTION (PP)

The tasks of production planning and inspection planning overlap in several areas during the integration of the inspection plan into the routing. Firstly, you will be somewhat surprised to find out that you do not have a separate inspection plan for Production. The inspection plan is fully integrated in the routing (the same applies to the line plan and recipe). It goes without saying, however, that the routing/inspection plan is provided with all of the functions contained in the inspection plan for Purchasing that we have already discussed. Here you can also work with sampling procedures and dynamic modification rules for inspection lot processing.

In most cases in the area of Production, inspection lot creation is initiated by the event 'Release production order'. The sole exceptions here are the production-specific inspection types such as 'Goods receipt/goods issue for production' etc., which create inspection lots in the event of material movements. With these inspection types, a transfer of goods from the warehouse to the production order, for example, creates the inspection lot.

Since in the case of quality planning with the aim of sample determination for the inspection lot, the processes are similar to those in Purchasing, in this practical example we will now turn our attention to a specialty of the in-process inspection: statistical process control (SPC). The main components of the SPC process are graphical charts which enable inspectors to document their processes and to operate within the *intervention limits* as far as possible. In spite of criticism of this work method from various quarters, it must be said in its defence that, under certain circumstances (relatively large series or continually recurring orders for the same machines), very high success levels are always achieved in process improvement. The prerequisites for a successful SPC process are listed in Fig. 6.46.

Translated into SAP language, we refer to inspection lot processing with so-called 'Inspection points'. A further feature that distinguishes it from the inspection lot in Purchasing is the usage decision, which remains without influence on stock management. The production stocks are recorded only on confirmation of the production order.

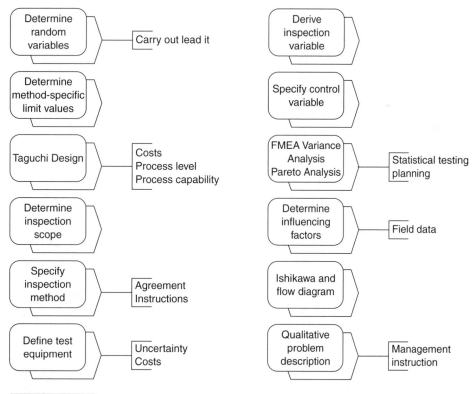

FIGURE 6.46 Procedural model for quality planning with statistical process control

From our examination of the goods receipt inspection of the CD cover, it would appear to be advisable to analyse this part with respect to its quality planning during production. We now find ourselves in the manufacturer's production, in the process stage 'injection moulding', where a diameter measurement should lead to a control chart. The diameter of 10 mm ± 0.1 is limited on two sides and is tested with a measuring device into which the component is inserted. Longitudinal probes determine the required dimension at three points, offset by 120°. A point on the control chart is to be created on the basis of the arithmetical mean of the three measurements on one part and with a constant sampling scope of three parts. Furthermore, we assume a normal distribution of the process which we have known for some time. The aim of the temporary use of a control chart is to reduce total scatter of the process. Our hypothesis is that we can achieve a minimization of the scrap share and an improvement of process capability using a process control based on intervention limits (as opposed to control within tolerance limits).

We record the measured values via an interface to the measuring probes with the help of the keyboard router and, for example, a 'Steinwald' interface box. This measuring equipment is described separately in Chapter 7, 'Quality inspection', in the section 'Interfaces'.

Quality planning for Production in the material master data

Starting once again with the material master data, this example requires that you enter the Quality Management view for the material. Other views required for production, e.g. the work preparation view, must also be updated. Since, theoretically, all views are options, we will limit ourselves again at this point to the Q view of the material.

TIP Sometimes it may be necessary for test purposes to enter a new material in your test system/client. With only a little bit of practice, this can be carried out intuitively. In short: CREATE MATERIAL | IMMEDIATELY, select all views and, using ENTER, make all the mandatory input from view to view. Then start the desired transaction, e.g. CREATE PRODUCTION ORDER. If you have forgotten entries in your material master data or have not created views, this is not a disaster. When the production order is running, the system constantly counterchecks whether the required data/views are already available. If this is not the case, a corresponding note appears in the status bar (bottom edge of screen). Although the material master data is a somewhat complex construction, users in our projects have never needed more than half an hour to provisionally prepare their material master record for a purchase order or a production order.

Similar rules apply to inspection type 05/03 as in inspection type 01, the difference being that it is not the movement of goods, but the release of the production order that generates the inspection lot (Fig. 6.47). The inspection lot is created no matter whether

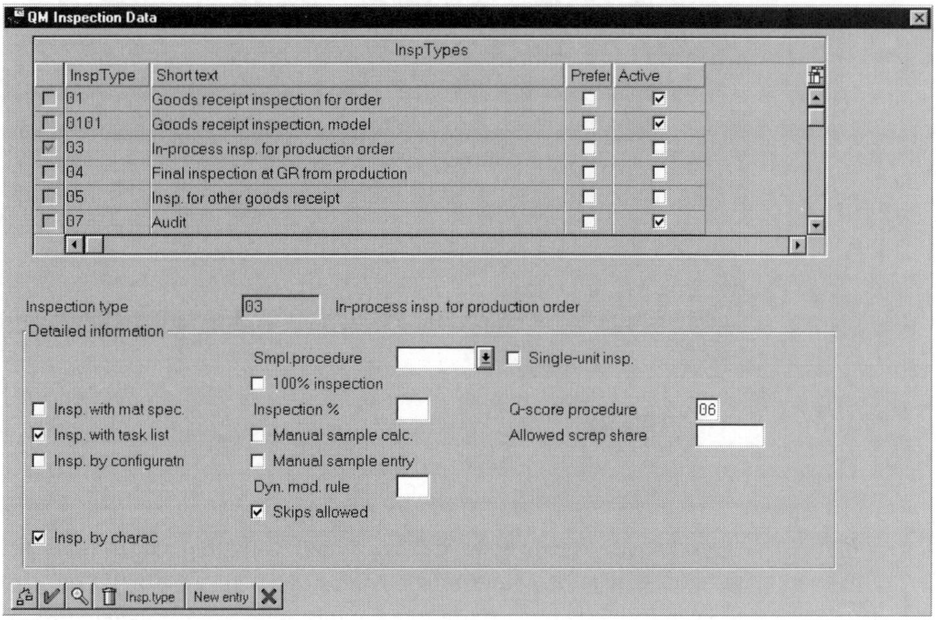

FIGURE 6.47   Inspection type 05: Intermediate inspection for production order with control indicator (© SAP AG)

the inspection plan is complete, not available at all or whether several are available. Each production order which is released or which is not yet concluded can be assigned only one inspection lot respectively. Here, it is of no significance whether it is created manually or automatically.

The inspection plan/routing with operations for the SPC planning

The basis of this example is a routing with various work operations. We will assume first of all that the inspection plan for the SPC inspections of this material has been previously illustrated in an external CAQ system. The specialist departments in our company get together to discuss the integrated routing /inspection plan that is now available and consider at what position the SPC inspections should be introduced.

TIP   This planning task is not always very easy in an implementation project and a certain amount of diplomacy is required on the part of Quality Management. In many cases, the routing structure has been well established for a long time and colleagues like to claim 'we don't need quality inspection in the routing', or there is recourse to the old argument 'we can do that later'. Show your colleagues the benefits of the process and, in order to generate the required acceptance, run it through as an example with the specialist departments.

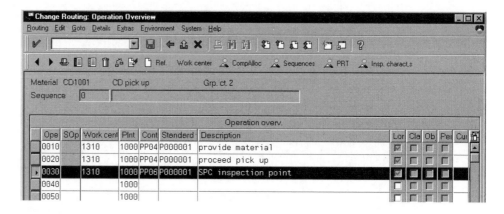

FIGURE 6.48   Operation overview with referenced operation set (inspection plan)
(© SAP AG)

In our case, however, we have included work preparation based on system ergonomics and lean management. The joint result is as follows: the inspection operation receives its own operation number and is prepared completely by Quality Management as a reference operation set.

During work planning, the reference operation set module, set up as a quality operation, only needs to be used by the work planner per *reference* (see sections 'Creating operations with a reference operation set' and 'Inspection operation' in this chapter). To prepare this step, we have compiled the reference operation set under the number '100, CD pick up', as shown in Fig. 6.48. The control indicator of the operation (PP01, QM01) has already been agreed in the preparatory discussions with work planning, as have the predefined work centre and the production resources/tools used. The SPC inspection characteristic has already been added to the operations in the reference operation set.

TIP   Another word on the *control key* in the operation. The control key does not change the actual inspection properties; only in the case of the plan check and printing of work papers that are the properties different to those of the pure routings. Take a close look at the control options together with the work planning department. It is no problem at all to develop a control key for the work and inspection operations that will do justice to the demands coming from both directions.

Planning objects

This inspection plan, again constructed similarly to the principles of quality planning described at the beginning of the chapter, has the following contents:

▨ *Material purchasing (in the routing)*

The assignment of the material has usually already been carried out by the work planner. The Material-plan allocation is only extended if a deviating routing is required for the material to be finished.

▨ *Inspection characteristic overview with inspection instruction*

For the operation 'SPC inspection', three results, i.e. the results of the three parts, are to be confirmed for each inspection point. This is the arithmetical average calculated in the respective inspection with the measuring device.

▨ *Scope of inspection (sample definition)*

We select a sampling procedure SPC01 with a fixed sampling scope of three units. In the sampling procedure, we also define:

– Sample type: fixed sample.

– Valuation mode: SPC inspection, where the valuation of the sample or characteristic is carried out according to the intervention limits of the quality control chart. The violation of an intervention limit (important – not the tolerance limit!) leads to rejection.

– Control chart type: Shewart, X bar/s.

– Sampling scope: three, fixed.

▨ *Inspection frequency*

Here it is essential that you enter the indicator 'SPC inspection' in the control indicators for the characteristic and that you set the attribute 'Inspection points' in the header data of the characteristic overview. Our definition of inspection frequency is one sample after each batch of 100 finished parts. Take note that in spite of this only a maximum of one inspection lot per production order is generated.

> **TIP** If, in addition to the SPC inspection, we want to inspect beyond our designated sampling scope for each inspection lot, then we can achieve this by using the *independent multiple sample*. The additional inspection is not included in the control chart update. To do this, the corresponding attributes must be set in the sampling procedure and in the control indicator of the characteristic.

▨ *Inspection data processing*

Results recording 'quantitative' in the characteristic is active (see section 'Control indicators of the inspection characteristic') with the attribute 'SPC inspection' (Fig. 6.49).

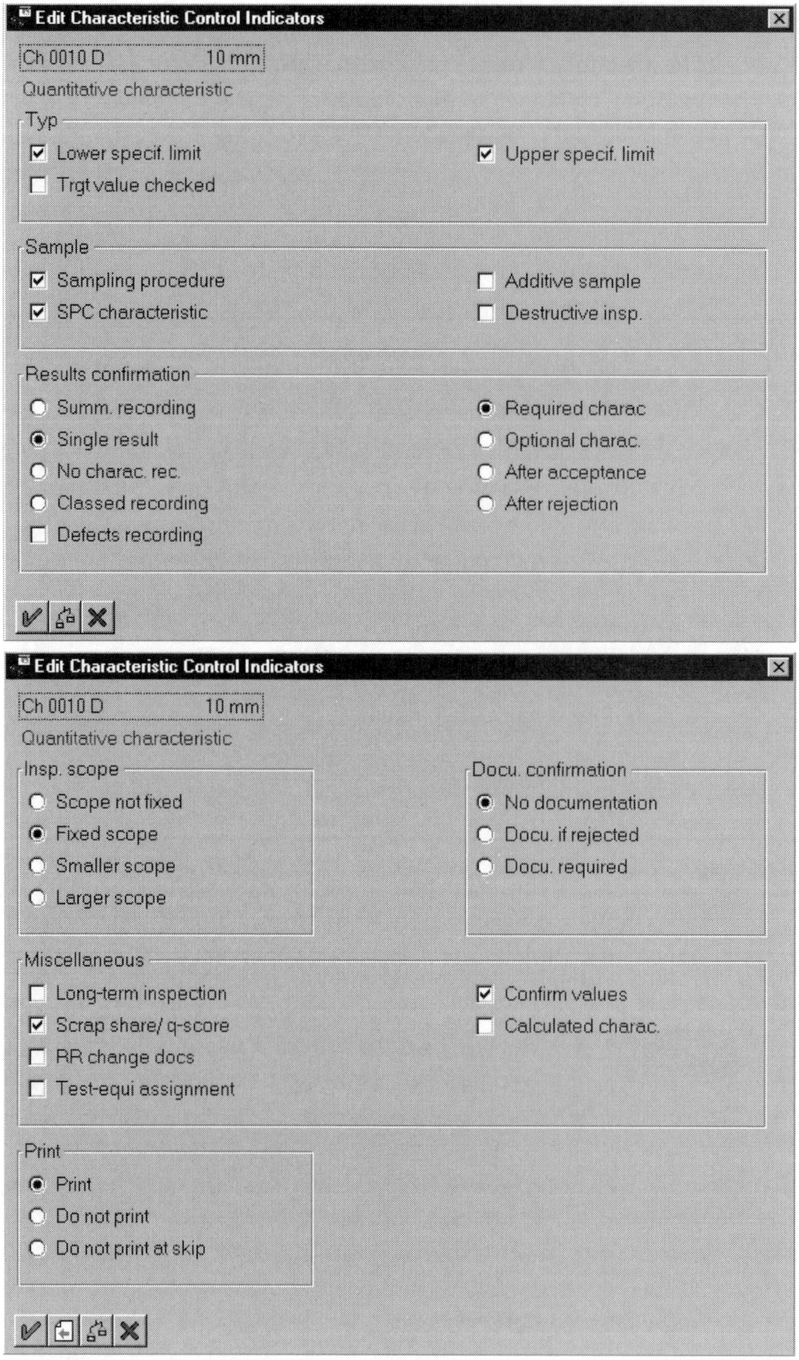

Edit Characteristic Control Indicators

Ch 0010 D   10 mm
Quantitative characteristic

Typ
- ☑ Lower specif. limit
- ☑ Upper specif. limit
- ☐ Trgt value checked

Sample
- ☑ Sampling procedure
- ☐ Additive sample
- ☑ SPC characteristic
- ☐ Destructive insp.

Results confirmation
- ○ Summ. recording
- ◉ Required charac
- ◉ Single result
- ○ Optional charac.
- ○ No charac. rec.
- ○ After acceptance
- ○ Classed recording
- ○ After rejection
- ☐ Defects recording

Edit Characteristic Control Indicators

Ch 0010 D   10 mm
Quantitative characteristic

Insp. scope
- ○ Scope not fixed
- ◉ Fixed scope
- ○ Smaller scope
- ○ Larger scope

Docu. confirmation
- ◉ No documentation
- ○ Docu. if rejected
- ○ Docu. required

Miscellaneous
- ☐ Long-term inspection
- ☑ Confirm values
- ☑ Scrap share/ q-score
- ☐ Calculated charac.
- ☐ RR change docs
- ☐ Test-equi assignment

Print
- ◉ Print
- ○ Do not print
- ○ Do not print at skip

FIGURE 6.49   Control indicator characteristic SPC inspection (© SAP AG)

The setting FIXED SAMPLE should be selected for the SPC inspection. Only with this control indicator is it possible to carry out SPC recording. (Fig. 6.50.)

■ *Necessity of inspection*

Is set by activating the inspection type in the material master data.

■ *Inspection sequence*

  – Inspecting with plan in the inspection type is active.

  – Results recording in the characteristic is active.

  The functional module for importing measurement data from the keyboard router is enabled. Once the results recording has been started, the required measured value is transferred to the R/3 system by means of a foot switch.

■ *Inspection method*

Inspection method can be assigned (optionally) for a more accurate description of the inspection sequence.

■ *Test equipment*

Can be assigned to the operation and characteristic as an option.

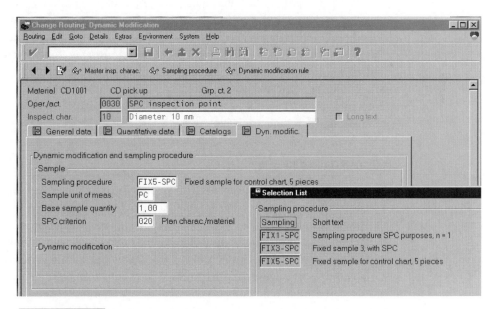

FIGURE 6.50 Sampling procedure for SPC (© SAP AG)

░ *Inspection lot processing/creation*

The control is via the input of the header data for the inspection plan (inspection point processing, inspection lot origin 03) and the inspection type. The inspection lot is generated by the release of the production order and the inspection type 03, Inspection in Production.

Valuation mode

You can select the valuation mode without any restrictions. There is, however, the special valuation mode 'SPC inspection', where the valuation of the sample or characteristic is carried out according to the intervention limits of the quality control chart. Here, the violation of an intervention limit leads to rejection. As long as intervention limits have not been calculated (lead time), the system automatically switches to manual valuation.

Starting the production order

The routing/inspection plan forms the basis for the 'Production order with material', which we will now create a simplified, but functioning, form. We navigate via the main menu LOGISTICS | PRODUCTION | PRODUCTION PLANNING and select ORDER | CREATE | WITH MATERIAL. After making our input on the material, the production and planning activities and, confirming with ENTER, we arrive at the item data of the production order. Now we enter the quantity that is to be produced and the scheduling dates, and confirm once again with ENTER. If our routing is correctly created, approved and, to some degree, error-free, the system will add this order via the routing selection to the routing we previously prepared. It is important to understand that the production order adopts the information/operations of the routing merely as a copy; we could now add or delete operations any way we wish.

Clearing the production order

In our example, however, we are satisfied with the operations and can clear the order via the menu bar or with the 'green man' icon. While doing this, we keep a close eye on the status bar at the bottom edge of the screen. The interaction of inspection type, inspection plan and production order generates an inspection lot which is indicated with 'Preparing quality inspection' in the status bar at the bottom of the screen. However, we still have two other options to monitor success. Firstly, the production order receives a further status called 'ILCR' (inspection lot cleared) which refers to an inspection lot creation and, secondly, the inspection lot number is displayed in the order header data.

Inspection lot processing

For inspection lot processing, we will turn to the 'Quality inspection' process described in Chapter 7, where we will confirm the measurement results. Each production order gives us a new point on the control chart graphics.

Plan variant 'Extended workbench'

If certain operations in a routing are not carried out in your own company, but you nevertheless wish to monitor success during a later delivery, there is a special function in the system for doing this. Using the operation control EXTERNAL PROCESSING and the subsequent settings, you initialize this process:

▦ Enter a control key for operations involving external processing.

▦ Enter an inspection type of origin 01, Goods receipt, in the detailed screen for external processing.

▦ Inspection type 01 is set in the material master data of the final product and activated.

▦ In Customizing, you can assign a special plan usage to each inspection type. This gives you the option of entering special inspection plans for external processing, and assigning them automatically to the inspection lot.

Inspection lot creation 'Extended workbench'

▦ With the release of the production order, a *requisition* is created for external processing and converted into a purchase order.

▦ When recording the goods receipt for this purchase order, the system checks whether there is an inspection type available in the operation and whether it is active for the material. If this is the case, an inspection lot is generated for the final product of the order.

▦ After the goods receipt posting, the inspection lot appears in the worklist for results recording, as is the case with purchased parts.

6.7 APPLICATION OF QUALITY PLANNING IN SALES AND DISTRIBUTION (SD)

The quality planning for Sales and Distribution is not usually directed toward repeat inspections of the manufactured goods but rather aims at a special type of qualification and, in many cases, a certified documentation. The following example depicts such a process.

Certificate for delivery

We will consider a situation in which two customers make different quality- and documentation-related demands on the same product. The customer Megatech Corp. would like a defined dimensional stability and certified documentation of the characteristic 'Diameter 10 mm ± 0.01' for every delivery. The customer Cheap-o-Matic Inc. simply expects a standard certification for the materials used, a so-called 'manufacturer's test certificate' (as per DIN 50 049) with characteristics. This certificate without characteristics is also to be issued for all deliveries to the customer Megatech Corp.

The goods issue inspection employs a standard inspection plan with operation 0010, Inspections as per specification, and the master inspection characteristics 020, Qualitative additional inspection as per customer specification, as well as customer Megatech Corp's requested additional, quantitative characteristic 010, Inspect diameter 10mm ± 0.01.

The shipment release is prepared with the help of the usage decision from the inspection lot, but only after successful completion of the inspection. In shipping, a certificate is then prepared using the characteristics from the goods issue inspection (Megatech Corp.). The general manufacturer's test certificate must be issued for every material.

Quality planning for Sales and Distribution in the material master data

The following inspection types can be used for the goods issue inspections:

- 13 Inspection on delivery to customer with order.
- 14 Inspection on delivery to customer without order.
- 15 Inspection on delivery to customer, general.

We select the inspection type 13, Inspection for delivery to customer with order, since the sales order accompanies us as the leading object through the entire Sales and Distribution process.

Processing customer information records/customer specifications

The customer information records are, as you have certainly noticed, the counterpart to the quality information records in Purchasing. There is, however, an important difference: the customer information record controls individual materials for a customer, whereas the customer specifications are valid for all materials from a customer. The example here uses a customer information record because we believe this enables an even better differentiation of material assignment (Fig. 6.51).

In the main menu, we select LOGISTICS | QUALITY MANAGEMENT | QUALITY PLANNING | SALES AND DISTRIBUTION. The screen for Quality Management in Sales and Distribution is displayed. We continue with QM CONTROL IN SD | CREATE. We

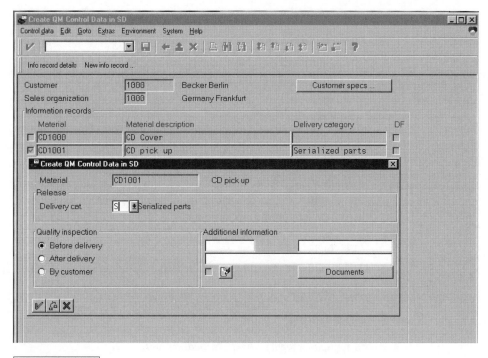

FIGURE 6.51   Q information record, Sales and Distribution (© SAP AG)

then fill in the customer and sales organization and select GOTO | CONTROL DATA. The screen for entering QM control data in SD is displayed. Via EDIT | NEW INFO RECORD, we arrive at the dialog window for entering QM control data in SD. In the dialog window that now appears, we make the following input:

- Material.
- Delivery category.
- Short text of additional information (optional).
- Set the quality inspection indicator.
- Save the customer info record.

TIP

If you are using the SAP-internal document management or another form of document management connected to the system, further workgroup objects are at your disposal. If you select DOCUMENTS, you have the further option of linking the quality information record to a quality document (e.g. quality assurance agreements, special specifications). In the dialog window for linking the QM information record with documents, use the input assistance to select the desired document.

Planning objects

▨ *Material purchasing*

The assignment of a customer is not necessary if all customers are inspected with the same plan. The Material-plan allocation is not extended!

▨ *Inspection characteristic overview with inspection instruction*

Various quantitative and qualitative characteristics are assigned to the operation 'GR inspection for series delivery'. The inspection characteristics are entered in a reference operation set and referenced in the operation, since this material is being managed in different variants with its own material number and own plan groups. The qualitative characteristics are updated as master inspection characteristics and used in the reference operation set.

▨ *Inspection scope*

The qualitative (QL01) and quantitative characteristics (QL02) each have a separate sampling procedure.

Calculation of the sampling scope with sampling scheme for the qualitative and quantitative inspection.

▨ *Inspection frequency (dynamic modification)*

Each delivery is to be inspected.

▨ *Inspection data processing*

Results recording in the characteristic is active (see control indicator of the inspection characteristic).

▨ *Necessity of inspection*

Is set by activating the inspection type in the material master data.

▨ *Inspection sequence*

Inspecting with plan in the inspection type is active; results recording in the characteristic is active; defects recording in the characteristic is active (generates Q notification with defect data record).

▨ *Inspection method*

Inspection method assigned.

▨ *Test equipment*

Can be assigned to the operation and characteristic as an option.

■ *Inspection lot processing/creation*

Control is via the input of the header data for the inspection plan (dynamic modification level 'Lot level', Inspection lot origin goods issue) and the inspection type 13, Outgoing lot in the material master data. The inspection lot itself is generated by means of the entry of the delivery in shipping and does not need to wait until the movement of goods 'goods issue'.

The delivery operation for sales order with inspection lot creation

This process also depends on the ability of Quality Management and the specialist departments to integrate (Fig. 6.52) and requires, of course, the cooperation of colleagues responsible for Sales and Distribution projects and their R/3 consultants. We would like show you an example from an area of Sales and Distribution (reduced to its core functions for the sake of simplicity) which you can simulate in your test system with your own data. The main emphasis in this section, therefore, will be on the inspection lot creation via the shipment operation. But first we will describe the business situation.

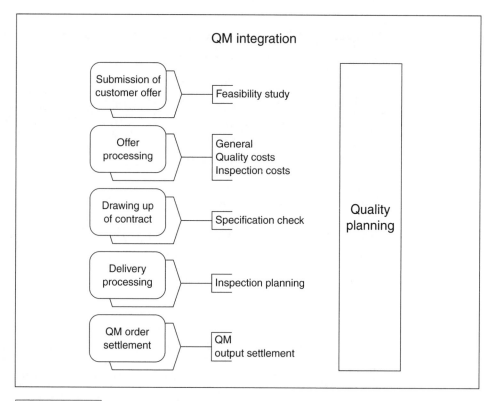

FIGURE 6.52   QM integration in the processes of Sales and Distribution

Our customer has ordered 1000 units of the material 'CD cover'. This gives us a sales order which we enter into the system. In order processing, we can save the order with or without delivery. We select 'without delivery' since we would like to describe the shipment operation afterwards in more detail. The delivery note for this order is prepared with a reference to a sales order. The sales order can then initiate a production order or the removal of material from the warehouse stock.

The delivery can also be prepared directly in Sales and Distribution (SD) without reference to a sales order. With the delivery, QM creates in the background an inspection lot for the delivery items relevant to the inspection. The control of the goods is now transferred together with the functions of the inspection lot and the usage decision to QM until the inspection is completed. The delivery can be released once this has been done, depending on the usage decision for the goods issue posting.

Influence of delivery processing on the inspection lots

If a delivery is prepared and processed in shipping, the SD operations on the delivery note also have an effect on the processing of inspection lots in QM. Key events include the following operations:

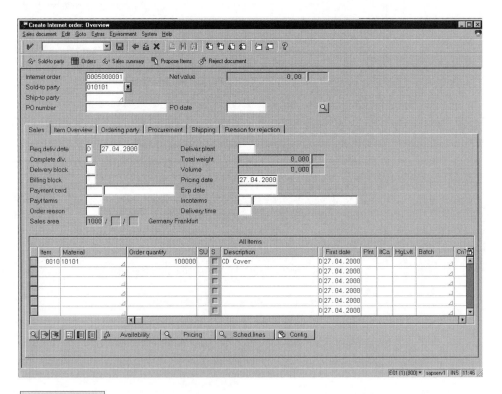

FIGURE 6.53 Create sales order (© SAP AG)

▓ *Preparation of delivery note*

If a delivery note for a material relevant to the inspection is prepared in SD, QM automatically creates an inspection lot for the material as soon as the plant is identified. The system indicates in the status bar that the quality inspection is being prepared.

▓ *Creating delivery for order*

We now provide the order that has just been created with the exact quantity stated in the order. The data is taken over from the predecessor record (purchasing document) and entered in the delivery (see Fig. 6.53).

To enter an individual delivery, we navigate as follows:

▓ In Shipping, we select DELIVERY | CREATE.

▓ An entry screen is followed by CREATE DELIVERY.

▓ We enter the SHIPPING.

▓ The SELECTION DATE is entered, or else the current date is automatically chosen as Selection date.

▓ In cases where only one specific order item is to be supplied, we enter the corresponding *item number range*. Use ENTER to post the operation.

The system compiles the delivery using the basic data of the order, material etc. The delivery quantity is set in the delivery according to availability. At this point, we could enter additional data, e.g. transport of goods or modified order data, in the header and item data. The delivery is saved with DELIVERY | SAVE. In the status bar at the bottom of the screen, we receive a message 'Preparing quality inspection' and the delivery number appears as soon as the document has been saved.

TIP   When you enter an individual delivery, you create exactly one delivery for one order. The delivery, however, contains only those order items which are due. You now have the option of making targeted modifications to the delivery (important for inspection lot creation), if the shipping situation should make this necessary.

Inspection lot processing

We can continue inspection lot processing in exactly the same way as in the areas of Purchasing or Production – with the results recording and the usage decision.

6.7.1 Certificate processing

A preliminary note: why is this section not to be found in quality control? The answer is simple: without targeted quality planning, it would be very difficult for us later to generate a certificate with data from the inspection lot. The most important basis for data transfer from the inspection lot into the certificate profile is work performed with master inspection characteristics or general characteristics. These characteristics must be entered in advance and assigned to the inspection plan. The description of how the characteristics are to be incorporated in the certificate follows immediately under CERTIFICATE PROFILE | ASSIGN MANUFACTURER'S TEST CERTIFICATE.

A complete description of business operations associated with certificate creation would be impossible within the scope of this book and this is, without a doubt, one of the more complex subjects in quality planning and quality control. In this example, therefore, we are looking at the relatively simple case of the assignment of a certificate for deliveries to the company mentioned at the start of this section, Megatech Corp., and printed output of the certificate on delivery.

The actual form with layout, formatting and contents of the certificates is defined in the interplay of certificate profiles and SAPscript forms. Processing one of these forms requires, just as with all forms, in-depth knowledge of SAPscript and is usually a task for your consultant/programmer. You should, however, be aware of the following:

■ The certificate profile (example: Q1001–01 with certificate type 'Manufacturer's test certificate as per DIN 50 049') controls the selection of inspection lots and partial lots and the selection of the characteristics.

■ The form (example: QM_QCERT_01) controls the page layout and the format of the data on the certificate.

■ A general purpose form can be linked with several certificate profiles.

■ Within the certificate profile, you determine the selection and sequence of the characteristics, the results of which are to appear on the certificate. You can vary the origin and the presentation of data for each characteristic.

In our example, we first prepared an uncomplicated certificate profile, geared to this material and with access to the characteristic data. In the next paragraph, the certificate profile will be allocated to the material and then, referenced to an inspection lot, it will be printed.

Creating a certificate profile

Our aim of listing a defined characteristic on the certificate for the material 'printed circuit board' is achieved by navigating from the main menu through LOGISTICS | QUALITY MANAGEMENT | QUALITY CERTIFICATE | CERTIFICATE PROFILE | CREATE. We enter the name of the layout set (QM_QCERT_01) in the field ASSIGNED LAYOUT SET. In the next step, the overview screen for entering the master inspection characteristics is opened by selecting CHARACTERISTICS. Following the selection of a characteristic, it is essential that the fields.

- Result origin
- Short text origin
- Specification origin
- Skip strategy
- Text element

are filled in, otherwise the system signs off during printing with a short dump (error log from the program). We now return to the header data of the certificate profile and save (see Fig. 6.54).

Assigning the Certificate Profile 'Manufacturer's Test Certificate'

In order to assign the certificate profile to

- A material or
- A material and a customer or a
- Customer only

we proceed as follows. We select from the main menu LOGISTICS | QUALITY MAN-AGEMENT | QUALITY CERTIFICATE | CERTIFICATE PROFILE | ASSIGNMENT | CREATE.

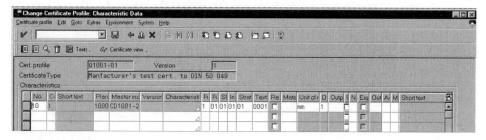

FIGURE 6.54 Defining characteristics for the certificate profile (© SAP AG)

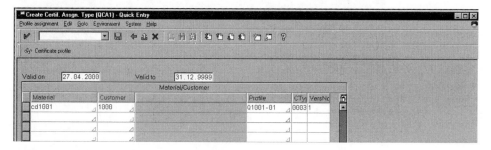

FIGURE 6.55 Assigning a certificate profile (© SAP AG)

The dialog window (Fig. 6.55) with the key combinations is displayed. In the title bar, we see that the Assignment Type QCA1 (condition type) is specified. We select one of the *key combinations* and arrive at the overview for multiple assignments via NEXT. The validity period specified here is decisive for all records that you enter at this point.

To obtain the assignment we want, we enter the name of the object (material). Then we specify the certificate profile, the certificate type and the version.

In the next step, we place the cursor in the column VERSION and receive a list of possible certificate profiles and then call up the 'possible entries'. If we now select a profile, the system copies the complete profile code into the recording overview.

The assignment is recorded via SAVE.

Printing certificate for the inspection lot

The quickest way to obtain a print preview of the certificate form is to select *test print* from the menu QUALITY MANAGEMENT | QUALITY CERTIFICATE | CERTIFICATE CREATION | FOR INSPECTION LOT. The prerequisite that the relevant characteristics are

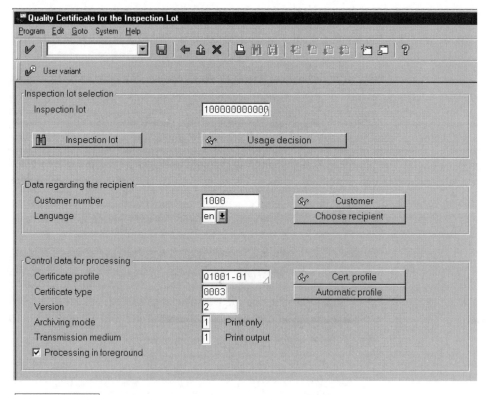

FIGURE 6.56   Create certificate for inspection lot (© SAP AG)

completed and valuated still applies. We select the creation variant FOR INSPECTION LOT, since this version does not require the entire delivery process to be completed, and the certificate can be printed out directly after conclusion of the inspection and consigned to the goods.

Before the print job can be carried out, the system demands input on the referenced inspection lot. The printout of the form which has just been created is then filled in completely with the order and customer data; the remainder is based on the assignment of the certificate profile from the last section (Fig. 6.56).

As a result, we receive the certificate printout (Fig. 6.57) with the data from the inspection lot, the order and the delivery. If the subject of certificate processing with your customer on the internet interests you, please refer to Chapter 12, 'Internet scenarios with SAP R/3 QM'.

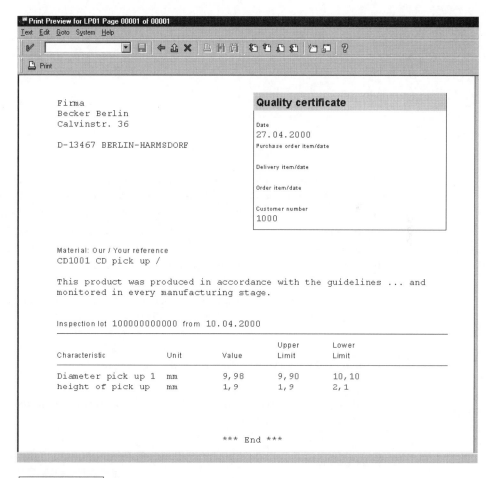

FIGURE 6.57   Certificate printout (© SAP AG)

CHAPTER 7

Quality inspection

Quality inspection is playing an increasingly important role in quality management. Once quality planning has created the preconditions, quality inspection can take place. Inspection lots are generated depending on the material movements, production orders, deliveries, or they are created manually. These inspection lots are then subjected to a quality inspection based on predefined characteristics. On inspection lot completion, important information is passed on to the quality information system and is available for quality control (Fig. 7.1).

The quality inspection comprises inspection lot creation, results recording, inspection lot completion, and appraisal cost processing.

7.1   BASIC PRINCIPLES

First of all, a few terms and a little background information is required so that you fully understand the next sections.

Inspection lot

Inspection lots are the requests to inspect a certain quantity of a material. Inspection lots are set up automatically or manually.

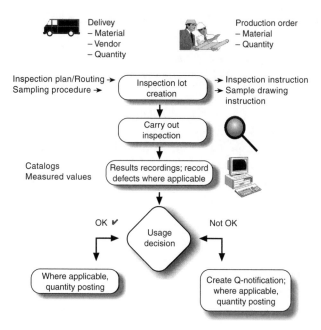

FIGURE 7.1 Sequence of quality inspection

In Materials Management, inspection lots can be generated by goods movements. Goods movements of this kind are:

▩ Goods receipt.

▩ Goods issue.

▩ Stock movements.

In Production, inspection lots can be generated by the release of

▩ Production orders.

▩ Process orders.

▩ Series orders.

▩ Goods issues production.

or by recurring batch inspections.

In Sales and Distribution, inspection lots can be created by the creation of the delivery for the customer or returns from the customer.

CUSTOMIZING TIP

In Customizing, you specify the events that cause an inspection lot to be created.

The size of the inspection lots is the total quantity of a material to be inspected. This must not be confused with the sample size, which specifies how many units of the inspection lot are to be inspected. Inspection lots are only created if an inspection type has been entered and enabled in the Q view of the material (material master data). The inspection lot contains, among other things, the following important data:

- Inspection specifications.
- Inspection results.
- Appraisal costs.
- Usage decision.

Types of stock

The stocks can be allocated to three types of stock:

- Released stock (material available for unrestricted use, which has either already been released or is not subject to a quality inspection – code: blank or F).
- Quality stock (material that is involved in the quality inspection – code: X or 2).
- Blocked stock (material that is currently blocked – code: S or 3).

An inspection lot can be either relevant to stock or not. This depends on the inspection lot creation and the inspection lot origin. Manually created inspection lots and the following inspection lot origins are, for example, not relevant to stock:

- 02 Goods issue.
- 03 In-process inspection.
- 06 Customer returns.
- 07 Audit.
- 10 Delivery for sales order.
- 11 Delivery without sales order.
- 12 Delivery, general.
- 13 Production order for series order.
- 14 Maintenance.

If a goods movement is a movement type that is relevant to stock, for example inspection lot origin 01 (Goods receipt for purchase order), the inspection lot quantity goes into the quality stock (Q stock). From the INSPECTION LOT STOCK in the usage decision, you can move the material from the quality stock into the released or blocked stock, or send it back to the vendor.

Ship to stock

If the quality capability of your vendor permits, you may wish to forego the goods receipt inspection completely or in part. Missing out individual inspections is referred to as 'skipping'. You can control this using the dynamic modification rules. If the vendor is located on the 'Skip' as regards a material, no goods receipt inspection is required. The inspection lot is automatically released after a set period and the quantity is shipped from quality stock into released stock.

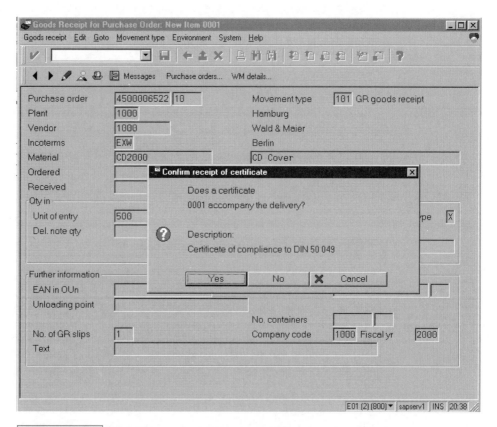

| **FIGURE 7.2** | Certificate query at goods receipt (© SAP AG) |

Delivery certificate

The QM module supports the administration of the receipt of certificates that must be enclosed with the delivery. Certificates of this kind can be, for example, plant inspection certificates, material certificates, prototype inspection reports or inspection confirmations. Receipt of the certificate(s) is confirmed on goods receipt. If the certificate is missing, no usage decision can be made initially (see Fig. 7.2).

The usage decision is the latest stage at which receipt of the certificate must be confirmed so that the material can be shipped to released stock.

System status

If you look carefully at the display of an inspection lot, you will probably notice the 'System status' field which, with various groups of four letters, shows the status of the inspection lot. It is worth paying a certain amount of attention to this status, as it provides some important details. It is particularly useful for troubleshooting if the system does not react in the way you expected. In many cases, observing the status can quickly provide the reason for this. Table 7.1 shows the long text for the status messages.

The long texts of the status can be displayed if you follow the EXTRAS | INSPECTION LOT STATUS menu path or click on the 'i' icon.

So that an inspection lot receives the status REL, i.e. is released for inspection, the following steps must be taken (usually, but there are always exceptions!):

▨ The inspection lot has been created (inspection lot number has been assigned).

▨ An inspection plan or a material specification has been allocated.

▨ The sample has been determined.

TABLE 7.1 **System status of inspection lots**

Short form	Meaning	Short form	Meaning
SPCO	Stock posting completed	ICCO	Inspection close completed
SPRQ	Quantity posting required	ICST	Short-term insp. completed
SPST	Stock posting started (partially posted)	INSP	Inspection active
PRII	Inspection instruction printed	QLUP	Quality level updated
PRSI	Sample drawing instruction printed	QLCH	Quality level relevant
RREC	Results confirmed	STUP	Statistics updated
CRTD	Created	CALC	Sample calculated
DEF	Defects were recorded	UD	Usage decision has been made
REL	Released	PASG	Plan/Specification assigned
CCTD	Insp. characteristics created	CROK	Certificate receipt confirmed
CRTD	Characteristics to be created	CTCM	Certificate conf. missing

The steps that have been performed can be seen from the inspection lot status. If it has not been possible to go through all the steps, the inspection lot does not appear in the worklist for results recording. What you should do in this case can be found below in the section entitled 'No inspection lot in the worklist'.

User status

The user status allows you to obtain a display of status information. Here you can obtain a display of, for example, whether a delivered material has the status 'Prototype', 'Series' or 'Revised model'. This status can also be influenced manually by the user.

Status profile

In addition to the user status, a status profile can be entered in the Q information record. An appropriately created status profile allows the user, depending on the status of a vendor relationship (prototype, series etc.), to control the inspection type, and thus also the use of a certain inspection plan.

7.2   INSPECTION LOT CREATION

A requirement for the opening (creation) of an inspection lot is that the basic data of the material has been updated. For this purpose, the Quality view for the material master data must have been created, and at least one inspection type must have been entered and enabled in the inspection data. Depending on the characteristics of the inspection type, there must be a valid inspection plan or a material specification. Whether and with what scope a sample is to be drawn depends on the specifications in the Quality view of the material, the quality level, and the specifications in the inspection plan or routing.

Inspection lots can be set up automatically or manually.

Manual inspection lot creation

Although we assume that inspection lots will usually be created automatically, it can certainly be required that an inspection lot be created manually. The reasons for creating an inspection lot can be:

▓ Retrospective inspection of a released material on suspicion.

▓ Inspection of a material whose receipt inspection was skipped.

▓ Inspection of a material due to a complaint from Production or from the customer.

The practical procedure involved in manual inspection lot creation, which we want to look at using a simple example from Materials Management, begins with the selection of the corresponding menu.

Starting at the R/3 main menu, we select:

LOGISTICS | QUALITY MANAGEMENT | QUALITY INSPECTION

and

INSPECTION LOT PROCESSING | INSPECTION LOT | CREATE

In the entry screen, we enter our MATERIAL (here: QM01–02), the PLANT (here: 1000) and the INSPECTION LOT ORIGIN (here: 01 = Goods receipt for purchase order). Pressing ENTER takes us to the CREATE INSPECTION LOT MANUALLY screen (see Fig. 7.3).

The system has already assigned the internal inspection lot number. All that needs to be done now is to fill in the mandatory fields INSPECTION LOT QUANTITY and VENDOR with the appropriate information. Note that the inspection lot quantity represents the total quantity of the goods, and that the size of the sample is determined from this in accordance with the sample rule or inspection percentage you have specified in the inspection plan.

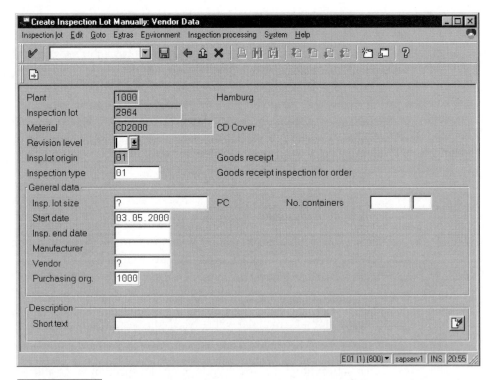

FIGURE 7.3   Creating an inspection lot for goods receipt manually (© SAP AG)

After you have filled out the mandatory fields and confirmed them with ENTER, the inspection lot is created and the sample determined, insofar as a valid inspection plan exists. Otherwise, the error message 'No plan could be assigned' appears. As soon as you SAVE the inspection lot, it is available for further processing.

It should be noted that the manual inspection lot for goods receipt does not change the stock type. If the material is already in the released stock, it remains in this stock type for as long as it is not posted elsewhere deliberately. As regards this point, the manual inspection lot is very different to the automatically created inspection lot for goods receipt.

You can also create a manual inspection lot for a production order. However, this is only possible if none has been created for the same production order, as a maximum of one inspection lot can be created per order (unless inspection points or batch inspections are planned). In the entry screen, you do not enter a material number in this case. Only the PLANT and the INSPECTION LOT ORIGIN (e.g. 03 = Production) are entered. After ENTER is pressed, a screen with a slightly different structure than for the inspection lot for goods receipt appears (see Fig. 7.4).

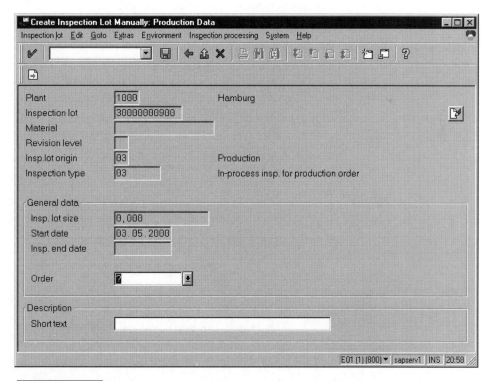

FIGURE 7.4   Creating an inspection lot for production manually (© SAP AG)

At ORDER, now enter the production order number. The system automatically obtains the other information such as material number and inspection lot size from the production order. If there is an inspection plan, the sample calculation can take place and an inspection lot is opened.

Automatic inspection lot creation

It is likely to be a great advantage to most companies to set the Quality Management module in such a way that a goods receipt for purchase order automatically creates an inspection lot. This can be seen at the goods receipt posting, as there the message 'Preparing quality inspection' is displayed briefly in the status bar. When the goods receipt posting is saved, the inspection lot is created and the inspection documents are printed.

If the inspection type is set appropriately, creating the inspection lots also posts the goods to the quality stock. As regards this point, the automatic inspection lot differs from the manual inspection lot, where the stock type of the goods does not change.

Inspection lots can also be created automatically in Production. For example, the system can be set in such a way that the inspection lot is created from Production on release of the production order or on goods issue.

In Sales and Distribution, the typical case would be that a goods issue would create an inspection lot.

If inspection lots are created for serialized materials, the serial numbers can be adopted in the inspection lot.

```
            S a m p l e   d r a w i n g   i n s t r u c t i o n
 05.05.2000                                             Page: 001
 --------------------------------------------------------------------
 Plant...: 0001                          Ins. lot.: 000000004224
 Lot text:                               Insp. plan: 6235
 Material: 53122                         Doc. no.: 4500003768
 --------------------------------------------------------------------


                         Samples to be drawn:


 Sample no.  Qty. in........  Sampling unit  Qty. in........  Base unit
 000000                8,000 PC                       0,000
                  Sample distribution to the laboratories:


 Sample no.IO    Inspection station Plant
```

FIGURE 7.5　　Example of a sample drawing instruction

Inspection Instruction

05.05.2000 15:59:50   Page 1

Material   53122   UCL-LABEL   13,7X46
Insp.lot   4224   Insp.period: 05.05.2000 - 05.05.2000

Inspection operation   0010   Inspection PA

Work center   5629980 / Plant 0001

Characteristic 0010 *General aspect*
Characteristic weighting: Major characteristic A
The characteristic must be inspected. Record summarized results.
Rejection no.:   1
Valuation rule: 10 Attributive inspection nonconf. units

Assigned test equipment: 0010 Visual check
To inspect: 8 *   1,00 PC
Selected set WE-MM-01 Characteristic attributes income insp.

Possible attribute codes:

WE-QS-01 WE01 OK   A
WE-QS-01 WE02 Certificate missing / incorrect   R 04
WE-QS-01 WE03 Part/assembly not according to SPEC   R 02
WE-QS-01 WE04 Failure in mech. assembly   R 02
WE-QS-01 WE05 Failure in electr. assembly   R 02
WE-QS-01 WE06 Measure failure   R 02
WE-QS-01 WE07 Surface failure   R 02
WE-QS-01 WE08 Material failure   R 02
WE-QS-01 WE09 Transportation damage   R 02
WE-QS-01 WE10 Wrong type   R 02
WE-QS-01 WE20 Other failure   R 02

Characteristic 0020 *Length 32,2 +-0,1*
Characteristic weighting: Major characteristic A
The characteristic must be inspected. Record summarized results.
Rejection no.:   1
Valuation rule: 10 Attributive inspection nonconf. units

Assigned test equipment: 0020 Digital caliper 0-200
To inspect: 8 * 1,00 PC
Selected set WE-MM-01 Characteristic attributes income insp.

Possible attribute codes:

WE-QS-01 WE01 OK   A
WE-QS-01 WE02 Certificate missing / incorrect   R 04
WE-QS-01 WE03 Part/assembly not according to SPEC   R 02
WE-QS-01 WE04 Failure in mech. assembly   R 02
WE-QS-01 WE05 Failure in electr. assembly   R 02
WE-QS-01 WE06 Measure failure   R 02

SAP AG, Walldorf

FIGURE 7.6   Example of an inspection instruction

Inspection documents

As soon as an inspection lot has been created, the associated work papers are printed (whether this is to take place automatically can be set in Customizing). These papers are:

■ *Sample drawing instruction*

This specifies whether a sample is to be drawn from the total quantity and, if so, its size (see Fig. 7.5). The printout also contains supplementary information, for example, the material document number, the material number, the inspection lot number, etc. (it is advisable to have the report customized to your own requirements).

■ *Inspection instruction*

In the case of an inspection with an inspection plan, this contains the inspection operations, inspection characteristics and test equipment, as well as supplementary information. If the work paper is structured in such a way, the inspector can note results on the inspection instruction (see Fig. 7.6).

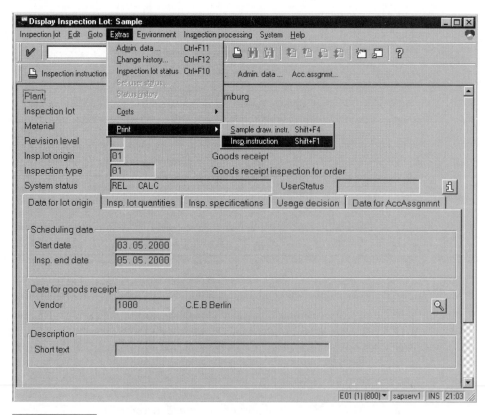

FIGURE 7.7   Display inspection lot (© SAP AG)

If your system is set so that the inspection instruction is not printed automatically, or you want to print one of the inspection documents again, start at the QUALITY INSPECTION view and select the following path:

INSPECTION LOT PROCESSING | INSPECTION LOT | DISPLAY

When you have specified the desired inspection lot number (if necessary, using FIND INSPECTION LOT), the inspection lot appears as shown in Fig. 7.7.

Now you can use the EXTRAS | PRINT menu path to choose whether you want to print the SAMPLE DRAWING INSTRUCTION or the INSPECTION INSTRUCTION.

On the basis of the sample drawing instruction, the sample can be drawn in goods receipt and sent to the QA department. The inspection is performed there on the basis of the inspection instruction.

7.3 RESULTS RECORDING

Results recording is used to document your inspection. If you want characteristic-based results recording, it must be possible to assign an inspection plan or a material specification to the inspection lot. Here, it should be assumed that you inspect according to the inspection plan, and that there is thus at least one inspection operation with one or more inspection characteristics.

The worklist

As is the case in many applications of the R/3 system, there is also a worklist for inspection lot processing. Before you can begin with results recording, the corresponding inspection lot must be located in the worklist.

You reach the worklist for results recording starting from the QUALITY INSPECTION screen, via WORKLIST | RESULTS RECORDING. As of Release 4.5, there are three options:

- General.
- For physical samples.
- Process-optimized (For all inspection lots, For inspection points, For master inspection characteristic).

We will restrict ourselves to the GENERAL submenu, and only enter the READ-IN MODE 1 (for 'All characteristics') there, in order to obtain a list of all inspection lots in the worklist. You can of course use this structure list to enter your own individual selection criteria. You can limit the selection using, for example, the date, material number, vendor number or work centre.

The other submenus enable an optimized display of the worklist for special applications, for example, the administration of physical samples in the processing industry.

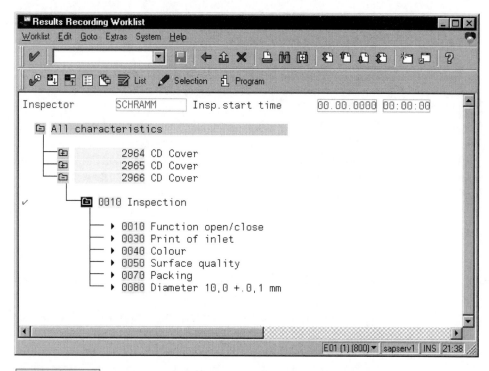

FIGURE 7.8   Worklist for results recording (© SAP AG)

Figure 7.8 contains an example of what a worklist of this kind can look like. Three inspection lots are shown, whereby the hierarchy tree has been opened for inspection lot number 2966 so that the operation (inspection) and the inspection characteristics (0010–0080) are also displayed below the inspection lot description.

No inspection lot in the worklist

Occasionally, although an inspection lot is created (status CRTD), it does not receive the status REL. The consequence of this is that it cannot be seen in the worklist, but only via the menu INSPECTION LOT PROCESSING | INSPECTION LOT | DISPLAY. If the inspection lot is not released, in most cases it has not been possible to assign a plan. This in turn can be for a number of reasons:

▨ The indicator for the automatic specification assignment is not set in the material master record.

▨ There is no valid inspection plan/material specification.

▨ The inspection plan/material specification is not released.

▨ The inspection plan is not valid yet or is no longer valid on the key date.

▨ The change of the material and of the inspection plan differ.

▓ The plan usage and the inspection type in the material master data do not match.

▓ The inspection plan has been assigned via the material plan allocation to a vendor other than the vendor who actually delivered.

▓ There are several inspection plans and thus no clear allocation is possible; etc.

In view of this list, which is not even complete, you can imagine that it might become a little tricky to find out the cause of a missing plan allocation. In this connection, consult Chapter 6, 'Quality and inspection planning'. Bear in mind that the read-in mode makes a selection when the worklist for results recording is displayed. The read-in modes intended for the standard version only allow the display of inspection lots with characteristics. Inspection lots without characteristics cannot be displayed with this transaction.

If the inspection plans have been set up correctly, the allocation should also work for inspection lot creation. However, if you find that the inspection lot is unable to find a plan, you can correct this problem retrospectively using INSPECTION LOT PROCESSING | INSPECTION LOT | CHANGE. To do so, use the above list as a check list and examine the error possibilities. When you have found the error and corrected the inspection plan, open the INSPECTION LOT | CHANGE menu and use EDIT | SELECT PLAN/SPECIFICATION to assign the altered or correct (if more than one) inspection plan. You will see immediately whether you have been successful when you press ENTER; the status changes from CRTD (created) into REL.

After the SAVE command, the inspection lot appears in the worklist and the inspection documents are printed.

TIP So that you do not have to make this inspection lot change too frequently, there is a way of detecting this danger at an earlier stage. As soon as a purchase order has been created, you can check whether the system can find a valid inspection plan for the ordered material.

To perform this inspection, open the INSPECTION PLANNING MENU and the EVALUATIONS | MISSING INSPECTION PLANS | IN PURCHASING submenus. In the selection screen, you can enter a range for the material numbers you are interested in. After starting the selection using RUN, you receive a list of purchase orders for which there is either no inspection plan or an unusable inspection plan (see Fig. 7.9). If 'No entries found' appears in the status bar, you do not currently have a problem, and all the inspection lots created for the purchase orders also appear in the worklist.

A convenient feature of this list is that you can jump directly to the Material view to check the entries there. Unfortunately, however, there is no function that enables you to view the associated inspection plan.

The EVALUATIONS | MISSING INSPECTION PLANS | GENERAL submenu works in a similar way, except that all the selected material numbers are checked there, independent of whether a purchase order has been created for them.

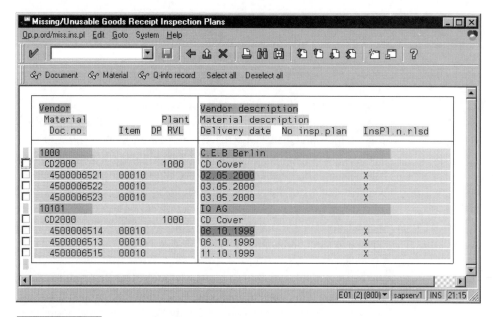

FIGURE 7.9 Missing inspection plans (© SAP AG)

It is recommended that you run this check regularly (for example, weekly) or, even better, that you plan a job that runs automatically every Sunday and relays the result list to you via SAPoffice.

7.3.1 Characteristic results

Assuming that you plan inspections, which is the case for every company with a quality management system, there will be inspection plans with at least one inspection operation and one inspection characteristic. As soon as an inspection lot has been created, it appears in the worklist. The simplest way of entering the recording of the characteristic results is to double-click on the operation (here: 'Inspection'). To do so, the hierarchy tree of the inspection lot must have been opened out, as you can see for inspection lot number 2966 in Figure 7.10.

If you are in the RECORD RESULTS: CHARACTERISTIC OVERVIEW screen (see Fig. 7.10), all the characteristics that you need to check are displayed.

You learned in Chapter 6, 'Quality and inspection planning', that you can plan characteristics for the inspection on an attributive and variable basis. Accordingly, the confirmation of the inspection results differs. In our example (Fig. 7.10), the results are to be recorded for three attributive characteristics.

After the CHARACTERISTIC OVERVIEW screen has been opened, we see the four tabs:

■ Summarized.

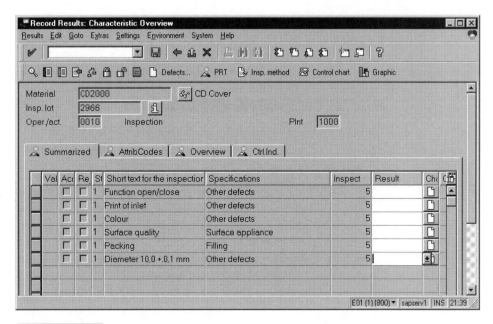

FIGURE 7.10   Screen for recording characteristic results (© SAP AG)

■ Attribute Codes (AttribCodes).

■ Overview.

■ Control Indicator (Ctrl.Ind.).

Instead of the summarized recording, the inspection planning can also have specified recording of classed values (i.e. the number of events within value classes) or single values (possibly with input of the inspection unit number). The name of the tab changes accordingly. There is a separate screen for the recording of single values. Here, you can enter the values for the characteristic for each single item or serial number.

If the inspection planning includes independent multiple samples, you can record results for several samples per inspection characteristic. It is even possible to input a greater number than the quantity specified in the sampling procedure.

Another planning variation for the attributive inspection are dual and multiple samples. In the case of inspections complying with AQL (ISO 2859), the result of a sample can lie between the accept and reject number. The consequence is that the sample is increased. After results recording for the new sample, there is a new valuation.

The inspection characteristic changes its status in the individual processing steps. Possible statuses (see Fig. 7.11) are:

■ Must/can be processed.

■ Skip.

- Processed.
- Valuated.
- Completed.

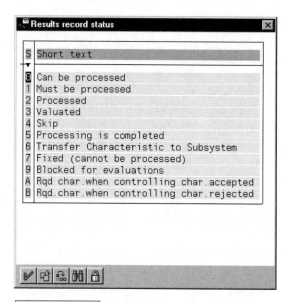

FIGURE 7.11 Characteristic status (© SAP AG)

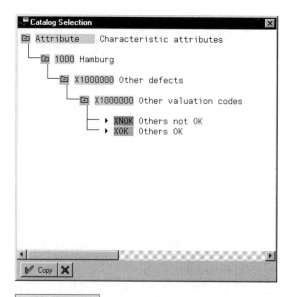

FIGURE 7.12 Simple catalog for the characteristic attribute (© SAP AG)

When the RECORD RESULTS screen is opened, the SUMMARIZED tab is in the foreground and the RESULT column is white, i.e. ready for input. You can begin to record the characteristic results.

Attributive characteristic results

In our example, the confirmation of attributive (qualitative) characteristic results is set. For the recording of qualitative results, you can only record the valuation Accept/Reject or the differentiated valuation on the basis of the catalog for characteristic attributes. An example of a simple characteristic catalog can be seen in Fig. 7.12.

In the case of defects, however, the statement 'Others not OK' is not very informative. This is why it is recommended to have a catalog that provides slightly more information. An example of this is shown in Figure 7.13. You can store an inspection comment for each characteristic as supplementary information.

During input in the CHARACTERISTIC OVERVIEW screen, the specification of the number of units to be inspected is adopted as the number of units inspected. Especially

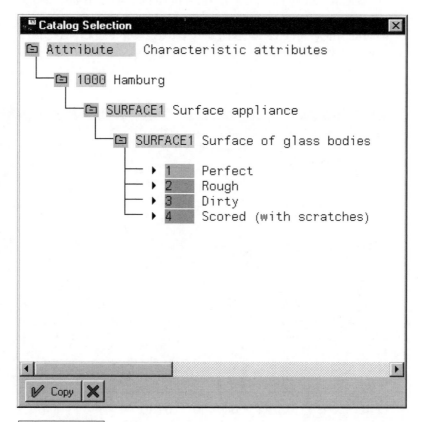

FIGURE 7.13   Catalog for characteristic attributes with specified defect types (© SAP AG)

in the case of defective characteristics, however, it is interesting how many units in the sample have the defect. In order to record this information, you need to select the characteristic by marking it and clicking EDIT | SELECT, or even simpler, by clicking the magnifier icon on the button bar. This selection takes you to the CHARACTERISTIC SINGLE SCREEN, where you can enter the precise number of units for INSPECTED and NONCONFORMING. An example of our CD cover characteristic 'Thickness' is shown in Figure 7.14. For this example, only 18 units were inspected instead of the required 20. On completion, this leads to the message 'You have not entered enough values for this attributive inspection'. However, this warning can be skipped using FORCE. The message is triggered by the control indicator for the inspection characteristic FIXED INSPECTION SCOPE.

At the end of results recording, the processing of characteristics must be completed. You can do this for each individual characteristic or for all characteristics at once. First of all, mark all the characteristics and then open the EDIT | COMPLETE menu.

If not all characteristics have been confirmed or if the number of units inspected deviates from the specification (as in Fig. 7.14), a message appears. You can skip this message and force completion. If no defect code has been specified for a characteristic and you force completion, the system demands a decision from you as to whether the characteristic is to be saved as accepted or rejected. This entry is important so that the system can make concrete proposals for the usage decision, as we will see later.

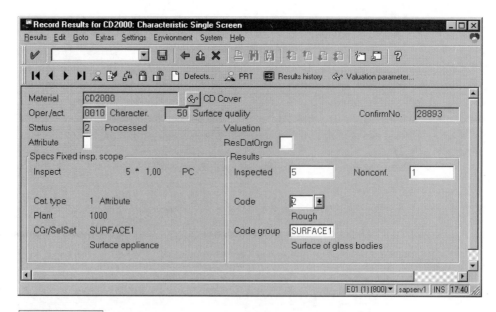

FIGURE 7.14   Characteristic single screen (© SAP AG)

Quantitative characteristic results

In contrast to the attributive (qualitative) characteristic results, you can also report back concrete measured values for quantitative (variable) characteristics. In doing so, it is of course possible to set both qualitative and quantitative characteristics under one inspection operation.

If there are quantitative characteristics, the CHARACTERISTIC OVERVIEW differs from that shown in Figure 7.10, as two additional tabs can be seen:

- Inspection unit.

- Measured values.

The reason for this is that when the characteristic was created in the inspection plan, the control indicator SINGLE RESULT was selected as 'Results confirmation'. This means you can number the inspection units (or use an existing serial number) and enter a

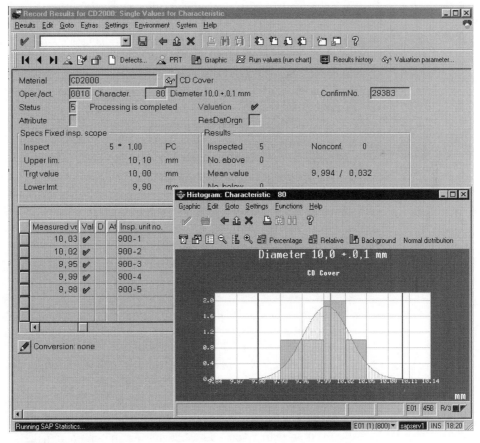

FIGURE 7.15   Record screen Single Values for Characteristic (© SAP AG)

measured value for each inspection unit. The most suitable screen for measured value input is SINGLE VALUES FOR CHARACTERISTIC. To do this, mark the characteristic and click on SELECT.

In addition to the single results for each inspection unit, you can also plan a summarized recording or a classed recording. Summarized recording only makes sense for variable measured values if you need a fundamental value, as the mean value is formed from the values entered. This type of recording could be of interest if, for example, you are measuring the diameter of a shaft at various points but only want to document the mean value. Classed recording is usually suitable if evaluation with the histogram is set, as the planned measured value classes are also used to form the histogram.

In our example with the CD cover, in which the characteristic '0010 Length' is set up as quantitative characteristic, Figure 7.15 shows the input value for a sample of five units.

On completion of the variable characteristic, some valuations are made, as can be seen in Figure 7.15. First of all, the result is valuated as regards Accept/Reject. As all the measured values were within the required tolerances, the valuation was completed with 'Accept' (shown with a green check mark). Furthermore, the fields have been set accordingly with INSPECTED and NONCONFORMING, and the mean value (X BAR) and the standard deviation (S) have been calculated. The HISTOGRAM function has also been started and the normal distribution for the measured values displayed. The process capability indices cp and cpk can also be calculated and displayed.

Another form of display for quantitatively recorded single values is the RUN CHART, which shows the course of the measured values of a characteristic as a curve. In this diagram, you can recognize trends and the situation relative to the tolerance limits, but you are not shown any intervention limits.

In many cases, these valuation and display options will be sufficient, and an external statistics program would be superfluous. Where the requirements of statistical evaluation are higher, the R/3 statistics interface (QM-STI) provides the possibility to process the data with external statistics software.

TIP   If it occurs relatively rarely that you have to record measured values as quantitative inspection results, input using the keyboard is acceptable. However, if this occurs frequently, it is advisable to use a keyboard router, across which the digital measuring equipment can be connected directly and thus measured values imported directly into the input screen. More information on this subject is available in this chapter in the section entitled 'Interfaces to external systems and measuring devices'.

In precisely the same way as with the attributive characteristics, you can force completion of the quantitative characteristics without having entered measured values. The system then warns you and asks whether the characteristic is to be accepted or rejected.

Required and optional characteristics

In inspection planning, the control indicators of the inspection characteristics can be used to specify whether results recording must take place (required characteristic) or can take place (optional characteristic). This can be seen in the RESULTS RECORDING screen from the status of the characteristic (0 = optional characteristic). The processing does not have to be completed, either. Completion is only absolutely essential in the case of required characteristics.

In an extended hierarchy tree, you can also recognize the status of the characteristics by their colour. Required characteristics are shown in yellow and optional characteristics in light blue.

Unplanned characteristics

Sometimes it is desirable to record results for a characteristic that was not set in the inspection plan. This is made possible by inserting a new characteristic in the results recording. There is, however, a catch: only master characteristics can be inserted.

TIP We simply create a master inspection characteristic 'Other characteristic' and can insert this as required as an ADDITIONAL CHARACTERISTIC.

Provided you have already created this master characteristic (otherwise you can do it immediately beforehand), open the EDIT menu and the RECORD RESULTS: CHARACTERISTIC OVERVIEW screen and the item CREATE ADDITIONAL CHARACTERISTIC. You enter the coding for the master inspection characteristic. The system asks for the sampling procedure for this new characteristic, and you can then use it for results recording.

Results recording with control charts

In the Quality Management module, you can use, for example, the following types of control chart (see Fig. 7.16):

- The mean value chart taking account of tolerance (acceptance chart).
- Shewhart chart for the mean value.
- Shewhart chart for the standard deviation.

The type of control chart used is already specified in inspection planning of the characteristics and the sampling procedure used. You can specify whether a separate control chart is to be used for each inspection lot, or whether you want to use one control chart for several inspection lots.

When the inspection lots are created, the control chart numbers are also created automatically for the characteristics for which a control chart is planned. In results

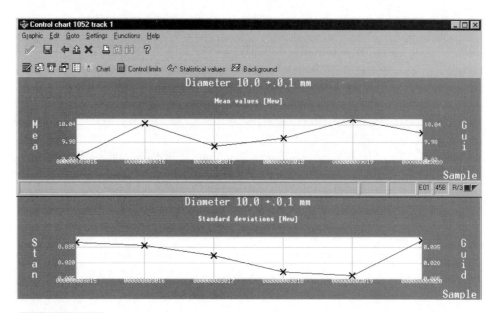

FIGURE 7.16   Example of an acceptance chart for mean value and standard deviation (© SAP AG)

recording, you can then enter measured values for these control charts, whereby a separate graphics window is opened for each track of the chart. There you see both the results already recorded from the previous inspection lots as well as the newly entered ones.

If set in the appropriate way, the system computes the intervention and warning limits from the lead-in or from the measurement results, or you specify these.

The valuation of the results recording can take place automatically, whereby exceeding or falling below the intervention limits will lead to rejection of the characteristic. However, you can also perform the valuation manually.

If you want to complete a control chart, this occurs in a very similar way to that for completing an inspection characteristic. At the next inspection lot, a new control chart is opened with a new number. This means that you should not complete the control chart if it is still to be used for the next set of inspection lots.

Inspection without a plan

So far, we have assumed that inspections are performed on the basis of an inspection plan. This is not absolutely essential. In the inspection data, you can also quite simply omit the check mark at INSPECTION WITH PLAN for the material concerned (in the material master data), and an inspection without plan is possible. As the sampling procedure for each characteristic is in the plan in the case of 'Inspection with plan', it must be entered in the inspection data for inspection without plan.

With these settings, for example, an inspection lot is created for a goods receipt. Unfortunately, this inspection lot does not appear in our worklist for results recording, as only inspection lots with characteristics are displayed there. However, as we have no plan, there are of course no characteristics for which a result is to be recorded.

We therefore have to switch directly into the usage decision for an inspection lot of this type, without confirming inspection results. This is also why only the two tabs DEFECTS and INSPECTION LOT STOCK appear in the recording screen for the usage decision. Of course defects can be recorded for the usage decision (inspection lot), as described in section 7.3.2, but only defects for the inspection lot and not for the operation or characteristic, as this is only possible in the case of 'Inspection with plan'.

Valuations

When a characteristic is completed, it is valuated and a decision is made on acceptance or rejection. The valuation is clearly indicated by a green check mark (Accept) or a red X (Reject). You can set various types of valuation:

▨ Manual valuation.

▨ Valuation based on the codes from the catalog of characteristic attributes.

▨ Valuation based on the defective units or number of defects.

▨ Valuation based on the tolerance range in the case of variable characteristics.

▨ Valuation based on the violation of intervention limits in the case of quality control charts.

If automatic valuation was planned but could not be performed because, for example, no or too few characteristic results were confirmed, an input window appears with the request to perform a manual valuation.

7.3.2 Defects

The input of the characteristic results as measured values or by means of an attribute code of the characteristic catalog is also referred to as planned characteristic results. In contrast to this, unplanned characteristic results are the creation of a defect data record. Here, this must not be confused with the negative characteristic results reflected in the characteristic catalog. The input of defects is an independent operation that opens up other possibilities and, for example, is very suitable for meeting the standard requirements of ISO 9000ff as regards corrective and preventative measures.

Defects can be set up on various levels of results recording for the inspection lot. We distinguish between:

▨ Defects for characteristic.

▨ Defects for operation.

▨ Defects for inspection lot.

We want to run through the creation of the defect data record using 'Defects for characteristic' as an example, and thus show the possibilities of this instrument.

In the RECORD RESULTS: CHARACTERISTIC OVERVIEW screen, you will see a paper icon at each characteristic in the DEFECTS FOR CHARACTERISTIC column. As soon as you click this icon, the input screen for defects recording opens. This is of course also possible using the menu structure. Open the EDIT menu and you will find the above defect input options at DEFECTS.

Before input of a defect, you are first asked to select a defect code from Catalog 9 'Defect types'. This is not the same catalog as Catalog 1 'Characteristic attributes', which we already know from the recording of the characteristic results. The advantage of this defects recording is obvious: you can specify several DEFECTS, the NO. OF DEFECTS in each case and a text DESCRIPTION for each characteristic. An example of this is shown in Fig. 7.17.

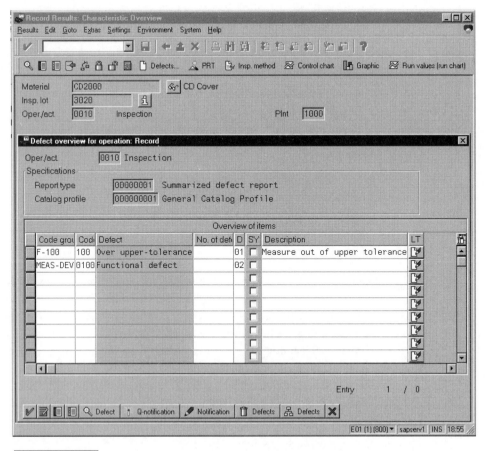

FIGURE 7.17   Defects recording for characteristic (© SAP AG)

TIP Practical experience has shown that setting up the defect catalogs for the 'Characteristic attributes' and the 'Defect types' is effective, as each characteristic which is not OK can also be assigned a defect type.

Finally, a quality notification can be activated manually or automatically from each level of the defect creation. This enables you to inform an internal or external partner quickly of defects that have occurred. If several defects have been recorded, for example, for various characteristics and the operation, a list of these defects appears in the quality notification. The automatic creation of a quality notification is to be used with caution, as this setting rapidly creates a large quantity of open messages in the system, and these must be worked through systematically. This is why manual creation of the quality notification for the defect has proved best in practice. Further details on the topic of quality notifications can be found in the chapter of the same name, Chapter 9.

7.4 INSPECTION LOT COMPLETION

With COMPLETION of the characteristics and SAVE, the results recording is completed and a valuation of all characteristics as regards acceptance or rejection is available. So that the inspection lot can be completed as such, the usage decision and, in the case of inspection lots relevant to stock, posting of the inspection lot stock is required.

The following actions are involved in inspection lot completion; these are performed manually, or automatically by the system:

- Valuation of inspection results.
- Calculation of defect share per lot.
- Determination of quality scores.
- Update of the quality level.
- Making usage decision.
- Posting of stocks.
- Calculation of appraisal costs.
- Update of scores in the QM information system.

As many of the above-mentioned actions of the inspection lot completion are directly related to the tasks of quality control, they are described in detail in Chapter 8, 'Quality control'.

Inspection results

So that a well-founded usage decision can be made regarding an inspection lot, the inspection results must be available. The RECORD USAGE DECISION screen provides all the important information for reaching a decision in the form of tabs (Fig. 7.18):

▦ Characteristic results overview.

▦ Defect overview.

▦ Inspection lot stock overview (insofar as the lot is relevant to stock).

▦ Inspection points overview (insofar as inspection points were planned).

Double-clicking on individual characteristics displays further details of the characteristic results and entered inspection comments.

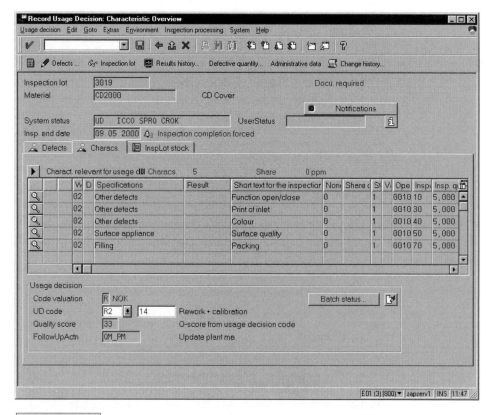

FIGURE 7.18   Screen for usage decision with characteristic results (© SAP AG)

```
                              Inspection report

Inspection lot        000000003025
Material              CD2000          CD Cover
Vendor                10101           IQ AG
Status                No usage decision made/No defects present
Origin                01    Goods receipt
Inspection type       01    Goods receipt inspection for order
Task list             CD Cover Inspection Plan
Inspection period     06.05.2000 - 09.05.2000
Lot size                       100  PC
Sample size                      5  PC

--------------------------------------------------------------------------------

Inspection operation 0010Inspection

--------------------------------------------------------------------------------

        Characteristic  0010      Function open/close
        Status          Processing is completed
        To be inspected 5 * 1,00 PC            Inspected     5    Nonconforming    0
        Attribute       The result is valid
        Code            X OK      Others OK
        Valuation       Accept


        Characteristic  0030      Print of inlet
        Status          Must be processed
        To be inspected 5 * 1,00 PC


        Characteristic  0040      Colour
        Status          Must be processed
        To be inspected 5 * 1,00 PC
```

FIGURE 7.19   Inspection report (© SAP AG)

Inspection report

The inspection report shows you on the screen or in the form of a printout the inspection results and comments for each characteristic. This means it is also suitable for providing an overview of the inspection performed, or can be used as the basis for the usage decision. It can also be used as an appendix to a quality notification to the vendor or to internal departments, to provide detailed descriptions of the deviations of the individual characteristics according to type and scope in the event of defects.

To display the inspection report, open the RESULTS | PRINT menu from the QUALITY INSPECTION view. The PRINT RESULTS selection screen appears.

If you know the inspection lot number, you can enter it directly; otherwise, the selection can be restricted using known parameters such as material number, vendor, date, etc.

Figure 7.19 shows an example of how an inspection report of this kind could appear on the screen. This inspection report can of course be printed.

The tasks of quality management also include the analysis of quality-related costs. In many companies, these costs can make up a significant proportion of expenditures. By recording and evaluating quality-related costs, improvements can be introduced that lead to increases in the efficiency and profitability of the company (see Fig. 7.20).

The quality-related costs are usually split into the following categories:

- Appraisal costs.
- Defect prevention costs.
- Defect costs.

The collection and evaluation of the costs incurred in the company take place in the Controlling (CO) module. There, the quality-related costs that have been recorded in the Quality Management module as inspection and defect costs are merged and can be processed for the quality valuation. Various order types are used to record costs from the applications in Controlling. Cost recording from quality management of the QM order is covered by the order type 06. The QM orders are subdivided into:

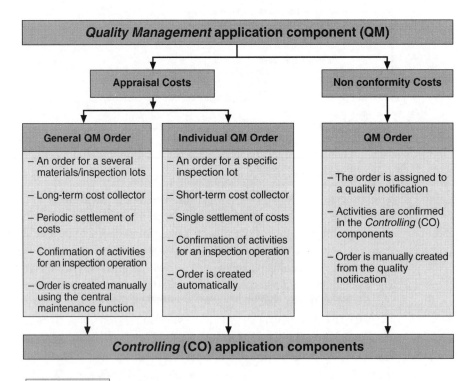

FIGURE 7.20 | Recording of quality-related costs

- General QM order for appraisal costs (an order for a number of materials/inspection lots).

- Individual QM order for appraisal costs (an order for a certain inspection lot).

- QM order for defect costs (an order for a quality notification).

The appraisal costs cannot be specified directly in amounts of money; they are calculated via the confirmation of output times for the inspection operation in the Controlling module from the set rates. As in work planning, the output times are composed of personnel, equipping and machining times. The confirmation of the outputs comes with the results recording or usage decision. In Production, it takes place together with the confirmations for the production order.

The defect costs are recorded with the processing of the quality notification. To do so, the QM order must be created manually in the quality notification as a cost collector. In this, the assigned order in the notification header, you can record the costs incurred, for example reworking, sorting or warranty costs. This means you can determine all the types of defect costs related to the quality notification and assign these to their cause, as well as analyse them further in Controlling.

The defect prevention costs, which mainly include training measures, are recorded via the Human Resources Management (HR) module.

7.6   SAMPLE MANAGEMENT

In the processing industry (e.g. in the chemicals, pharmaceuticals and food industries), the drawing and administration of physical samples is very important. The generation of physical samples can be necessary at goods receipt or during production. The R/3 sample management meets the requirements of good manufacturing practice (GMP) in the processing industry.

Your system supports the following types of sample creation:

- Automatic creation of physical samples on inspection lot creation.

- Manual creation of physical samples (if appropriate, with reference to an inspection lot).

- Manual creation of inspection lots for existing physical samples.

Sample data record

A so-called sample data record is created for each physical sample; this contains the following essential information:

- Sample number.

▨ Physical sample type (from goods receipt, from production, from the customer complaint).

▨ Sample category (drawn sample, mixed sample, reserve sample).

▨ Sample origin (material, batch, order).

▨ Detail data.

Planned physical samples

If the physical samples have been planned in a sample drawing procedure, they are created automatically on inspection lot creation. The sample drawing procedure specifies how many samples are to be drawn, their scope in each case, whether the sample drawing is to be released, and which sample category is to be used. Here, this procedure is logically assigned to the inspection plan or routing. With the generation of the physical sample, the inspection lot creation can also be used to print a sample drawing instruction that contains detailed information on how the sample is to be drawn.

The following sample categories can be selected:

▨ Drawn sample (taken directly from a material/batch stock. You can inspect these samples or form mixed samples from them).

▨ Mixed sample (created by mixing other physical samples of the same material/batch).

▨ Reserve sample (drawn from a material/batch stock and kept back for other inspections).

If materials are delivered in different package types, you can store appropriate instructions depending on the package type.

Unplanned physical samples

In the process of sample management, it can also become necessary to draw physical samples that were not planned. This can take place in two ways:

▨ You can create a completely new physical sample manually.

▨ You can create a physical sample manually for an existing sample data record.

Manual inspection lots

For every existing physical sample, manual inspection lots can also be created. These can be used, for example, to perform additional investigations of reserve samples or samples about which a customer has complained.

As already explained in section 7.2, no stocks can be managed using manual inspection lots.

Release

The sample drawing procedure can be used for automatically created physical samples to specify whether these are to be released automatically or manually. With the release of a drawn sample, all the associated physical samples are also released. To comply with the security requirements of good manufacturing practice (GMP), a manual release can be necessary. In addition, there is the possibility of entering a digital signature, which ensures that certain activities (such as the release) can only be performed by authorized employees.

Manually created physical samples must always be released manually.

Label printing

In the case of automatically created physical samples, you can print labels for the samples. You can design these labels to comply with your own wishes and requirements, printing information such as description, date, time, batch, sample number and inspection lot number, and possibly even adding a bar code. Naturally, label printing for the sample data record can also be started manually.

Results recording and usage decision

Results recording for the physical sample takes place in the same way as inspection lot results recording. The physical samples are located in a special worklist (work centre or user-related) for results recording, and can be worked through at that location. There can be one or more physical samples per inspection lot. It is only when all the physical samples of an inspection lot have been processed and valuated that you are able to make the usage decision for the inspection lot.

Unplanned (manually created) physical samples must first be released manually before you can record results.

| 7.7 | **APPLICATION IN SALES AND DISTRIBUTION** |

Inspection lot creation and results recording in Sales and Distribution differs only slightly from the processes in Materials Management. Instead of the inspection lots for goods receipt, the inspection lots for goods issue are generated for certain goods movements (for example, for a return), or for a customer complaint. Here, too, there is the possibility to create inspection lots manually.

Inspection lot creation can be linked to the material or the customer, which means that the agreed inspections are only performed for certain customers or certain materials.

Results recording in Sales and Distribution corresponds to the process already described.

Certificates

Different customers require certain certificates, e.g. regarding assured properties, material properties, plant inspection certificates or confirmation of inspection. You can set the system is such a way that these certificates are created, printed or faxed automatically for the relevant customer and their delivery.

7.8   APPLICATION IN PRODUCTION

The basic process of quality inspection in Production corresponds to the inspection in Materials Management, but there are a few essential differences.

The inspection in Production is based on the idea that the inspections are to be performed during the production process and are the responsibility of Production (self-inspection). This is why the quality inspection is integrated in Production and in Production Planning. As you already learned in Chapter 6, 'Quality and inspection planning', the operations in quality inspection in Production are contained in the routing. The inspection operations are thus not fundamentally different from other production operations in the routing. It is only in the next level, in which the inspection operations are also assigned inspection characteristics, sampling procedures and characteristic catalogs, that the additional functions of the Quality Management module become apparent. An example of a routing with an inspection operation can be seen in Fig. 7.21.

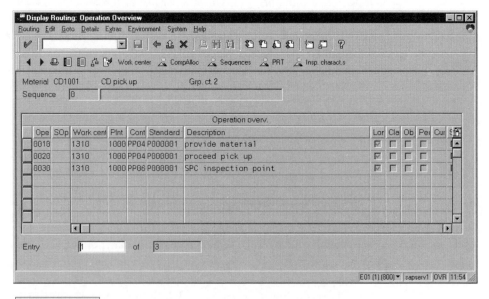

FIGURE 7.21   Routing with inspection operation (© SAP AG)

With the release of a production order, the inspection lots are generated for the inspection operations. The total quantity can also be split into partial lots. The inspection documents (sample drawing and inspection instruction) are printed along with the work papers. The sequence of the inspection steps in the routing can be used to form both intermediate and final inspections.

For Production, inspection lots can be created both manually and by goods movements or a goods receipt from Production.

The integration of the inspections in the routings requires close cooperation between inspection planning and work planning, insofar as these tasks are not performed centrally or by one person. The test equipment appears in the production operation 'Inspection' as production resources/tools. No separate inspection plans are required.

The inspection results are confirmed for each inspection lot and for each inspection characteristic in precisely the way described above (see Fig. 7.22). Here, there is no difference between the inspection in Production and other applications.

Completion of the inspection also involves a usage decision (see also Chapter 8, 'Quality control'), whereby the quantity confirmation does not take place in the usage decision but in the production order for the corresponding operation. There, enter the appropriate quantities 'To unrestricted use', 'To rework' or 'To scrap'. There is the possibility of partial confirmation, final confirmation and automatic final confirmation. Consequently, you can first inspect and confirm one part of the production lot and inspect and confirm the rest later (final confirmation).

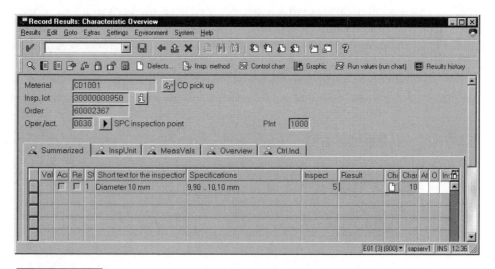

FIGURE 7.22   Results recording for a production order (© SAP AG)

Inspection points

If you want to perform inspections at certain intervals, at certain points in time, after the production of certain production quantities, or based on events, then you need inspection points. Events of this kind can be, for example, a change of container for finished parts or a change in shift. A typical occasion for setting up inspection points would be the hourly inspection of a sample from the production as it runs.

To set up inspection points, the following minimum entries are required in the routing:

- Plan header – parameters for inspection points.
- Operation (inspection) – inspection interval (quantity, time).
- Characteristic – sample size (fixed size).

The inspection points also enable you to create partial lots as well as to allocate the partial lots to batches.

Control charts

Control charts are normally used in Production in the case of SPC inspection. If the Quality Management module is configured appropriately, you can use the R/3 system as an instrument for *statistical process control in Production*. Direct measured value input (see the section entitled 'Interfaces to external systems and measuring devices') can be used in conjunction with control charts and inspection points to optimize the monitoring of the production process without the need to invest in special SPC software. The existing IT structure of the R/3 system can be used 'as is' for measured value recording in Production, which means that the hardware costs remain within acceptable limits.

The description of control charts can be found in the section entitled 'Characteristic results'. There is a detailed section on the topic of SPC in Chapter 8, 'Quality control'.

Batches

If you have planned to use batch administration for your materials, you can assign batches to the partial lots and/or group a number of partial lots to form a batch. The inspection results of the partial lots can be passed on directly to the batch and used for batch classification. The inspection results can also be used directly to create quality certificates.

TIP So that inspection results can be transferred to the batch classification, a material specification must also be maintained for material specification requiring batches.

Inspection in the QA department

If independent inspections in a quality assurance (QA) department are planned, this can be set up without a great deal of effort. In Production, inspection lots can also be generated by goods movements. With the appropriate Customizing, a goods movement leads directly to an inspection lot, or an inspection lot can be created manually.

As the inspection in this case is separated from production planning, an inspection type and the associated plan usage must be set in the system. Furthermore, an inspection plan with this plan usage must have been created. A suitable inspection type, for example, is inspection type 04 (Goods receipt from production), as set in the standard version.

This case is thus very similar to the 'Goods receipt for purchase order'. As described above, the results are recorded for the planned characteristics.

EXAMPLE We shall illustrate the process of a self-inspection using an example from a company's own plastics injection plant. We make the following assumptions:

- We inject a plastic part in our own production (lot manufacturing).
- The quality inspection is enabled for the material.
- There are attributive characteristics for an inspection operation within the framework of the plant self-inspection.
- With the release of the production order, an inspection lot was created automatically.

Consequently, this inspection lot must be in the worklist. We therefore open the selection screen for RESULTS RECORDING | GENERAL, as described in this chapter in the section entitled 'Results recording'. In order to restrict the list of inspection lots to those originating from Production, it is a good idea to enter the inspection lot origin (03 = Production) in the selection screen beforehand.

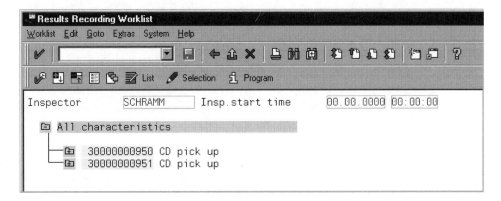

FIGURE 7.23   Example of a worklist of inspection lots from Production (© SAP AG)

If you compare Fig. 7.23 with the worklist from Materials Management (Fig. 7.8), you will see that there are, in principle, no differences between the two, apart from the number range of the inspection lot numbers. There is also no difference in the remaining inspection and results confirmation. For this reason, please refer to the appropriate process in section 7.3.1, 'Characteristic results'.

7.9   APPLICATION IN MATERIALS MANAGEMENT

As the explanations provided so far have mainly focused on the processes in Materials Management, we will now examine in more detail two special cases, which nonetheless can occur on a daily basis.

SCENARIO   *Changing the status of a material after goods receipt from 'subject to inspection' into 'not subject to inspection'.*

We assume the following situation: an overzealous colleague has entered some materials as 'subject to inspection' in the R/3 system, although these materials do not require inspection. Initially, this error goes unnoticed. The purchaser can create and dispatch the purchase order and no problems arise. One day, the material, for example, a pallet of toilet paper, is delivered and as soon as the goods receipt posting is made, the goods are in the quality stock. Depending on the configuration of the system, an inspection lot is also created right away. At the last minute, when someone wants to withdraw the toilet paper from the warehouse stock, it becomes apparent that it is located in the quality stock and has been erroneously planned for a goods receipt inspection.

In order to remedy this situation, first of all a usage decision is made for the current inspection lot and the goods are posted from the quality stock into the 'Released stock'. This makes the goods available and they can be withdrawn. So that this unwanted inspection lot does not falsify the scores, the inspection lot is then cancelled, which is easy to do using USAGE DECISION | CHANGE and USAGE DECISION | FUNCTIONS | CANCEL LOT.

In order to correct this error for subsequent deliveries, it is sufficient to disable the inspection type in the Quality Management view for the material by deleting the check mark from the ACTIVE field. If the inspection type is no longer active, the material is no longer subject to inspection. As the inspection type in the Quality Management view of the material master data does not make much sense for material of this kind, it is even better to delete the inspection type completely.

Under certain circumstances, the matter is not yet fully resolved: if Purchasing has ordered a large quantity and only a part delivery has been made, perhaps due to a split in the delivery, the same problem occurs with the next goods receipt. This even happens if the inspection type has been deleted in the meantime! 'How can that be?' we hear you ask. The explanation is that the temporal validities have be taken into account in each case. The purchase order from Purchasing is based on the state of the material (subject to inspection) at the time of placing the order. If the material, as in our case, is later changed into 'not subject to inspection', this does not affect the current purchase order; it only applies to new purchase orders.

TIP   If a material that was planned for quality inspection is changed in such a way that it is no longer subject to inspection, then check whether there are any open purchase orders for this material. If this is the case, the change only takes effect for new orders. However, if you want the change to take immediate effect, the current purchase order must be changed. To achieve this, the check mark in the QUALINSP (quality inspection) field in the CHANGE PURCHASE ORDER menu must be removed and the order saved. Beforehand, however, the inspection type must have been disabled in the Q view of the material master data.

SCENARIO   *Changing the status of a material after goods receipt from 'not subject to inspection' into 'subject to inspection'*

The reverse case is also not so unusual. We are assuming that, after a goods receipt has been posted, it was noticed that this material should really always be subjected to a goods receipt inspection. So that the following scenario of a retrospective goods receipt inspection makes sense, we assume that the goods are still accessible, so that, on the one hand, a sample can be drawn and, on the other hand, the goods can be blocked in the event of a negative inspection result.

This case is relatively easy to handle: you perform the required activities of inspection planning retrospectively for this material, then cancel the goods receipt and run a new goods receipt posting. The change from 'not subject to inspection' into 'subject to inspection' takes effect immediately here, i.e. the new goods receipt posting now creates an inspection lot and the goods are posted in the quality stock. This also applies to all further purchase orders and goods receipts, as long as you do not reverse the settings in the inspection planning.

7.10   INTERFACES TO EXTERNAL SYSTEMS AND MEASURING DEVICES

Initially, the input of measured values using the keyboard is perhaps the simplest solution, but it is certainly not the most economical. Of course, this depends on the requirements within the company and the local circumstances.

The R/3 system provides interfaces for special tasks in quality inspection and control, which can be used to connect additional external systems to the Quality Management module. It will help you to determine whether or not you need a connection of this kind if you ask the following questions:

▨ How frequently do measured values have to be recorded?

▨ Are digital measuring devices already in use?

▨ Which statistical evaluations are required?

▨ Does the measured data recording take place in a coarse environment (production hall, processing centre) or in a laboratory environment?

▨ Are systems for measured data recording or evaluation already in use – for example, CAQ systems : Computer Aided Quality Assurance; SPC systems (Statistical Process Control); LIMS (Laboratory Information and Management System)?

When you have sorted out these questions and analysed the conditions in the company, and defined the resulting requirements, one of the following possible solutions can be applied:

▨ Measured value processing in the R/3 system.

▨ Inspection handling in an external CAQ or LIM system.

▨ Online measured data recording.

▨ External statistics program.

Measured value processing in the R/3 system

From the point of view of system integration, complete results recording and processing in the R/3 system is the best possible solution. Provided the numerous evaluation possibilities in the QM module are sufficient to meet your needs, you only have to ensure that the measurement results are transferred to the system. In the case of attributive characteristic results for an inspection plan, codes have to be entered from a characteristic catalog. The simplest way to handle this is using the keyboard. The variable characteristic results can be transferred by means of a direct connection to a digital measuring device. The simplest solution here is to use an interface box (keyboard router); these are available on the accessories market for this purpose. This device is placed between the keyboard and the computer, and linked to the measuring device. In this way, a measured value can be entered using the keyboard or transferred directly from a digital measuring device to the computer. Measuring devices can be, for example, digital measuring gauges, timers, bar code scanners or electrical multimeters with interfaces. An advantage of this low-cost solution is that neither changes to the system nor additional software are required, as only the keyboard input is simulated (see Fig. 7.24).

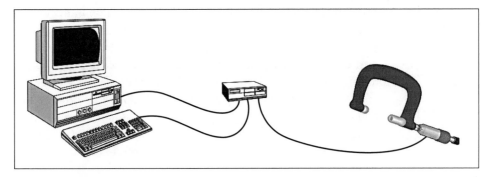

FIGURE 7.24 Measuring device connection via keyboard router

Inspection handling in an external system

If you want to continue to use an existing external CAQ system, this is also possible. These systems are connected via the QM-IDI (Inspection Data Interface) implemented in the R/3 system. Physically, this can take place across a local network (LAN) or the serial interface of a client PC. The appropriate drivers are installed in the R/3 system (host) and at the client.

The separation of tasks between the R/3 system and the CAQ system could take the form indicated below:

▓ The integrated functions are handled in the R/3 system (for example, appraisal costs, usage decision, quantity postings, stock types).

▓ In the subsystem, the inspection operations and measured values are processed.

The RFC (Remote Function Call) can be used to exchange data with the subsystem in both directions. If data is transferred to the external system, this is referred to as a download. The following information would be possible for the download:

▓ Worklist (open inspection lots for a work centre).

▓ Catalogs (characteristic attributes, defect types).

▓ Inspection plan data (operations, characteristics, inspection severity).

Data that could be interesting for an upload, i.e. transfer from the subsystem to the R/3 system, includes:

▓ Single results.

▓ Characteristic results.

▓ Sample results.

▓ Inspection points.

▓ Usage decisions.

▓ Defect codes for each of the result types.

During the processing in the CAQ system, the operation in the R/3 QM is blocked. After the inspection has been completed in the subsystem, the results are reported back to the R/3 system. The interface programs check the consistency of the data.

An external system can be required, for example, if very large quantities of measurement data are generated. If, for example, measurements have to take place in cycles of one second or fractions of a second, this can only run on the subsystem. The data is evaluated there; the results of the evaluation might trigger immediate actions (e.g. machine stop). At regular intervals (inspection points), the compressed data (e.g. mean value, minimum or maximum values) are transferred to the R/3 system.

Online measured data recording

Measuring machines, processing centres or other systems for measured data recording can also be connected to the R/3 system. In the case of an external CAQ system, the measurement data is picked up at the external system by means of a remote function call (RFC) and assigned to the corresponding result type in the R/3 system (see above). In this way, for example, the characteristic results can be imported directly. Special drivers for the data import are required both on the R/3 side and at the external system. SAP AG provides sample drivers. The effort and overhead involved in a solution of this kind are not excessive.

External statistics program

The R/3 system already provides you with several statistical evaluation possibilities such as mean value, standard deviation, process capability indices, to name but a few. However, if you have other requirements that go beyond these possibilities, you can also use an external statistics program. The required data is transferred by the R/3 system to the subsystem via the QM-STI (Statistical Interface) with the remote function call (RFC). There, you can then perform additional evaluations. You can transfer the following data:

- Inspection results (measured values).
- Specifications for the statistical evaluation (tolerance limits, intervention limits, etc.).
- Reference data (sample numbers, inspection lot numbers, material numbers, etc.).
- Additional data (descriptions, units, etc.).

Certified interfaces

Third-party providers can have themselves and their products certified by SAP AG. This ensures that the interface of the SAP application functions with the interface to the external application. Certification of interfaces is definitely an advantage for users, for

SAP AG and for third-party providers. The user can rely on the fact that the interfaces have been checked by SAP AG; SAP AG can refer customers to efficient subsystems from third-party providers; and the third-party providers themselves can exploit the advantages of the inclusion of their software in the integrated R/3 system.

TIP   The third-party providers certified by SAP AG are referred to as Complementary Software Partners (CSP). If you want to find out which companies are registered as CSPs, the internet is the best method. On the SAP AG homepage (`www.sap.com`), you will find a list of partners and their product information under 'Partners' and 'Complementary software'.

Program interfaces (BAPI)

So-called business application programming interfaces (BAPIs) are provided for programming; applications use these interfaces to access data and processes. BAPIs are defined for the objects 'Inspection lot', 'Quality notification' and 'Quality certificate'.

CHAPTER 8

Quality control

BASIC PRINCIPLES

According to DIN EN ISO 9000–1, quality control comprises working techniques and activities with the purpose of monitoring processes and removing the causes of unsatisfactory results. To remove these causes, corrective and quality-promoting measures must be initiated to effectively prevent recurrence.

The SAP R/3 system provides numerous tools for quality control:

- Usage decision.
- Quality level.
- Quality notification.
- Vendor evaluation (vendor assessment).
- Statistical Process Control (SPC).
- Dynamic modification of inspection frequency and severity.
- Batch log.
- Quality costs.
- Quality information system.

As the topics 'Quality notification' and 'Quality information system' are very extensive, they each have their own separate chapter (Chapters 9 and 10).

8.2   THE USAGE DECISION

The usage decision (UD) usually completes the inspection of an inspection lot and is therefore often referred to as the inspection lot completion, although the inspection has already been completed with the confirmation and completion of all characteristic results. However, the inspection lot only disappears from the worklist when the usage decision for the inspection lot has been made.

In addition to the task of completing the inspection lot, the usage decision leads to automatic or manual triggering of several other functions, or these can be started as options. For example, the vendor evaluation and quality level are influenced automatically, and the quality information system is updated. Manual tasks that can be performed include stock postings, confirming inspection output, recording defects, and creating quality notifications.

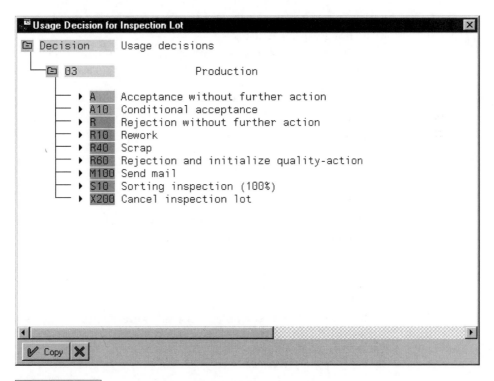

FIGURE 8.1   Catalog for usage decisions (© SAP AG)

As stock posting, recording of defects for the usage decision and the creation of quality notifications are corrective and improvement measures designed to increase the quality of products and processes, the usage decision is discussed here in Chapter 8, 'Quality control', and not in Chapter 7, 'Quality inspection'.

Possible usage decisions

When the inspection of all characteristics of an inspection lot has been completed, a decision as to the usability of the inspection lot is made on the basis of these inspection results. You thus make a decision as to whether the inspection lot can be used (Accept) or is to be rejected (Reject). Other levels are possible in the UD, and these are specified in the basic data via Catalog 3, 'Usage decisions'. A typical catalog for a usage decision is shown in Figure 8.1.

Quantity posting

An important function in the case of stock-relevant inspection lots (e.g. goods receipt from vendors) is the quantity posting. With quantity posting, some tasks that are more or less part of quality control are performed. For example, the decision 'Reject' with the quantity posting 'Return delivery to vendor' or to 'Scrap' means that goods of low quality do not get into circulation.

During the inspection, the goods are in the quality stock. The usage decision involves the following postings which are relevant to Materials Management:

- *Released stock (unrestricted use)*

  You post a quantity from the quality stock into stock available for unrestricted use.

- *Scrap*

  Unusable material can be posted directly to scrap.

- *Sample*

  In the case of a planned destroyed sample a proposal appears here, but you can also post unplanned destroyed quantities.

- *New material*

- *Reserves*

  If you want to put a sample to one side for evidence, the stock handling can take place here.

- *Return delivery to vendor*

  In the case of a return delivery for reasons of quality, the quantity is entered here.

You can perform the quantity postings before, during or after the usage decision is made. Partial quantities can also be posted. However, in the case of manually created inspection lots and inspection lots for the production order (cf. the section on 'The usage decision in production'), no quantity postings are required.

The material documents are frequently of particular interest in the context of quantity postings. You can view the material documents for the inspection lot directly from the current menu via EXTRAS | MATERIAL DOCUMENTS.

Additional interesting information in connection with the quantity posting is provided by the Stock Overview, which can also be opened from the current menu via ENVIRONMENT | STOCK OVERVIEW. In this overview, you will see the material quantities that are available for unrestricted use, contained in the quality stock or those which are blocked, structured according to Plant, Storage Bay and Batch.

Defects for the usage decision

Defects recording and tracing are valuable tools for quality control. The evaluations can be aligned to the defect location, type and cause, as user-defined catalogs can be created for these categories. The existence of an inspection plan or a material specification is not a requirement for the recording of the defect data.

Defects can be recorded for the inspection characteristic, the inspection operation, and for the usage decision. If serious defects are discovered during the inspection, which might have to be reported in the form of a quality notification, it is advisable to record these defects in the usage decision, as a quality notification for the defect can also be created from this point. If the quality notification is created from the usage decision for the inspection lot, the advantage is that all the relevant data of the inspection lot, such as the inspection lot number, goods receipt number, vendor and purchase order number, is automatically adopted into the quality notification. This makes the evaluation with the quality information system more effective, as there is a relationship between the inspection lot and the associated quality notification.

At first, the defect type is entered before the defects. If a quality notification is also created for this defect, this input can be extended to include the defect location and defect cause when the quality notification is processed further.

TIP The expression 'defect location' (see Fig. 8.2) can be understood in different ways. It can be understood as the position on a part or assembly where the defect was localized (e.g. scratches on the front). Another interpretation of defect location is the place where the defect was discovered (for example, goods receipt, in assembly, at the customer). This version of the expression 'defect location' enables more useful evaluations than the first option (cf. Sobotta, H.: 'The simple solution also leads to the target'. *Sobotta*, 1999, p. 76).

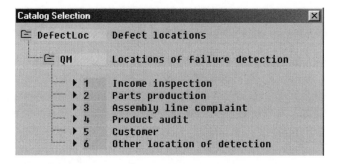

FIGURE 8.2   Catalog 9 'defect locations' (© SAP AG)

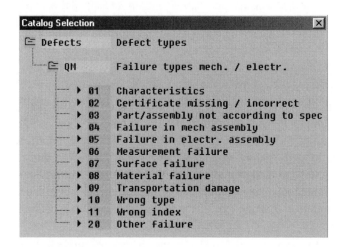

FIGURE 8.3   Catalog E 'defect types' (© SAP AG)

As already mentioned in Chapter 7, 'Quality inspection', it is advisable to set up Catalog 9, 'Defect types' (Fig. 8.3), and Catalog 1, 'Characteristic attributes' in the same way, as these two catalogs correspond closely to one another.

The whole thing becomes very interesting when a quality notification is created for the defect or defects. In Customizing, it is possible to set the type of quality notification this should be. It is usual in the case of an inspection lot from Production to create an 'Internal quality notification' (notification type Q1), and in the case of an inspection lot from goods receipt a 'Complaint to vendor' (notification type Q2). The quality notification can be used to provide an even more precise description of the defect – with defect location, defect cause and various supplementary texts. There is also the fact that measures and actions can be monitored accurately, as described in detail in Chapter 9, 'Quality notification'.

A quality notification on the defect can be activated in defects recording, which takes place as in the recording screen by clicking the Q-NOTIFICATION (ACTIVATE) button (see Fig. 8.4).

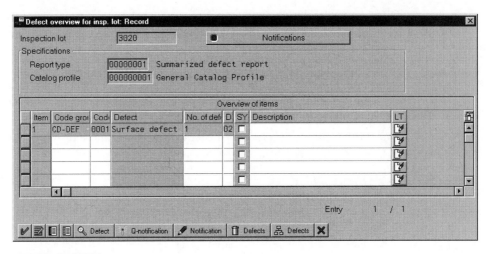

FIGURE 8.4   Creating defects from the usage decision (© SAP AG)

The quality notification should then be extended to include additional input (defect location, defect cause, clerk, comments, etc.).

Important! Always enter the defects first and activate the associated quality notification; only then should you make the usage decision. If you try to do this in the reverse order, the system will display the message 'The function you selected cannot be carried out'. The reason for this is that, with the usage decision, the system regards the inspection as already completed and no defects (and no characteristic results) can be recorded retrospectively.

Views in the usage decision screen

In the usage decision screen, you will see various tabs, the number and appearance of which can vary depending on the inspection planning and results recording.

■ *Characteristic view*

Entry view with the relevant inspection characteristics and the associated inspection results.

■ *Stock view*

Only for inspection lots relevant to stock.

■ *Defect view*

In Release 4.0, this only appears if defects have been recorded.

■ *Inspection points*

Only if inspection points or physical samples are planned.

In the Characteristic view, only the required characteristics are displayed initially. Optional characteristics or skipped characteristics are suppressed, but can also be displayed by clicking the ALL CHARACTERISTICS button. If characteristic results have been confirmed and completed beforehand, the valuation of the characteristics is also visible. Accepted characteristics are marked with a green check mark and rejected characteristics with a red cross.

By double-clicking or using the magnifier icon, you can obtain details of the data from the various overviews. Further information can be displayed using the function keys and the ENVIRONMENT menu:

- Inspection lot data.
- Results history.
- Defective quantity.
- Batch status, batch and batch usage.
- Administrative data.
- Inspection specifications.
- Material data.
- Quality level.
- Stock overview.
- Production order or sales order.
- Master data of the vendor or manufacturer or customer.
- Vendor evaluation or cost report.

This wealth of information and data can be called up quickly for the usage decision and included in the process of making a decision.

Influence of the usage decision on the quality score

When the usage decision (UD) is made, the quality score (QS) for the material and vendor, and thus for the vendor evaluation, is updated. Whether and how the individual usage decision affects the quality score is specified in Customizing and in the 'Usage decisions' catalog. This is covered in more detail in the 'Vendor evaluation' section. As soon as the usage decision that has been made is entered in the input field and confirmed with ENTER, the system uses the set method to calculate the quality score of the inspection lot and displays it in the QUALITY SCORE field (see Fig. 8.6).

Influence of the usage decision on the quality level

The usage decision updates the quality level (Q level) for the material and vendor. This is important mainly when you have defined dynamic modification rules which, for example, stipulate an increase in the severity of the inspection in the event of rejected characteristics or, in the event of a number of positive inspection results, permit skipping inspections. It is only when the usage decision is made that the quality level is updated, which means that the modified Q level can affect the creation of a new inspection lot. A modified Q level does not affect inspection lots that have already been created, even if the inspection lots were created later. Further details can be found in the 'Quality level' section.

Influence of the usage decision on the quality costs

Within the Quality Management module, the quality costs incurred can be recorded at various positions. During results recording and making the usage decision, the overhead incurred at the work centre for equipping times and personnel can be confirmed, and the costs can be determined in the Controlling (CO) module. However, in order to be able to enter confirmations for types of action, a QM order must have been created beforehand. If this is the case, you can confirm the individual activities using the menu EDIT | CONFIRMATIONS and CONFIRM ACTIVITIES. The costs of a QM order incurred so far can be seen in the menu EXTRAS | COST REPORT QM ORDER.

Certificate receipt

If you have planned the receipt of certificates, for example a manufacturer's test certificate (see Fig. 8.5) for certain goods receipts in the material master data (Q view), this must be confirmed before you can make a usage decision. This makes sense insofar as you can only decide on the use when the certificate has been received. If you try to make the usage decision without confirming the certificate receipt, an error message appears.

Batch administration

You can also draw on the usage decision to perform various actions for batch administration. These include:

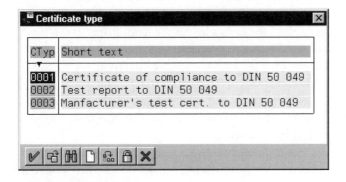

FIGURE 8.5   Possible certificate types (© SAP AG)

- Changing the batch status.
- Displaying the batch list.
- Displaying the batch usages.
- Displaying batch values.
- Posting batches as new material.

In the case of stock-relevant inspection lots, you can use this method for negative usage decisions to change the status of the batch from 'released' into 'not released'. To do so, open the menu GOTO | BATCH STATUS. You can maintain a proposal for posting the batch status with the catalog 'Usage decisions' (catalog type 3).

The list of batches can be displayed using GOTO | BATCH LIST.

The composition of batches or, the other way around, the use of raw materials in finished batches, can be determined via the batch use. The menu path for this evaluation is EXTRAS | BATCH USE | TOP-DOWN or BOTTOM-UP.

In order to be able to compare the characteristic values of a batch with the inspection results, display the name of the characteristic, the characteristic value in the batch, and the inspection result. To do so, select EXTRAS | BATCH VALUES.

If a batch is to be posted as new material, select the menu GOTO | OTHER MATERIAL. The system automatically assigns a new batch number, but you can also overwrite this with a number of your own.

The automatic usage decision

If you skip inspections using dynamic modification rules, the 'automatic usage decision' is an option open to you. This can become active when the inspection is in 'skip' or when the inspection is completed in full and no characteristic has been rejected. Another requirement is that the receipt of necessary certificates has been confirmed.

The 'automatic usage decision' is performed if the above requirements are met, if the indicator 'automatic usage decision' is enabled in the material master data (Q view – inspection type) of the materials concerned, and a job has been planned for this. In this way you can, at night for example, complete all inspection lots with the 'automatic usage decision' if the above requirements are met.

You plan a job for the 'automatic usage decision' using the menu LOGISTICS | QUALITY MANAGEMENT | QUALITY INSPECTION and WORKLIST | INSPECTION LOT COMPLETION | AUTOM. UD GENERAL | PLANNING OF JOBS or AUTOM. UD ORDERS | PLANNING OF JOBS. GENERAL refers to inspection lots from Procurement and ORDERS are inspection lots from production.

After the job has been terminated, a printout is created to inform you about which inspection lots were completed without problems and where errors (for example, due to a missing certificate receipt) occurred.

Usage decision for a manual inspection lot

When a manual inspection lot is created, this is not linked to a goods movement or reposting. This means that the stock type of the goods does not change, either. As a rule, the goods are and remain in released stock and are not posted to the quality stock. Consequently, no quantity posting to released stock is required after the inspection has been performed.

If the inspection makes a special action necessary, for example rework or return delivery to the vendor, these goods movements are controlled by means of special movement types, which (outside the QM module) have to be set up in Customizing and handled in Materials Management.

Usage decision without previous inspection

Usually, the usage decision follows completion of the results recording. This includes the confirmation of the characteristic results, e.g. by means of an attribute code and the completion of the characteristic. If all the required characteristics are completed, the inspection is completed. Whether characteristics are completed can be seen from the characteristic status and by the colour of the inspection lots in the worklist. If the inspection lot is yellow, more characteristic results are expected.

However, you can also make a usage decision without waiting for all characteristics to be completed. In this case, you receive the warning 'Requested inspection still open!'. Either you complete the inspection first, or you ignore the warning and make the usage decision nonetheless. There are no disadvantages in the case of a positive usage decision. In the case of a negative usage decision, a lot-based dynamic modification that might have been planned does not take place, as it takes its orientation from the characteristic results. In order that – in the event of a negative inspection result – the dynamic modification rule leads to an increase in the severity of the inspection for the next inspection lot, you must confirm at least one rejected characteristic with the negative inspection result.

Mandatory documentation

If documentation of the material is set as mandatory, a usage decision must always contain a comment if no previous inspection took place, if the inspection was only performed in part, or a positive usage decision (Accept) has been made although characteristics were rejected. If a usage decision is changed retrospectively, this is only possible 'with history', i.e. with the creation of a change document.

Expiration of a usage decision

After all of this dull theory, we now want to run through a usage decision using a practical example. The example describes a usage decision for a 'Goods receipt for purchase order'. The typical entry point would be the worklist for results recording, which we reach on the following menu paths:

LOGISTICS | QUALITY INSPECTION and WORKLIST | RESULTS RECORDING

By entering '1' (all characteristics) in the READ-IN MODE field and selecting PROGRAM | RUN in the selection screen, the entire worklist is displayed. The inspection lots for which you can make a usage decision without any further actions are colour-coded in light blue. Inspection lots that contain required characteristics still to be inspected are yellow. A double-click on a light-blue inspection lot number leads you directly to the input mask for the corresponding usage decision (see Fig. 8.6).

TIP If there are a great many inspection lots, the display quickly becomes a little complicated. It is then advisable to specify other selection criteria, for example, lot origin, material number or work centre, to find the desired inspection lot more quickly.

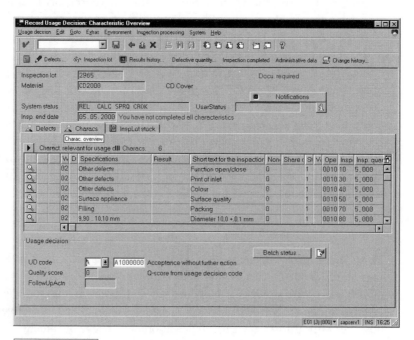

FIGURE 8.6 Record usage decision: Characteristic overview (© SAP AG)

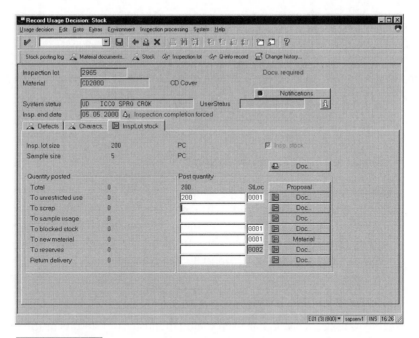

FIGURE 8.7   Record usage decision: Stock (© SAP AG)

A manual usage decision is now to be made for the inspection lot shown in Figure 8.6. When the screen is opened, the cursor is already in the 'UD code' field, where you can enter directly the code from Catalog 3, 'Usage decisions' (see Fig. 8.1) or select from the selection screen. As soon as you press ENTER, the associated quality score is displayed. If you now go to SAVE, you are automatically moved into the next view, namely 'Record Usage Decisions: Stock'. This view is shown in Fig. 8.7.

If no defects were detected in the inspection, you will post the entire inspection lot quantity TO UNRESTRICTED USE. Using SAVE once more, the usage decision and the quantity posting are saved and you are returned to the view of your worklist. After you have updated the view, you will see that the inspection lot has disappeared from the worklist.

TIP

If you have to make a large number of usage decisions on a daily basis, and do not want to select each individual inspection lot, you can also create a list of inspection lots and make usage decisions for them all at one time.

TIP

When editing Catalog 3, 'Usage decisions', you can also assign fixed posting instructions for the inspection lot stock to individual decisions. For example, it makes sense to firmly assign the posting 'to unrestricted use' to the decision 'Accept'. The result of this is that with this usage decision the quantity posting is dealt with right away, eliminating another entry in the 'inspection lot stock' view. This setting is not recommended for the other usage decisions, as you might want to make different postings depending on the material situation.

Follow-up actions for usage decision

If the relevant Customizing settings have been made, you can trigger appropriate follow-up actions in the input screen RECORD USAGE DECISION. If the display MANUAL appears, this means that no automatic follow-up action is planned, and any such actions have to be started manually. An example of an automatic follow-up action is the sending of an e-mail to Purchasing in the event of a negative usage decision.

Changing a usage decision

Once a usage decision has been made, the inspection results of the inspection lot can no longer be changed. However, this does not apply to the usage decision itself, which can be changed retrospectively, for example in the light of new information. There are two methods that permit a retrospective change:

- With history.
- Without history.

In the case of a change with history, information on the changes and the status prior to the change is saved by the system in a change document. In the case of material with mandatory documentation, a change of the usage decision is only possible with history.

Usage decision in Sales and Distribution

In Sales and Distribution, a usage decision is used to decide whether or not goods can be shipped to the customers. Your catalog will therefore differ from the catalog for goods receipt, e.g. 'Delivery release' takes the place of 'Accept'.

Usage decision in Production

The usage decision in Production refers to inspections during or after the production process.

The usage decision in Production is different from the others in that the stock view is missing. All stock postings are performed in the Production Planning (PP) module using the confirmation for production order. In the QM module, decisions are only made via 'Accept' or 'Reject' of an inspection lot.

Usage decision in Materials Management

The usage decision in Materials Management usually refers to inspection lots that have come about through goods receipt from a vendor. The goods receipt means the goods can be posted into the quality stock (stock code Q). Via the stock posting in the usage decision, good quality goods are posted into the released stock and defective goods are usually returned.

The usage decision in Materials Management directly affects the vendor evaluation (with the appropriate settings in the material master data and in Customizing).

| 8.3 | **QUALITY LEVEL** |

The quality level is a data record containing information on the inspection stages of the characteristics, the inspection lots, the material and – in the case of purchased parts – also on the vendor. The quality level is only relevant if you are using dynamic modification rules to regulate a change in the inspection severity or inspection skips. The quality level is, in a manner of speaking, a reminder of how the next inspection is to be treated.

In the case of a planned dynamic modification, the system automatically creates a quality level (Q level) with the next inspection lot. For the first inspection lot, the inspection severity is taken from the initial stage of the dynamic modification rule. A distinction is made between characteristic-based and lot-based dynamic modification, which can be specified in the inspection plan header.

Updating the quality level on lot creation

If no quality level exists yet, it is created automatically on lot creation. The valuation is set initially to 'Accept' and the relevant counters are increased. The characteristic-based results recording has no initial effect on the valuation. The valuation might be changed with the usage decision. If only one characteristic is rejected (worst-case principle), this leads to a 'not OK' valuation (NOK) in the case of lot-based dynamic modification. It is therefore not the usage decision (for example, 'Reject') that influences the dynamic modification, but rather it is the rejection of the characteristic. In the case of characteristic-based dynamic modification, only the valuation of the relevant characteristic has an effect.

Updating the quality level with usage decision

Here, too, the quality level is created automatically (insofar as it does not exist yet) as soon as a dynamic modification rule is used. With the usage decision, the quality level is updated in accordance with the characteristic valuations. If the dynamic modification is lot-based, the lot is rejected if only one characteristic is rejected (worst-case rule). In the case of characteristic-based dynamic modification, the valuation of the relevant characteristic has an effect.

TIP
This worst-case rule also makes the following tip easy to understand: if you make a usage decision without confirming characteristic results (which is possible), the dynamic modification cannot function in the case of a characteristic rejection. So that the dynamic modification can work as intended, at least one characteristic must be confirmed and completed with a negative result.

Manual creation of the quality level

As already mentioned, the quality level is created automatically as soon as it is required for the dynamic modification. However, it can be desirable to create the quality level manually beforehand. A possible reason for this would be that, for a certain material, a start phase other that that set in the dynamic modification rule is to be used. A Q level can only be created manually for lot-based dynamic modification.

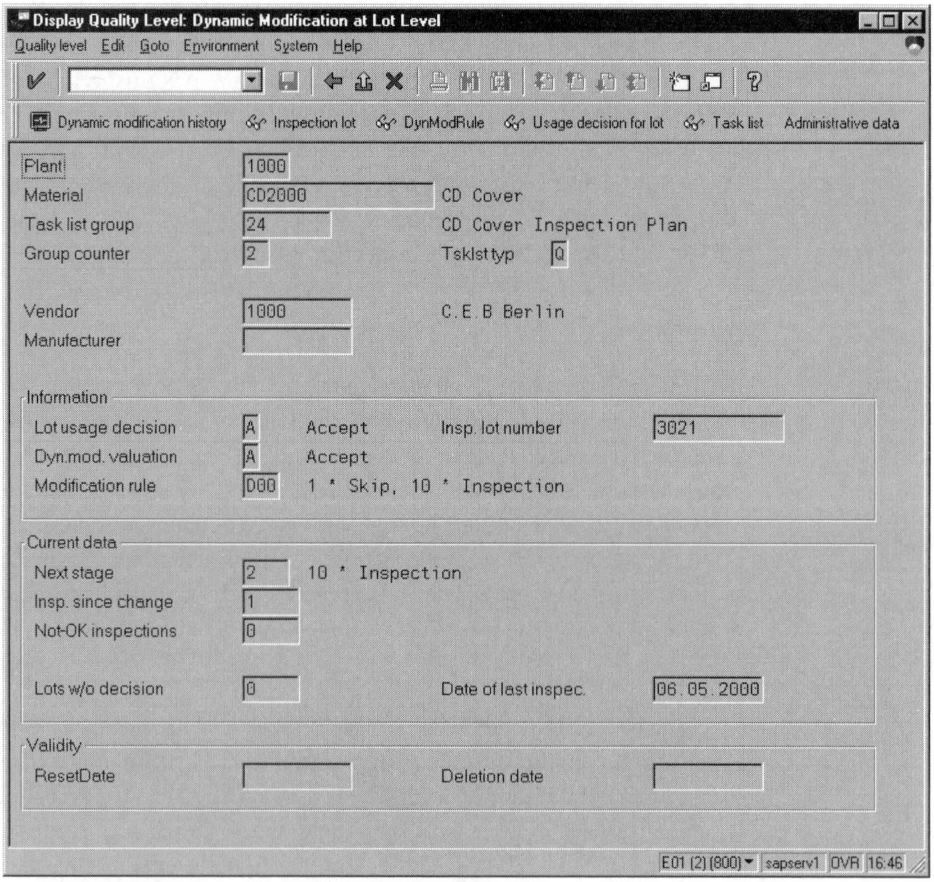

FIGURE 8.8   Quality level (© SAP AG)

Creation of the Q level is quite simple via the menu path LOGISTICS | QUALITY MANAGEMENT | QUALITY INSPECTION and QUALITY LEVEL | CREATE. There, enter the necessary details in the appropriate fields (see Fig. 8.8).

8.4   VENDOR EVALUATION

The vendor evaluation makes it easier for Procurement and Quality Management to pursue their objectives by means of comprehensible figures. These objectives could be:

- To establish the actual status of a supply relationship.
- To show the vendor the extent to which the requirements of the purchaser are met.
- To create the basis for vendor selection or vendor reduction.
- To provide assistance in decision-making in obtaining quotations and extending the supply relationship.
- To provide assistance in decision-making in setting the emphasis on goods receipt inspection and inspection planning.
- To provide background information leading to conclusion of a quality assurance agreement.

In vendor evaluation, subcriteria and main criteria are used to form scores that permit the assessment of individual criteria and the formation of a ranking list for the overall score. These scores can be used as the basis for initiating targeted corrective and improvement measures. In this way, a useful vendor evaluation is not restricted to determining the actual state of affairs, but also creates the starting point for future quality improvements.

8.4.1 Basic principles

An essential component of quality control is vendor evaluation. It is required in Element 6, 'Procurement' of the quality management standard DIN EN ISO 9001. The R/3 system provides you with flexible tools for assessment of your vendors. These tools meet the requirements of the standard, and they can easily be adapted to the circumstances in your company. As it is the main topic of this book, our description will focus on the quality criterion.

Vendor evaluation is positioned somewhere between Purchasing and Quality Management, as it incorporates the information and criteria from both a commercial and a quality point of view. In the R/3 system, you will find the vendor evaluation in Materials Management (MM), as the majority of the criteria are assessed from a commercial point of view, and vendor evaluation is assigned to the Procurement element in the series of standards DIN EN ISO 9001–9003. It also accesses master data and movement data from Materials Management, for example the material master records and vendor master records. The vendors are evaluated on the purchasing organization level. One or more plants are assigned to the purchasing organization.

Vendor evaluation enables every vendor to be assessed with a quality score. This quality score is a summary of all criteria, which means that a ranking list of vendors can be drawn up. However, each criterion can also be regarded individually. In addition, the quality score can be formed regarding a certain material or various vendors for a material.

Vendor evaluation covers not only vendors of material; vendors of services, for example maintenance services, cleaning services, trade services, etc., can also be assessed.

8.4.2 Master data

The master data on the system is accessed for vendor evaluation. This includes, in particular:

- Vendor master record.
- Material master record.
- Purchasing information record.

The vendor master record contains the name, address and contact information, as well as the terms of payment and the currency applicable to the vendor.

The material master record and its various views contain all the information regarding the material. The following factors, among others, are relevant for vendor evaluation: unit of quantity, order unit of quantity, purchasing group, under- or over-delivery tolerances and the inspection types.

The purchasing information record (also referred to as the information record) defines the relationship between the vendor and the material. This contains information not only on which materials were offered and delivered by which vendor, but also on the associated prices and terms, delivery period and other data regarding quotations and purchase orders.

8.4.3 Evaluation criteria

The standard version of the R/3 system provides five main criteria and other subcriteria for the assessment of vendors.

The main criteria are:

- Quality
- Price
- Delivery
- General service/support
- Service

The main criterion 'quality' has the following subcriteria:

▓ Goods receipt

Determination of the Q-score from the quality of the inspection lots of the individual goods receipts.

▓ Audit (system audit)

Determination of the Q-score from one or more audits.

▓ Complaints (shopfloor complaints)

Determination of the Q-score from the complaints to the vendor.

CUSTOMIZING TIP

This default setting can be changed so that it appears more suitable for your company. For example, the main criteria or subcriteria can be supplemented or removed. A total of up to 99 main criteria and 20 subcriteria per main criterion are possible. The weighting of the various criteria can also be set. It is even possible to set various weightings ('Equal weighting', 'Unequal weighting') which can then be selected from the WEIGHTING KEY field. The setting for weighting can be found in Customizing (path: TOOLS | BUSINESS ENGINEER | CUSTOMIZING) in the SAP reference IMG at MATERIALS MANAGEMENT | PURCHASING | VENDOR EVALUATION | SPECIFY PURCHASING ORGANIZATION DATA FOR VENDOR EVAL. At the navigation point WEIGHTING, you can now enter the corresponding weighting factors. If all the main criteria are to be weighted equally, enter '1' in each case; this defines the weighting ratio as 1 : 1 : 1 :1. If a main criterion is not to be weighted, then select a '0' instead of '1'. An example is shown in Figure 8.9.

Figure 8.10 shows you how to set the subcriteria to obtain weighting in accordance with Table 8.1. For the AUDIT, the check mark at MANUAL MAINT. creates the possibility of entering the quality score from the vendor audit manually.

The quality score is formed from bottom to top, which means that the individual subcriteria are evaluated first. These are summarized according to the weighting key, and they provide the quality score of the corresponding main criterion. The main criteria and their weighting keys are included in the overall score.

The quality score of the subcriteria can be determined automatically, semi-automatically or manually. In the case of goods receipts or complaints, automatic calculation would be normal. For a system audit, manual input makes sense, as here the quality score can be adopted from the audit result. Semi-automatic calculation is mainly relevant to the subcriteria of service and general service/support, as no automatic calculation is possible there.

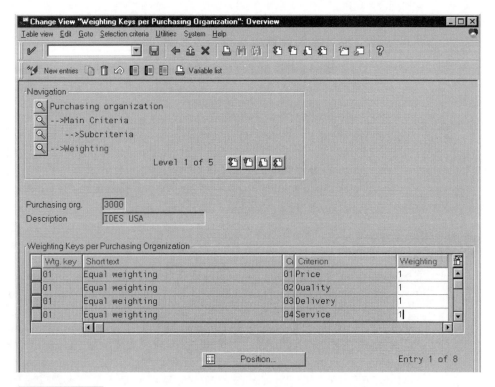

TABLE 8.1 Main criteria and subcriteria with examples of weighting factors

Main criteria		Subcriteria	
	Weighting		Weighting
Quality	60 %	Income inspection	50 %
		Audit	10 %
		Complaints	40 %
Delivery	40 %	On-time delivery	50 %
		Quantity reliability	50 %

Calculation of scores

The calculation of scores will be explained using examples. Table 8.1 shows typical settings which can be selected in Customizing on a company-specific basis.

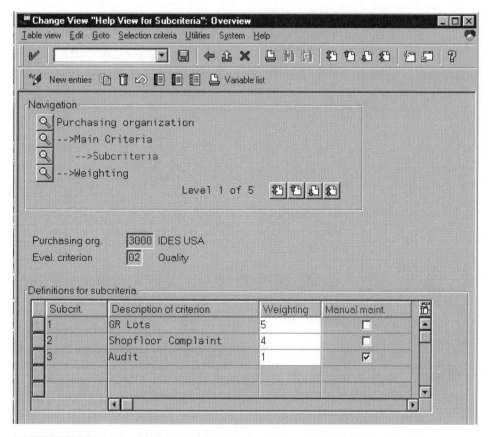

FIGURE 8.10 Setting the subcriteria according to the example from Table 8.1
(© SAP AG)

Subcriterion 'goods receipt inspection' (income inspection)

The usage decision on an inspection lot is relevant for the score calculation of the subcriterion for goods receipt inspection. You can specify a weighting factor for each usage decision (Accept, Reject, Sorting). The decision 'Accept' is usually evaluated with 100 points and 'Reject' with 1 point. The quality score is then the arithmetical mean of the weighting factors of all usage decisions for the goods receipt inspection lots in the period of analysis (Fig. 8.11).

EXAMPLE If five inspection lots have been created from goods receipts in the period of analysis, four of which were accepted and one of which was rejected, the subcriterion 'income inspection' receives a Q-score of (100 + 100 + 100 + 100 +1)/5 = 80.2 points (Fig. 8.11).

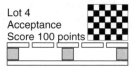

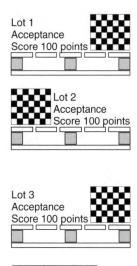

FIGURE 8.11 Goods receipt (GR) lots with the valuation from the usage decision

Subcriterion 'audit'

The subcriterion 'audit' can be calculated automatically if the system has been set in Customizing to generate audit inspection lots for each audit. From the usage decision via the audit inspection lots, the number of points in the catalog is used to calculate a quality score for audits. The advantage here lies in the summary of several audits to form a quality score.

The simpler method is manual input of the quality score of the last system audit of each vendor. It is taken for granted that you can also apply a process or product audit instead of a system audit, or create a separate subcriterion for each audit type. Here, all the scores should be standardized to the same maximum number of points (typically 100 points), so that meaningful figures are also created after the subcriteria are summarized.

TIP If you do not perform any system or process audits yourself, the results can be documented at this subcriterion from a vendor self-assessment, a VDA 6.1 Audit or other audit evaluations.

Subcriterion 'complaints'

As soon as a quality defect for which the vendor is responsible is discovered, whether in the goods receipt inspection, during production, at the final product or even at the final customer, a quality notification is created as a complaint to the vendor. This subcriterion allows you to include the number or value of complaints (quality notifications) in the vendor evaluation.

As a rule, this subcriterion is used to indicate shopfloor complaints separately. A shopfloor complaint is a defect in the delivered goods that is only discovered during processing in Production, not at goods receipt.

TIP If you are using the subcriteria 'goods receipt inspection' and 'complaints' at the same time, bear in mind that under certain circumstances the quality score is reduced twice. On the one hand, the negative usage decision influences the vendor evaluation and, on the other hand, it affects the relevant quality notification that is created. It is therefore advisable to use only one of these two subcriteria for the vendor evaluation. The decision as to which subcriterion is more suitable depends on the processes in your company.

Main criterion 'quality'

The quality score of the main criterion 'quality' is calculated from the above-mentioned subcriteria. To achieve this, each subcriterion is weighted according to the set factor. Provided the weighting factors have been selected in such a way that the total is 100 per cent (if not, it is standardized to 100 by the system), each subscore is multiplied by he factor and the total is the sum of the subtotals.

EXAMPLE In Table 8.2, you will find the accepted scores for the three subcriteria and a weighting factor for each. The subtotal values are calculated from the scores of the subcriteria multiplied by the weighting. The quality score for the main criterion is the total of the subtotals. This means that the result for the main criterion 'quality' in this example is 40 + 9.5 + 36 = 85.5 points.

TABLE 8.2 Example of weighting the subcriteria for the main criterion 'quality'

Subcriteria	Score (Q-score)	Weighting	Subtotal
Goods receipt	80	50 %	40
Audit	95	10 %	9.5
Complaints	90	40 %	36

TIP It has proved effective in practice to weight only the subcriterion that is most important for your company with 100 per cent and all other subcriteria with 0 per cent. In this way, although all the subcriteria are recorded, only this particularly important subcriterion influences the calculation of the main criterion from the subcriteria, and it can be used in the 'ranking list' (see below) as a sorting criterion.

Main criterion 'delivery'

The main criterion 'delivery' in Table 8.1 is composed of the subcriteria 'quantity reliability' and 'on-time delivery', which have been set in the example with equal weighting (but can also be weighted differently). For each delivery, it is established how accurately the specifications for adherence to the correct delivery date/time and the correct delivery quantity were met. In the same way as with the main criterion 'quality', the score for the main criterion 'delivery' is calculated from the evaluation scores of the subcriteria.

Another criterion from the default setting of R/3 is the shipping instructions. You can assess how precisely your vendor adheres to the instructions for the shipping type and packaging. For example, it is frequently the case that returnable packaging, packaging suitable for ESD or a maximum weight per pallet are prescribed.

Main criterion 'price'

This criterion can be used to evaluate the price level of this vendor in relation to the average market price. If the price is lower, the evaluation is better; if the price is higher than the market price, this results in a poorer evaluation.

The requirement for an assessment of this kind is of course that comparison prices of competitors supplying the same materials are available and have been entered in the system.

Service

The criterion 'service' also refers to the material shipment. Typical subcriteria are:

- Reliability
- Innovation
- Flexibility

As can be seen from the nature of these subcriteria, they cannot be determined automatically by the system, as they include subjective estimations that depend on the branch of industry and many other factors. For subcriteria of this kind, semi-automatic determination of the quality score is possible. Deliveries are assessed by the specialist departments responsible, taking account of the set subcriteria, and the result is entered manually. When updating the vendor evaluation, the system summarizes these individual assessments automatically into a score.

Main criterion 'general service/support'

The criterion 'general service/support' is used for the assessment of services. The qualitative performance of the service is assessed. This assessment cannot be performed automatically by the system, but takes place when the work performed is inspected or on conclusion of the work; it is entered into the system manually. Examples of services of this kind are the maintenance of machines or the car fleet by external companies, cleaning, maintenance of outdoor facilities, and much more.

The trend towards outsourcing an increasing number of service tasks means that the assessment – and the comparison of assessments this enables – is becoming increasingly important.

Overall score

Finally, the overall score (overall quality score) is calculated from the individual main criteria. This uses the same procedure as for the calculation of the main criteria from the subcriteria.

In practice, it has become apparent that the representation of an overall score via the main criteria has relatively low significance. Although it can be used to set up a sequence (ranking list) of vendors, if there is a negative assessment the question as to why? crops up, and this is followed by the question as to which main or subcriterion is responsible for the poor assessment. In day-to-day work, and in pursuing the aim of continuous improvement, the analysis of the subcriteria is of much greater interest.

TIP   Do not select too many main and subcriteria! A small number of criteria increases the level of acceptance and comprehensibility. Simply begin with the criterion 'quality' only, for example, and the subcriterion 'goods receipt inspection' with the usage decision as the basis of the quality score (cf. Federation of German Automobile Industry, VDA, 1998 Volume 2).

8.4.4 Evaluating vendors

The practical performance of vendor evaluation on the system can be shown very easily with an example. The starting point for vendor evaluation is the PURCHASING screen. Select the path LOGISTICS | MATERIALS MANAGEMENT | PURCHASING

In the MASTER DATA submenu, you will find the VENDOR EVALUATION menu with its options. To assess a vendor, you must first open the VENDOR EVALUATION MAINTAIN menu (Fig. 8.12).

Maintain vendor evaluation

In the entry screen, specify the number of the purchasing organization and the vendor for which you want to create the vendor evaluation.

The first time a vendor who has not yet been evaluated is called up, the fields of the main criteria are not yet filled out, which can be seen from the fact that no quality score

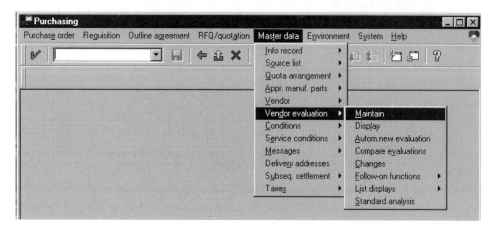

FIGURE 8.12 Opening the menu 'maintain vendor evaluation' (© SAP AG)

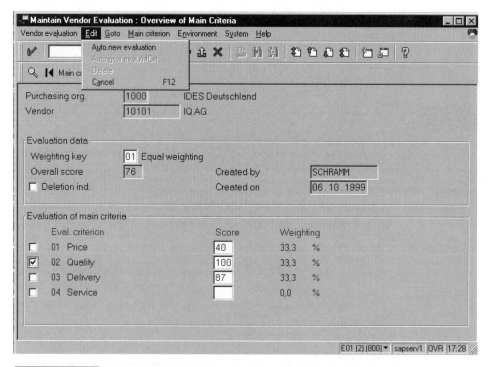

FIGURE 8.13 'Maintain vendor evaluation' with evaluated main criteria (© SAP AG)

has yet been determined. First of all, select a weighting key (here: 01 = equal weighting) and then start the command EDIT | AUTOM. NEW EVALUATION. This first recalculates all the subcriteria and then all the main criteria and the overall score for the current date.

After the AUTOMATIC NEW EVALUATION, the fields of the overall score and the main and subcriteria are filled with the current quality score (Fig. 8.13).

If the main criterion GENERAL SERVICES/SUPPORT appears, it is defined in grey (disabled), as it is only relevant for service providers. This example, however, deals with a material vendor and this criterion does not apply.

The criterion SERVICE could be maintained manually here, but it is not required for this example.

With SAVE, the status of the vendor evaluation is stored and is directly available the next time it is opened. It is advisable to perform AUTOMATIC NEW EVALUATION at regular intervals, for example at the end of the month or quarter. However, it can be updated at any time in between. All the relevant events over a certain period, which can be set in Customizing (e.g. to one year), up to the day of the new evaluation are included in the calculation.

How often you maintain the vendor evaluation depends on what you need it for. For negotiations with vendors, visits to vendors and the revision of inspection plans, short-

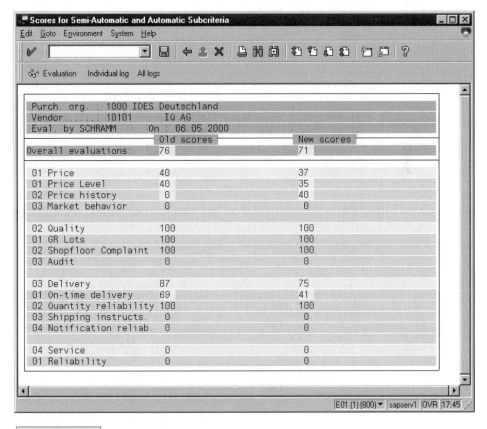

FIGURE 8.14 | Log after an automatic new evaluation (© SAP AG)

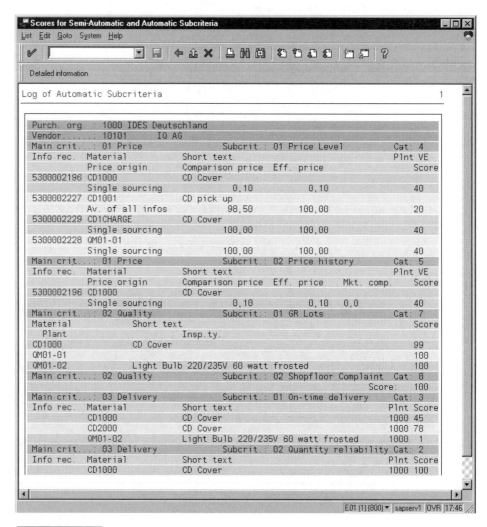

FIGURE 8.15   Display of all logs (© SAP AG)

term (monthly) maintenance is required. For vendor selection or for the purpose of reducing the number of vendors, mid-term maintenance, for example per quarter or every six months, would make sense.

Displaying vendor evaluation

The VENDOR EVALUATION | DISPLAY menu allows you to view the vendor evaluation that was saved using the MAINTAIN menu.

Vendor evaluation – automatic new evaluation

In the submenu AUTOM. NEW EVALUATION of the VENDOR EVALUATION menu, you can trigger the new evaluation of all main criteria. In the entry screen, you have to again enter the VENDORS and the PURCHASING ORGANIZATION of your company. As an option, a setting can be made in the entry screen with the effect that only vendors who have not been evaluated since a certain date are newly evaluated (VENDS. NOT EVALUATED SINCE ...). Press ENTER to start the calculation of all criteria.

In Figure 8.14, you can see the result of the automatic new evaluation. It provides a comparison of the scores between the last and the current assessment for the overall score and the main and subcriteria.

For an analysis of the reasons for each assessment, further details are interesting. Clicking on the ALL LOGS button provides you with a list of the scores for each material number (Fig. 8.15).

By marking the material number, clicking on DETAILED INFORMATION, marking the material number again and clicking the DISPLAY INSP. LOTS button, you receive a display containing a list for each material of the inspection lots relevant to the vendor evaluation, with the date of the usage decision and the associated quality score (Q-score) (Fig. 8.16).

Evaluation comparison

The COMPARE EVALUATIONS submenu from vendor evaluation permits determination of the quality score of a vendor only in relation to a material or a goods group and comparison with the quality score of all supplied materials.

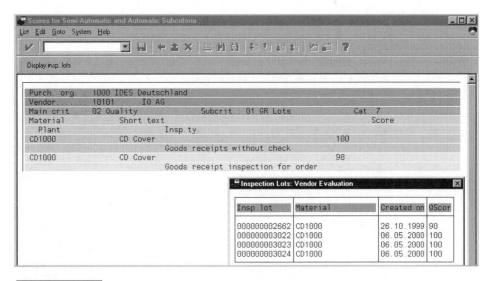

FIGURE 8.16 Detailed information on the material with additional inspection lots screen (© SAP AG)

Changes

Each new vendor evaluation is also a change to the existing one. You can use the sub-menu CHANGES to find out who created a new vendor evaluation, and when they did so, and view both the old and the current values.

Follow-on functions

The submenu FOLLOW-ON FUNCTIONS leads on to three submenus that provide additional functions (Fig. 8.17).

Evaluating vendors in the background (Evaln. in background)

Here, you can maintain a job that runs regularly in the background and, for example, performs a new evaluation of your vendors monthly. You can specify when the background evaluation is to run and at what intervals it is to be repeated. For information regarding the creation and use of 'jobs', contact your system administrator.

Vendors without weighting key (Vendors w/o wtg. key)

If you use the automatic vendor evaluation in the background, it is possible that the allocation of the weighting key is missing. An allocation of this kind is required if you have evaluated vendors with different weighting keys in the above background evaluation or have not specified a weighting key. With this menu item, you can then supply the background evaluation with a weighting key retrospectively.

Printing the evaluation sheet (Print evaln. sheet)

This menu can be used to print the documentation of the current assessment of a vendor with overall score, main and subcriteria. An evaluation sheet of this kind is often sent to

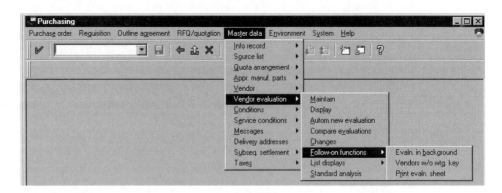

FIGURE 8.17   The follow-on functions menu and submenus (© SAP AG)

the vendor to inform them of their current status. To do this, the form provided with the standard version usually has to be adapted to your needs by an SAPscript programmer. The appearance is normally revised with a view to complying with the corporate identity (company logo, company lettering). In this context, you also have to decide whether the printout is to appear on company letterhead paper or on normal paper.

8.4.5 Evaluations

The menus encountered so far are used mainly to create, update and display a vendor evaluation. The section below contains descriptions of menus that enable more detailed evaluations (Fig. 8.18).

List displays

All list displays have in common that parameters can be used for selections. These parameters can have the effect, for example, that only certain vendors are displayed. The listing operation is always started with RUN. It is possible to branch into more detailed screens (spectacles icon) from the resulting lists (Fig. 8.18).

Ranking list of vendors

With the RANKING LISTS menu item, starting from the entry screen, you can obtain a display listing vendors with their overall scores and the scores for the main criteria (Fig. 8.19). You can select which vendors you want to see in the entry screen by specifying, for example, the number range of the vendors or by restricting the vendor class.

The ranking list can be sorted, which means that you can have a display of the list of vendors which is sorted in descending order based not only on the overall score but also on the main criteria. By marking a vendor and clicking on the EVALUATION button,

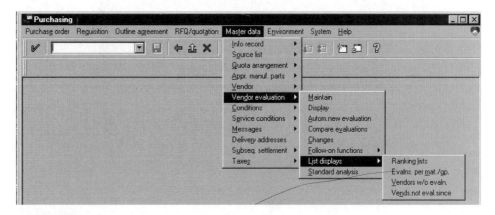

FIGURE 8.18 Submenus for the list displays menu (© SAP AG)

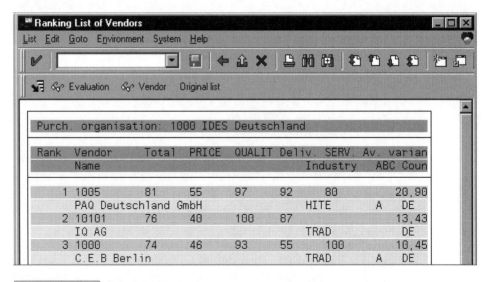

FIGURE 8.19   Ranking list of vendors (© SAP AG)

you receive a detailed assessment of this vendor based on the main and subcriteria. Furthermore, you can use the VENDOR button to display the vendor master record. The ORIGINAL LIST button returns you to the initial display.

Evaluation per material/group (Evalns. per mat./gp.)

This menu generates a ranking list of the vendors, whereby the vendor evaluation refers to a special material or group of goods. This is mainly of interest if you purchase the same material from different vendors.

Vendors without evaluation (Vendors w/o evaln.)

This evaluation enables display of a list of vendors for whom no vendor evaluation has yet been performed.

Vendors not evaluated since (Vends. not eval. since)

Here, you receive a list of vendors for whom no vendor evaluation has been performed for a certain period. To get this list, you have to enter the purchasing organization and the number range of the vendors to be evaluated, as well as a key date. The list then shows all the vendors that have not been newly evaluated since this date.

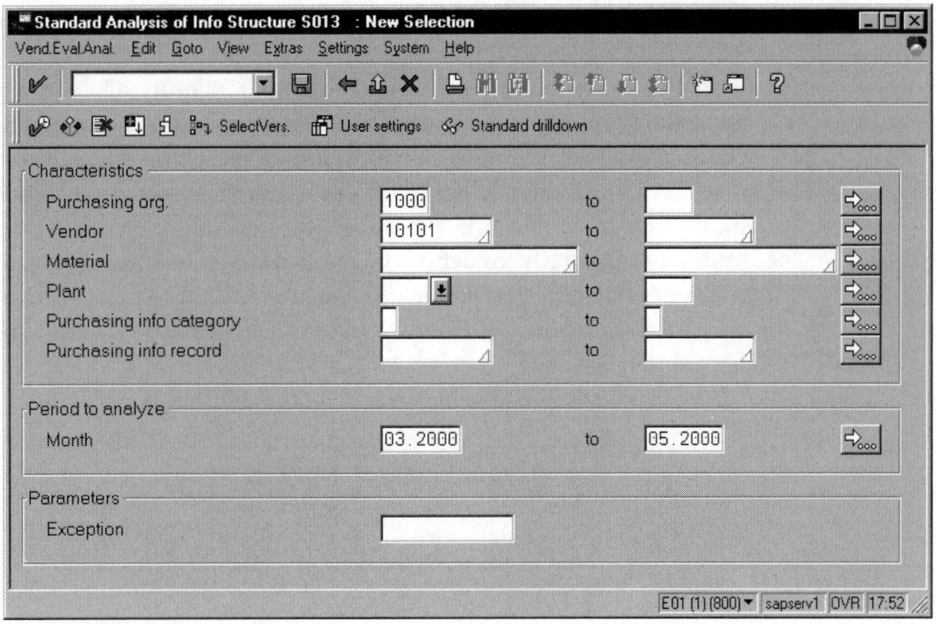

FIGURE 8.20 Standard analysis for vendor evaluation (© SAP AG)

Standard analysis

The standard analysis is integrated in the logistics information system (LIS). It contains a selection screen that can be used (with parameter setting options) to display vendors and their evaluation (Fig. 8.20). The scores can be evaluated over the total period (set in Customizing) or over a partial period (for example, one month or quarter).

Scores that can be used for the evaluation include:

- Quantity reliability.
- On-time delivery.
- Notification reliability (deviation from delivery advice).
- Delivery advice (not continued in Release 4.0B).
- Shipping instructions.
- Quality audit (not continued in Release 4.0B).
- Quality of general service/support.
- Timing of general service/support.

Unfortunately, the most frequently required evaluation, namely the evaluation based on quality of the goods receipt inspection, is not included in the standard version. To obtain this, you have to have the report modified by a programmer or have a new report created according to your own wishes.

8.5   STATISTICAL PROCESS CONTROL (SPC)

Each process is subject to deviation. Here, a distinction is made between random deviation and systematic deviation. In the case of random deviation, small deviations occur continuously, depending on the process parameters in each case, e.g. tools, operators, material, etc. Systematic deviation occurs on an irregular basis, and it can often be traced back to certain influences such as temperature or tool wear. A process that is under control is only influenced by random deviation. The systematic influences were removed during the development of the processes into a controlled process. Figure 8.21 shows a process with systematic deviation, indicating an increase in frequency at the upper tolerance limit.

The process improvement can be structured into three activities:

- Process analysis.
- Process monitoring.
- Process improvement.

In the process analysis, the process is observed and set using statistical methods. This includes a process efficiency analysis. If the process is stable, it is monitored using the methods of statistical process control, and any existing systematic deviations are removed. Finally, an attempt is made to optimize the process. To achieve this, statistical process monitoring methods are used to determine where random deviations occur and how these can be removed. These three focal points are run through several times to improve the process on a continuous basis and achieve control.

There is a wide variety of methods and tools available for process monitoring and improvement:

- Control charts.
- Histograms.
- Normal distribution.

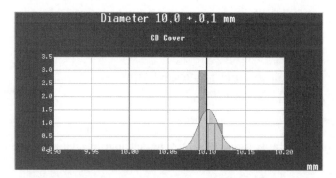

FIGURE 8.21   Example of a process with systematic deviation (© SAP AG)

- Run charts.
- Ishikawa diagrams (cause–effect diagrams).
- Pareto diagrams.
- Variance diagrams.
- Process efficiency analyses.

The Quality Management module of the R/3 system provides solid support for some of these tools.

Control charts

The core of statistical process control is the use of quality control charts (QCC). With statistical process control (SPC), you are able to analyse, monitor, control and improve processes.

The quality control charts are based on a technique developed by an American, Walter A. Shewhart (1891–1967), in 1924. With his 'control chart', the Western Electric Co. achieved a substantial reduction in the overheads required for inspection.

Usually, a control chart is used to monitor the production process. It can be used to establish very quickly whether a process is controlled or how changes have affected the process. However, it is also possible to use a control chart in the procurement process, for example in the case of multiple goods receipt inspections according to the delivery plan with regular call-ups. Here, the control chart can indicate whether the manufacturing process was controlled. In practical application, the critical variables are specified, samples of identical size are taken at fixed time intervals, the control variable is determined by measurement and calculation and entered in the control chart in graphical form. Normal control variables are:

- Mean value x.
- Standard deviation s.
- Range (R).
- Median (central value).
- Original value of a sample.
- Number of defective parts.
- Number of defects.

Each control variable can be selected as a track for a control chart. If two control variables are selected, this is a dual-track control chart. A typical example of a dual-track control chart is the x/s control chart (mean value and standard deviation). Depending on the type, a centre line, tolerance, warning and intervention limits can be entered in a control chart. The warning and intervention limits are calculated from a lead-in under real process conditions and entered in the control chart.

The classical types of control chart for quantitative (variable) characteristics are:

- *Acceptance chart* (e.g. mean value chart with tolerance). This takes its orientation from the tolerance and controls the scrap share of the process.
- *Shewhart chart* (e.g. standard deviation chart). This uses internal process parameters without taking account of the tolerance limits.

Typical control chart types for attribute (countable) characteristics are:

- In the case of defective units
    - p chart (share).
    - np chart (number – with constant sampling scope).

- In the case of defects per unit
    - u chart (share).
    - c chart (number – with constant sampling scope).

Figure 8.22 shows a few types of quality control chart that are already set up in the standard version.

In addition to these chart types, other quality control charts, for example, the pre-control chart, are also used in industry.

The control chart can therefore be used, in accordance with the definition of quality control, to monitor and analyse your processes, and finally to plan corrective measures. For the analysis, it is necessary to evaluate the created control charts regarding the following points:

- Is a natural process involved here?

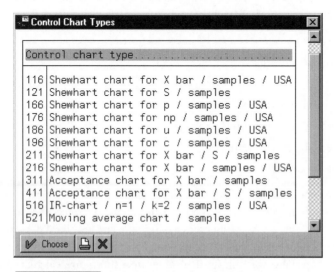

FIGURE 8.22 Types of quality control chart (© SAP AG)

■ Is there a recognizable trend (rising or falling tendency)?

■ Are there systematic or periodical fluctuations?

■ Do jumps in the flow of the process occur?

■ Does the process situation change over time?

■ Do strong, short-term deviations in the control variables occur?

■ Is the process stable (no unnaturally strong fluctuations)?

If the analysis or other quality information indicate that the process is not producing the desired results, it has to be changed, or all appropriate measures have to be taken to achieve a stable and controlled process. The success of these changes can, in turn, be checked using a quality control chart.

Histograms and normal distribution

A very indicative and useful tool (available without any special settings in the standard version) is the graphical display of the variable measured values as a histogram. In addition, the EDIT submenu can be used to show the normal distribution. An example is shown in Figure 8.23.

From the SAP graphic the GOTO | STATISTICAL VALUES submenu also enables you to calculate and display the process efficiency. In addition to the mean value and the standard deviation, the cp and the cpk values are determined if the target value and tolerance limits for the characteristic have been updated. These two values are the

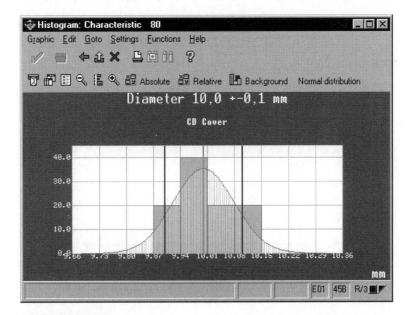

FIGURE 8.23 Histogram with normal distribution (© SAP AG)

process efficiency indices, whereby one is a measure of the deviation width of the processes (Is the process controlled?), and the other describes the position of the mean value of the distribution in comparison with the tolerance limits, thus indicating whether the process is efficient. For a controlled and efficient process, both values should be above 1.33. In many branches of industry, the minimum requirements for a process efficiency index are now 2.0 and higher!

A requirement for using the histogram is thus the variable recording of characteristic results as single values or classifications, as well as the maintenance of the tolerance limits and target value. It is not necessary to run a control chart to use the histogram. In the case of single values, the class division for the histogram is calculated by an internal algorithm. If the inspection results are already recorded in classes, this classification is also used as the basis for the histogram.

Run chart

The run chart is a simple method that can be used to indicate certain tendencies over time. This also makes it possible to display the measurement results of one or more samples, as can be seen in Figure 8.24.

In the SAP graphic, the target value and the upper and lower tolerance limits are shown as coloured lines. In the EDIT submenu, the measured points can be linked by a line or a regression line (using the smallest square method) can be set through the measured points.

It is also a requirement for this evaluation that variable measurement results have been recorded as single values.

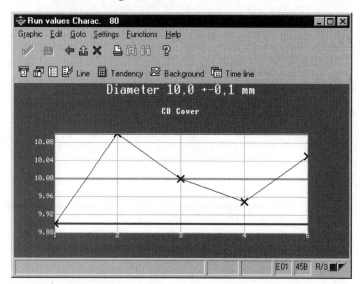

FIGURE 8.24 Run chart (© SAP AG)

| **8.6** | **DYNAMIC MODIFICATION OF INSPECTION SEVERITY AND INSPECTION FREQUENCY** |

The dynamic modification of inspection severity and inspection frequency is an ideal instrument of quality control. Starting from past experience (last inspection result or results), a rule can be set up to control the intensity of the next inspections. The basic principle here is quite simple: the better the quality, the lower the inspection overhead, i.e. the inspection severity and inspection frequency are reduced, including the skipping of inspections. If the quality is lower or if it has deteriorated, the inspection severity and inspection frequency are increased.

You can define so-called dynamic modification rules for these changes to the inspection intensity. These rules automatically alter the inspection severity and inspection frequency.

DIN ISO 2859–1 classifies inspection severity in the following levels:

- Reduced
- Normal
- Increased

With the dynamic modification rule, you specify not only the dynamic change between these inspection severities depending on the inspection result, but also whether goods receipt inspections or inspection characteristic are skipped entirely. Although the definition of these rules is not so simple, it can be achieved by an experienced inspection planner without too much effort.

If inspection plans are being used, the setting of the dynamic modification rules takes place in the inspection plan header. Here, you specify whether you want to have dynamic modification at lot level or at characteristics level. At lot level means that all the characteristics of the lot are inspected 'more intensively', even if only one characteristic result is defective. In the case of characteristic-based dynamic modification, each characteristic can change its inspection severity individually – dependent on each result. If there is no inspection plan, the dynamic modification can also be entered in the Quality view of the material master data.

You can use various dynamic modification rules to take account of the quality capability of a vendor in individual cases. For example, a vendor with full quality capability and a good audit result is assigned a dynamic modification rule that allows reduced inspection severity and frequent skipping in the goods receipt inspection. In the case of a lower-grade vendor, the inspections take place without skipping and with normal or intensified inspection severity until the vendor improves the delivered quality.

The switch between the individual inspection severities in the dynamic modification rule is referred to as a stage change. The current stage of a supply relationship can be seen in the quality level. By changing the quality level, it is also possible to change the stage of the dynamic modification rule manually. If, for example, the skip stage has been reached, the next inspection lot does not have to be inspected. Now, however, the inspection stage can be changed manually in the quality level in such a way that the next inspection lot does become subject to inspection.

Bear in mind that although the quality level is updated with the usage decision, this does not have a direct effect on the dynamic modification. Only the characteristic results are relevant to the dynamic modification. If, for example, you reject an inspection lot per usage decision without confirming defects in the characteristic beforehand, the dynamic modification rule acts as if everything were OK. It is only when at least one characteristic has been rejected that the dynamic modification rule of the setting reacts for the Not-OK case.

TIP The dynamic modification rule can be entered in the inspection type in the material master data in the case of inspections without a plan. However, if there is an inspection plan, it is more flexible to define the dynamic modification rule in the plan header. Every change to the plan that is made for the purposes of quality control thus has a direct effect on the next goods receipt. Changes in the material master data, on the other hand, only take effect for the next purchase order for the material.

8.7 BATCH LOGS

A central requirement of good manufacturing practices (GMP) for pharmaceutical products is that a processing log is to be created for each manufactured batch.

The GMP guidelines originate from the United States, where they were issued by the Food and Drug Administration (FDA) and are legally binding for the pharmaceutical industry. Over the years, the guidelines have developed into an internationally applicable standard, which must be complied within a great many countries.

TABLE 8.3 Data in the batch log

Data of the batch log	Allocation in the R/3 system
The relevant parts of the manufacturing instruction and process instruction	Process order and bill of materials
In-process and post-process checks, the names of the inspector, and the inspection results	Inspection lot for in-process inspection and for goods receipt
Actual data for the process	Process notifications and manufacturing instructions

In the R/3 system, the GMP guidelines have been followed to the extent that the requirement for a processing log has been met. This has been implemented in the Production Planning Processing Industry (PP-PI) module by the batch log (see Table 8.3).

The origins of the batch log are the process order and the quality-relevant data that is created in this context. The essential requirements of the GMP guidelines are met in the associated print list. These include the identification of each printed page with the batch number, material number and sample quantity, numbering of the pages, and a special identification of the last page.

The batch log is only created when the production and inspection of the batch has been completed. It can then be transferred to an optical archive using SAP ArchiveLink. The archived logs are approved with a digital signature. The system can be set in such a way that the usage decision for the goods receipt inspection lot of the batch can only be made and the batch status can only be changed to 'released' after approval of a batch log.

8.8 QUALITY COSTS

8.8.1 Basic principles

There are a variety of important reasons for dealing with the subject of quality costs in the context of quality management (cf. Steinbach W. and Masing, *Manual of Quality Assurance* 1998):

- The quality costs, resulting from the costs of quality inspection, the additional costs caused by defective products, and the costs of quality planning and control, amount to a significant proportion of the total manufacturing costs.

- The quality costs are an important indicator of quality-related and thus commercial weaknesses in the company. Analysing these means exposing starting points for improvement in the quality of the products and the efficiency of the company.

- Top management is more willing to appreciate the necessity of projects and measures for quality improvement and quality promotion if the arguments are underscored by business data such as costs and profitability.

The quality costs are usually split into the following categories:

- Appraisal costs.
- Defect costs.
- Defect prevention costs.

Appraisal costs are the costs of product inspections within the framework of quality assurance. These include the inspection personnel, costs for premises and infrastructure, as well as costs for measuring equipment and facilities. Appraisal costs can include:

- Goods receipt inspection.

- Quality inspection in Production.

- Intermediate and final inspections.

- Audit inspections and product audits.

- Laboratory analyses.

- Approval inspections for prototypes and pre-series.

Defect costs are costs incurred when products do not meet the set quality requirements. In the case of defect costs, a distinction is made between internal and external defect costs:

- Internal defect costs:

  - Scrap.

  - Rework.

  - Value reduction due to low quality.

  - Defect costs due to short quantities.

  - Defect costs due to sorting and repeat inspections.

- External defect costs:

  - Handling complaints to vendors.

  - Settling warranty claims.

  - Consequential costs due to reconstruction, delay and standstills.

  - Product liability costs.

Defect prevention costs are costs that come about due to measures within the framework of quality assurance designed to prevent the occurrence of defects. Some examples of defect prevention costs:

- Personnel for quality management.

- Quality planning, inspection planning.

- System audits, vendor audits.

- Quality capability studies.

- Quality reporting and quality analysis for quality control.

- Quality promotion and quality training (KVP, CIP).

- Vendor evaluation and assessment.

- Vendor development and promotion.

8.8.2 Cost and output accounting

The data for quality costs comes from the company accounting department, in particular from cost and output accounting. This will be explained at this point (cf. Steinbach W. and Masing, *Manual of Quality Assurance* 1998).

Costs are money values of quantities of production factors (output, resources and materials) as well as money values of third-party services, taxes and duties that are used to generate the company output.

Cost types

In a first step, cost accounting – as so-called 'cost-type accounting' – records the production factors consumed in the company, then evaluates them and classifies them into cost types according to their origin. The most important groups of cost types are:

- Wage costs (wages, salaries, taxes).
- Material costs (raw materials, resources and consumables).
- Investment costs (depreciation, interest).
- Costs for services (power, water, cleaning, etc.).

Cost centre accounting

In the second step, the cost accounting function uses cost centre accounting to distribute the costs of the individual cost types in a period to the individual areas of the company that incurred the costs. For this purpose, the various areas and departments are divided into so-called 'cost centres'. The recording of the appraisal costs and the quality planning and control costs is based on the figures for these cost centres.

Cost unit accounting

Finally, in the third step, the costs distributed to those who caused them are allocated by cost unit accounting to the individual company output, i.e., the manufactured products or services provided. Two important items of information are used by cost unit accounting for the quality cost appraisal:

- In order to ascertain the defect costs of scrap and rework parts, the manufacturing costs determined by cost unit accounting for the various process steps of the part are used.
- Ascertaining the manufacturing costs per unit enables the evaluation of the output of a manufacturing area per accounting period. The figures are required as reference variables for analysis of the quality costs.

With these three partial accounts, the company cost and output accounting provides the most important data for the quality cost elements.

8.8.3 Recording quality costs

For cost centre accounting, separate cost centres for the various types of quality costs must have been set up. In this context, it is relatively simple to allocate the appraisal costs in Procurement to a goods receipt inspection department or inspection area. This clear allocation is falsified by non-related activities that are usually performed in these departments, for example sorting work, which should really be allocated to the defect costs. It becomes more difficult when allocating planning tasks for the recording of costs for quality planning. As the tasks in planning are part and parcel of the general management tasks of staff from Development, Construction/Engineering, Quality Assurance and Production, allocation to cost centres is not possible. Frequently, the costs of the cost centre quality assurance and goods receipt inspection are roughly apportioned in equal measure to quality inspection and quality planning.

In the final analysis, cost accounting is not very suitable for recording defect costs, as the costs are incurred either as additional costs in the various cost types and cost centres or as reduction in earnings. Reduction in earnings means that the manufacturing costs of a product incurred have no corresponding revenue from the market and thus no corresponding credit.

In order to record the various defect cost types, a supplementary system must be set up. The system must be able to record the defect causes and to distinguish between the various defect cost types. One possibility is cost unit accounting, whereby the costs over and above the manufacturing costs are reported as defect costs. Another possibility is in recording the defect costs by means of separate orders, which are grouped and allocated accordingly at a later date.

8.8.4 Evaluation of quality costs

In order to be able to use the recording of quality costs for quality control and for the purpose of continuous improvement, meaningful evaluations are required. These are intended to indicate quality-related and commercial weaknesses and to provide support in locating these weaknesses. This is why the quality cost reports should be clearly laid out and presented with informative and appealing graphics.

Comparisons are a frequently used method of analysing weaknesses:

- Comparison between different areas/companies (internal/external).
- Comparison of various periods or over the course of time.
- Comparison between planned and actual costs.
- Comparison between different products.

Evaluation tools such as ABC analysis or Pareto diagrams can be used to determine the main causes and reduce the weaknesses with targeted measures.

The quality cost evaluations should be current (weekly/monthly), should be sent to a fixed distribution list and have a uniform structure in order to ensure quick orientation and good comparability over a certain period.

8.8.5 Implementation possibilities with R/3

The integrated R/3 system supports the above-mentioned business requirements or wishes in a wide variety of ways with the close interaction of its Quality Management (QM) and Controlling (CO) components.

Cost centre accounting can be performed in full using the Controlling (CO) component, without involving the Quality Management (QM) component. However, when the R/3 Quality Management component is used, the inspection planning and assigned work centres can be used to achieve much more accurate recording of appraisal costs. In precisely the same way as the times for inspection equipment in work planning, setting up and inspection times of personnel can be planned for each inspection operation and recorded with confirmations. This means that the appraisal costs can be recorded in relation to material or orders and are thus available for more detailed evaluations.

The QM order is a tool that is available for recording defect costs. In conjunction with the quality notification, you can create QM orders and confirm the same expenditure in the form of personnel (times) and material (costs). By allocating the QM orders, you can distinguish between internal and external defect costs, as well as group and evaluate the costs according to various criteria such as material, vendor and customer. The cost report for a QM order can be displayed from the USAGE DECISION screen.

CHAPTER 9

Quality notification

BASIC PRINCIPLES

The communication of quality-related complaints is one of the touchstones of every customer–vendor relationship, whether this is an internal or external relationship. First of all, events of this kind are always accompanied by more or less unpleasant circumstances, which means that people are unwilling to go into the details of the subject of 'complaints handling'. Even the standard reference works on the topic of quality assurance are pretty wary of the subject. In the course of adopting customer-oriented processes, the experts have approached complaints essentially from the point of view of Sales and Distribution, and have formulated suitably flashy slogans such as: 'Exploit complaints to improve your business relationship!' Methods with a practical approach have emerged primarily in the automobile industry. In this context, the method of the 8-D Report developed by Ford is a milestone in the standardization of complaint procedures.

The will to re-engineer the complaints process is not enough on its own. Anyone who examines the overall business context will notice how complaints represent a draw on resources for the areas of Materials Management, Production Planning and Control, Sales and Distribution and of course Quality Management. This mainly generates the need for smooth organization, supported by suitable tools, such as computerized notification systems. Furthermore, there are not only external customer complaints, but just as many internally reported problems and complaints directed at vendors (Fig. 9.1).

FIGURE 9.1   Notification types for Quality Management

From a business point of view in the areas of Production Planning and Control, detecting and remedying faults in the manufacturing chain at the earliest possible stage is decisive. As a rule of thumb, you can expect one cost concentration per work step. A suitable notification system in the production environment supports manufacturing, unmasks process weaknesses, and provides the necessary transparency as regards the amount of errors and defects.

In most cases, several areas of a company and members of staff are involved in handling a complaint. When a customer complaint is registered, the process moves from a starting point outside the company, through the processing by the addressee, and returns to the external exit point. This requires intra-company communication with the appropriate communication channels.

At the outset, a complaint is provided with a number to ensure its clear identification. This is supplemented by reference objects, for example the sales order, customer number, delivery note number, etc., and additional reference data. In the ideal case, the organizational responsibilities with regard to further processing are clearly defined. One person should be appointed to bear the main responsibility; the others involved should have clearly defined tasks when a complaint occurs. Basically, complaints handling is similar to a small project with a defined start and a – hopefully – successful end.

The main factors in the internal chain of events are fast and effective information distribution and immediate initiation of the correct measures. The basis for correct decisions is formed by both experience and access to the knowledge acquired from cases of complaint that have already been dealt with. The measures taken and the handling period now constitute the information that has to be passed on to the complaining party at lightning speed and – very important – in the right form. The evaluation of the number of complaints then provides us with important indications of the weak points of the products concerned and the performance capability and efficiency of the company. The fact that all of these requirements have to be met gives you some idea of the complexity of the task. Without the deployment of high-performance software, complaints management and handling would be inconceivable in large companies.

Of particular interest with regard to an improved customer orientation is the use of a computerized complaints management in service companies, energy providers, banks, insurance companies, etc. (cf. Drewes in Masing, *Quality Assurance in the Banking Business*). The examples below are based on logistic core processes, and can thus be applied without any special effort in all commercial areas of use, whether in retail and wholesale, production or services.

9.2   QUALITY NOTIFICATIONS IN THE R/3 SYSTEM

The official allocation of the quality notification to the QM application component gives the initial impression that it is a separate QM application within the logistic processes. The notification system within the R/3 system is in fact intra-modular. In its shipped version, the R/3 system contains the notification types listed in Table 9.1.

In the area of logistics, the R/3 notification system provides worthwhile integration potential. In contrast to business events, where it is often the case that only one organizational unit is involved in the processing in a software system and an organization change does not improve the process, it must be the aim of a quality notification to structure a workflow process across several specialist departments. The main task of the

TABLE 9.1	Notification types (quality notifications printed in bold)	
F1	**Customer error**	**Quality notification**
F2	**Vendor error**	**Quality notification**
F3	**Material error**	**Quality notification**
M1	Maintenance request	Plant maintenance
M2	Malfunction report	Plant maintenance
M3	Activity report	Plant maintenance
MQ	Malfunction report from QM	Plant maintenance
Q1	**Customer complaint**	**Quality notification**
Q2	**Vendor fault list**	**Quality notification**
Q3	**Internal problem notification**	**Quality notification**
S1	Service notification	Service notification
S2	Activity report	Service notification
S3	Service request	Service notification
S4	Service: Mat/SerNo	Service notification
S5	PM Service request	Service notification
Z3	**Gen. i. problem notif.**	**Quality notification**

R/3 notification system is to manage external and internal complaints concerning vendors and customers and to trace problems in the production environment (Fig. 9.2).

As the quality notification is mainly used in the context of 'non-quality', a few more aspects of active quality control using the R/3 notification system are listed below:

▨ Organization of the company notification system.

▨ Coordination with the customer in the automotive field with regard to the QS 9000 requirements.

▨ Support of processes initialized by the FMEA team.

For the above areas, your own notification types can be added to those of the shipped version of the system, thus enabling an individualized notification structure. Each notification type can be set in many ways to suit the requirements of the user and, as of Release 4.5, they each provide simple possibilities to communicate with applications outside the R/3 system, for example e-mail applications. As far as its performance capability is concerned, the R/3 notification system fares well when compared with external systems specially developed for this purpose. The advantage of an integrated application is particularly strong as regards the quality notification. Practically all of the data from logistics that has to be processed can be loaded into the application by mouse-click, and it is possible to navigate in the logistics objects involved simply by selecting them.

Furthermore, the notification system also extends to the PM (Plant Maintenance)

FIGURE 9.2   The interplay of the components and objects of a quality notification enable processing of the quality problem

and SM (Service Management) application components. The special features of customer service tasks have developed their own forms of notification, which are nonetheless based on the same systematic structure as the quality notifications.

As described in Chapter 1, 'Management systems, standards and SAP R/3', the notification system can be used to implement the requirements of corrective and preventative measures in ISO 9000ff.

9.2.1 Scenario: Complaints management with the quality notification

We shall now use a typical case to trace the course of a customer complaint. In this example, it will become apparent that the company Duff & Sons Ltd has again delivered parts that are only a very fine line away from the specification you have set.

The case study deals first of all with a notification of the type Customer complaint Q1 from a delivery of 10,000 assemblies of the CD cover, the same example as used in Chapter 6, 'Quality and inspection planning'. It is the CD pick up inside the assembly that is causing problems. The pick up does not hold, and the CDs fall out when the cover is opened. You have already used part of the materials, assembled finished units for a sales order, and delivered to your customer. The customer is extremely dissatisfied. In this case, the purchaser lodging the complaint contacts your Sales department and demands an immediate new shipment, otherwise it is assumed that this customer will threaten to impose a contractual penalty.

Table 9.2 provides you with an overview of the events surrounding the notification to help you arrange the subsequent tasks.

We will use a standard installation of the R/3 notification system to monitor the case and create a complete documentation and defect analysis in the notification, involving the following aspects:

- Defect type.
- Defect location.
- Defect cause.
- Tasks.

The aim should be to satisfy the customer as quickly as possible and to eliminate the defect in the future, if possible in the course of preventive quality assurance. Our flow organization (any other sequence could also be used) dictates that an incoming customer complaint with reference to a sales document is first processed by Sales and Distribution. As complaints usually arrive here, the notification header and the subject of the complaint are also filled out by Sales and Distribution.

In the processing flow for this example, it was also agreed that the Quality department should be responsible for all subsequent inputs and completion of the notification. The consequence of this in our case is that the responsibility for monitoring tasks lies in the area of quality management, thus relieving the Sales

TABLE 9.2	Diagram of a quality notification flow		
Individual step	**Content of activities**	**Navigation in the notification**	**Flow of work**
Receipt of the complaint			
Start of relationships	Select reference objects Select reference documents Select organizational unit Select partners	Notification header, reference	Start
Transfer of descriptions into the notification			
Document the subject	Select type of notification Description of the subject Enter quantities concerned	Subject	Transfer
Record and analyse defects			
Defect analysis	Select defect type Select defect location Select cause	Items	Transfer
Task administration			
Initiate and monitor tasks	Create immediate task Schedule immediate task Create other tasks Schedule other tasks	Tasks, item tasks	Transfer
Activities administration			
Define other activities	Create activities Schedule activities	Activities	Transfer
Conclusion of complaint and archiving			
Conclude complaint	Perform completion check Perform check of success Determine costs Set completed flag	All areas	End

department of any further management of the notification. In your company, complaints handling can of course be organized in a completely different way. We therefore strongly recommend in this context that you perform a precise business process modeling together with all those involved. In the section 'Quality notifications in Sales and Distribution' later in this chapter, we have illustrated a simple example.

After you have been able to obtain a description of the situation from your customer by telephone, ask the customer to send a short written note by fax or e-mail, so that you can make reference to it in the quality notification.

Creating a notification

A notification is created during the first telephone call. This is achieved in the menu path LOGISTICS | QUALITY MANAGEMENT | QUALITY NOTIFICATIONS | CREATE QUALITY NOTIFICATION. Select the notification type Q1, Customer complaint. This opens a dialog window (see Fig. 9.3), in which you enter the document numbers from the sales

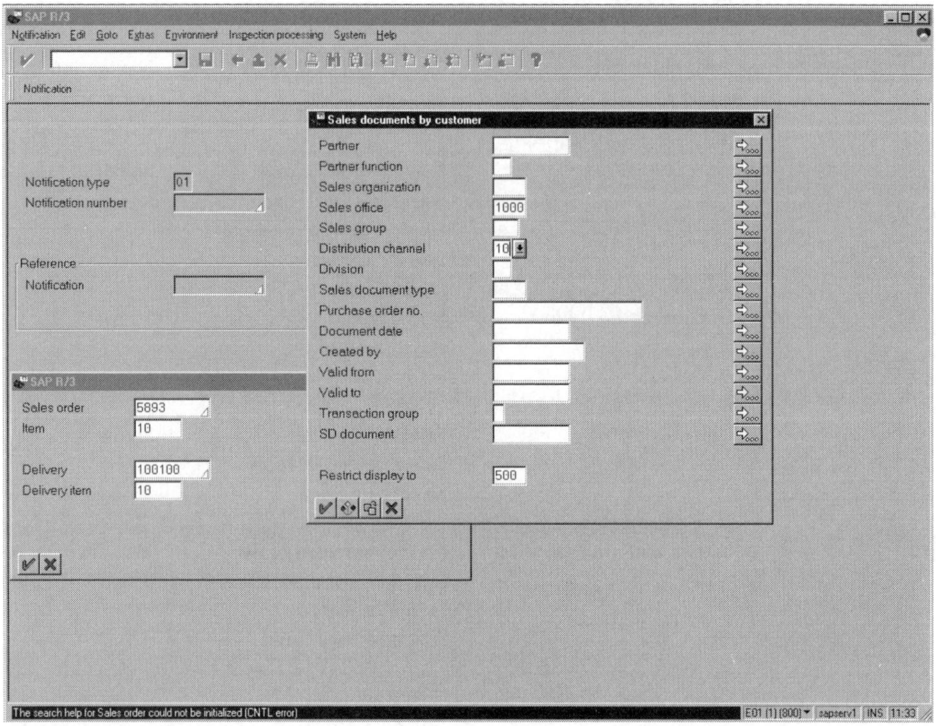

FIGURE 9.3   Entry dialog for the notification type Q1, Customer complaint (© SAP AG)

order or delivery. Here, it is important also to enter the item numbers, as the system is otherwise unable to find the content of the document, for example the material ordered, and cannot then include it in the notification. If you now press ENTER to confirm, the system transfers the most important document data for the quality notification into the notification header.

CUSTOMIZING TIP

The dialog you have just seen can be adapted to your process with relative precision using the Customizing tables. For the example, we have chosen 130, Sales documents, as the entry screen. There are a total of eight different customer subscreens available, and they are described in detail in the context help. For the notification types with reference to Procurement, Production, and Sales and Distribution, there are separate entry points with references to the documents in each case. However, filling out the subscreens is not mandatory, and this can be skipped without causing any problems if, for example, the data is not at hand. The document data can also be used to adopt targeted information into the notification retrospectively.

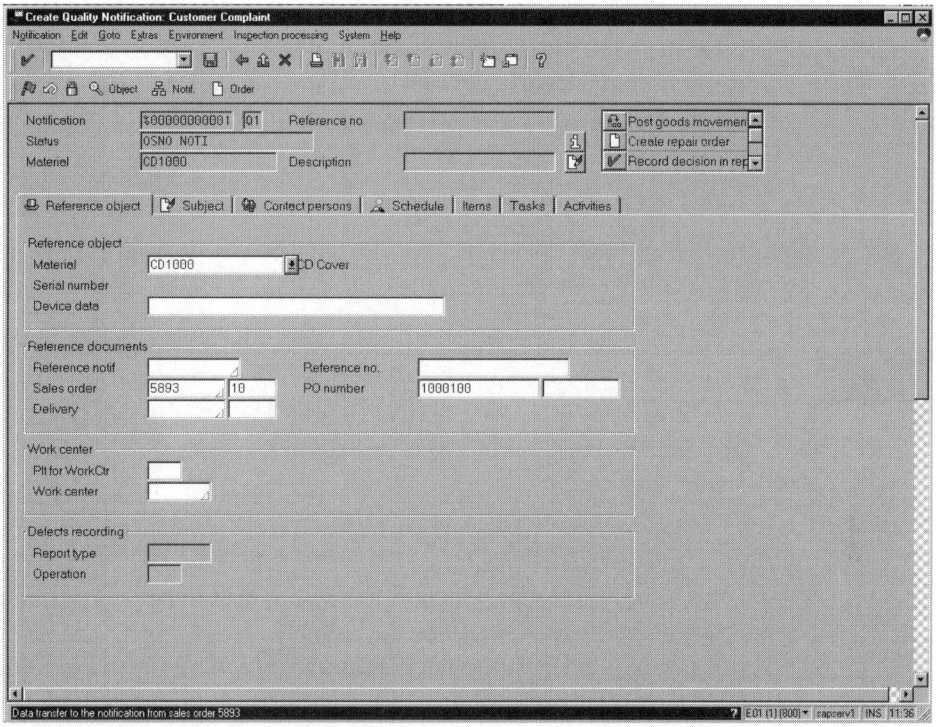

FIGURE 9.4 Notification header with the reference objects of Sales and Distribution
(© SAP AG)

Note

As of Release 4.5, the user interface of the quality notification has been changed to tab index cards in the QM application component. The screens shown in this chapter have all been created using this release. If a tab is mentioned below, a section (usually framed by a thin line) is meant in the context of Releases 3.x to 4.0. NOTIFICATION HEADER refers to the area above the tabs and the REFERENCE OBJECTS tab (see Fig. 9.4). Up to Release 4.5, these two areas belonged together in the HEADER DATA section of a quality notification.

The notification number is assigned by the system in accordance with our settings of the number range interval. With the input of the sales order, we already reference - depending on the system setting – the associated data such as purchase order number, material number, production date, delivery quantity, delivery date, etc. If there are already notifications for the same material or customer, a message is issued, and we obtain an overview of similar complaints with the same reference.

The customer already assigned a master data record in the R/3 system is all that is required as the mandatory partner (see section 'Partner data of the notification' below) of the customer complaint. It is of course possible to set other partners of the notification as mandatory or optional partners in Customizing beforehand. As we do not yet know at this stage – on conclusion of the telephone call – where the defect lies, other steps and a more precise analysis must take place. To achieve this, the department performing the initial activities – in our example Sales and Distribution – adds additional information to the tab (section) SUBJECT.

Filling out the notification header

In the notification header, we fill out the tab (section) SUBJECT: here, the entry COMPLAINT is selected from the CODING (i.e. the subject) selection list.

TIP

For the sake of clarity, where possible, place only two or three logically separate entries in the basic data catalog CODING in the selection list (see Fig. 9.5). Here it is a question of determining as quickly as possible whether a complaint is really involved or whether it is only a normal inquiry or even only a note.

In the description field, we enter: 'CD pick up set too soft'. The long text could be: 'Defect cause not yet known, but Duff & Sons delivered material with this defect on two occasions last year. However, as the last five deliveries were without defects, the inspections are in the Skip mode (inspection waiver) and this is why they were not inspected.'

With this entry, processing of the notification in our example on the part of Sales and Distribution is concluded for the moment. Here, it is assumed that measures will

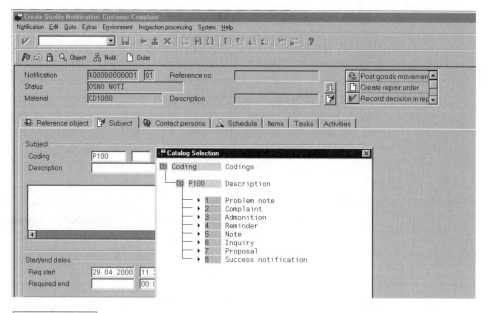

FIGURE 9.5   Subject of the notification (© SAP AG)

now be initiated and monitored by Quality Management. Naturally, we believe it is important to agree on how the complaint can be processed quickly, but now it is the turn of the QM department, who have to perform a defect analysis. Perhaps a more detailed analysis will discover the defect quickly, and under certain circumstances an appropriate task that is carried out rapidly will prevent further damage.

Defect analysis

We begin immediately with an initial defect analysis to exclude the possibility that the same defect occurs once again in the current deliveries. In the processing of the quality notification, it is also possible to initiate an immediate task first (e.g. 'Deliver new parts immediately' or 'Delivery stop') and then to continue with the defect analysis.

We navigate through the menu bar of the notification to the ITEMS tab, where we can perform the defect analysis. We create a defect item by selecting an entry from the selection list of defects. A double-click on a list entry sets up the detailed view. The structure of the quality notification provides a defect item for each defect in a complaint. We will therefore refer to *items* or *notification items* from now on. The defect analysis relies on a well-prepared defect catalog structure and demands the selection of a defect code for each item. However, you can add a freely defined text in short or long form to each entry. The same applies to the defect location and the defect cause, which we assign to the item next. The number of defects can refer to the number of defects on one or more parts, but does not yet mean the number of defective delivery units (pieces, packages, etc.). These entries are made in the fields DefQty (intern.)/DefQty (extern.).

A detailed examination of the sample sent by our customer has shown that the CD pick up does not perform its intended function, as the circumference of the pick up is too small. We create one or more defect items by selecting the individual codings from the catalogs already created, for example:

- Defect loc.: Inner case with CD pick up.
- Defect: Function CD hold.
- Defect cause: Material vendor (see Fig. 9.6).

Displaying assemblies

If a defect in a material from an assembly is involved, selecting DEFECT ITEM | DETAIL | ASSEMBLY ICON enables you to enter the material number of the defective part of an assembly as supplementary information. The term 'assembly' refers to the bill of materials (CD1000); the graphical display of the associated bill of materials appears (see Fig. 9.7). In the case of more complex assemblies, this function allows the defect location to be shown in a hierarchy. On the first level, a part of the assembly is specified as the defect location; on the second level, selection of an entry from the defect location catalog shows the occurrence of the defect in more detail.

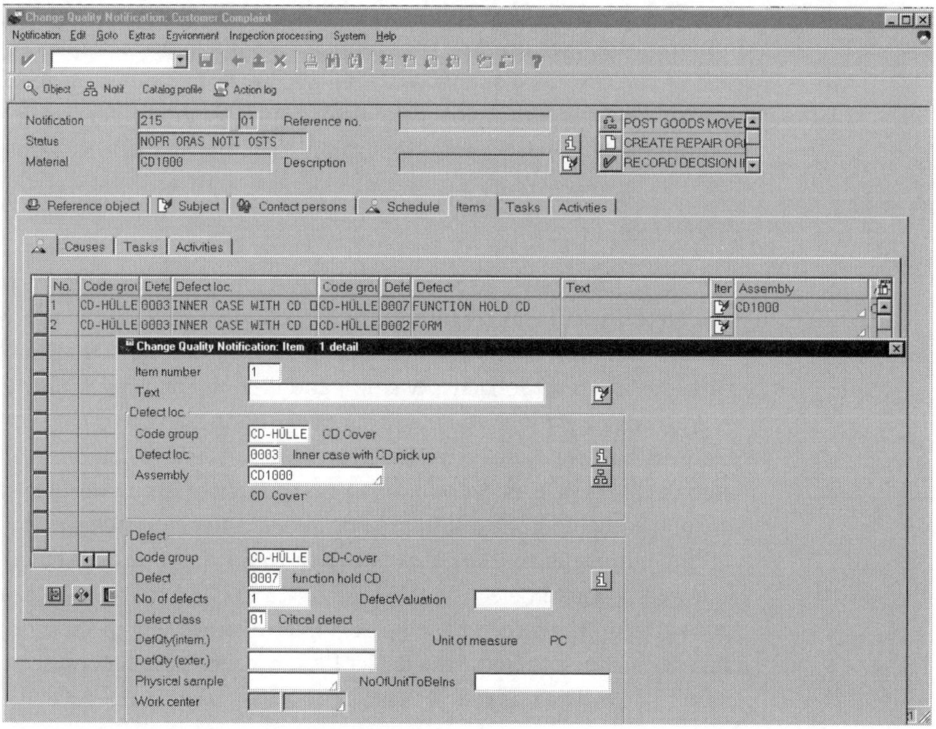

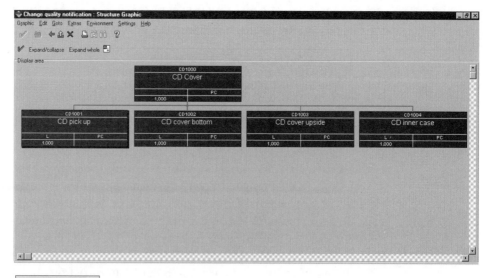

FIGURE 9.6   Item detail (© SAP AG)

FIGURE 9.7   Defect Item with reference to the bill of materials (© SAP AG)

CUSTOMIZING TIP

Unfortunately, the catalog types used do not provide the function SELECTED SETS. This means that the a code must always be selected from the entire pool of code groups. However, particularly in large companies, a separation between various business areas makes sense for a defect analysis; here, a selection of all the existing defect codes would quickly become confusing.

The solution lies in using a catalog profile. First of all, a defined catalog profile has to be assigned to certain code groups in Customizing. In our example, we could create our own notification type for domestic and foreign sales units on the basis of the Q1 standard notification. In the next step, we create a separate catalog profile that is suitable for each notification type, and assign it to the notification type, as can be seen in Table 9.3.

Filling out the fields for defective quantities or the simplified summarized defects recording enables us to evaluate the extent of damage later.

Informing customers using the 8D report

One of the most important tasks of a customer-oriented notification process is the report to the complaining party regarding the general situation, the processing status and the reference number that can be used to call up further information regarding the complaint. In this connection, the generally recognized 8D report method from the automobile industry can be of service. As of Release 4.5, the standard version provides support with a separate form for the 8D method. If you are planning a release change for later, the 8D report can be mapped using form programming in SAPscript; the example in Fig. 9.8 might provide you with a model. All the values in the fields are taken from the quality notification and processed using SAPscript programming.

TABLE 9.3   Allocation of notification type to catalog profile

	Notification type short text	Catalog profile	Catalog profile short text	Catalog type	Code groups
CD	Customer complaint, domestic	CUSDOM	Customer complaint, domestic	5	1–2
				9	1–2
				E	1–2
CF	Customer complaint, foreign	CUSFOR	Customer complaint, foreign	5	3–4
				9	3–4
				E	3–4

Problem description

The solution of operational problems or the implementation of proposed improvements, e.g. within the framework of a continuous improvement process (CIP), often fails due to a lack of systematic procedures and consistent documentation and examination of the individual solution steps. The 8D method and the 8D report can provide valuable assistance here. The application of the 8D report has already proved very effective in many companies and branches of industry, for example in the automobile industry.

What is the 8D method?

The 8D problem-solving method (also referred to as the 'eight-step plan') is a sequence of eight steps (disciplines) that should be run through as soon as a problem becomes apparent. If it is handled correctly, the method helps to find a prompt and complete solution to the problem involved. Its fundamentally fact-oriented approach ensures that solutions, decisions and planning are based on hard data, guaranteeing that the real core of the current problem is solved and that the symptoms are not merely covered up. At the same time, the 8D report that is to accompany the process serves as a monitor of progress and a catalyst that ensures that all the steps of the 8D processes are run through in full.

Creating the 8D report

The 8D report is updated and provided with the associated enclosures by a single person on conclusion of each stage. It reflects the current status of the problem solving and is a dynamic document. The report filled out in this way is stored in a generally accessible archive system and is available to teams and individuals who might one day have to deal with similar problems.

The basic principle is that 8D is a problem-solving process supported by a certain form of report, thus specifying and ensuring a uniform standard for the company and the vendors.

Reasons for ineffective problem solving

The 8D process was developed to increase the efficiency of problem solving in the areas of production and development. Ineffective problem solving is caused by any of the following factors:

- *Incorrect description of the problem*

  A clear, detailed description of the problem is necessary. An unambiguous description and strict definition is a requirement that must be met before a team can process a problem effectively.

░ *Rushing the problem-solving process*

In the problem-solving process, steps are skipped inappropriately in order to enable a rapid solution.

░ *Poor cooperation in the team*

Not all members of the team work actively on the problem, which means that the team cannot record all the causes of the problem.

░ *No logical sequence in the process*

There is no systematic approach to setting priorities, performing analyses and investigating the problem.

░ *Lack of technical skills*

The persons involved lack knowledge of the working techniques and tools that support the problem-solving process.

░ *Impatience on the part of management*

A lack of knowledge of the problem-solving process and an underestimation of the required work overhead leads management to set an unrealistic schedule. This pressure leads to the employees' performing low-quality analyses.

░ *Errors in identifying the basic cause*

Sometimes a possible cause is prematurely assumed to be the basic cause, and the investigation of the problem is concluded. However, the problem crops up again later because the real cause was not properly clarified.

░ *No implementation of permanent improvement measures*

Although the basic cause may have been found, no or only inadequate improvement measures were initiated. For permanent improvement measures to be effective, support on the part of management in approving costs and implementation of the measures is required.

░ *Lack of documented information*

There is not enough information on the current problem or on similar problems that might have appeared in the past.

The eight disciplines (steps)

0 *Get a clear picture of the problem!* Consider what problem is involved from the point of view of the customer, and check whether a procedure in accordance with 8D is appropriate.

1 *Tackle the problem!* Enter the name of the person that started the 8D report and supplement the header data (problem, ref. no., start date, status on (date), part description).

2 *Describe the problem!* Define the problem of the internal or external customer as precisely as possible. Work out the core of the problem and quantify it. Collect and analyse statistical data.

3 *Initiate temporary measures (tasks) to limit the damage and check their effect!* Initiate measures (tasks) that, where possible, keep the effects of the problem away from internal or external customers until a permanent solution has been found. Continuously check the efficacy of these temporary measures and, if appropriate, initiate more tasks.

4 *Determine the basic cause(s) and check whether you have found the right one(s)!* Check whether the task can be performed. Search for all possible causes that might explain the occurrence of the problem. Specify the likely cause(s) and use comparisons with the problem description and the existing data to check whether a likely cause is the basic cause. Prove your assumption with tests and experiments.

5 *Specify improvement measures (tasks) and check whether they work!* Search for all possible tasks that could remove the cause(s) of the problem and thus solve the problem. Choose the optimum permanent improvement measure(s) and prove by means of appropriate tests that the permanent improvement measures selected really do solve the problem from the customer's point of view and that there are no undesirable side-effects. If necessary, specify tasks for contingencies based on risk analysis.

6 *Introduce the improvement measure(s) and check on their effects!* Draw up a plan of action for the implementation of the selected improvement measure(s), and specify the continuous checks that are to ensure the cause of the problem has really been eliminated. Implement the plan of action, observe the effects and, if appropriate, implement the tasks planned for contingencies.

7 *Specify measures (tasks) that prevent recurrence of the problem!* Change the management and control systems, instructions and usual procedures to prevent recurrence of the same or similar problems. Identify improvement possibilities and initiate process improvements.

8 *Conclusion of the 8D report!* Completion by the Quality department head (date, name).

TIP The 8D report can in fact be used at any time within the notification process for customer information. In this context, it doesn't matter whether it contains all the relevant information. You can indicate the current processing status of the complaint on the form. This means that the 8D report is a 'living' form that you can use for a wide variety of communication purposes without deviating from a certain standard in form and sequence.

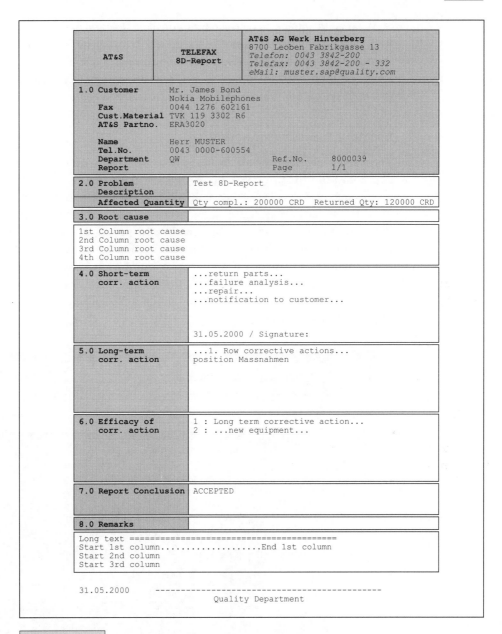

FIGURE 9.8   Example of an 8D form in the R/3 system

Immediate task

The next step is to extend the notification by recording an immediate task, depending on the cause of the damage and the precise defect analysis: select TASKS from the tab in the notification header.

What is the difference between an immediate task and an item task? The other tasks from defect analysis should not be used here, but rather, for example, tasks involving immediate distribution of information, submission of a complaint number to the customer, creation of a response plan, etc. You can therefore use this method to set up a two-stage programme of tasks if this appears to make sense for your complaints handling.

Control of tasks using the worklist

The system automatically places all the tasks we create within the notification in a special notification list, the WORKLIST (see Fig. 9.9). This assumes that the employee responsible performs his or her assigned task within the predefined framework and views the worklist. Here, 'traffic-light' functions signal the state of the individual tasks of the notification, and we are informed of the period for completion. We can immediately branch from the list into the notification by mouse-click. The worklist is a report that can be assigned parameters on an individual basis in many areas, i.e. it is well adapted to the needs of the user. Furthermore, there is also the option of creating simple graphics from the overview, providing information, for example, on the focal point of the list of tasks.

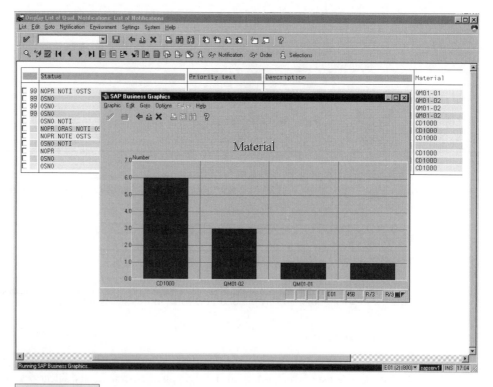

FIGURE 9.9 Worklist (© SAP AG)

The immediate task initiated contains not only the list but also detailed information that can be called up in a separate window by double-clicking on the item.

Here, as is the case for all list functions, it is a matter of taste whether you work with the detailed view or with the configurable table control list. After the planned start and finish of the task and a person responsible have been entered, the task is saved by returning to the notification header (see Fig. 9.10).

As Quality Management has extended the notification in our example to include an immediate task, the various specialist departments must now handle the case. At this point, we will start an internal workflow process in connection with the quality notification – as an alternative to the process control via the worklist illustrated above (see Fig. 9.9). We can run the workflow process with or without the SAP module BUSINESS WORKFLOW in R/3 and illustrate this in simplified form with three variations:

1   *SAP Business Workflow is already in productive use*
In this case, the SAP BW module is started with predefined rules. The employee concerned receives special workflow information via SAPoffice, for example: 'New notification with open tasks'. Further on in this chapter, you will find more detailed information on the topic of workflow.

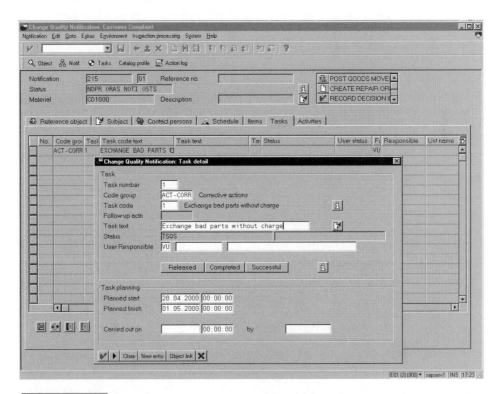

FIGURE 9.10   Overview screen of the immediate task (© SAP AG)

2 *The SAP BW module is not in productive use*
The employee concerned is then informed of new quality notifications using conventional communications technology and fetches the information from the relevant worklist.

3 *One of the components located in the Activities bar is used (as of Release 4.5, functions for other activities in connection with the notification)*
This communications component contained in the notification header is used to provide information for those who process the notification subsequently, e.g. per e-mail.

We shall assume case 3. Quality Management sends an urgent e-mail to Sales, asking for immediate processing and comment. The notification is then saved and closed.

When the e-mail arrives, the processing QA office process opens the notification from the worklist, from a selection list or directly using the internally assigned (by the system) or externally assigned (by the clerk) number. In addition, our Quality Management uses the TASKS tab to create another task. The TASK CODE is: 'Retrieve parts'. This is explained with the TASK TEXT: 'Definitely send a sample part with the relevant defect per express'.

However, we now stick to the task that was entered initially and perform a precise defect analysis by entering another defect item in the ITEMS tab to locate the defect more accurately.

Corrective task

The corrective task contains the same elements as the immediate task and only differs from it in that a certain group of task codes is selected in this case. You reach this via the ITEMS | TASKS tab in the menu bar of the item list.

This is now a targeted corrective task for the notification item. In contrast to the immediate task discussed above, this type of task is not assigned to the notification header, but directly to the defect item. The item tasks contain the next steps regarding removal of the defect. For our example, this means: as the CD inlets cannot be printed again within the allotted time, all the supplied CD covers are to be fitted with a new pick up (we have, of course, an assembly machine). We then create a task plan with the following content:

- QM-G1 – 0001: Subsequent delivery.
- QM-G1 – 0006: Rework.
- QM-G1 – 0014: Create repair order.
- QM-G1 – 0015: Enter goods movement for repair order (see Fig. 9.11).

When the tasks have been defined, this means that the tasks involved in remedying the defect are now distributed and, from the point of view of the Quality department, the customer complaint can be filed for the moment until the next events occur. As we have specified 'complaint to the vendor' as one of the tasks, the process must continue with

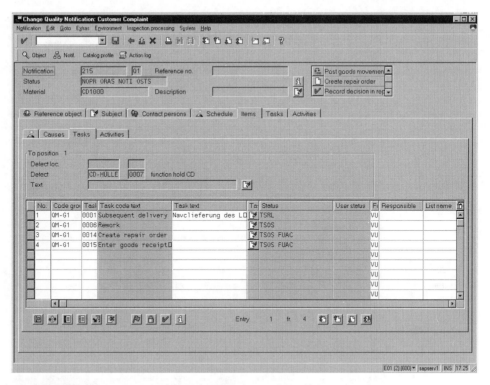

FIGURE 9.11 Task list on item level (© SAP AG)

the notification type Q2, Complaint to vendor (select via: LOGISTICS | QUALITY MAN-AGEMENT | QUALITY NOTIFICATIONS | CREATE QUALITY NOTIFICATION) and a new notification is started.

The detailed view of the task is opened with a double-click. At TASK PLANNING, we also schedule the start and finish of each task, and can thus monitor the current processing status for the rest of the process (Fig. 9.12).

Changing task status and completing notification

When the replacement delivery is received, an assembly order is started for the parts to be exchanged. When this activity has been completed successfully, we process the status of the immediate and item tasks in our notification.

By double-clicking on a task in the task overview, we receive a detail view and can change the status here (RELEASED, COMPLETED, SUCCESSFUL). We select COMPLETED, directly followed by SUCCESSFUL. The 'date carried out' is entered by the system itself based on the notification priority from the notification header (see Fig. 9.12). Each of the processing times for TASK PLANNING is assigned a certain priority in Customizing (Fig. 9.13).

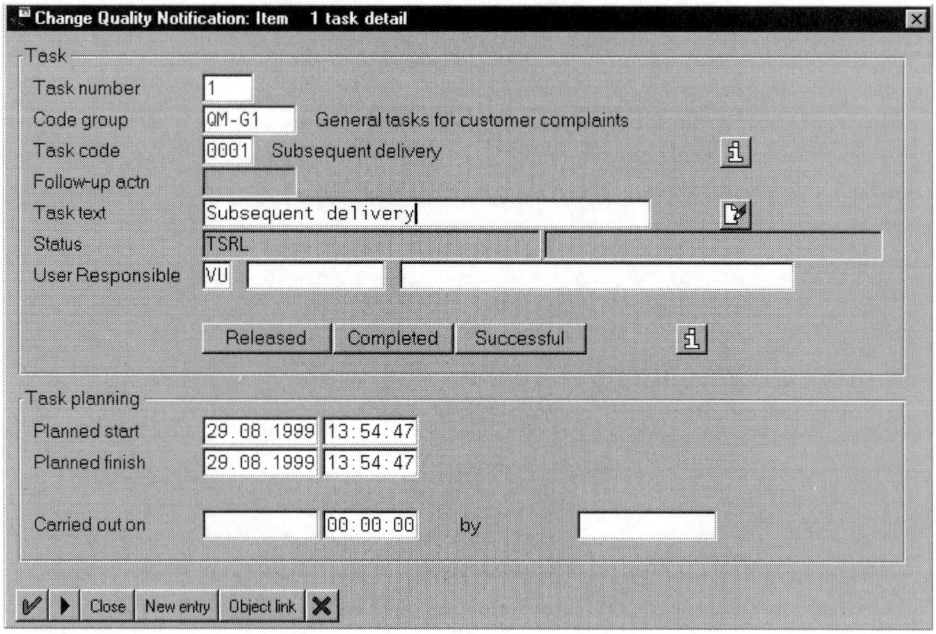

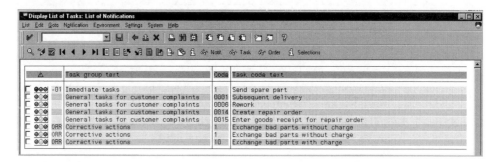

FIGURE 9.12 Task detail (© SAP AG)

FIGURE 9.13 Processing status of the tasks (© SAP AG)

When all the immediate tasks have been performed, we can select the remaining notification items and choose the associated tasks such as corrective tasks from the list, then mark them in the detail screen as 'completed'. Completion of a notification is only possible with completed tasks, which we do by selecting the menu from the quality notification: NOTIFICATION | FUNCTIONS | COMPLETE NOTIFICATION | EXTERNAL ORIGIN.

With this function, the notification receives the system status NOCO, 'Notification completed', and NOTE, 'Notification external'. The notification header then appears in grey and no more processing is possible. However, in the same menu path, there is the back door IN PROCESS AGAIN, although it makes sense to allow only a restricted circle of users with the relevant rights profile to use this function.

This example contains only the basic functions of processing notifications, but it makes it clear that modeling the business event beforehand is the fundamental basis for meaningful application of the R/3 notification system. In the next sections, we will deal with the most important remaining functions in connection with the quality notification (Fig. 9.14).

9.2.2 Functions and elements of the quality notification

Specified quantities in the quality notification

When order, document or delivery data is being transferred, the system enters the associated specified quantities of the relevant order items in the notification. The specified quantities are then listed in the section QUANTITIES of the SUBJECT tab. A further division of the defect quantity into 'internally' or 'externally caused', enables you to carry out an informative analysis of the occurrence of defects.

System status and user status

Two status forms can be used for the quality notification: the system status with its standard profile already defined in the shipped version, and the user status, which can also be set (see Fig. 9.15). Set accordingly, the user status is suitable for overriding the system status manually. In Customizing, the status profile is assigned to and set up in the structure of the quality notifications. Incidentally, the way the status profile functions is precisely the same as described in Chapter 6, 'Quality and inspection planning' in the section on the 'Q information record'.

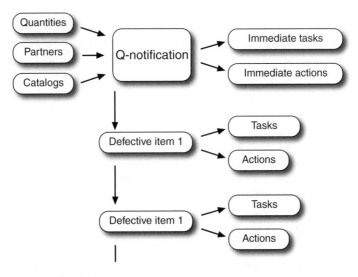

FIGURE 9.14   Structure of the quality notification (© SAP AG)

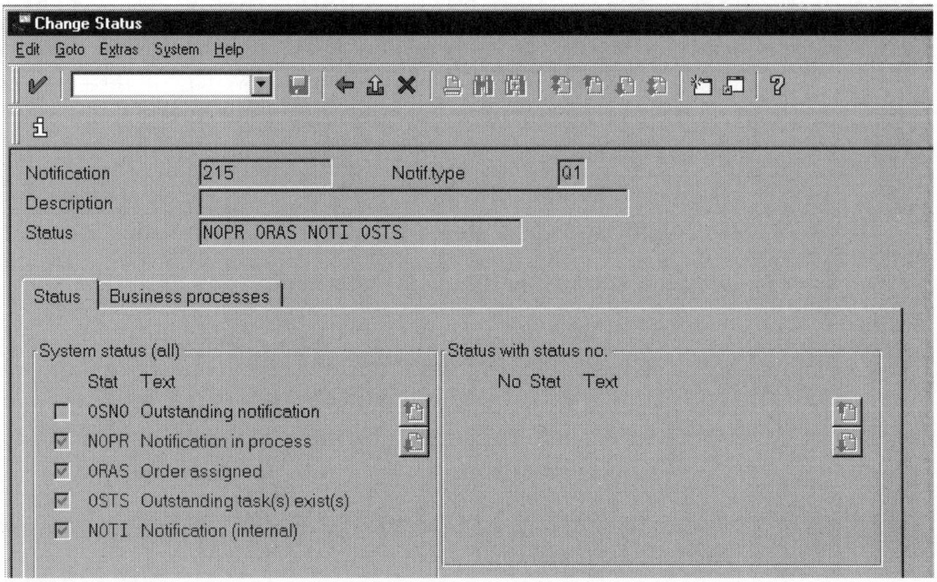

FIGURE 9.15 System status and user status (© SAP AG)

An overview of the status forms of your notification type can be obtained by clicking the INFORMATION button to the left of the status bar in the notification header and then navigating further in EXTRAS | OVERVIEW (see Fig. 9.16).

Activity

These functions in the menu bar of the notification header help provide a more precise differentiation between the task and other activities to be carried out (see Fig. 9.17). The activity refers to another catalog and is used to describe activities running parallel to the tasks.

Follow-up activity

The follow-up activity can be used to automatically trigger linking system functions such as extended quality inspections, changes to the vendor relationship, opening another notification and other logistic processes. The function is selected in the task detail from a catalog and then activated when the task is saved. Basically, the follow-up activity is the start of a function module. In your system, there is a template for it in the corresponding Customizing table. Based on the template, a suitable function module is programmed for you; in principle, this can start all system transactions. As of Release 4.5, various follow-up activities can be grouped in a follow-up activity list using a collection function, and these can then be run consecutively in the system.

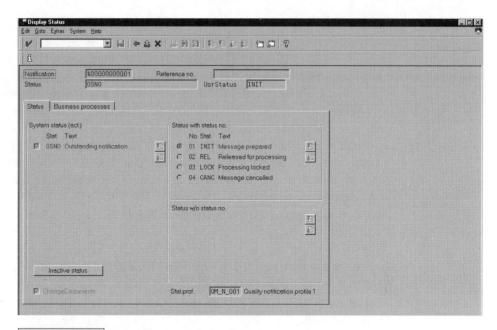

FIGURE 9.16 Status overview (© SAP AG)

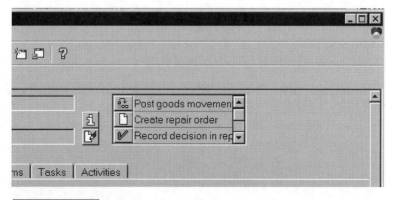

FIGURE 9.17 Activity bar (© SAP AG)

Quality order in controlling/quality costs

The individual activities and costs incurred in the context of complaints handling can provide important feedback regarding the overhead due to mistakes and errors within the company. With a dedicated allocation of quality costs, for example, a clear distinction can be made between quality costs caused externally and those caused internally. However, this type of overhead analysis is only possible if the activities have been allocated to accounts according to the rules of business management. The main components of an order are the clearing accounts and the activity types. Activity types can be machine hours, wage hours in quality management, laboratory examinations and other quality inspections. The cost centre sending the information usually specifies the cost centre of Quality Management (see Fig. 9.18). Table 9.4 clearly illustrates a simple allocation to an order.

If you have to use additional external services in complaints handling, another activity on the part of Controlling is required. The costs of, for example, external processing are posted to the quality order and, in the case of commercial order completion, are added to the internal activities to produce the total costs of the quality order. The quality order is a complete, accountable order in the CO module, with the separate order type QN01, quality order. In the SAP system, the ORDER function in the notification header generates an order of this type, along with an order number, and creates the basic data for the order. The activity allocation, i.e. the actual costs, are to be recorded for this order.

To avoid confusion, we have covered the topic of quality costs separately. The appraisal costs are described in detail in Chapter 7, 'Quality inspection'. Chapter 8, 'Quality control', provides you with an overview of quality costs. In this chapter, 'Quality notifications', the quality costs that are closely related to the quality notification are covered.

The activity allocation screen can be reached via LOGISTICS | QUALITY MANAGEMENT | QUALITY NOTIFICATION | COSTS | ACTUAL POSTINGS | ACTIVITY ALLOCATION | RECORD. The document items are filled out as shown in Table 9.4.

As soon as the activity allocation has taken place, the order can be analyzed as regards costs using the function COSTS | ACTUAL POSTINGS in the menu path LOGISTICS | QUALITY MANAGEMENT | QUALITY NOTIFICATION | COSTS | ACTUAL POSTINGS.

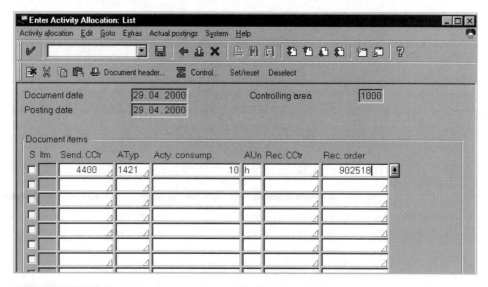

FIGURE 9.18 Activity allocation for quality costs (© SAP AG)

TABLE 9.4	Activity allocation	
Field content	**Meaning**	**Entry in example**
Send CCtr	The cost centre (of quality management)	4400 quality management
Enter activity type	For example, an activity type set up specially for notification processing	1421 notification processing
Acty. consump.	AUn	10 h
Rec. CCtr.	Enter either a receiving cost centre or, in the next field, name the receiving order	If required
Rec. order	Here, the order number of our quality order from the Q-notification is usually entered.	909518

TIP

For many quality notifications, the costs incurred are the real focus of later analysis, which means they are an important component for company management from the beginning of the R/3 project. However, from the point of view of Controlling, this fact causes some difficulty. The expenses of quality assurance are usually allocated to the overhead costs. If additional quality costs are now recorded, there is a double recording of quality costs in the profit and loss account. After one accounting period at the latest, in which the quality costs have been recorded in detail, it is therefore possible to allocate the activities from the quality order type. For Controlling, a switch from overhead accounting to unit cost accounting for quality management means a considerable expenditure, which is usually unplanned in implementation projects.

In order to be able to use the Q order in spite of this, it can be used temporarily as a neutral cost collector. To achieve this, CO only needs to create cost centres and allocation types, which are used exclusively by Quality Management. It is advisable, with the agreement of Controlling, to create a reasonable number of accounts and activity types that enable simple activity allocation within the company. A division of this kind enables an initial separation of the costs of the quality notification from the operating result, and means they can be viewed as statistical costs.

Work papers

The individual forms and lists that belong to a quality notification can be printed, faxed or sent by e-mail (as of Release 4.5, from the Activities bar). Documents with an external effect in particular must certainly be adapted to the company-specific corporate design, and they must meet the requirements as to information content. The desired changes can then be implemented with ABAP and SAPscript programming. For form changes that are of more than a cosmetic nature, plan in around two to four days per form of additional work, and plan this work in good time. As a rule, the programming resources for implementation projects are scarce. The documents in the shipped SAP version are, for obvious reasons, only to be regarded as suggestions.

You will find:

▦ Form, Notification overview

The notification overview is a printout of all the information of a quality notification (see Fig. 9.19).

▦ Form, Item list

The item list contains either a part of or all of the defect items in the quality notification. You can include individual defect items in the printout or exclude them.

▦ Form, Complaint to vendor

This form is recommended for a vendor who delivers defective or incorrect goods. The work paper is only relevant for the quality notification type Q2, Complaint to vendor. In addition, other company-specific work papers can be defined in your company. The control tables for the print functions are defined centrally in your company in such a way that you can use the online help functions to display the relevant work papers and select the desired work paper:

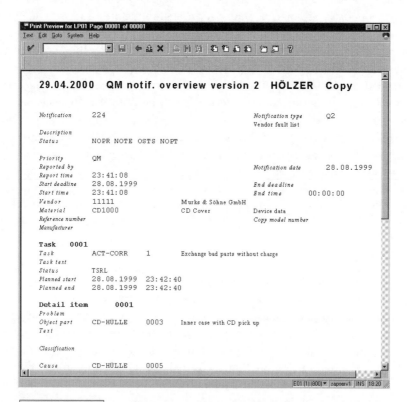

FIGURE 9.19 Notification overview (© SAP AG)

   – Process note to the customer.

   – 8D report (as of Release 4.5).

   – Interim report.

   – Concluding report.

Partner data for the notification

Partners are companies or people who are closely associated with the notification. The vendor and the clerk responsible are the set mandatory partners for the notification type Q2, Complaint to vendor, without which a notification cannot be saved. Logically, the customer and the employee are the mandatory partners for the customer complaint. The mandatory partners of the notification are entered in the tab CONTACT PERSONS (up to Release 4.0, 'Notification header' section) (see Fig. 9.20).

Alternatively, you can enter the partners in the quality notification via the menu bar GOTO | PARTNERS in a selection list. Moreover, at the menu item PARTNER DATA, information partners can also be specified, insofar as these have been assigned to the partner profile of this notification type in Customizing. The selection of the partner can subsequently be used to create informative analyses.

Reference objects

Reference objects are the data that have a business relationship to the notification. Examples of this are the sales order for notification type Q1, Customer complaint, or

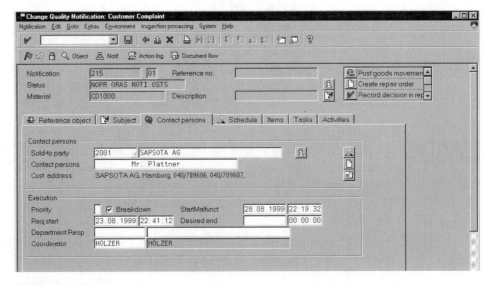

FIGURE 9.20   Contact persons tab (© SAP AG)

the material document from goods receipt for the notification type Q2, Complaint to vendor. We have listed the default reference objects in this chapter in sections 9.3, 9.4 and 9.5 in connection with the quality notification in Sales and Distribution, Production and Procurement. The reference objects of quality notification can be changed retrospectively on entering the header data.

Response profile

If the function for automatic determination of tasks is enabled, the system can propose on the basis of the predefined parameters in the response profile or standby profile the tasks to be carried out first. The response profile and standby profile specify the times and period within which there is to be a certain response to a notification in the form of a task.

EXAMPLE You create a notification at 10 o'clock. In the response profile, a period of two hours is defined for the task code 'Call customer' and a period of four hours is defined for the code 'Check whether technician is at customer'. The times defined in the standby profile are from 8 to 12 o'clock and from 2 to 6 p.m. In this case, you must call the customer back by 12 o'clock to discuss or clarify the problem. If the customer needs technical support, a technician must arrive there by 4 p.m. You can use the automatic determination of tasks to define a number of standard tasks for immediate response (a task of this type can, for example, require that a customer is called back with priority 2 within two hours).

Report profile in general

In larger corporations, there is frequently a separation between the catalog groups defect type, location, cause, task, etc. of the same notification type. This can be achieved by adding other notification types with identical character to the basic settings of the shipped system version in Customizing and assigning these a report profile.

EXAMPLE Internal quality notification Plant 1 and internal quality notification Plant 2 are each allocated to a code group from DEFECT LOCATIONS and then, on selecting their notification type, have an appropriately tailored selection of defect codes.

In the same way, the report profile can also be assigned materials. In the case of an existing report profile on notification level and on material level, the report profile of the material has priority.

Workflow

If the R/3 module SAP Business Workflow is used, the system takes over the preset tasks of information distribution in the context of notification data. Depending on the status of the notifications or tasks, it places 'work items' in the SAPoffice mailbox of the partner responsible and directly provides the users with the required functions and the individual work steps. The processing status is now transparent for those involved in the notification; uncompleted tasks are visible immediately and can be followed up. From the displayed work item, you can use the RUN icon in the menu bar to branch directly into the notification processing (Fig. 9.21).

Although the workflow component of the R/3 system is included in the shipped version, it requires intensive customizing and numerous settings before it can be used completely, and should be set up by an experienced consultant (see Fig. 9.22). For Quality Management, SAP has already prepared a few scenarios that you can view in Customizing at BUSINESS | MANAGEMENT | SAP BUSINESS | TASK-SPECIFIC CUSTOMIZING or activate on a test basis. Incidentally, up to Release 4.0, the R/3 workflow component is the only way for the quality notifications to leave the R/3 system environment in external e-mail. In principle, the SAP Business Workflow module can be used to operate all external mail and workgroup programs such as Lotus Notes or MS-Outlook, which is not possible directly from the R/3 QM application. As of Release 4.5, there are comprehensive extensions for these activities in the Activity bar.

Lists and evaluations

By navigating in QUALITY NOTIFICATION | WORKLIST | NOTIFICATION | CHANGE DATA, then QUALITY NOTIFICATION | EVALUATION, you reach reports and selection lists that can be configured for further processing of notifications. The time line analysis can be used to obtain a nice graphical display of the number of notifications in a certain period, depending on the various selection parameters (see Fig. 9.23).

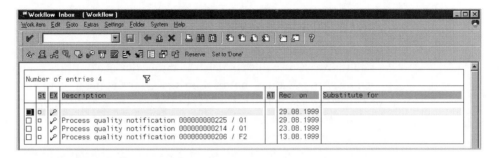

FIGURE 9.21 Workflow step log in SAPoffice (© SAP AG)

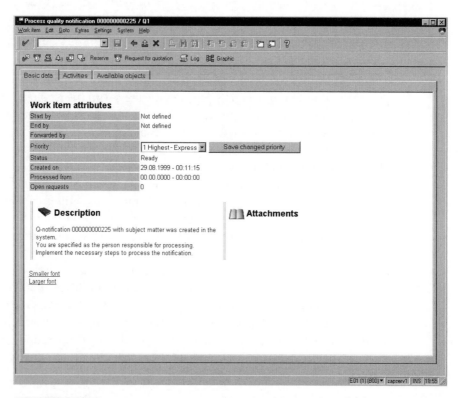

FIGURE 9.22 Predefined workflow tasks as work items (© SAP AG)

In other analysis functions, you can use the INFORMATION SYSTEM branch to leave the EVALUATIONS menu and enter the QMIS (Quality Management Information System), which will be discussed in more detail in Chapter 10, 'Information systems and evaluations'.

Archiving and deleting quality notifications

Once a notification has been created, the requirements of data integrity mean that it is not quite so easy to archive or delete it at the click of a button. If you want to use these functions, first set a new notification status on the menu path EDIT NOTIFICATION | FUNCTIONS | DELETION FLAG | SET. In the second step, use QUALITY MANAGEMENT | ARCHIVE | MOVEMENT DATA | ARCHIVE/DELETE to organize the data as desired. As these activities were placed in this path from the base administration, we strongly recommend that you seek the advice of your system administrator, as it is unlikely that the expertise required for this task will be found in the area of Quality Management.

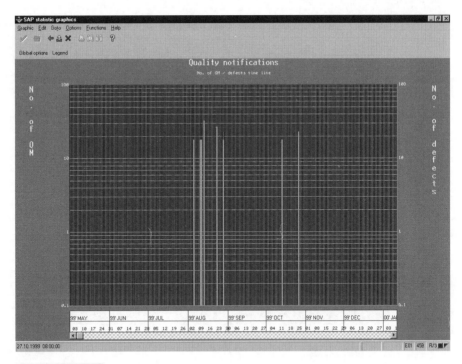

FIGURE 9.23   Overview graphic of number of notifications as time line diagram
(© SAP AG)

Internal number assignment

For the purposes of identification, the system creates a separate number for each quality notification. The basic settings provide for internal number assignment (i.e., the system specifies consecutive numbers) with a predefined number range.

CUSTOMIZING TIP

A problem that occurs frequently when tracing quality notifications is the internal system number assignment with 'buffering'. To avoid placing a load on system performance, some numbers are placed in a buffer; the notification itself then takes one of these numbers from the buffer. This makes sense when a great many documents have to be created within a short space of time; without the buffer, the system would have to generate individual numbers in a separate process. However, the disadvantage of buffering is that there is an undefined jump in the number sequence, for example 100 is not followed by 101 but by 105 or 111.

Action Log						

Message no : 000000000215
Created by:
Malfunction start: 28.08.1999 22:19:32
Malfunction end: 00.00.0000 00:00:00

Created by: 23.08.1999 22:41:12
Des. start: 23.08.1999 22:41:12
Des. end: 00.00.0000 00:00:00

Date	Time	Changed by	Subobject			Field changed	Field contents (new)/(old)
	23:19	HÖLZER	Task		0001	Status	Task outstanding
			Notif.			Status	Outstanding task(s) exist(s)
			Task	0001	0002	Status	Task outstanding
			Notif.			Catalog type - codin	D
			Notif.			Code group - coding	QM
			Notif.			Coding	1
	22:21	HÖLZER	Notif.			Material number	CD1000
			Notif.			Unit of measure	PC
			Item		0001	Unit of measure for	PC
			Item		0002	Unit of measure for	PC
	22:19	HÖLZER	Notif.			Account number of cu	2001
							1000
			Notif.			Customer purchase or	1000100
			Notif.			Distribution channel	10

FIGURE 9.24	Action log (© SAP AG)

In order to eliminate this effect, a small change in the settings of the productive system is required. With the transaction SNRO, you reach the input screen of the number range object directly. Here, enter the object QMEL_NR, select EDIT NUMBER RANGE and then EDIT | SET BUFFERING | NO BUFFERING. The notification number is now written consecutively without jumps.

Processing overview with the action log

The action log (Fig. 9.24) provides you with a detailed overview of all the user actions in a quality notification via EXTRAS | DOCUMENTS FOR NOTIFICATION | ACTION LOG.

9.3	QUALITY NOTIFICATIONS IN SALES AND DISTRIBUTION

Notification type Q1/F1, Customer complaint

In principle, the range of functions and the operation of the various quality notification types are the same. The main differences come from the reference objects of the header data and, of course, the individual processing scheme of the company using the program. You have already seen an example of this in the customer complaint scenario above. Furthermore, the partner scheme is also equipped with separate partner roles for each notification type. It is advisable to retain the mandatory partners from the shipped version – the customer and the clerk responsible.

Reference objects of the notification type 'Customer complaint' are:

- Customer (mandatory partner).
- Material.
- Sales order.
- Sales organization.
- Division.
- Distribution channel.
- Delivery.

When you select certain reference objects using the entry screen shown in the example, the system transfers other data from a document (sales order, delivery) into the notification, which means that the input required for the creation of the notification can be kept at a low, user-friendly level.

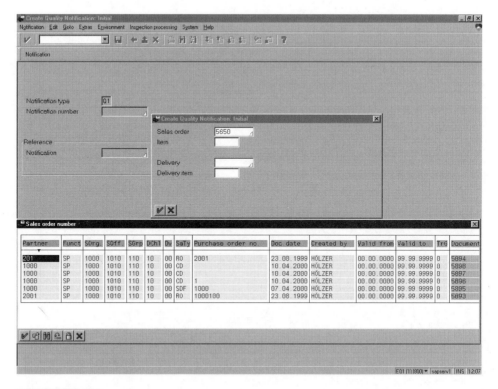

FIGURE 9.25 Creating a notification via entry screen 130, delivery (© SAP AG)

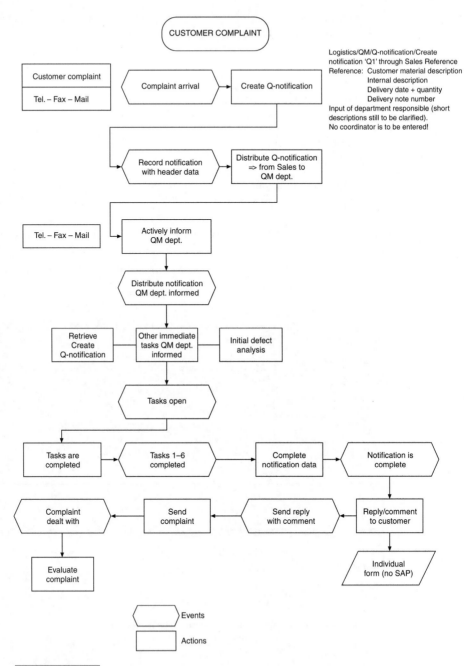

FIGURE 9.26 Flow diagram of a customer complaint in simplified form

Initiating the customer complaint

Selection via: LOGISTICS | QUALITY MANAGEMENT | QUALITY NOTIFICATIONS | CREATE QUALITY NOTIFICATION. Select the notification type Q1, Customer complaint. Selection via: LOGISTICS | QUALITY MANAGEMENT | QUALITY NOTIFICATIONS | CREATE QUALITY NOTIFICATION. Select the notification type Q3, Complaint to vendor. With ENTER, either a dialog box appears for input of the document data (customizing required via the entry screen CHANGE QUALITY NOTIFICATION | QM03_CREATE_QMEL_WITH_WINDOW | SCREEN 130) or the notification processing at header level is opened (Fig. 9.25).

In most cases, this notification type is created manually, following a telephone or written complaint from the customer. It can conceivably be opened using an SAP

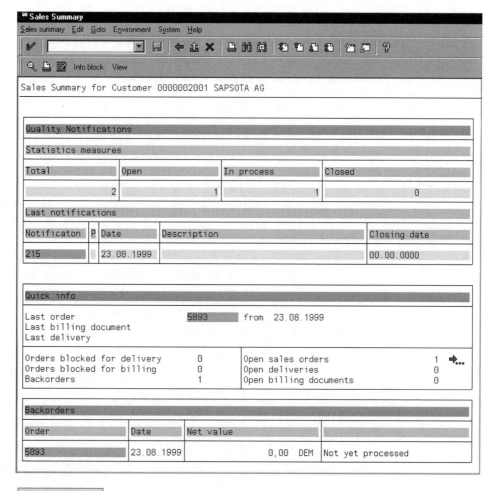

FIGURE 9.27   Sales summary (© SAP AG)

Business Workflow function. The most important step in implementing this notification type is a consistent design of the business process. We have illustrated a simplified example in Fig. 9.26.

Sales summary

Another interesting function from the customer complaint is the display of the sales summary (Fig. 9.27), which you can reach by selecting ENVIRONMENT | SALES SUMMARY. Here, you will find comprehensive information from the movement data of the customer, combined with current details of the course of the complaint and the last notifications. As the sales summary is an interactive report, a double-click on the notification number enables immediate viewing of the quality notification.

9.4   QUALITY NOTIFICATIONS IN PRODUCTION

Notification type Q3/F3, Internal quality notification

Selection via: LOGISTICS | QUALITY MANAGEMENT | QUALITY NOTIFICATIONS | CREATE QUALITY NOTIFICATION. Select the notification type Q3, Internal quality notification. With ENTER, either a dialog box appears for input of the document data (customizing required via the entry screen CHANGE QUALITY NOTIFICATION | QM03_CREATE_QMEL_WITH_WINDOW | SCREEN 140) or the notification processing at header level is opened (see Fig. 9.28).

An internal problem notification (see Fig. 9.29) refers to problems that occur within your own company (e.g. defects confirmed during the production process for a material or a work operation). It can also be used for all events that occur in the company

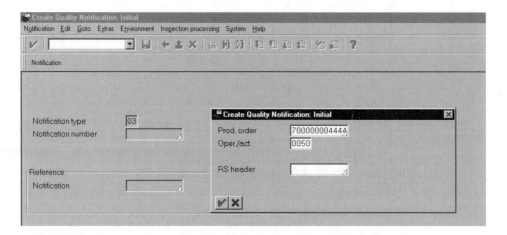

FIGURE 9.28   Creating a notification via entry screen 140, production order (© SAP AG)

and have to be traced and assigned tasks. As of Release 4.5, there are additional functions that exert defined influences of the internal quality notification on the complaint. For example, the internal notification for a production order can directly trigger a complaint and change the quality score of the vendor.

Reference objects of the notification type 'Problem notification' are:

- Internal partners.
- Material, batch (mandatory partner).
- Production order or series order.
- Work centre.
- Inspection lot.
- Author (mandatory partner).

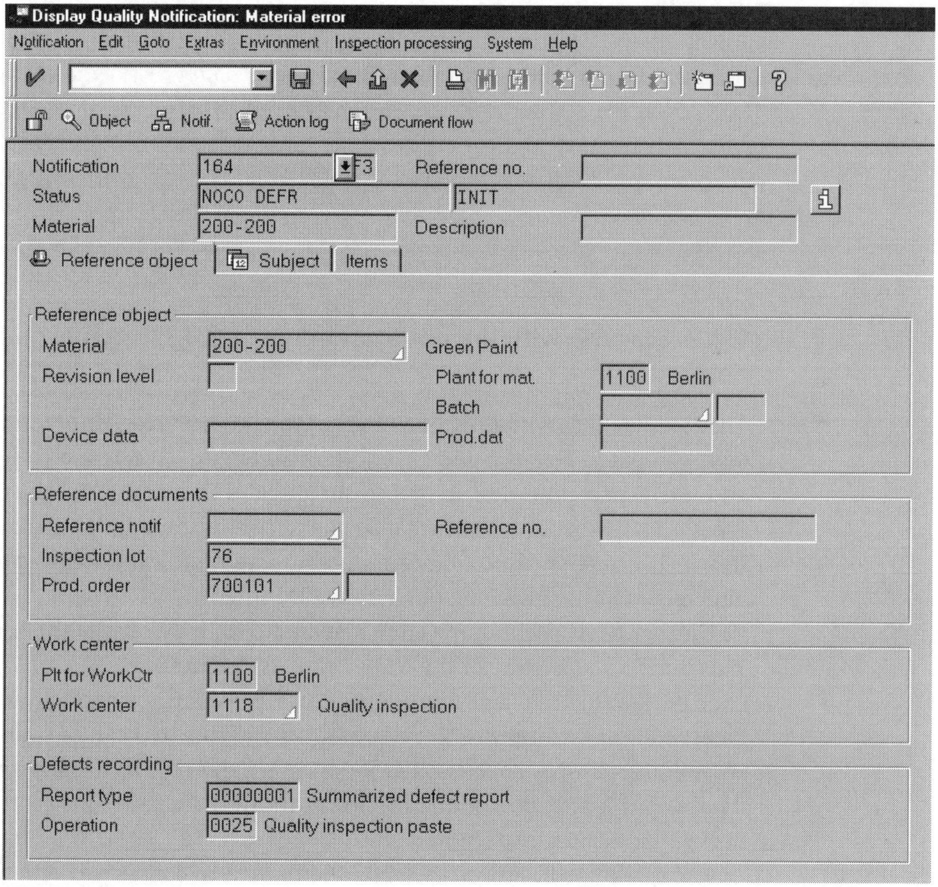

FIGURE 9.29 Notification header of the internal problem notification (© SAP AG)

Initiating the internal problem notification

To create notifications from Production, there are both manual and automatic functions as well as the initialization from other QM components, such as creating the notification via the usage decision or the inspection lot in the event of defects occurring.

CUSTOMIZING TIP

Generate the notifications automatically by means of batch input (program that simulates a manual input via the application). In this way, for example, a small ABAP utility can create a separate notification for each confirmation of the work run with defective quantities in the PP module or from an external application. The origin of the automatically created notification can be implemented simply using a partner scheme with reference to the user data. In the meantime, SAP has developed a separate program (RIIBIB00) for this case, and it can be reached directly in the application via the menu path LOGISTICS | QUALITY MANAGEMENT | QUALITY NOTIFICATIONS | ENVIRONMENT | DATA TRANSFER. RIIBIP00 is a general tool for data transfer, which is used to enter information in the SAP system using standard transactions and functional modules. Chapter 14, 'Migration concepts' provides you with more detailed information on this topic.

9.4.1 Scenario with the notification type Q3/F3, Internal quality notification

The internal quality notification refers to the occurrence of errors and mistakes in your own company. The two most important reference objects are the production order and the inspection order. The processing logic is the same as for the other notification types from the field of quality management. In this scenario, we shall look at a situation in which a quality inspection in Production automatically creates an extended defect data record in the form of a quality notification.

During the inspection, the employee has to roughly classify the defect on discovery. This is achieved by way of the inspection task requesting input of a predefined defect code if the valuation 'defective' appears. Here, the inspector only selects an applicable defect code and completes the inspection step. This step can of course be repeated for several inspection characteristics. We have set the system in such a way that a defect data record – and thus a quality notification – is created for each defect valuation during the quality inspection.

The quality notification (see Fig. 9.30) already contains the header data and the required reference objects for subsequent processing. In our case, it is planned that quality management trace the number of Q3 notifications. This is achieved by regular

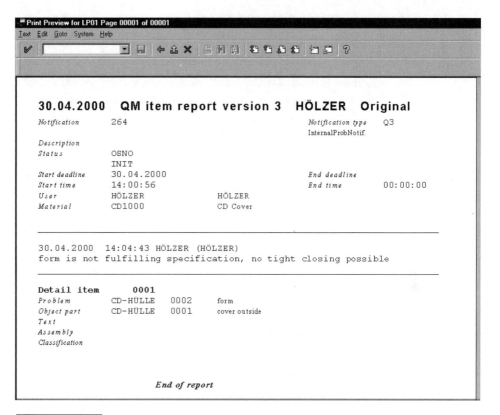

FIGURE 9.30   Sample printout of an internal Q-notification (© SAP AG)

observation of the worklist and thus becomes a task to be performed by the Quality department employee responsible. We can tailor the list individually to the task of a certain person, which means that the overview only contains the items to be processed at the relevant centre. Later in the process, the QM clerk or other people involved give the notification the necessary information to remedy the defect and make an evaluation.

Frequently, the defect discovered is not the fault of Production, but was caused by a defective delivery from an external vendor or an upstream manufacturing step. If this occurs, the notification system offers to adopt the data from the previous notification when creating a new notification (complaint or other internal quality notification). This systematic approach ensures tracing of the notification all the way to the origin of the defect at any time.

QUALITY NOTIFICATIONS IN PURCHASING

Notification type Q2/F2, Complaint to vendor

Selection via: LOGISTICS | QUALITY MANAGEMENT | QUALITY NOTIFICATIONS | CREATE QUALITY NOTIFICATION. Select the notification type Q3, Complaint to vendor. With ENTER, either a dialog box appears for input of the document data (customizing required via the entry screen CHANGE QUALITY NOTIFICATION | QM03_CREATE_QMEL_WITH_WINDOW | SCREEN 100) or the notification processing at header level is opened (see Fig. 9.31).

The complaints to vendors or other external partners are handled and managed in the notification types Q2/F3. In this way, the complaint is also made to the vendor.

The complaint to the vendor provides Quality Management with a comprehensive tool for quality control in Materials Management. The opened notifications can influence not only the standard functions but also the vendor evaluation and cost analyses for overheads in connection with complaints. There are also separate forms for communication with the vendor (raw versions) for this notification type.

Reference objects of the notification types Q2/F3 'Complaint' are:

- Goods receipt document.
- Material, batch.
- Vendor (mandatory partner).
- Purchasing organization.
- Inspection lot.

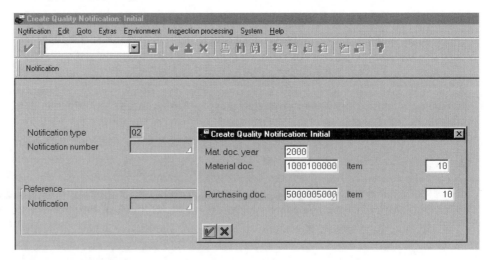

| **FIGURE 9.31** | Creating a notification via entry screen 100, Purchasing documents |

(© SAP AG)

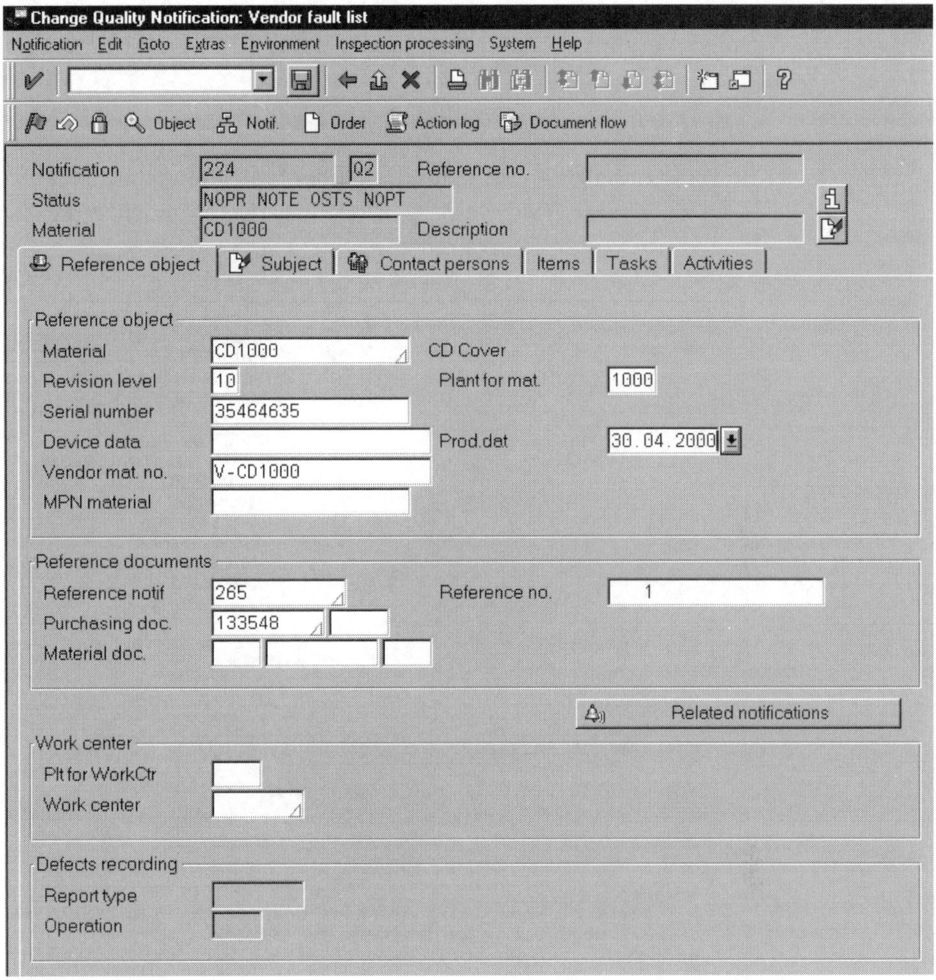

FIGURE 9.32 Notification header of the complaint (© SAP AG)

Initiating the complaint

In the sample scenario described above, the complaint would be initiated by means of an item task from the defect analysis and generated via the CREATE NOTIFICATION function. Opening from the SAP Business Workflow component – manually or automatically – can also be implemented.

Cost check

When a quality order is created from the notification, a cost check of the quality problem as regards your vendor is possible. Connections to R/3 workflow items are also an option for creating complaints. The initialization of the notification from the inspection lot or the usage decision is also possible for this notification type.

Effects of the complaint on the quality score

In the Customizing section for the vendor evaluation (cf. Chapter 8, 'Quality control', section 'Vendor evaluation'), you can negatively influence the quality score of the vendor with every complaint issued.

```
                                        PURCHASE VOUCHER / POSITIONS NO:
                                        4500000858 / 00030
                                        MATERIAL VOUCHER / POSITIONS NO:
                                        50002432 / 0001
                                        MATERIAL NO.: 47882
                                        CONTROLLER              T3016*M
                                        QUANTITY / RETURN TO VENDOR
                                         1.000 PC    1.000 PC
                                        SUPPLY NO.
                                        1006241
                                        AUTHOR / PHONE NO.
                                        Schramm / 07308/80-299
                                        FAX NO./E-mail
                                        07308/80-553


Problem report


DESCRIPTION
---------------------------------------------------------------------
Measurement failure

Measure 122,5 +-0,1 out of tolerance
---------------------------------------------------------------------



REMARK
All parts of the sample are with one measure out of tolerance.
We well send back the delivery for rework.
We expect your written comments within the next 10 working days.




With best regards
Tally Computerdrucker GmbH


i.V. Schramm              i.A.
```

FIGURE 9.33 Sample printout for a customer-specific complaint to the vendor (quality report)

Buyers negotiation sheet

The buyers negotiation sheet is the counterpart of the sales summary from Sales and Distribution and it is available both via navigation in the area of Procurement and in Quality Management. Selecting LOGISTICS | QUALITY MANAGEMENT | QUALITY NOTIFICATIONS | ENVIRONMENT | BUYERS NEGOTIATION SHEET allows you to view the report involved. Here, you will find comprehensive information from the movement data and master data of the vendor, combined with current details of the course of the complaint and the last notifications. As the buyers negotiation sheet is an interactive report, a double-click on the notification number enables immediate viewing of the quality notification. All functions in relation to the notification are of course also available to Purchasing.

CHAPTER 10

Information systems and evaluations

10.1 BASIC PRINCIPLES

Many processes and quality elements of the ISO 9000 series of standards require the recording and documentation of inspections and inspection results. Everything you enter in or feed back to the R/3 system is available to you for this verification. In order to find this data quickly and analyse it further, the system provides various information systems, reporting techniques and graphical preparation options.

In general, the evaluation options in R/3 system can be divided into four groups:

▦ Evaluation of the results history (see Fig. 10.1) with integrated trend analysis.

▦ The information system.

▦ Report lists which can be created without programming overhead using

   – the Report Writer for flexible analyses.

   – the ABAP query (database query).

▦ Report lists programmed using ABAP

The most important information systems of the R/3 system are:

▦ The Executive Information System (EIS).

▦ The Logistics Information System (LIS).

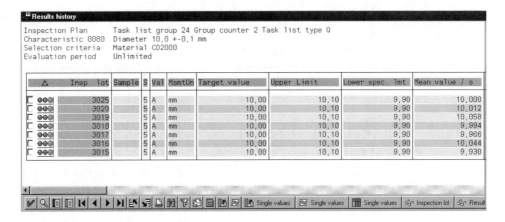

FIGURE 10.1   Results history (© SAP AG)

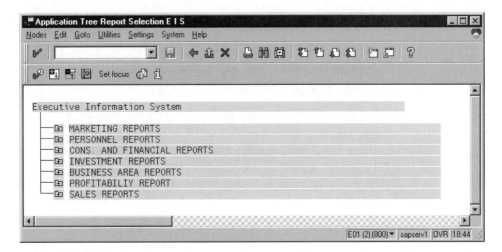

FIGURE 10.2   Report selection from the Executive Information System (EIS) (© SAP AG)

▨ The Financial Information System (FIS).

▨ The Human Resources Information System (HRIS).

The information systems can be started from the relevant application.

10.2   EXECUTIVE INFORMATION SYSTEM

The INFORMATION SYSTEMS menu item in the menu bar catches the eye in the entry screen. The first submenu there is the EXECUTIVE MENU with the Executive Information System (EIS).

The Executive Information System is aimed at upper levels of management and employees in Accounting and its main purpose is to provide evaluations of data from the various information systems in a uniform view (see Fig. 10.2). This data can be, for example, from the Financial Information System, the Logistics Information System and the Human Resources Information System.

10.3   LOGISTICS INFORMATION SYSTEM

The Logistics Information System (LIS) provides a considerable amount of information for quality management. It in turn consists of various information systems:

- Stock Controlling.
- Purchasing Information System.
- Sales and Distribution Information System.
- Production Information System.
- Transport Information System.
- Plant Maintenance Information System.
- Quality Information System.

Important data from the business transactions and events is compressed and saved in the information structures. Various types of analyses can be used to open up and display this compressed data via the information systems.

There are various ways of reaching the information systems of logistics: first, via LOGISTICS CONTROLLING from the LOGISTICS menu and, second, via the relevant application.

> LOGISTICS | LOGISTICS CONTROLLING | STOCK CONTROLLING or
> PURCHASING INFORMATION SYSTEM or
> SALES AND DISTRIBUTION INFORMATION SYSTEM or
> PRODUCTION INFORMATION SYSTEM or
> TRANSPORT INFORMATION SYSTEM or
> PLANT MAINTENANCE INFORMATION SYSTEM or
> QUALITY INFORMATION SYSTEM

As an example of starting from the application, we will select Quality Management.

10.3.1 Quality Information System

We reach the QM Quality Information System via the path

> LOGISTICS | QUALITY MANAGEMENT | INFORMATION SYSTEM.

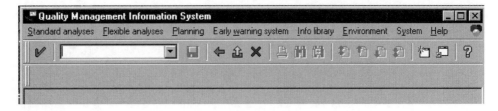

FIGURE 10.3   Menu bar of the Quality Management Information System (© SAP AG)

Figure 10.3 shows the various submenus, to be explained below.

Standard analyses

Here you can run the standard analyses that are predefined in the R/3 system (see, for example, Fig. 10.4). However, these can only be adapted to the relevant requirements to a limited extent as regards depth of information and the selected key figures.

You can use the standard analyses of the Quality Management Information System (QMIS) to evaluate data from the inspection lot processing and quality notifications. The views of the material, of the vendor or of the customer provide the following analyses:

- Lots
- Results
- Defects
- Notifications

You can start other functions from the list displays of the analyses in the EDIT menu, for example, CUMULATIVE CURVE, CORRELATION, ABC ANALYSIS, CLASSIFICATION, SEGMENTATION or also ranking lists. Finally, the results can be displayed in diagram form.

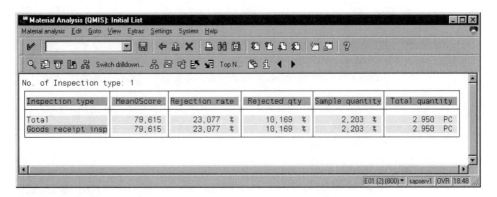

FIGURE 10.4   Example of a standard analysis for material (© SAP AG)

SCENARIO

You would like to find out when IQ Corporation received a quality notification in a certain period (for example, in the fourth quarter of 1999).

To do so, select the Quality Management Information System via the path LOGISTICS | QUALITY MANAGEMENT | INFORMATION SYSTEM. In the menu item STANDARD ANALYSES, select VENDOR | NOTIFICATION OVERVIEW. After entering the vendor number and the analysis period, you receive an overview of all the notifications to this vendor, whereby they are still structured according to processing status (open, in process, completed). Via the submenu EXTRAS | Q-NOTIFICATIONS, you receive a list of the associated quality notifications with date and inspection lot number in an additional display window (see Fig. 10.5).

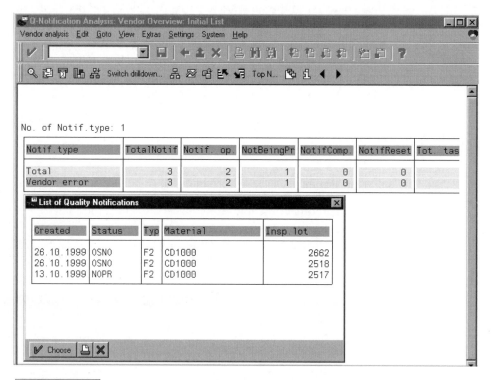

| **FIGURE 10.5** | Notification analysis for vendor with list of Q-notifications (© SAP AG) |

Flexible analyses

Here, you can define and perform analyses and evaluations. The FLEXIBLE ANALYSES enable simple entry into the Report Writer. The Report Writer is a tool that can be used to create individual reports for various applications. Within the flexible analyses, some of these functions are used.

The information structures supplied with the standard version can be evaluated and the key figures that are of interest compiled into individual reports. The individual key figures can be linked with one another using formulas and inserted in a report with a layout that can be adapted to requirements (see Fig. 10.6).

Planning

Here, plan data can be entered and forecasts created. Within the framework of the standard analyses, you can then compare the actual and plan data.

Planning in the information systems is based on the information structures already mentioned in the context of the flexible analyses which are supplied with the standard version or can be defined by users.

Early warning system

The early warning system enables searches for weaknesses and exceptions in Logistics, and it can be used for all applications in Logistics.

Exceptions consist of the definition of characteristics or characteristic values (for example material, vendor) and conditions. The following can be defined as conditions:

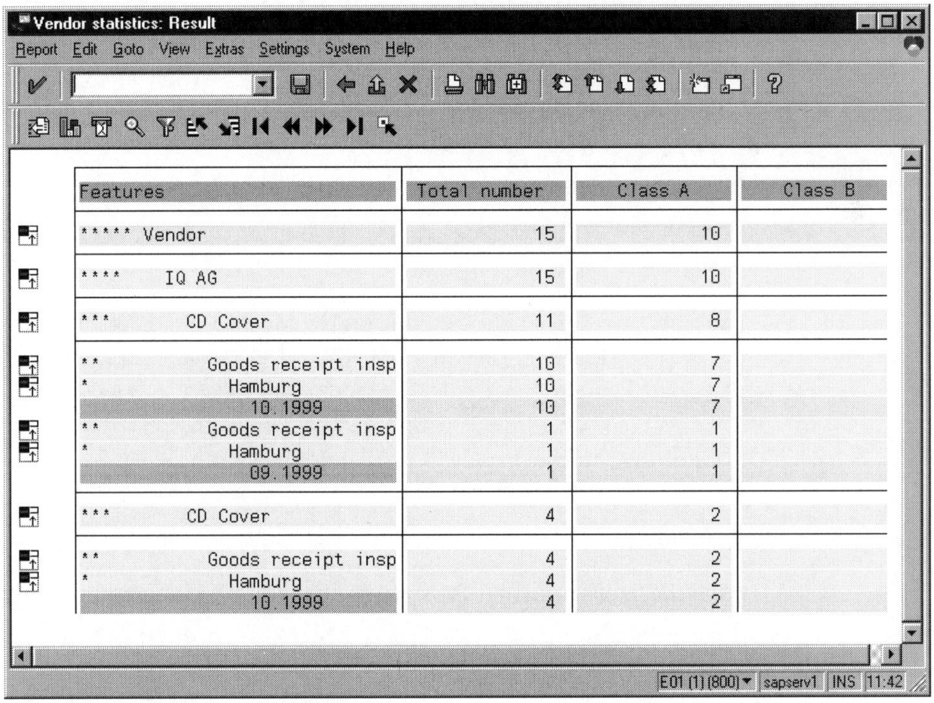

Features	Total number	Class A	Class B
***** Vendor	15	10	
**** IQ AG	15	10	
*** CD Cover	11	8	
** Goods receipt insp	10	7	
* Hamburg	10	7	
10.1999	10	7	
** Goods receipt insp	1	1	
* Hamburg	1	1	
09.1999	1	1	
*** CD Cover	4	2	
** Goods receipt insp	4	2	
* Hamburg	4	2	
10.1999	4	2	

FIGURE 10.6 Evaluation result of a flexible analysis (© SAP AG)

- Threshold value.

- Trend.

- Plan/actual comparison.

In the search for exceptions, there are three possibilities:

- Standard analysis.

- Exception analysis.

- Periodic analysis.

In the case of the standard analysis, the exception is highlighted in colour in the display. The exception analysis filters out the standard cases, i.e. only shows the exceptions, which are highlighted in colour. The periodical analysis automatically performs an analysis of the exceptions at previously defined intervals (hourly, weekly, monthly) and informs of their occurrence by e-mail, fax or workflow.

Info library

With the logistics information library (LIB) as part of the Logistics Information System, you can record, classify or select data and key figures. You cannot create new key figures using the LIB, but it is easy to use information that already exists in the system.

The logistics info library offers the following advantages:

- Access to all key figures.

- Simple availability of information.

- Convenient searches.

- Simple user guidance.

- Possibility to group information into info sets.

In a similar way to a search engine on the internet, it is possible in the INFO LIBRARY to use the KEY FIGURE RETRIEVAL | USING TEXT STRINGS menu item to search for and display a key figure. For example, the search for VENDOR and EVALUATION leads to a list of the possible key figures. Selection of 'Vendor evaluation for vendors from Purchasing' leads directly to the display of the vendor evaluation.

Environment

From the 'Environment' submenu, you can jump to other important transactions in the usual manner.

10.4   REPORT LISTS

The Report Writer

You use the Report Writer to create special reports if the range of functions of the standard analyses is insufficient. You can use this tool to select and evaluate special data on a more individual basis, and configure it into the desired form. The Report Writer provides you with the following possibilities, among others, for your reports:

■ Calculation of key figures, percentages and deviations.

■ Classification of reports into various categories.

■ Data comparison (for example, plan/actual or previous year/current year).

■ Download of report data to the PC (for processing).

■ Sending reports by e-mail.

The Report Painter

The Report Painter is a simpler version of the Report Writer, with a limited range of functions. In forgoing some of the functions of the Report Writer (for example, the sets) and with a graphical report structure as the basis of the report definition, the Report Painter is easier to understand and operate.

ABAP Query

ABAP Query can be used to create reports without the need to program in ABAP. 'Query' refers to a database query. As the system creates an ABAP report internally from the database query, the whole is referred to as an ABAP Query. There are three types of report available:

■ Initial lists.

■ Statistics.

■ Ranking lists.

These types can of course be combined with one another.

ABAP reports

With the programming of evaluation programs in ABAP/4, the programming language for the R/3 system, you have a great deal of flexibility and breadth of variation in creating an evaluation or a report. The price for these virtually unlimited possibilities is that detailed system skills and knowledge of this programming language are required in order to be able to program a report of this type. If these skills are available in your IT department, or can be sourced from outside, you can create reports that are specifically adapted to the needs of the company.

10.5 SAP OPEN INFORMATION WAREHOUSE

SAP Open Information Warehouse (OIW) is a grouping of the following information systems under one roof:

▪ Executive Information System (EIS).

▪ Logistics Information System (LIS).

▪ Financial Information System (FIS).

▪ Human Resources Information System (HRIS) (see Fig. 10.7).

A special catalog is used to specify which data is to be obtained for the SAP Open Information Warehouse (OIW) across which access path from the R/3 information systems. This data can be transferred across a programming interface and the front-end for Microsoft Excel to the spreadsheet program and processed there, or other database queries can be run via the OIW browser directly from Excel.

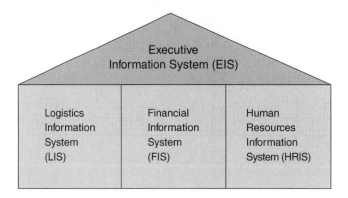

FIGURE 10.7 The SAP Open Information Warehouse

CHAPTER 11

Test equipment management

11.1   BASIC PRINCIPLES

Test equipment monitoring is an essential element of the ISO 9000ff quality management standards. As a result, there is a close relationship between test equipment monitoring and a functioning Quality Management system: reliable and carefully monitored test equipment is required to ensure quality!

The significance of test equipment management for quality management is also reflected in the SAP R/3 system. The menu structure provides direct access from Quality Management to test equipment management (see Fig. 11.1).

On the basis of the functions of the PM (Plant Maintenance) and QM (Quality Management) modules, the R/3 system as of Version 4.0 provides integrated test equipment management, which combines the important planning and handling functions of both modules. This is not an independent module, but rather a user interface that groups the suitable functions of the various modules for test equipment management/monitoring and makes them available to the user in a compact form.

An integrated software system such as the R/3 system is available at most points in the company and is extensively integrated, offering not only the core functions of the various modules, but also the following advantages for test equipment management:

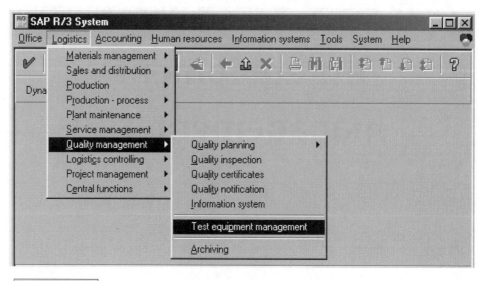

FIGURE 11.1 The menu structure shows the close relationship between test equipment management and Quality Management (© SAP AG)

- Intra-modular information and evaluations.
- The same system for all basic data of the company.
- Permanent access to information on every R/3 work centre.

The functions of the Plant Maintenance module are to be described in this chapter in sufficient detail for proper implementation of test equipment management. However, it is not possible to go into every conceivable variation. We shall restrict ourselves to typical applications, similar to those that have already been put into practice. At various points, you will nonetheless find notes and tips on how you can meet your own special requirements as regards test equipment management with the R/3 system.

11.2   DEFINITION OF THE BUSINESS TASKS

The administration of test equipment using the Plant Maintenance module is described below. As there are various possibilities for implementation using the SAP R/3 system, we shall first of all define the typical tasks in a business and then put these into practice.

It is our aim to meet the requirements of the 'Control of inspection, measuring and test equipment' element of ISO 9001. To achieve this, it is necessary to record the test equipment, including details of the device type, unambiguous identification, location of deployment, inspection frequency and method, acceptance criteria as well as tasks to be performed in the event of unsatisfactory results. Furthermore, the inspection results of calibration of the test equipment must be recorded, evaluated and stored.

As regards the company environment, we assume that there is an external calibration system or that there are calibration devices which, however, are not directly linked to the R/3 system. The inspection specifications are available either in the external systems or on paper in the form of inspection instructions or calibration instructions. The calibration results following the calibration should also be stored externally in electronic form or on paper. These assumptions apply to companies that have so far organized their test equipment monitoring themselves with a PC system or commissioned an external service provider with the calibration.

The R/3 system should be deployed to meet the standard requirements regarding recording, identification, location of deployment, inspection frequency and next calibration date, inspection status, tasks, and recording and storage of the inspection results (but only good/bad).

Although the definition of these tasks does not exhaust all the possibilities of the R/3 system, it means that a productive status can be reached relatively quickly, and this can be extended at a later date. The special feature of the above task definition is that it is not an assumed scenario but one that is actually implemented.

11.3	MASTER DATA

In the R/3 system from SAP, test equipment is used at various points within the framework of Quality Management of the QM module. For example, test equipment can be specified in routings or inspection plans for the purposes of planning or documentation.

Test equipment is managed within the framework of quality planning as so-called production resources/tools (PRT). These can be defined in the R/3 system by various types of master data records:

- Production resources/tools master record.
- Material master record.
- Document master record.
- Equipment master record.

The variability of the production resources/tools means that there are also various reference points for the mapping of test equipment in the R/3 system. Depending on the functions required, the test equipment data can be mapped as one or more of the above types of production resources/tools. Depending on the mapping variation chosen, specific functions for the test equipment for each type of production resource/tool are also available.

Test equipment as production resources/tools master data

On setting up production resources/tools, it is possible to store not only the usual administration data in the R/3 system but also information on status and location. There is also the possibility to group the test equipment and arrange it in sets.

The master record for production resources/tools contains very little data, which places strict limits on the related functions in the R/3 system. Essentially, test equipment that is mapped as production resources/tools is only recorded very roughly as regards master data. No other logistic functions are supported.

The mapping variation of test equipment as production resources/tools master records is thus the simplest case, enabling only pure evidence of use and no further functions. The test equipment is not normally recorded on an individual basis but in relation to its attributes (e.g. caliper gauge 0–150 mm).

Test equipment as a document

With the PRT master record, there is either a reference to document master records or the document master records are used directly as production resources/tools. The interfaces and functions of document management can be used to access drawings and other documents directly.

By mapping the test equipment to document records or using/integrating document records in the other types of production resources/tools, test equipment can be used in the sense of documents, for example drawings, descriptions.

This method is also used primarily for the planning and documentation of the use of test equipment. It features special functions of document management.

Test equipment as material

If general logistic functions such as procurement, storage or quality inspection are desired, it is possible to map the test equipment to material master records (see Fig. 11.2).

The material only defines the type of test equipment. This is sufficient for the handling of purchasing and the planning of operations (routings, inspection plans, etc.), as the individual items of test equipment of one type usually have the same properties and are thus interchangeable. The individual items of test equipment are not relevant to stock administration, only their total number.

A material can be serialized, thus enabling the mapping of individual items of test equipment. The material itself in this case would correspond to a certain attribute of an item of test equipment, and the serial number could represent the individual item of test equipment.

When mapping the test equipment to material, extensive functions of the R/3 system such as procurement, receipt inspection, stock management, etc. can also be used for the test equipment.

FIGURE 11.2   Possible views of material master data

Test equipment as equipment

The best range of functions is provided by mapping the test equipment as equipment. Equipment master records are maintained in the Plant Maintenance (PM) module and provide the option of defining individual devices and assigning them a hierarchical structure. This allows mapping of individual items of test equipment or grouped test equipment or more complex measurement apparatus.

The PM module provides comprehensive functions for administration, monitoring, maintenance and calibration of equipment. If equipment is integrated in routings, it is possible to check on release of production lots whether all the items of equipment involved are available.

Serialization of the material numbers is an elegant option in the SAP R/3 system to define both master records in one run and to link them at the same time. First of all, the material number is recorded or an existing number is selected. Then, the serialization function is used to generate a new serial number. In the displayed dialog, you can switch directly into the Equipment view and add specific data to the equipment master record.

The evaluations provided include the results history, graphical trend analyses and usage lists.

TABLE 11.1	Advantages and disadvantages of the alternatives for administration of production resources/tools	

Mapping option	Advantages	Disadvantages
Production resources/tools	Simple data recording	Generally low functionality No individual items of test equipment are possible
Documents	Filing of documents Functions of document management (display, archiving, etc.)	Generally low test equipment-specific functionality
Material	Extensive functionality in the areas of Logistics, Recruitment, Quality Management	Careful creation and maintenance of master data required
Equipment	Very extensive functionality suitable for test equipment	Complex data model and thus complex operation Plant Maintenance structures must be defined in the system (plant, work centres, etc.) Plant Maintenance orders and inspection processes must be revised

Summary

Due to the many varied ways of mapping test equipment in the R/3 system (see Table 11.1), there should be a very precise preliminary check as to which requirements the test equipment management is to meet. This is the only sensible way to weigh the various mapping options against one another and to find the optimum solution for the desired area of application.

11.4 THE R/3 MODULE CONFIGURATION

The different alternatives for creating production resources/tools are based on different module configurations (see Fig. 11.3). The possibilities for implementating test equipment management are thus closely related to modules that are or can be used productively for each company. If the priority is to implement a consistent concept for test equipment management, this places demands on the use of the required modules.

Variation 1: Plant Maintenance module without Materials Management module

Plant Maintenance can be used to record test equipment as equipment, to structure it hierarchically and assign it to a detailed maintenance plan. This can be used to monitor and process inspection deadlines and maintenance orders. Using the functions for capacity planning, it is possible to control the entire inspection laboratory.

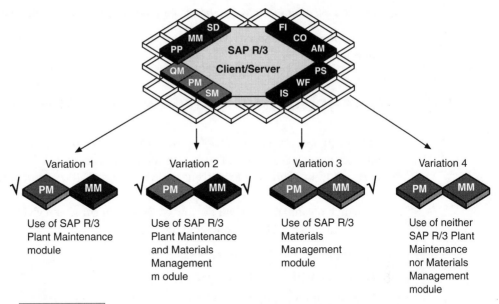

FIGURE 11.3 Possible module configurations for test equipment management

Items of equipment can be created and managed independently of the material. The special functions of Materials Management such as order, goods receipt and storage are omitted in this variation.

Variation 2: Plant Maintenance module with Materials Management module

This is the most complex but also the most efficient variation. The implementation example below is based on this.

If both modules are being used, the functions of both modules can be combined. An item of test equipment can be ordered as material and posted to goods receipt. It can then be serialized and managed as equipment.

Variation 3: Materials Management module without Plant Maintenance module

A very interesting variation that enables test equipment management with limited functionality.

Materials Management provides the opportunity to create materials also for test equipment, and thus to handle the entire administration of requests, orders and goods receipts. In addition, the materials created for the test equipment can be integrated in the various plan types in the same way as the production resources/tools.

This variation lacks the special functions of Plant Maintenance, for example the calibration deadline monitoring.

Variation 4: Neither Plant Maintenance module nor Materials Management module

This variation only permits very restricted administration of test equipment as production resources/tools.

11.5 SCENARIO FOR TEST EQUIPMENT MANAGEMENT

The following sections take their orientation from a scenario as successfully practised in a company using Release 4.0 B. The description of the individual steps is therefore to be understood in the context of the scenario, whereby not all the variations and setting options can be discussed in detail. Some points were set up in Customizing for this scenario, which means that you will not always find identical screen views in your system.

The scenario describes the following processes:

- Creation of test equipment master data.
- Procurement of the test equipment.
- Planning of test equipment monitoring.
- Performance of test equipment monitoring.

11.6 EDITING THE MATERIAL MASTER DATA

The basis for test equipment management is processing the material master data (see Fig. 11.4). Processing the material master data comprises both creating new material master data and changing the material master data.

We select MATERIAL, because the serialization, as we will see later, provides us with the possibility to create several items of test equipment under one material number with different individual serial numbers. The benefit of this variation will become clear in the example below. There are 30 dial gauges of type 0–10 mm in a company. For this type of dial gauge, there is a uniform material number but 30 different serial numbers. This gives us the opportunity to record the data of the dial gauge in the material master data and the individual data, such as the location of a certain dial gauge, at the serial number. This procedure is also required to reference an item of test equipment in the inspection plan (cf. Chapter 6, 'Quality and inspection planning'), as we do not want to refer to the individual dial gauge of 'Mr Black' but to a dial gauge of type 0–10 mm.

For each measuring device that we create using the material and serial number, the system assigns an internal equipment number, which does not interest us further. Figure 11.5 is intended to make this clear.

First of all, we create the material master data for our measuring device. To do so, we select the path LOGISTICS | QUALITY MANAGEMENT | TEST EQUIPMENT MANAGEMENT and then TEST EQUIPMENT | MATERIAL | CREATE.

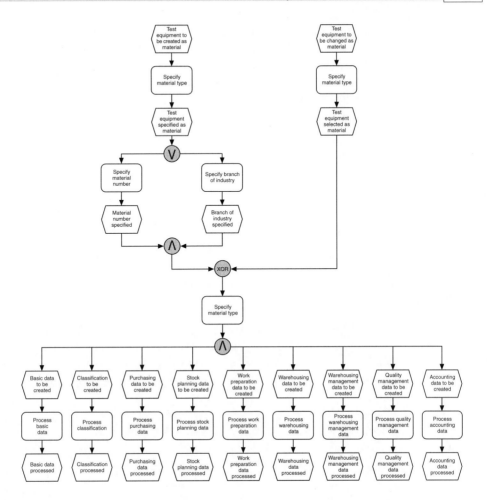

FIGURE 11.4   EPC for processing the material master data in the MM module

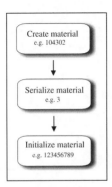

FIGURE 11.5   Relationship between material, serial and equipment number

Assuming that the system is set for external number assignment (which is advisable if you want to continue using an existing test equipment number system), enter the MATERIAL (test equipment number), the BRANCH OF INDUSTRY (here: M) and the MATERIAL TYPE (PRT = production resources/tools). When you press ENTER, the SELECT VIEW(S) dialog appears (see Fig. 11.6).

Mark at least the following views for creation:

■ Basic data 1.

■ Purchasing.

■ Production resources/tools.

■ Storage 2.

If you want to use the option of test equipment procurement and warehouse management, other views have to be created.

In the BASIC DATA view, update the MATERIAL (here: 'dial gauge 0–10 mm'), the BASE UNIT OF MEASURE (usually 'pieces') and the MATERIAL GROUP (see Fig. 11.7).

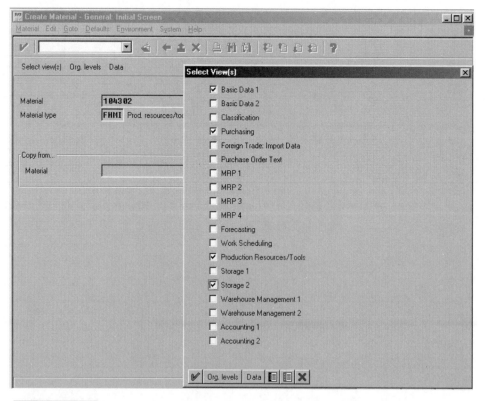

FIGURE 11.6　Views to be created for material test equipment (© SAP AG)

TIP For the material group, it is recommended to group the measuring devices into, for example, mechanical and electrical measuring devices and subdivide them into cylinder gauges, caliper gauges, dial gauges etc. or in multimeter (3½ positions), oscilloscopes, etc. This division into material groups makes later searches much easier.

In the PURCHASING view, enter the PURCHASING GROUP. By maintaining the Purchasing view, you enable Purchasing – in the event of a purchase order for other measuring devices of this type – to include the master data in the purchase order automatically.

We then come to the PRODUCTION RESOURCES/TOOLS view (see Fig. 11.8). There, we enter the TASK LIST USAGE (009 = usage in all task lists), as we want to integrate the test equipment in our inspection and task lists. For CONTROL KEY, select 'Print' (2).

Finally, in the STORAGE 2 view, the SERIAL NUMBER PROFILE (here: Z999) must be entered so that the subsequent serialization is possible. The serial number profile is required because the serial numbers are used in various R/3 components. The profiles are based on various business operations specified in Customizing. The serial number profile used here has been set up for test equipment monitoring.

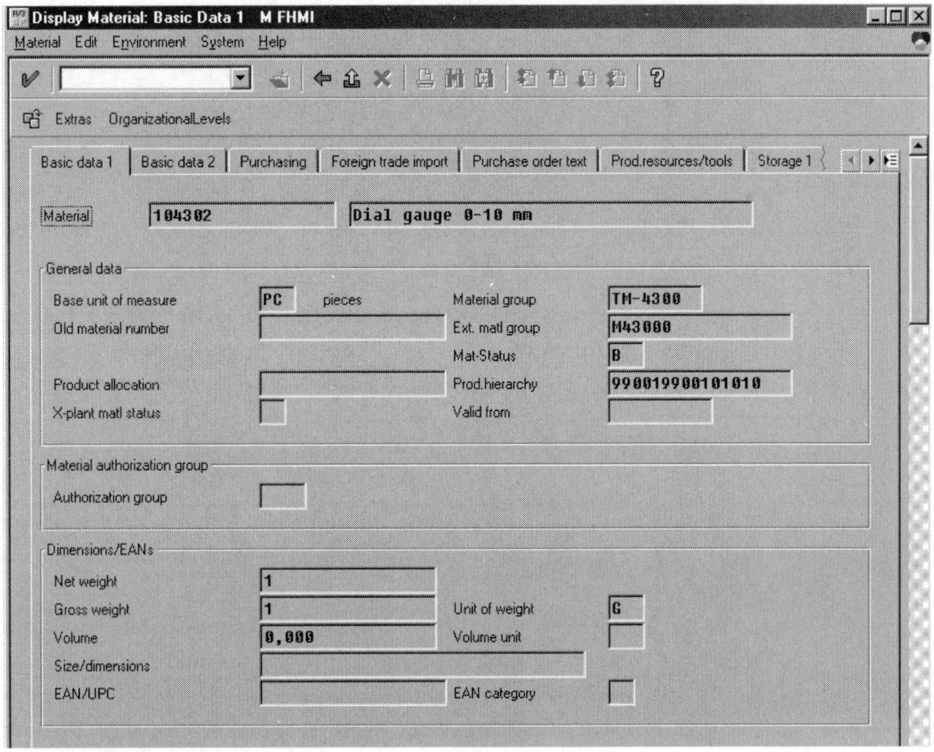

FIGURE 11.7 BASIC DATA VIEW in the material master data (© SAP AG)

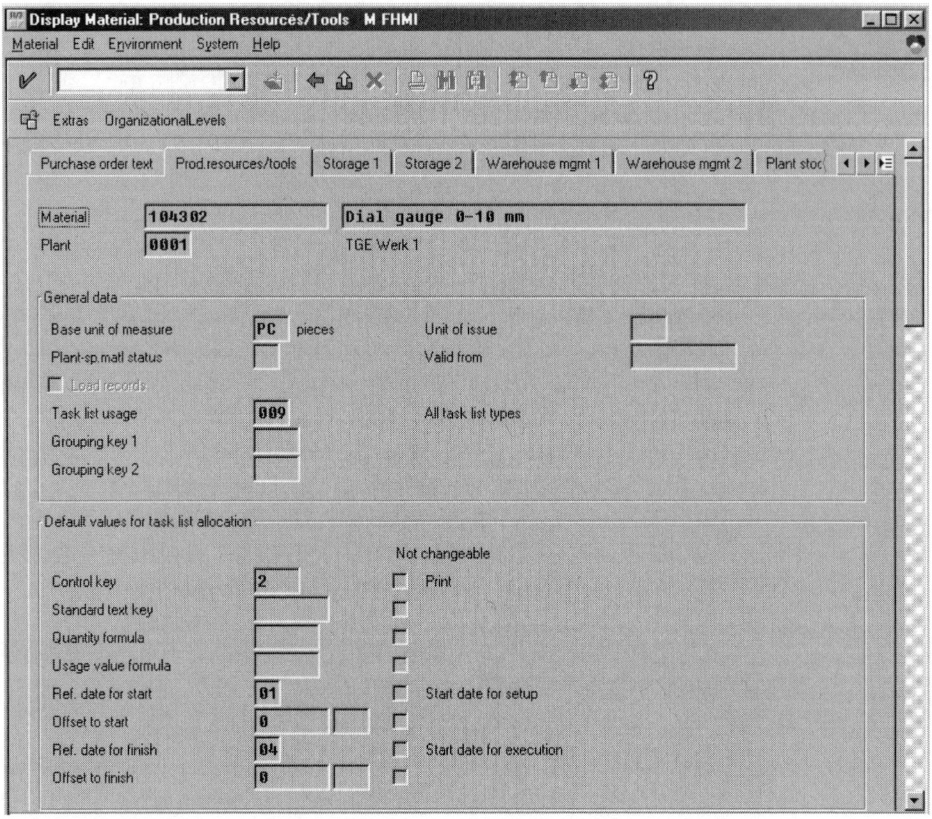

FIGURE 11.8 PRODUCTION RESOURCES/TOOLS view in the material master data
(© SAP AG)

After the views have been set up, the creation of the material master data for the test equipment is complete.

11.7 PROCURING TEST EQUIPMENT

After the master data of the test equipment material has been updated, the test equipment material can be procured. The basic flow of the procurement process is shown in Figure 11.9.

In the business process shown, it is assumed that the test equipment is procured as warehouse material. Each procurement process normally begins with a requisition that can be issued by the department that requires the test equipment. The requisition is a two-part process, consisting of the processing and approval of the requisition. The requisition then goes to Purchasing. There, the purchase order is processed (e.g. selection of vendor, etc.), approved, and sent to the vendor. After the delivery period, the ordered

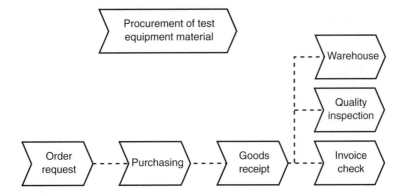

FIGURE 11.9   Procurement process for test equipment

goods are delivered to the company, and a goods receipt with reference to the generated purchase order is processed. After posting in goods receipt, three different part processes are started up:

- Goods receipt inspection
  - Inspection lot creation.
  - Inspection lot processing.
  - Inspection lot completion.

- Warehouse management
  - Storage.

- Invoice processing
  - Invoice processing with reference to the goods receipt.

When the test equipment has been procured, it is serialized as equipment, creating a fixed relationship between the existing serial number or the serial number to be attached to the test equipment and the management system.

11.8   SERIALIZING MATERIAL

First of all, a quick note: although you can create the test equipment as material in the path LOGISTICS | QUALITY MANAGEMENT | TEST EQUIPMENT MANAGEMENT and TEST EQUIPMENT | MATERIAL | CREATE, you cannot serialize it. To do so, you need to enter via the MATERIALS MANAGEMENT menu, i.e. LOGISTICS | MATERIALS MANAGEMENT | MATERIAL MASTER DATA. Only then will you find the submenu SERIAL NUMBER | CREATE or DISPLAY in the ENVIRONMENT menu.

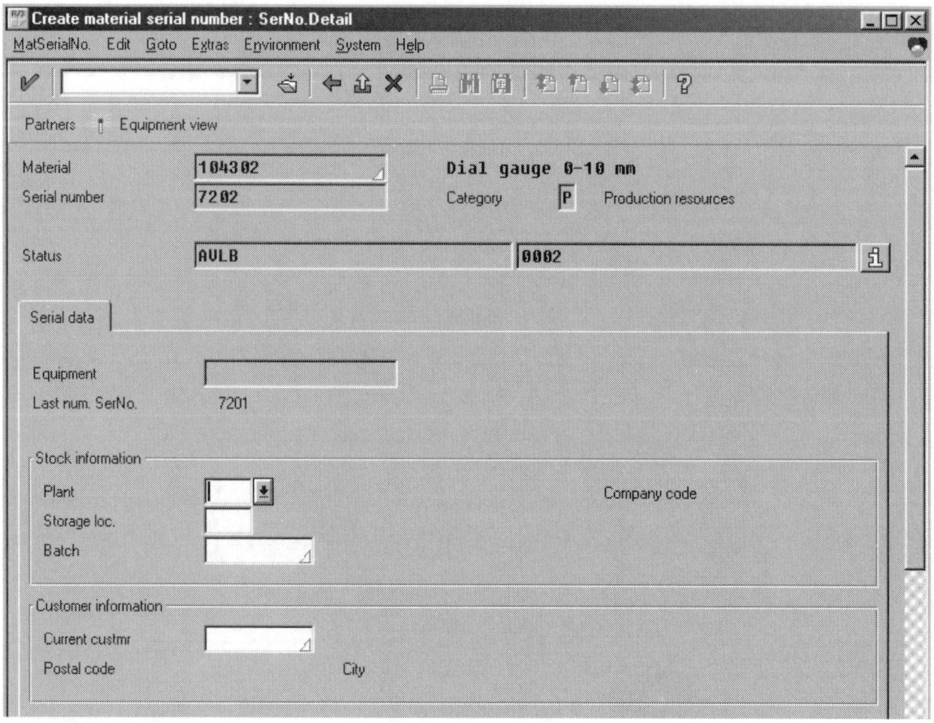

FIGURE 11.10 Serial data for material on creation (© SAP AG)

Now enter the material number (in our example: 104302) in the MATERIAL field. If you deliberately want to assign a certain SERIAL NUMBER because the test equipment already has a series number, enter this in the appropriate field. If you leave the field blank, the system automatically assigns the next serial number in the sequence. Finally, an input is required in the CATEGORY field (here: P = production resources/tools).

After you press ENTER, the detail view for the serial number appears, as shown in Figure 11.10. There, fill out the fields PLANT and STORAGE LOCATION with the appropriate values. The specified storage location is the location where the test equipment is stored when it has not been issued to a user.

11.9   CREATING MATERIAL AS EQUIPMENT

The function key ACTIVATE EQUIPMENT VIEW allocates the test equipment with material and serial number to a fixed equipment number. At the same time, other tabs appear on the screen: GENERAL, LOCATION and PM DATA as well as SERIAL DATA, whereby the equipment number is meanwhile displayed in the EQUIPMENT field. This begins the extension of the material master record to become the equipment master record.

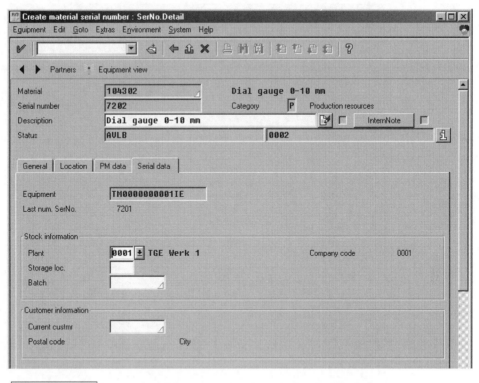

FIGURE 11.11   The four tabs of the equipment master record (© SAP AG)

The creation of the test equipment is completed by filling out some of the fields in the four tabs, as can be seen in Figure 11.11. On the GENERAL tab, the EQUITYPE field (equipment type) is filled out.

Next, select from the button bar the CLASSIFICATION function. Via the selection of the CLASS TYPE (002 = Equipment class), the CLASS TEM (Test Equipment Management) and the function key EVALUATION, you enter the CHARACTERISTIC EVALUATION screen (Fig. 11.12). The fields in this screen have been set up in Customizing in such a way that the input data meet the company requirements.

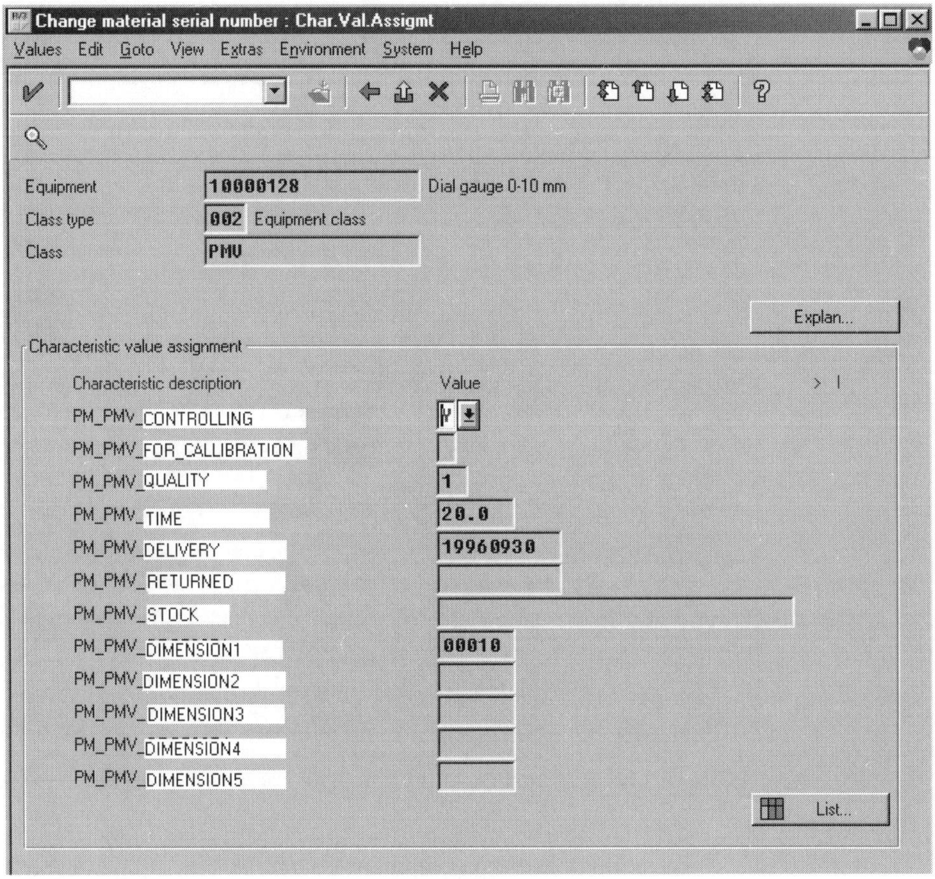

FIGURE 11.12 Characteristic evaluation screen (© SAP AG)

The input fields listed below are set in the CHARACTERISTIC EVALUATION screen; you can add to them or remove them to meet your requirements:

▨ Mandatory monitoring

An entry is made here to specify whether the test equipment is only to be recorded or also monitored on a regular basis.

▨ Quality class

Input option for the quality class, for example, for measuring instruments, gauge blocks.

▨ Time required for calibration.

▨ Issue date (from test equipment store to user).

▨ Return date (from user to test equipment store).

▓ Storage bay number

Organizational aid for the test equipment store.

▓ Variable fields

Organizational and search assistance for certain items of test equipment, for example, cylinder gauges or gap gauges.

The next function from the button bar that you process is PARTNERS. As you saw in Chapter 9, 'Quality notification', partners can be defined for certain tasks within the R/3 system; these are placed in groups (so-called 'roles'). Two groups of partners have been set for test equipment management:

▓ Internal users – partner role ZB – these are the users of an item of test equipment.

▓ Processor – partner role ZM – these are the people responsible for the calibration of the test equipment.

The corresponding employees with their personnel numbers are selected from the two roles. The master data of the employees is taken from the Human Resources Management module (HR). For reasons of data protection, only the name of the employee is accessible at this location, which in turn is only accessible to a restricted circle of users in the test equipment management functions.

The LOCATION DATA group is beneath the LOCATION TAB. There, fill out the fields LOCATION PLANT (here: 0001) and WORK CENTER (here: 5629983). WORK CENTER is the same field as you have seen in the inspection or routings. In practice, the administration of this field enables simple localization of an item of test equipment if it is to be inspected.

The ALLOCATION group is where you enter only the cost centre to which the test equipment is allocated in accounting terms. From here, with appropriate customizing, costs can be transferred to Accounting.

You enter the STATUS submenu by clicking on the 'i' button or selecting EXTRAS | STATUS. Clicking on the function key SET USER STATUS opens a selection menu of permitted USER STATUSES (see Fig. 11.13). The user status has been tailored to the requirements of our example in Customizing.

The most important statuses are:

▓ 0001 – test equipment located in warehouse.

▓ 0002 – test equipment is in use.

▓ 0008 – test equipment is being checked (in the company).

Finally, you have to fill out the PM (Plant Maintenance) DATA tab. You will find this abbreviation at various positions, as the test equipment management uses not only the Quality Management component but above all elements from the 'Plant Maintenance' component. At the PLANT MAINTENANCE DATA group, we enter the PM PLANNING PLANT, the PM PLANNER GROUP and the work centre responsible (RESPWKCEN). This

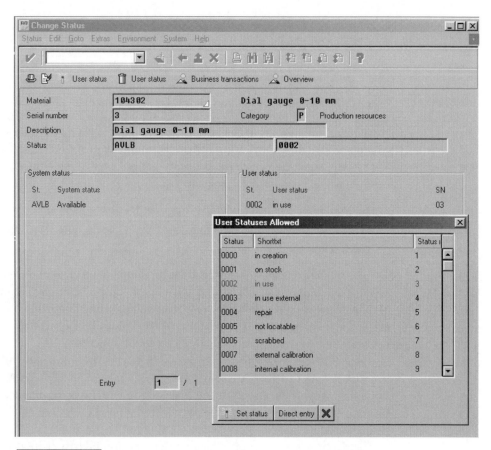

FIGURE 11.13   The user status (© SAP AG)

input corresponds to the input we already got to know in Chapter 6, 'Quality and inspection planning', as Plant, Planner group and Work centre.

After we have completed the input, we select SAVE and our test equipment has been completely set up.

11.10   PLANNING OF TEST EQUIPMENT MONITORING

The R/3 system has two instruments for the planning of test equipment monitoring. Firstly, the maintenance plan, which specifies when and in what cycle items are to be calibrated and, secondly, the plant maintenance task list (PM task list), which specifies what is to be done during the calibration.

Consequently, each item of test equipment must be clearly assigned a maintenance plan and a plant maintenance task list. Theoretically, several items of equipment can be assigned a joint maintenance plan if they all have exactly the same maintenance cycle. In our example, however, a separate maintenance plan is available for each item of equipment. Each item of equipment can also be assigned a separate plant maintenance task list. In our example, we have set up a shared task list, namely 'Calibrate by task list', as we assume in our scenario that the individual calibration task list is available on paper. For other scenarios, detailed individual plant maintenance task lists can be implemented. Figure 11.14 shows the relationship between equipment, maintenance plan and PM task lists.

11.10.1 Plant maintenance task list

First of all, we have to create a plant maintenance task list (PM task list). This is a kind of work plan for the maintenance or calibration work. This is why, at some points in the R/3 system, the expressions 'routing' or 'maintenance work plan' are used.

In principle, the corresponding sections in Chapter 6, 'Quality and inspection planning' apply to the plant maintenance task lists. For this reason, we will only briefly discuss the required input. You can create operations for the individual work steps, assign work centres and production resources/tools to the operations, plan equipping and work times, and thus also record the costs.

For this example, we assume that a simple plant maintenance task list is sufficient for all the equipment, as the detailed calibration specifications are available outside the R/3 system. It is an advantage that we only need one task list (PM task list) at the beginning, and this is assigned to all maintenance plans. At a later time, the calibra-

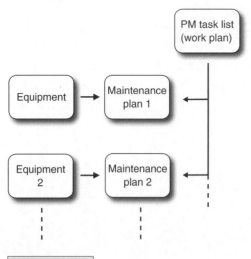

FIGURE 11.14   Planning of test equipment monitoring

tion specifications available, on paper for example, could be entered gradually in the R/3 system as individual task lists and then assigned. We also assume that there is only one central calibration point with one work centre. The costs are recorded at a flat rate by cost centre accounting and dependent on the duration of calibration. This provides us with a scenario that can be implemented relatively easily, but which can also be expanded at any time after the productive start and adapted to growing requirements.

Starting from the menu TEST EQUIPMENT MANAGEMENT, we select the path CALIBRATION PLANNING | MAINTENANCE TASK LISTS | GENERAL TASK LIST | CREATE. We enter the header of the task list and enter the task list name 'Task list for calibration' and fill out the other mandatory fields, PLANT and STATUS (see Fig. 11.15).

The next task is to create the operation. For a description of the operation, we select 'Calibration according to specification', and for work centre the calibration point is entered (Fig. 11.16). The control key set in Customizing (here: PM01) is also important. It can be used to control special functions such as confirmations.

After we have saved our plant maintenance task list, we can create the maintenance plans for the individual items of test equipment.

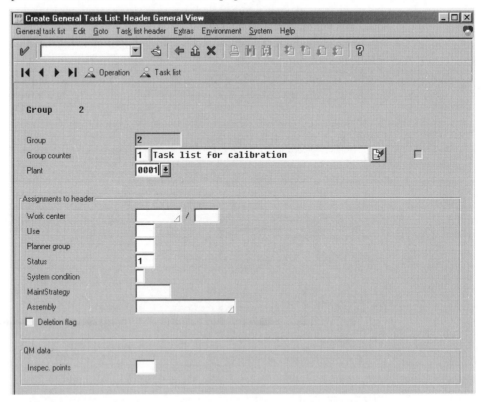

FIGURE 11.15 Example of a plant maintenance task list (© SAP AG)

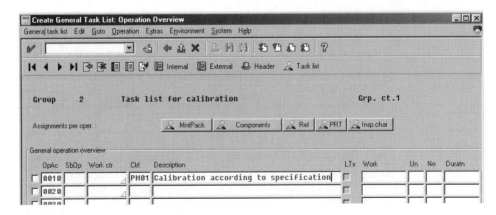

FIGURE 11.16   Operation of a general task list (© SAP AG)

11.10.2 Maintenance plan

The maintenance plan is used to plan the schedule and cycles for the calibration. In our example, we are using only time-dependent planning. However, the system also supports output-related planning (for example, calibration after 500 uses) or a combination of both (e.g. inspection after one year or 500 uses). Order specifications or maintenance strategies can also be assigned. The type of activity is specified by a reference in the maintenance plan to the associated task list.

A requirement for the creation of the maintenance plan is that we have created the test equipment that we want to calibrate with this plan and the associated task list (plant maintenance task list).

Starting from the menu TEST EQUIPMENT MANAGEMENT, we select the path MAINTENANCE PLANNING | MAINTENANCE PLAN | CREATE. In the entry screen, only the MAINTENANCE PLAN TYPE (here: PM) needs to be entered. In the ITEM DATA screen, we begin again with the DESCRIPTION field.

TIP   Instead of a text, select a combination of material and serial number, which makes it easier to search for a special maintenance plan later. For example, dial gauge 104302 with serial number 587 would receive the maintenance plan description 10430200587 (see Fig. 11.17).

In the REFERENCE OBJECT group, we enter the serial and material number for our test equipment in the appropriate fields. Then we fill out the TASK LIST group. The connection between this maintenance plan and our plant maintenance task list is set up here. If you know the plan type, the plan group number and the plan group counter of your plant maintenance task list, you can enter these directly in the appropriate fields. Otherwise, you can also use the binoculars icon to find the PM task list and transfer the data. Here, make sure that you have plan type R (as in Routing). In Chapter 6, 'Quality and inspection planning', you encountered plan types I (as in Inspection plan) and O (as in Reference Operation set).

After the fields in the TASK LIST group have been filled in, the system automatically transfers the available data into the PLANNING DATA group. You do not need to make any more entries there.

Then, the CYCLE field in the INTERVALS group must be filled out. This value specifies the time that elapses before the next calibration. Typical values are three months, six months or one year. In Figure 11.17, the entry is 365 days.

Finally, the scheduling parameters must be set. You reach the relevant submenu from the current screen via the GOTO menu item. This is where you specify when an item of test equipment that is planned for calibration is to be included in the worklist and

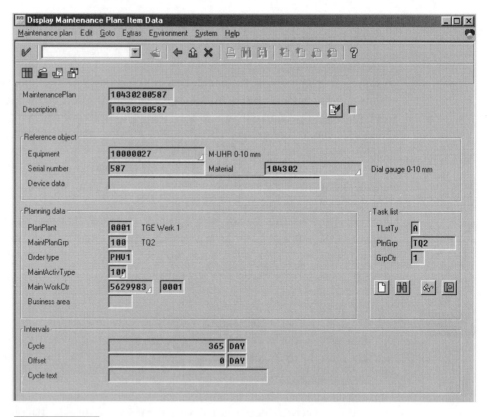

FIGURE 11.17 Example of a maintenance plan (© SAP AG)

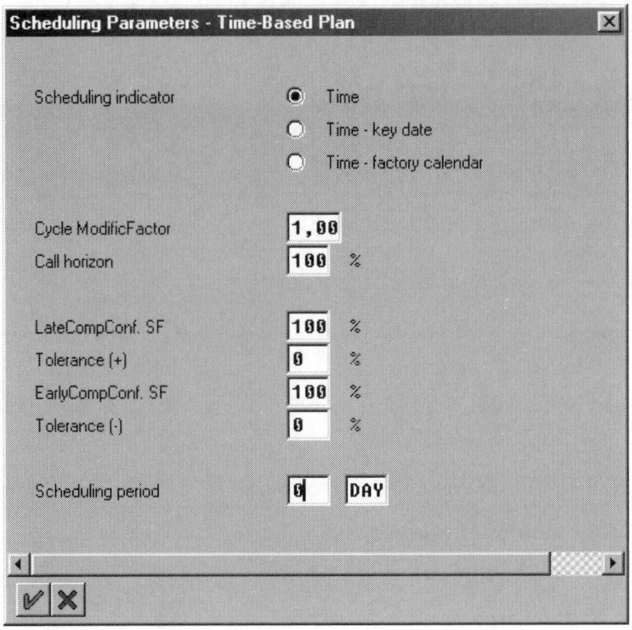

FIGURE 11.18 Scheduling parameters (© SAP AG)

when the next cycle is to start after the calibration. It would be possible, for example, that the calibration appears in the list as early as six weeks prior to the set date. For our example, the entries as shown in Figure 11.18 have proved effective in practice.

After the input has been confirmed with ENTER and SAVE, the creation of the maintenance plan is complete.

If test equipment is to be recorded but not regularly calibrated, it is not necessary to create a maintenance plan for them.

11.10.3 Scheduling

So that the automatic monitoring of the calibration deadlines can start, the scheduling for an item of test equipment and its maintenance plan must be started after creation. This takes place via the menu CALIBRATION PLANNING | MAINTENANCE PLANNING | SCHEDULING (Fig. 11.19).

Scheduling requires the input of the internal maintenance plan number. As you are unlikely to know this, open the selection window to search for the number. If you have assigned the combined material-serial number for the maintenance plan number, this advantage now comes into play. Enter this in the MAINTENANCE PLAN TEXT field, click on RUN, and you receive the required maintenance plan immediately.

After pressing ENTER and SAVE as usual, the cycle is started on the current date.

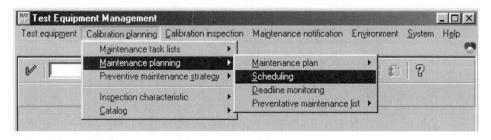

FIGURE 11.19 Menu guidance to scheduling (© SAP AG)

11.11   CALIBRATING AND CHECKING TEST EQUIPMENT

The following tasks are involved in handling the test equipment calibration:

- Release of the calibration orders.
- Performance of the calibration.
- Recording of the inspection results.
- Making the inspection decision.
- Completion of the order (inspection completion).

So that you receive calibration orders, you must start up the schedule monitoring of the system, starting from the TEST EQUIPMENT MANAGEMENT screen, manually via the path CALIBRATION PLANNING | MAINTENANCE PLANNING | SCHEDULE MONITORING (see Fig. 11.19). In practice, however, automatic start of a batch program has proved effective. This starts the schedule monitoring once a week, for example, and enters the test equipment to be calibrated in the order list.

11.11.1 Calibration orders

All the test equipment planned for calibration is located in the order list. The list is filled automatically by the periodic batch program for schedule monitoring. The list is edited manually.

Again, we start at the TEST EQUIPMENT MONITORING screen and now select the path CALIBRATION CHECK | ORDER | ORDER LIST | CHANGE. Naturally, we could also have selected DISPLAY, but as we want to start work immediately we decided in favour of CHANGE. One of the selection screens for the list display appears (Fig. 11.20).

It is important to mark the ORDER STATUS OPEN box, as all the new inspection orders initially receive the status 'open'. Following RUN, we receive a list of test equipment planned for calibration, as shown in Figure 11.21.

In order to be able to begin with the calibration of the test equipment, you must first

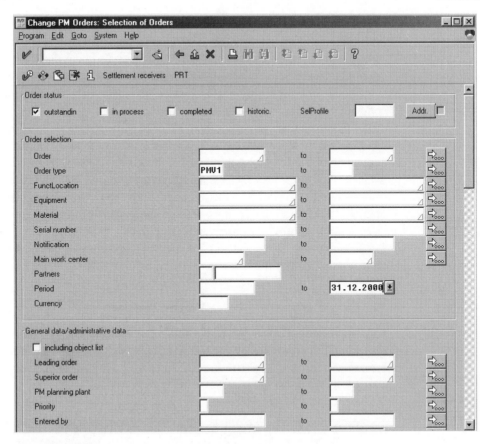

FIGURE 11.20 Selection for open calibration orders (© SAP AG)

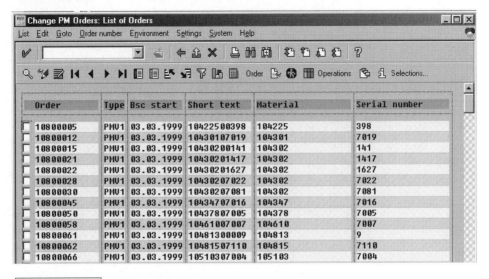

FIGURE 11.21 List of test equipment to be calibrated (© SAP AG)

release the order using ORDER | RELEASE ORDER. This creates an inspection lot with all of the data required for the calibration check. At the same time, the status of the order changes to IN PROCESS. This manual release can also take place automatically if the appropriate settings are made in Customizing.

Although the list of calibration orders is suitable for the calibration centre in the company, not every employee has the possibility to consult the system on a continuous basis to see if the test equipment he or she is using appears on the list and has to be calibrated. In spite of the aim to work only without paper, a print list for each cost centre is the suitable tool for this task. This list can be sent by internal mail, and the recipient thus finds out which test equipment is planned for calibration. To achieve this in our scenario, an ABAP/4 program has been created; this arranges all the test equipment to be calibrated according to cost centre and prints it with the number and description. This program can also run as a weekly batch program or can be started in the path SYSTEM | UTILITIES | REPORTING; it then prints a monitoring list (the users have been hidden in the list in Fig. 11.22).

11.11.2 Results recording and usage decision

You can use the worklist for the equipment to record the results for the individual inspection lots and items of test equipment. In our simplified scenario, the inspection results are documented in the external system, which means that the results recording in the R/3 system can be eliminated.

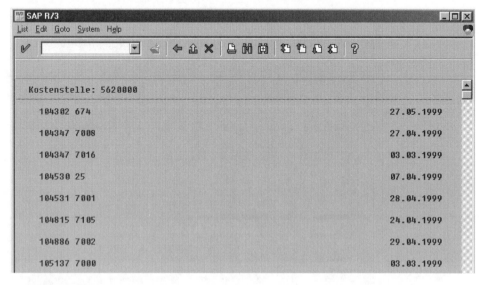

FIGURE 11.22   Calibration list (© SAP AG)

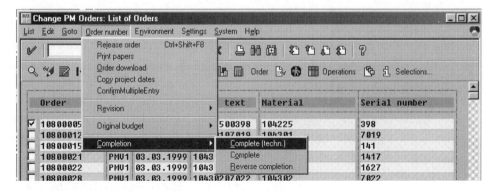

FIGURE 11.23   Order completion (© SAP AG)

It is also configured in the R/3 system that a usage decision is made for each inspection lot. We encounter the same procedure as, for example, in the case of goods receipt inspection (cf. Chapter 7, 'Quality inspection'). You use the usage decision to specify whether the test equipment can be deployed again or whether it requires repair.

The benefit of results recording and usage decision with the R/3 system is the complete documentation of the inspection in the same system. However, both tasks can be skipped if the system is set accordingly, which would mean that, following the order release and inspection, you can move on to inspection completion.

11.11.3 Inspection completion

As soon as the calibration of the test equipment has been completed, we select all the test equipment from the above screen with the status IN PROCESS. Selecting ORDER | COMPLETION | TECHNICALLY COMPLETE notifies the system that the marked items of test equipment have been fully calibrated. However, full completion of the calibration order includes the commercial completion, which you initiate via ORDER | COMPLETION | COMPLETE. Only then is the calibration order completed in full for the R/3 system, and the next cycle begins (Fig. 11.23).

If the calibration operation extends over a longer period, for example due to movement to an external calibration centre, do not forget to set the user status in the Equipment view of the serialized material accordingly (see Fig. 11.13). In this context, do not confuse the status of the PM order with the user status of the equipment.

11.12 EVALUATIONS

As in all applications, evaluation is both required and possible. Virtually any number of evaluation options are conceivable, for example total number of measuring devices, usage lists for measuring devices in certain departments/with certain people/planned for calibration/in storage, costs of calibration, number of calibration orders, and defects detected. You can use the results history to obtain a display of the changes to certain characteristics of a measuring device over defined periods. This can be shown as a run chart. In this way, following a thorough analysis, a forecasting statement can be formulated as to when a cylinder gauge will be so worn down that it exceeds the tolerance limit.

The evaluation options of the standard configuration of the R/3 system cover most of the requirements. As an example, we will show the cost centre-related usage list. It will be of interest to managerial staff to identify the measuring devices located at certain points in their own cost centre.

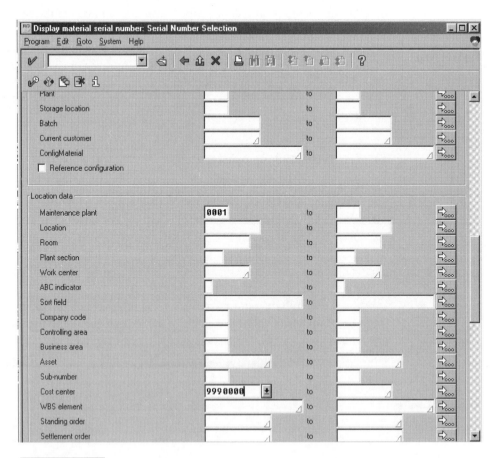

FIGURE 11.24 Test equipment search via serial number selection (© SAP AG)

In order to find this out, we start with the paths LOGISTICS | MATERIALS MANAGEMENT | MATERIAL MASTER DATA and proceed with ENVIRONMENT | SERIAL NUMBERS | LIST PROCESSING | DISPLAY. These paths take us to a selection list for serial numbers, which we are familiar with from other applications. In this selection list, you can make selections based on numerous criteria. As we want to make a selection of measuring devices in the cost centre for our example, we fill out the PLANT, LOCATION PLANT and COST CENTRE fields with the required values. Although PLANT and LOCATION PLANT are not required fields, the search time can be significantly reduced in the case of large data stocks and multiple locations by restricting the search range (as here, to the plant) (Fig. 11.24).

After clicking RUN for the selection, you receive the list of test equipment in the cost centre.

11.13 THE USE OF SUBSYSTEMS

The exclusive use of the R/3 system for test equipment monitoring has many advantages resulting from the system integration. On the other hand, a requirement is that, where possible, the Materials Management (MM) module is used and also that the Plant Maintenance (PM) module is used for the calibration planning. This would make an existing external calibration system superfluous.

If, for example, the Plant Maintenance module is not in use or you want to continue to use an efficient calibration system, you have the option of integrating the existing calibration system or a new one as a subsystem.

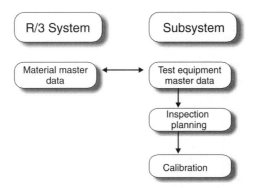

FIGURE 11.25 Test equipment master data administration in R/3 – inspection planning and inspection in the subsystem

The tasks of test equipment management and calibration, namely master data maintenance, calibration planning and calibration checks, must be divided between the R/3 system and the subsystem, and the data interchange must be assured. Two variations are conceivable:

- Variation 1: Material master data in R/3 – calibration planning and inspection in the subsystem.

- Variation 2: Master data and calibration planning in R/3 – inspection in the subsystem.

Variation 1: Material master data in R/3 – calibration planning and inspection in the subsystem

The master data is created in the R/3 system in Materials Management. This is necessary so that test equipment is known in the R/3 system, and can be ordered and included in routings and inspection plans.

The serialization of the material numbers for individual items of test equipment takes place in the subsystem, as do the administration of location and user, the inspection planning, the scheduling of inspections and calibration, as well as inspection and results recording (see Fig. 11.25).

Data interchange is required for comparison of the material master data. For this reason, the subsystem must have a defined interface to the R/3 system. The data comparison can, for example, take place every night. The inspection results remain on the subsystem. Under certain circumstances, the evaluations are also performed on the subsystem.

In principle, this variation is suitable for mapping the flow with an external calibration

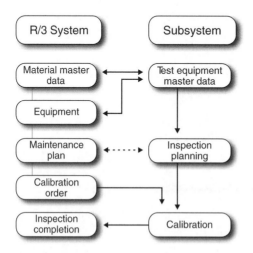

FIGURE 11.26   Test equipment management in R/3 – inspection in the subsystem

centre. In this case, the external calibration centre stands for the external subsystem. The comparison of master data can take place either using printed lists or also online.

Variation 2: Master data and calibration planning in R/3 – inspection in the subsystem

If both the Materials Management module and the Plant Maintenance module are used, the advantages of both modules can be exploited. The functions of Materials Management can be used to handle procurement, and Plant Maintenance handles test equipment management and monitoring. The inspections are then performed in the subsystem.

This variation requires more intensive data interchange between the R/3 system and the subsystem, as the material master data and the equipment data of the serialized material have to be transferred to the subsystem and the calibration result from the subsystem into the R/3 system (see Fig. 11.26). As a rule, however, it is also sufficient here to run the comparison on a nightly basis.

This variation is very suitable for including an existing calibration system in the R/3 installation, which means that the familiar working environment can be retained. The connection of the subsystem can be implemented on various levels. In the scenario described above, for example, manual input of the inspection completion was assumed, eliminating the need for implementation of an interface. However, there is a risk in forgoing the comparison of master data: the data in the R/3 system and that on the subsystem could drift apart as time goes by.

CHAPTER 12

Internet scenarios with SAP R/3 QM

BASIC PRINCIPLES

Within the SAP system, numerous business operations can be mapped and handled across the internet. As it is only in very rare cases that an SAP web server is set up especially for Quality Management, it is advisable – where required – to look for coalitions in the company for internet use, and then to work out a joint strategy. From a certain company size onwards, and in view of the relatively low expense involved, we even believe that a separate web server would be justified. The applications described here are included in the shipped version. Internet connection of course initially requires configuration and installation of the web server. In the simplest case, this involves a PC of the appropriate power with MS Internet Information Server 4.0 and the SAP Basic Tools. The computer is linked across your company network to the productive SAP R/3 domain. Your customers also need internet access, and you have to provide them with access rights in the form of user IDs and passwords. Consequently, access by your customer to the complaint data of other companies is normally impossible.

The standard internet applications – as usual with SAP – can be extended using your own programming, and should thus not be viewed as rigid specifications. The supplied scenarios provide good possibilities for you to transfer your familiar business processes and gear them to the new requirements of internet communication.

If you wish to highlight your customer orientation, allowing your customers to handle quality matters across the internet is practically a 'must'. Communication difficulties in notification processes, in particular, frequently generate misunderstandings regarding the allocation of complaint objects and the associated defect descriptions. By working on the same notification across the web, these problems, for example, would no longer have the same significance.

As of Release 3.1x, SAP provides two internet scenarios specifically for Quality Management. These are described below:

- Handling of quality certificates.
- Recording of quality notifications.

The abbreviation IAC, which you might encounter in the course of your project engineering, stands for 'Internet Application Component'. IACs comprise R/3 transactions, as well as external data that is required for an internet application.

12.2 RECORDING QUALITY NOTIFICATIONS

In our view, the most important aspects in recording a quality notification over the internet are conformity of the reference objects (material, order, etc.) and the defect descriptions. This procedure significantly reduces the processing overhead, which will lead on both sides to a faster and 'leaner' business event. The internet notification can be activated by the customer at any time, and information on the processing status of a notification is always available. As this form of notification handling is by no means standard in industry at the moment, your company stands out in a positive light by using this method, and a corresponding competitive advantage is one of the pleasant side-effects.

The quality notification is imported via the internet application directly into the appropriate notification type in the SAP system, where it is available for further processing. For the clerk processing the notification, this generates a backlog of work for further processing, which can be extended by an additional workflow connection in an active workflow item.

12.2.1 Requirements in the R/3 system

The quality notification is issued by an employee of the customer, the company supplied with goods, which is set up in the customer master record of our R/3 system, with the employee entered as contact.

In the internet transaction, the contact involved (which could be more than one) receives a number stored in the customer master record and an internet ID of the type BUS1006001 (business partner staff). This number and code is passed on to your customer in the course of business communication, but the best way is to hold a small workshop on the subject. If your customers agree, they can use the internet method of complaints handling from that moment on.

Customizing requires specification of the initial notification type for the transaction *QM01* (Create quality notification); this is the only way that the correct notification type can be found in the case of notification creation across the web. The system also checks whether all of the mandatory partners of the notification have been supplied. As the notification type Q1 (Customer complaint) is involved here, the sold-to party (STP) and the contact must be defined as mandatory partners in Customizing. No other mandatory partners may have already been created, as you cannot serve these partners across the web.

Scenario example

Based on our example of a customer complaint in Chapter 9, 'Quality notification', we now run through the alternative of notification handling over the internet.

Contact starts the internet application

In a delivery to an important corporate customer, a defect occurred on the CD cover. Instead of a telephone call with an accompanying fax or e-mail, the person lodging the complaint starts up the internet application for notification handling and logs on with number and password. In the next step, the employee specifies whether he or she wants to create a new notification or query the status of older notifications. At logon, the customers naturally only have access to materials supplied by their own company or for which notification handling is set up. The permitted materials must be defined beforehand in the customer material information record.

Creating the customer complaint

After selecting a material from the list of options, the customer starts to describe the problem. By switching to the web page provided for this purpose, the customer starts the defect description in the same way as in our R/3 system – by selecting a defect from the defect catalog. The notification is completed with the input of the catalog-supported defect location and a defect description in text form.

If the internet quality notification method has been successfully coordinated with the customer, the customer is now willing to help by providing an indication of the posting document (delivery note or purchase order number). This can be used to identify the delivery more specifically at later stages in notification handling. The options for the defect codes and the defect locations displayed here have also been assigned to the materials beforehand. In this way, when assigning defects, the customer only sees the codes that affect his or her materials. The next task is to save the notification on the web page. After saving, the notification is given a notification number which is displayed immediately. This notification number can be used from then on by the customer and the recipient of the complaint to identify and trace the notification (see Fig. 12.1).

Other processing in the R/3 system

It should be our principal task to confirm receipt of the notification as quickly as possible, and to specify and initiate an immediate task. This can be done without any difficulty using the various lists for the worklist. The setting of a certain number range interval can separate the internet notifications from all other notifications. By selecting notifications with a certain status, the newly created notifications can in turn be selected. If your working method involves hourly reading of newly created notifications, the first step towards rapid processing has already been taken. In special cases, of course, a parallel telephone call or other communication would not be superfluous. In most cases, however, the customer has at least the possibility of making a complaint very quickly and without a great deal of effort, and the complaint contains concrete information that could be decisive for your subsequent course of action (see Fig. 12.2).

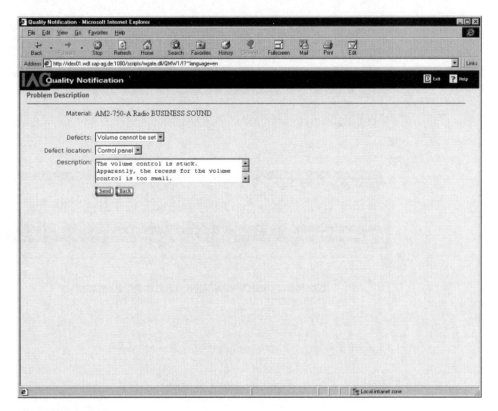

FIGURE 12.1   Notification processing on the internet (© SAP AG)

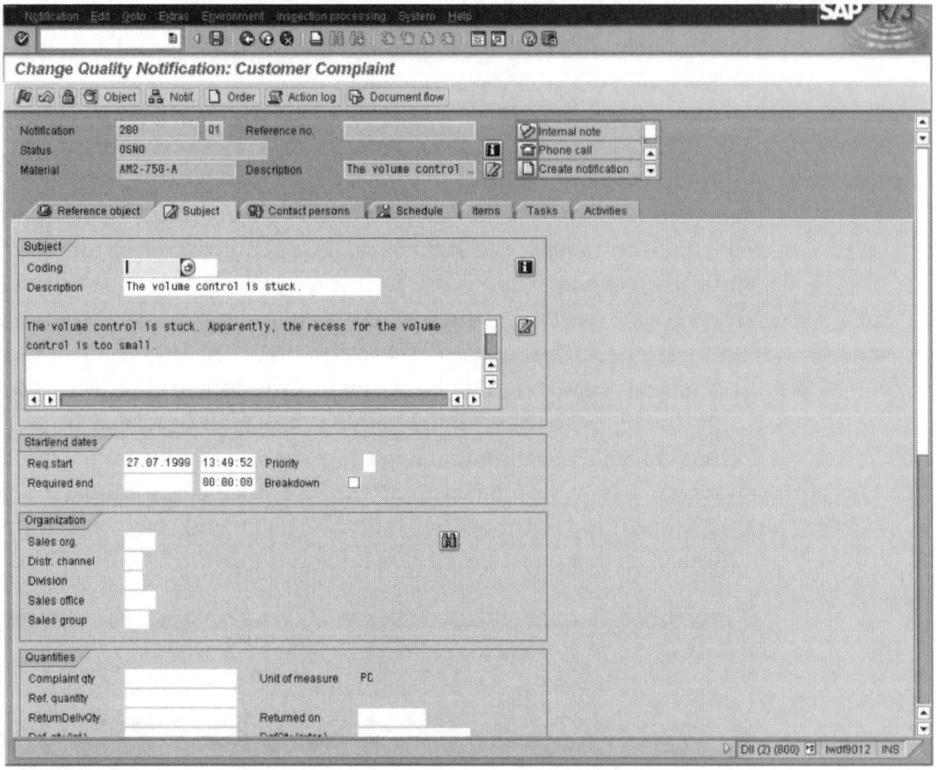

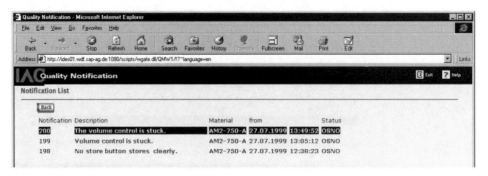

FIGURE 12.2 Processing a notification in R/3 4.6 (© SAP AG)

FIGURE 12.3 Display notification status (© SAP AG)

Displaying the notification status

The customer can use the web transaction to query the processing status based on the status of the notification number (see Fig. 12.3). The list of quality notifications contains all the information specified by the customer, such as material, defect coding and, in addition, the defect description. The defect description could also contain the name of the complaint recipient, which enables the customer to obtain detailed information on the processing status at any time from the person responsible.

12.3	CREATION OF QUALITY CERTIFICATES

For all vendor/customer relationships in which an exchange of material certificates plays a decisive role, it is advisable to use the SAP IAC (Internet Application Component) for provision of quality certificates. A well-known recurring problem of certificate processing is the lack of prompt provision of the certificate form for delivery of the goods. In many cases, the customer has to verify the values on the certificate or analyse the goods once again under their own laboratory and plant conditions. The results of the inspections are then compared and batches are classified in order to make a final decision on the usage of the goods. For described processes, the certificate is essential; the goods are worthless to the customer without the right certificate.

Incidentally, the difficulties in certificate processing already mentioned occur not only in the processing industry, but also in mechanical and plant engineering. In these branches of industry, in the case of parts and components in plants where safety is critical (nuclear power stations, petrochemicals, etc.), a separate certificate is often demanded for each individual valve, each section of pipe. The certificates must always be available and are to be submitted when a plant of this nature is inspected on completion. We know of projects in which the expenditure for certificates and documentation amounted to almost a quarter of the total project costs.

The internet application 'creation of quality certificates' enables the customer to access the agreed certificates conveniently across the internet. The reference object for finding the certificate is the 'batch'. Depending on what case is involved, this expression can refer to an order number or another code number of a delivery, allowing the customer to see the reference to their goods.

Requirements in the R/3 system

The basis of the procedure is formed by the certificate definition from Chapter 6, 'Quality and inspection planning'. Here, the content and appearance of the certificate are defined. It is certainly possible to use several certificate forms for internet handling. Certificate profile configuration and the content agreed with the customer are defined in advance, so that the customer receives the designated certificate form on selection of a batch. Without the configuration of certificate profiles in the R/3 system's

SCENARIO Here, we will use the example of a transmission assembly with casing components made of aluminum. To ensure that no corrosion occurs in special areas of use (drilling rigs), the specification requires a certificate documenting analysis of a certain proportion of alloy. When the product is used on 'drilling rigs', the alloy proportion must be less than one per cent to ensure corrosion resistance in sea water; for use in 'mechanical engineering', the specification is identical, but the alloy component does not need to be documented in the form of a certificate. The certificate is to be enclosed with every delivery to the purchasers demanding 'corrosion resistance in sea water'.

Customizing it is not possible to use the internet application.

So that an employee of the supplied company can view the quality certificate, the following settings must be considered:

- This customer is created in the customer master record of the R/3 system and the employee is entered as contact.

- The configuration of certificate profiles has been set up.

Requirements for the customer

A normal internet access option with a standard browser (MS Internet Explorer, Netscape etc.) is used here. For display and printing of certificates, a PDF (Portable Document Format) browser is required. A common product is, for example, the one made by Adobe™, which can be downloaded from the internet as shareware. Moreover, the Acrobat Reader™ program is on the enclosed CD.

Customer starts the internet application

The customer logs on with his or her number and password. At logon, the customer only has access to materials they have supplied or for which certificate handling is set up.

Certificate selection via batch number

All certificates must be allocated in advance to a batch. With the internet application, you do not search for the certificates directly, but by batch number. In order to select the right batch, the following search criteria are provided (see Fig. 12.4):

- Product group (in the R/3 system = material group): all batches of a material group are listed.

■ Search string: with this search, the suitable materials are identified by means of the short text of the material; a generic search with * (any character string) and + (for one character) is permitted here.

■ Batch number – for direct input.

A combination of the criteria is also possible. The search criteria are then linked by means of a logical AND link.

The search is started using the SEARCH button. The list that is then displayed shows the materials found and the allocated batch but does not show the certificates yet. All result lists are displayed with material, batch and, if applicable, sell-by/use-by date.

Creation of certificates

Selecting a batch from the result list provides the customer with the certificate containing the information from the certificate profile configuration of the R/3 system. The profile already takes account of the customer-specific formats and results layouts. The

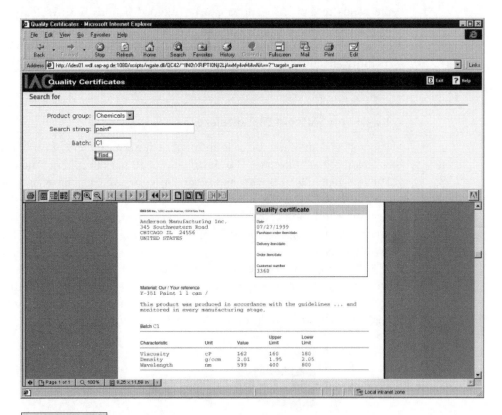

FIGURE 12.4   Quality certificate on the internet (© SAP AG)

display is in PDF format, and is thus available for filing or printing. The certificate created using the internet application is identical in form and content to the certificate of the R/3 system, and is based only on concluded inspections. This method provides an identical basis of data and ensures that the content of documents can be matched.

12.4   MYSAP.COM

mySAP.com is the new, comprehensive solution concept of SAP for optimum integration of all relevant business processes across the internet (see Fig. 12.5). mySAP.com provides a seamless and consistent integration of SAP-internal and SAP-external solutions, starting with initial contact and covering all business processes. mySAP.com thus provides a complete business environment for electronic commerce (Fig. 12.6).

For quality management, mySAP.com represents a configurable environment for the exchange of all quality-relevant data along the logistic chain. For example, multiple goods receipt inspections can be avoided if both business partners call up the inspection data of the traded product using a shared application on the internet. Results of current production provide the business partner with information not only on the quantity already manufactured, but also on the product quality.

mySAP.com consists of four essential elements.

12.4.1 mySAP.com Marketplace

The mySAP.com Marketplace is an internet community which is the central point for companies in all branches of industry and of all sizes to transact their business in full. The internet address is *www.mySAP.com*. Anyone can use a browser to access the open environment of the global mySAP.com Marketplace and find new business partners or customers and contact them. SAP customers can expand their business processes on the internet by linking existing SAP applications with the Marketplace. This protects your investments.

SAP has many years of experience in handling integrated, industry-specific business processes. SAP is also able to provide a large network of partners with fast solutions. Moreover, SAP has a comprehensive list of customers who will have a large share of business-to-business trade on the internet in the future.

FIGURE 12.5   Internet applications with mySAP.com (© SAP AG)

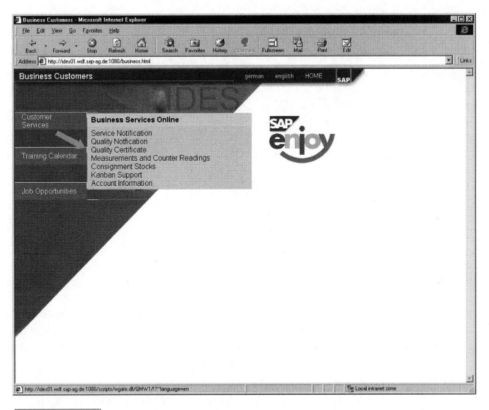

FIGURE 12.6   mySAP.com – one-step business for quality management (© SAP AG)

SAP has also formed partnerships with leading external technology providers to create an open market environment based on internet standards.

The mySAP.com Marketplace offers:

- The possibility of one-step business handling at any time, in any place, with any business partner.

- An inter-industry, horizontal marketplace as the basis for cooperation between business partners in general; a range of vertical and regional marketplaces for specialized trade between groups with similar interests, for example, the oil and gas industries.

- Comprehensive business information and detailed news from specific industries (see Fig. 12.7).

The inter-industry marketplace provides horizontal applications such as auctions, commodity trading and matching of vendor inquiries. These horizontal applications can be used independently of the branch of industry. This includes, for example, trading in goods and services and general information (news, company profiles, stock market quotations, etc.).

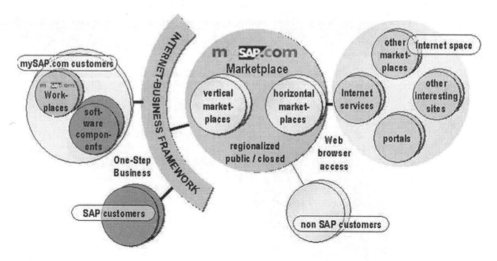

FIGURE 12.7 mySAP Marketplace (© SAP AG)

The vertical and regional marketplaces offer tailored applications for each target group. The vertical applications comprise industry-specific trade with goods and service as well as industry-specific information and internet communities. All users of the global marketplace have access to the available information and communities, and can customize them to meet their own requirements. Individual industry- or region-specific functions can be protected and made accessible to only a selected group of people.

Components for business-to-business trade

The mySAP.com Marketplace also supports a number of specific, preconfigured applications for cooperation in the area of electronic commerce.

Business directory

The Business Directory provides a variety of information for buyers and sellers on general company data, product catalogs, contact addresses and target markets. Every company can enter itself in the central business directory of the mySAP.com Marketplace. In addition to specifying addresses and contact information, each company can have itself allocated to certain product and service categories. This allocation allows potential vendors and customers to find the company more easily.

The Business Directory uses the internet standard protocol LDAP (Lightweight Directory Access Protocol) to access the directory service. The DUNS number of the database provider Dunn & Bradsteet is used to identify companies. DUNS numbers are the most widespread categorization numbers available in the world for company information searches.

Document Exchange

The Document Exchange enables smooth information interchange between buyers and sellers on the mySAP.com Marketplace. The company can maintain additional data fields here. This supplementary information is used for seamless handling of business processes. In a buyer–seller scenario, the selling party can add to the data in the Business Directory master data regarding creditors and vendors. On the buyer side, this information is used on creation of a vendor master record in their system in the background. This operation takes place during the requisition. This helps to integrate the requisition in the accounting process of the buying company.

Distributor Reseller Management

The web-supported business scenario Distributor Reseller Management (DRM) simplifies the individual steps from the introduction through the negotiation to the conclusion of agreements between manufacturers and their distributors. The DRM function in mySAP.com reduces the costs in electronic commerce to such an extent that even small companies remain competitive.

RFP and RFQ matching

The mySAP.com solution is a central node for matching vendor inquiries. From here, vendor inquiries can be posted, distributed and matched; administration costs in Purchasing and Sales are considerably reduced. mySAP.com enables the requirements

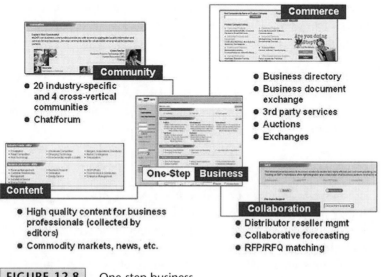

FIGURE 12.8   One-step business

of buyers to be matched by means of a sophisticated classification system to the capacities of the vendors. Furthermore, companies can pass on changes to vendor requirements without having to create and dispatch a copy of the new document every time.

Auctions

mySAP.com gathers both buyers and sellers in two types of market: inter-industry markets and industry-specific markets. In both areas, mySAP.com provides open and private markets. The customer can use these markets, for example, to reduce overcapacities.

Services

The mySAP.com Marketplace currently offers 20 different internet services from partners from the areas of Customer Relationship Management, Office, Travel, Careers, Personnel, Reference Works and more. All mySAP.com Marketplace users have access to these services. The services provide the option of 'single sign-on', which means that users only have to log on to mySAP.com Marketplace once, and then can use the various services without the need to log on again (Fig. 12.8).

Architecture of the mySAP.com Marketplace

The mySAP.com Marketplace is a combination of infrastructure technology, web applications and web services. It is a safe, high-performance and scalable access point for all types of information and services, providing an open, distributed and decentralized environment that enables the integration of other services. To protect the data, mySAP.com uses SSL protocols (Secure Sockets Layer). SSL guarantees confidentiality, integration and authentication of data. Verisign and other certificates are supported. The transfer of transactions is assured by means of a Message Store Service. As a trustworthy, independent third party, mySAP.com provides a service that enables all business-to-business purchase orders and confirmations to be logged and saved. In addition, the mySAP.com Marketplace is seamlessly integrated in the security of the SAP R/3 system.

Messaging backbone

The messaging engine of the mySAP.com Marketplace uses publish-and-subscribe technology for communication. This enables reliable and transparent transfer of current information. The messaging engine also supports query and reply operations, enabling scalability and error tolerances.

The messaging engine of mySAP.com receives, saves and transmits business documents in the XML format, using both synchronous and asynchronous messaging protocols. This makes it one of the most sophisticated engines on the market.

12.4.2 mySAP.com Workplace

The mySAP.com Workplace is a company portal that provides the user with fast, simple and convenient web-based access to all internal and external applications, including content and services, that are required for day-to-day work. The mySAP.com Workplace supports employees by providing the right information and applications by mouse-click – by means of an interface that is easy to understand, customize and use. The following are some features of the mySAP.com Workplace:

- Single point-of-access to applications by means of web browser.
- Content and services.
- A personalized and role-based user interface.
- Convenient integration.
- Openness and flexibility.
- Access is from everywhere and possible at any time.

Single point-of-access with a web browser

The mySAP.com Workplace provides all users with a central starting point (see Fig. 12.9). From there, they have access to everything they need to perform their day-to-day

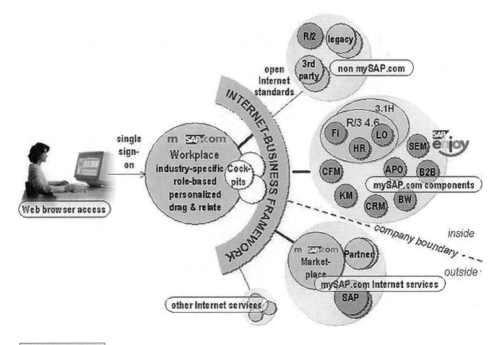

FIGURE 12.9   mySAP Workplace (© SAP AG)

tasks. Via a web browser, the users can profit from the advantages of a single integrated company portal.

With a pleasantly simple screen design and corresponding functions, the mySAP.com Workplace grants access to all the SAP and non-SAP applications and internet services. At the same time, the user has access to intranet and self-service applications as well as extranets and existing applications – and all of this with one web browser.

Personalized and role-based user interface

As no two users are the same, the mySAP.com Workplace is preconfigured for the relevant roles (employee, controller, purchaser, order clerk, manager) and can be fully customized to individual requirements. There are configuration options at all levels: specific to the individual, role, company and branch of industry. They ensure that the relevant information, services and functions are available for precisely the right area of activity.

The users can assume various roles to take part in different business scenarios. For example, the user can assume the role of the employee and create procurement requests, thus automatically taking part in the business scenario 'e-procurement'. Another participant in this scenario, in the role of the buyer, has the possibility to execute this purchase order. Various functions, contents and services are required, and

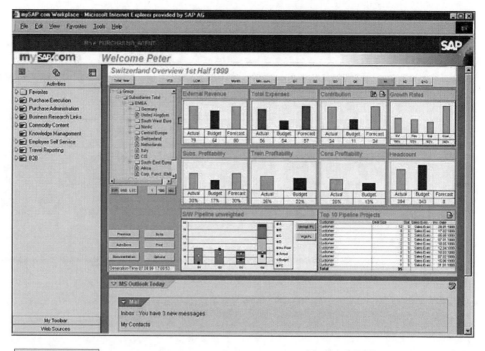

FIGURE 12.10 Convenient overviews (© SAP AG)

these are supplied by the mySAP.com Workplace depending on the role the user assumes. The mySAP.com Workplace is supplied with different, predefined roles, which are used as the starting point for company-specific customizing. In addition, each user can customize the mySAP.com Workplace to his or her personal needs, e.g. by adding links to special, frequently used transactions or web pages.

Convenient integration

With the mySAP.com Workplace, long searches and repetitive tasks, as they are frequently encountered in today's IT environments, are a thing of the past. The user can 'drag & drop' between different applications – with a simple mouse-click (Fig. 12.10).

With the internet, intranet, extranet and other applications, users can feel over-powered by the flood of information and the technical possibilities, many of which are only vaguely related to the actual task of the employee. Consequently, users waste a great deal of time on repeated password inputs, on searching through mountains of information and files, and switching between different user interfaces. The lack of integration between web-based resources and business applications reduces the productivity of the user. It is precisely this challenge that is met by the mySAP.com Workplace and its 'drag & drop' functions between business software and web pages.

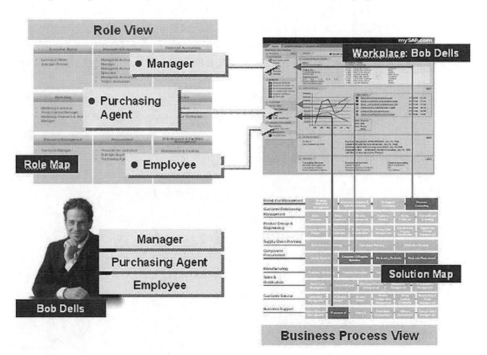

FIGURE 12.11   Ergonomic workplace configuration (© SAP AG)

For example, a purchaser can use the mySAP.com Workplace to drag an overdue order and drop it on the icon of an express delivery service within the same screen window. This simple act causes the mySAP.com Workplace to access the web page of the forwarder automatically to record all the details concerning the overdue consignment. This integration saves the user several steps: clicking on the web browser, input of the web address of the forwarder, logging in to the web page and re-entering the order data.

The user also profits from the complete integration in the mySAP.com Marketplace, an open electronic marketplace for business partners. For example, a purchaser might require raw material prices on a regular basis, and these are offered on the mySAP.com Marketplace or other web pages. Instead of repeatedly entering expressions in various search engines, the integrated access enables the purchaser to run a targeted search across several resources – direct from a material request list.

Openness and flexibility

An essential characteristic of the mySAP.com Workplace is the open and flexible infrastructure, which groups the resources according to the role and personal requirements of the user within the company. A centrally located and administered server as well as excellent security mechanisms enable the user a convenient single sign-on. The mySAP.com Workplace is one of the latest possibilities for shared work across the web that is supported by the Internet-Business Framework. It provides easy access, permits simple changes and enables effortless cooperation. The Internet-Business Framework is a flexible and open infrastructure based on web standards for all mySAP.com solutions, and is supported in this by XML-based web messaging and web flow.

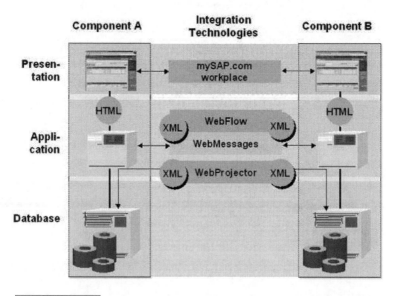

FIGURE 12.12 Complete integration in the IT landscape (© SAP AG)

CHAPTER 13

Customizing

BASIC PRINCIPLES

The expression 'customizing' can be defined as customer adaptation, and it is part of the standard vocabulary for R/3 implementations. If you draw a parallel between the content of this activity and certain areas in everyday life, you will notice that we perform 'customizing tasks' relatively often. Consider, for example, putting together a new car, a kitchen, or building a house. Let us remain briefly with the example of buying a car: car dealers – in simple terms – take on the function of consultants, showing the different variations in the ways a car can be put together. They describe the optional extras that can be combined, which combinations make sense, and the expense involved in realizing your 'customizing'. It is therefore easy to understand that the interplay between customers and consultants runs all the more smoothly if the following factors are ensured:

- The consultant is able to identify with the wishes of the customer.
- The customer is informed about all the possibilities.
- Customers clearly formulate their requirements.
- The feasibility of the requirements/wishes is examined by experts.
- The resources for the customer adaptations are available.

This is only possible, of course, if the customer and the consultant 'speak the same language'. In the example 'buying a car', the shared context of consultant and customer has usually grown over a number of years, making understanding slightly easier. For an R/3 implementation project, communication on the subject of customizing is a little more difficult. The reason for this lies in the fact that the customer has no clear conception of either the principles of the procedure in Customizing nor of its possibilities. You encountered one method as a common level in Chapter 2, 'Modeling QM business processes using the EPC method'. Other shared points of contact worth mentioning in this context are the work packages and activities involved in the Customizing functions, and the SAP procedural model, where business know-how and system-specific knowledge meet. You could even call it a human interface, i.e. a communication platform that enables exchange across many specialized fields. It is therefore essential for customers who want to properly understand the system and the implementation concept to take an active interest in Customizing.

The example we mentioned above of 'new car customizing' can be applied to the project work of an R/3 QM implementation – except that the content is more comprehensive and certainly slightly more complicated than the act of 'buying a car'. However, the essential difference is that an R/3 QM project consists of a large number of business processes and functions. The process 'buying a car' is relatively simple from the point of view of the purchaser, and the combination options are generally more transparent.

The path towards completion of Customizing is usually iterative, i.e. it approaches the initial concept in individual steps and across several project phases. In the example 'buying a car', within the definition of customizing, the order is normally handled and concluded in a few steps.

In order to implement customer-specific requirements, an R/3 system contains the Implementation Guide (IMG). For the area of QM alone, there are over 200 different possible settings, many of which have reciprocating effects within QM and with other components. Figure 13.1 shows an 'expanded' REFERENCE of the IMG for the area of Quality Management.

Properties of the Customizing functions

We divide Customizing of the R/3 system roughly into two areas of focus:

▓ Customizing the business settings.

▓ Customizing the operative (QM) processes.

Particularly when setting basic business data in the area of QM, the reciprocating effects with all the components of Logistics must be checked accurately. Although this content is not separated in Customizing, it is recommended that you check every setting within the framework of the QM implementation as to whether neighbouring processes are affected.

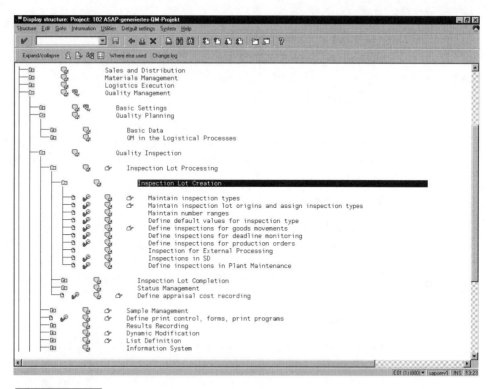

FIGURE 13.1 IMG screen for the area of QM (© SAP AG)

IMG (Implementation Guide)

The Customizing model is set up in graphic form as a structure tree, and is filed in the system as REFERENCE IMG. As required, individual projects can be created from the REFERENCE IMG. The Customizing settings should be made and documented in the projects.

TIP

The REFERENCE IMG usually contains all the available components of the R/3 system. However, it can occur that, at the beginning of a QM project, the QM component is invisible and the installation appears to be incomplete. In this case, however, the QM component is simply not a part of the IMG project. The program is definitely already on your system. The QM component is part of the standard scope of every logistics system. In order to make the QM work package visible, your SAP system administration only need to regenerate the REFERENCE IMG for the QM area in a new project.

The structure is based on the PROCESS FLOW VIEW of the R/3 reference models, which you encountered in Chapter 2, 'Modeling QM business processes using the EPC method'.

SAP provides powerful tools for systematic Customizing of the R/3 system.

Procedural model

The procedural model contains text descriptions of the processes for implementation of an SAP system. Checklists and project components for the individual subprojects and the complete implementation project can be called up from the functions.

Reference model

The R/3 reference model lists all the activities and functions of the system with a view of the system component or, alternatively, process designs. Each of the various functions contains reference processes with event-controlled process chains (EPCs). The possibilities provided by the EPC method are dealt with in detail in Chapter 2.

Implementation guides (IMGs)

Together with the Customizing transactions, the IMG forms the core of Customizing activities. Its structure is identical to that of the process flow view of the reference model. The work packages contain descriptions of the setting activities which, viewed as a whole, form an Implementation Management Guide.

Customizing transactions of the IMG

In the IMG structure, the RUN icon leads to the Customizing transactions. Here, the necessary settings are made directly in the system according to the information from the Implementation Management Guide.

Project steering and documentation of the IMG

With the functions of project steering, SAP places the most important instruments for project management directly in the execution area of Customizing. Resources, specified times and the relevant status can be entered for the procedural model and the project IMG. In addition, project documentation can be assigned to the activities of Customizing and to the work steps of the project.

Transport

As Customizing settings initially have a prototype character, they remain in the test or development system until they are completed in full. The transfer to the consolidation

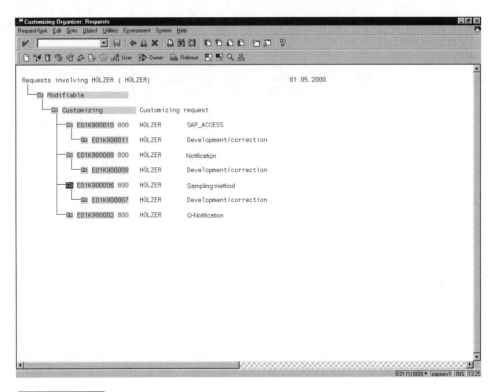

FIGURE 13.2   Transport of Customizing orders (© SAP AG)

system, and later to the productive system, takes place with so-called 'transport orders'. The transport orders of each resource are listed here; they receive a status such as 'released' to indicate that they are sufficiently 'mature' for transfer (see Fig. 13.2).

13.3   FUNCTIONS IN CUSTOMIZING

You reach the CUSTOMIZINGS overview on the menu path TOOLS | BUSINESS ENGINEERING | CUSTOMIZING. After selection, the entry screen appears as shown in Figure 13.3. In the standard version, the FIRST STEPS IN CUSTOMIZING screen appears first. In the main window of Customizing, you will see an overview of the existing projects. Double-clicking on the project displays the project IMG as shown in Figure 13.1. The IMG is explained in more detail in the course of this chapter.

The following sections provide you with an overview of the most important operations within the framework of QM Customizing. We have deliberately omitted any special illustration of the QM Customizing functions.

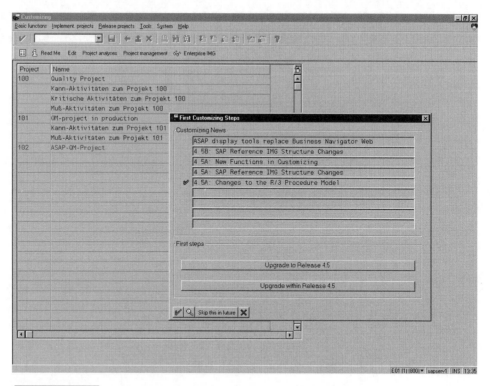

FIGURE 13.3 | Main window for Customizing (© SAP AG)

13.3.1 Procedural model

The procedure provided by SAP is basically divided into the four phases of a classical IT project (excerpt from the SAP procedural model). As of Version 4.5, there is no graphic display, but the very clear structure diagram remains. SAP AG will continue to develop with a customer orientation in the area of implementation concepts, and merge the procedural model with the specialized versions in a component-related implementation model (ASAP, AcceleratedSAP).

Phase 1: Organization and conception

The most important foundation stone for smooth project work is the organization of the teamwork (cf. Kuba, 1987). The individual steps involved are described in the work package PREPARING THE PROJECT. From the results of Phase 1, the target concept can be extended to become a real specification. Only proceed to Phase 2 once you have worked through the points listed here regarding QM-specific system settings. In the case of complex defined tasks, consider the possibility of subdividing your QM project into other individual projects, for example, 'QM in Sales and Distribution', 'QM in Production' or 'QM in Procurement'.

- Prepare the project.
- Set up the development system.
- Train the project team.
- Specify processes/functions.
- Design interfaces and system extensions.
- Target Concept Quality Inspection.

Phase 2: Detailing and realization

In this project phase, the content of the target concept is transferred to the R/3 system. This is where Customizing work is truly at home. By matching the requirements arising from the process with those originating from the user dialog, the individual enterprise system comes about iteratively.

- Make global settings.
- Map the enterprise structure.
- Map the basic and master data.
- Map processes/functions.
- Implement interfaces and system extensions.
- Map the report system.
- Map the archive administration.
- Map the rights administration.
- Perform a concluding test.
- Application System Quality Inspection.

Phase 3: Production preparation

- Prepare productive setting.
- Develop user documentation.
- Set up the productive environment.
- Train users.
- Organize system administration.
- Transfer data into the productive system.
- Productive System Quality Inspection.

Phase 4: Productive operation

▨ Support productive operation.

▨ Optimize system use.

13.3.2 Implementation guides (IMG)

With the implementation guides, SAP has certainly assumed a pioneering role in the area of customer orientation within standard software systems. Where it normally used to be necessary to implement setting variations to a software system in a higher-quality text editor, the R/3 system provides a separate application for this task. Within the IMG, the central functions of Customizing take place in process-oriented form. The structure takes its orientation from the process flow view of the SAP reference model from Chapter 2. The documents of the Implementation Management Guide are stored within the IMG, which means that the implementation process can be continuously matched up to the SAP guides. The implementation activities are supported by the following functions:

▨ Direct execution of Customizing transactions to process the setting parameters.

▨ Accompanying project documentation for each step in Customizing, editing of own notes on the individual activities.

▨ Status administration for each work step in Customizing for project steering.

▨ Accompanying documentation with the Implementation Management Guide.

IMG versions

All IMG versions appear in a structured display, each line of which represents either nodes or activities. Clicking on the nodes 'expands' them into further structures. In the final level, the actual Customizing activities are indicated by the RUN ICON. The functions in the structure screen are to be selected in the key according to Table 13.1.

Depending on the IMG selected, you will see more information in the line. In Customizing, the implementation guides are available with different scopes:

▨ *Reference IMG*
You select the Reference IMG via the menu path TOOLS | BUSINESS ENGINEERING | CUSTOMIZING | DISPLAY REFERENCE IMG. Here, as is also the case in the Reference Model, all functions of all components are present. The Reference IMG (also referred to as Reference Guide) is used as the starting point for the project activities, and it exists in the shipped version of every SAP system precisely once. No changes are made in the Reference IMG and no user documentation is stored. It is used primarily as a template for the Enterprise and Project IMG. If settings in the Enterprise and Project IMG lead to unwanted reactions, the Reference IMG can be accessed and used to recover the original status.

TABLE 13.1	Functions in the structure display of customizing

Icon	Meaning
⊞	Expanding is possible with a single click on the icon or with the function 'Expand/collapse'
⊟	Collapsing is possible with a single click on the icon or with the function 'Expand/collapse'
🗋	Nodes without subnodes

Customizing-specific icons

Node title

Icon	Meaning
🗨	Double-click branches to the description of the activity
🗨	Single click branches to the maintenance of notes on the node
🖈	There is an executable function for this node. Single click on the field runs the associated function.
✔	Single click on this field branches into status maintenance
☞	There is release info for this node. Single click on the field to show the release info.

▨ *Enterprise IMG*

In precisely the same way as the Reference IMG, the Enterprise IMG applies to the whole company and is a subset of the Reference IMG. This IMG is also in the system only once. In the Enterprise IMG, the IMG structure is equipped with the necessary components and activities from the Reference IMG on client level. This ensures that the individual projects only contain the components that are planned for the implementation of the R/3 system. However, there is the possibility to generate components in the Enterprise IMG retrospectively at any time without losing existing information.

▨ *Project IMG*

Where possible, the real work in Customizing should take place in the Project IMGs. For this purpose, the IMG projects can be divided according to the specifications of project organization. For each subproject, the required component and activity share is created on the basis of the Enterprise IMG. Depending on the scope, the project structure for Quality Management can contain all activities or only subareas such as QM in Production. It is also conceivable to run projects only for a certain project stage in order to install a prototyping or test operation as an example. If you are following recommendations and working with several systems, and have a test system available, it is certainly possible to experiment with various settings without disrupting a parallel productive operation.

13.3.3 Creating a Project IMG

Via the menu path in CUSTOMIZING IMPLEMENTATION PROJECTS | PROJECT MANAGEMENT | CREATE PROJECT, you reach the window for maintenance of the Project IMG (Fig. 13.4).

The mandatory fields are indicated with question marks and are filled in according to your definitions. It is advisable to select 'Yes' in the area PROJECT MANAGEMENT, as this option button enables the functions available here. In particular, you use the status information and resource assignment during the activities in Customizing. The created projects can be changed at any time.

When you select the GENERATE PROJECT IMG function, the selection structure of the

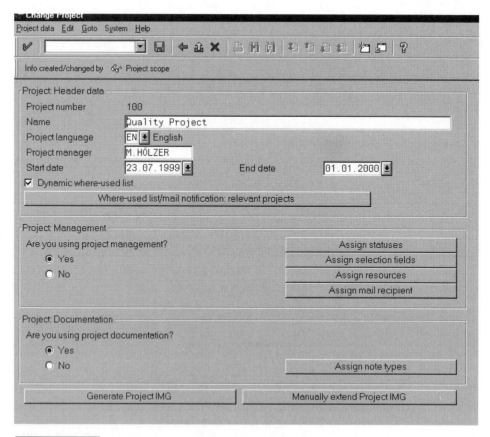

FIGURE 13.4 Creating a Project IMG (© SAP AG)

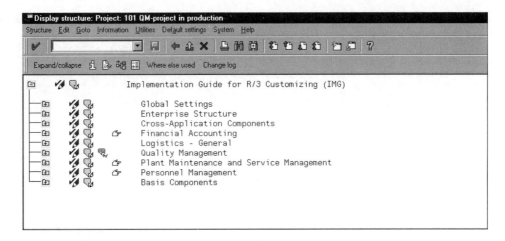

FIGURE 13.5   Project IMG for Quality Management in Production (© SAP AG)

components and activities appears. You mark the necessary components with mouse-clicks and then SAVE generates a PROJECT IMG (see Fig. 13.5). The result is a new project with the selected components and the areas required for the execution of the project. The system automatically generates these IMG areas at the same time. Following this, a line with the project number and the description of the added project appears in the overview of the project management.

TIP   If you have generated a new project, as in our example, the project management is of course empty, the new project not yet being 'in process'. However, this should not distract from the fact that the settings made in other projects are already included in this new project. By the same token, changes in the newly generated project affect all other projects of the same system.

TIP   For users of Microsoft Project®, the function for the transfer of project activities and their status information in the Microsoft Project® is an option. Selecting the UPLOAD/DOWNLOAD function in the PROJECT MANAGEMENT window takes you to another dialog window that expects the input of the desired file name, the directory and other selection criteria. The system creates an MPX file with the activities from the IMG, and this can be processed using Microsoft Project® Version 3.0 or higher.

Work in the IMGs

The functions described here are available in all IMGs. The icons of the function bar in the IMG are self-explanatory and can be operated by mouse-clicks. The IMGs permit printouts in several levels of detail and can be configured individually at the menu item DEFAULT SETTINGS. Selecting the menu item INFORMATION in Customizing provides

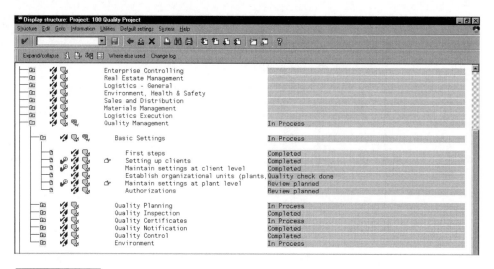

FIGURE 13.6 | Supplementary information on the Customizing activities (© SAP AG)

you with a variety of supplementary information regarding Customizing activities (Fig. 13.6), for example the assigned status from the project notes or the reference to the corresponding activities in the procedural model.

The most important functions of the menus in the DISPLAY STRUCTURE window are described in more detail below:

▓ Menu EDIT | SEARCH

Here, you can run targeted searches for texts and entries in the structure.

▓ Menu GOTO | WHERE ELSE USED

A particularly interesting function is WHERE ELSE USED. This function can be used to check in which activities identical Customizing objects are used. This enables an initial check of the functional and business effects on other components, which protects against incompatible settings.

▓ Menu INFORMATION | TITLE and IMG INFO

▓ NOTES

If a note has been entered, it is displayed here.

▓ RELEASE INFORMATION

You can recognize the presence of this supplementary information from the icon with the blue hand and use the function to display the release note.

▓ DOCUMENTATION OF DEFAULT SETTINGS

Apparently, work still in progress ...

■ NEED FOR ACTIVITY

Divides the activities into 'mandatory activities' and 'optional activities'.

■ CRITICAL ACTIVITY

Divides the activities into 'critical activities' and 'uncritical activities'.

■ ASSIGNMENT OF PROCEDURAL MODEL

Shows the assignment to the activities from the procedural model.

■ COUNTRY ASSIGNMENT

You see the assignment to a country if you have selected this when creating the project. If no country is displayed, the settings apply for all countries.

■ APPLICATION COMPONENT

Shows the assignment to a module of an application component.

■ EXTENSIONS

In the right-hand column, the IMG activities are displayed that are possible for customer-specific function extensions.

TIP What is involved here are either existing function modules or so-called 'user exits' for which a change or the docking on of a separate program have already been preconceived at SAP. Particularly in the case of release changes, these extensions are not as critical as extensions to original SAP programs or function modules for which no customer extension is planned. SAP continuously maintains the program interfaces specified here for all release changes.

■ CLIENT DEPENDENCE

In the right-hand column, you can read off which Customizing tables are client-dependent.

■ TRANSPORT TYPE

In the right-hand column, you can read off which Customizing tables are connected to the transport:

– MANUAL TRANSPORT

In this case, there is no transport connection, i.e., changes to the Customizing tables are not automatically recorded in a change order. You have to move the change manually into a change order.

– AUTOMATIC TRANSPORT

In this case, there is a transport connection, i.e., changes to the Customizing tables are automatically recorded in a change order.

▧ LANGUAGE DEPENDENCE

In the right-hand column, you see which Customizing tables are to be translated where required:

– Tables not language-dependent

Means that you do not have to translate this Customizing table.

– Translation via standard translation method

You have to translate these tables. Use the internal SAP translation transaction for the translation. You will find this transaction in the entry screen at TOOLS | ABAP WORKBENCH | UTILITIES | TRANSLATION | SHORT AND LONG TEXTS.

▧ RESOURCES

Shows the use of resources from the entry in the project management.

▧ SELECTION FIELD

In the right-hand column, you can see which selection fields have been assigned to your project.

13.4 PROJECT STEERING WITH THE IMG AND THE PROCEDURAL MODEL

In the structure models, you have a great many possibilities for monitoring and controlling the activities in Customizing and in the general project procedure. You use most of the functions for project steering directly from the structure display of the procedural model and the IMG.

▧ You use the procedural model to steer the project flow.

▧ In the IMGs, you control the specialized activities.

The various projects can then be evaluated with regard to the activities, status information and according to individual criteria.

13.4.1 Project steering with status information

You specify the status depending on the processing status of a work package or an activity. In order to show the 'Status' icon (blue check mark with pencil), enable the PROJECT MANAGEMENT as described in the section 'Creating a Project IMG'. No project statuses have been stored yet, so enter them retrospectively. To do so, start at the CUSTOMIZING window and select PROJECT MANAGEMENT | CHANGE PROJECT and enter the desired status at ADMINISTRATION | ASSIGN STATUS as shown in Figure 13.7. Several useful statuses are already available in the standard shipped version, but it is also possible to design your own status records and store them here.

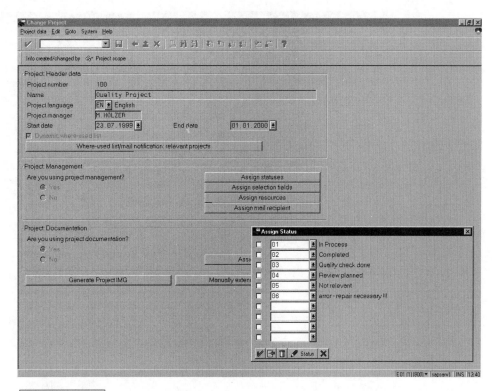

FIGURE 13.7   Entering possible statuses for a project (© SAP AG)

Editing status information

With a single click on the STATUS icon in the IMG or procedural structure, you reach the input window for the status information (Fig. 13.8).

■ Status

Selection of the desired status from project maintenance.

■ Percentage complete

Enter a percentage value here. Alternatively, the system calculates this itself if you enter the proportion of actual and remaining work.

■ Resources

Selection of the desired resources from project maintenance This is usually a member of the project team.

■ Planned, Actual, Remaining work

You can schedule the tasks/activities in the relevant fields. The remaining work is set automatically when you press the ENTER key.

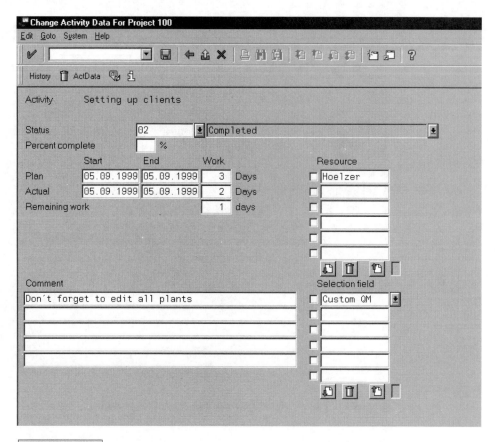

FIGURE 13.8 Status information for Customizing setting (© SAP AG)

▨ Selection field

In this field, you choose an additional selection criterion which simplifies the overview according to a certain focal point. A separate evaluation is possible via these selection fields.

▨ Comment

Short additional comment for this activities/procedural item.

Change logs

Change documents are written in the system for each change to the status information. The system creates change documents with the following content:

▨ Change date.

▨ User name of the person making the change.

▨ Old and new field contents.

13.4.2 Maintaining notes for the IMG

In this context, notes are the text documentation associated with the procedural model or IMG. You recognize that there is a note by the text icon with the spectacles in the structure graphic and jump there directly with a single click. If there are not yet any notes, you can create them by selecting the icon CHANGE STATUS INFORMATION | ICON CHANGE NOTES | CHOOSE NOTE TYPE. With the project documentation, the system enables central administration of written records, notes and other information related to the project work. The permitted note (documentation) types are also edited in the IMG project maintenance. A selection of two or three note types is usually quite sufficient; otherwise the administration quickly becomes confusing (see Fig. 13.9).

When you have selected a note type, the window in which the texts are edited appears. Do not be surprised at the standard setting of the SAPscript line editor! Once you have got used to working with this type of editor, it is really quite a practical tool. An alternative would be to use MS-Word® as editor. To do so, open the Customizing menu and select BASIC FUNCTIONS | EDITOR FOR MS-WORD®.

Another advantage of the SAP editor types is that you are normally not even tempted to experiment with any of the countless layout/formatting variations of an

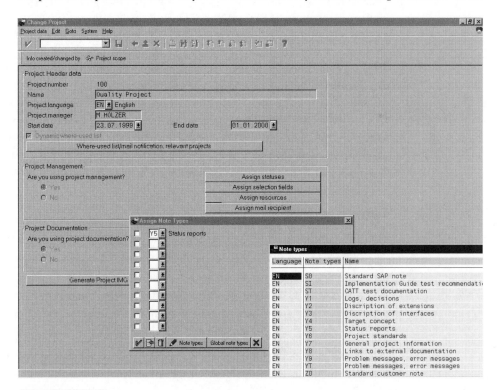

FIGURE 13.9 Selection of note types in the IMG project maintenance (© SAP AG)

Office application, whereby the functions of the formatting can often cause headaches. Incidentally, even if you use MS-Word®, most functions are disabled, so that the only advantage is the slightly more familiar menu control.

13.5 SCENARIO

There is a very good reason why we have not described any details of QM Customizing so far in this chapter: even without the rest of the SAP online documentation, the Implementation Guide (IMG) is almost 200 pages long, and is conceived for the individual setting of SAP QM. In order to provide you with a practical explanation of the basic Customizing procedure, we will use a 'genuine' example from an implementation project at a large supplier to the automobile industry. Please read through the whole example, as it illustrates the dangers of special Customizing settings.

Analysis of the general conditions

An SAP R/3 system is productive for Materials Management in the company. QM is planned as an extra SAP component. During the analysis of the interface of QM to the other R/3 components, it turns out that the influence of the QM component in the area of goods movements causes problems in the case of a stock-relevant inspection type (INSPECTION TYPE 01 – INSPECTION OF GOODS RECEIPT FOR PURCHASE ORDER). With the inspection type active, QM posts with the CONTROL INDICATOR 'POST IN THE QUALITY INSPECTION STOCK' with the stock type QUALITY INSPECTION STOCK and creates an inspection lot. The operation is initiated by goods movement 101, Goods receipt for purchase order. This has the effect on the stock management that only the usage decision in QM can be used to post from this stock back into the RELEASED STOCK.

Customer specification

1 There must be an inspection type that enables dynamic modifications and sampling schemes on the characteristics level for the inspection lot.

2 With the active inspection type for the goods receipt inspection and the goods movement, QM is not permitted (due to postings and interfaces to external systems) to take over the sole management of the quality inspection stock!

3 Nevertheless, goods movement 101 should post automatically to the quality inspection stock and permit manual postings to Released or Other.

4 Where possible, only original programs should be used.

Implementation problems

At first glance, the customer specifications seem impossible for the following reasons:

■ Inspection types that are not relevant to stock have no inspection lot origin 'goods receipt', and therefore do not create an inspection lot at goods receipt. The standard inspection types that are stock-relevant do not permit dynamic modification at the characteristics level.

■ The standard inspection types are also used for the stock management of a quality inspection stock, if one exists. A transfer via the transactions of goods movement is then not permitted.

Solution with the Customizing settings?

In Customizing, we assign settings to an inspection type, and these settings meet all the criteria from the specification. We can use various tests to determine that one criterion, namely the 'automatic posting to quality inspection stock', could not be implemented together with the other criteria. In order to enable automatic posting, the idea was to install a small supplementary program which posts the delivered quantity with the movement type 321 directly into the quality inspection stock. This program is started by each goods movement 101, Goods receipt for purchase order.

INSPECTION TYPE 01 – INSPECTION AT GOODS RECEIPT FOR PURCHASE ORDER cannot be used as this inspection type definitely takes over the administration of the quality inspection stock.

We use inspection type 89 – OTHER INSPECTION because dynamic modifications and sampling schemes are already set and the first criterion is met. We rename the short text of the inspection type in 'Goods receipt inspection'. For special Customizing, we navigate in our Project IMG as in Figure 13.10 all the way to MAINTAIN INSPECTION TYPES.

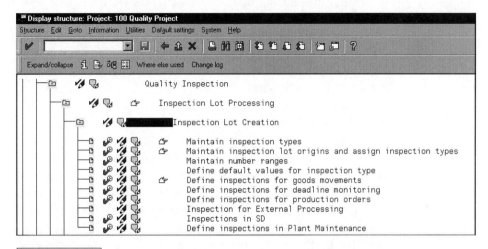

FIGURE 13.10 Navigation to MAINTAIN INSPECTION TYPES (© SAP AG)

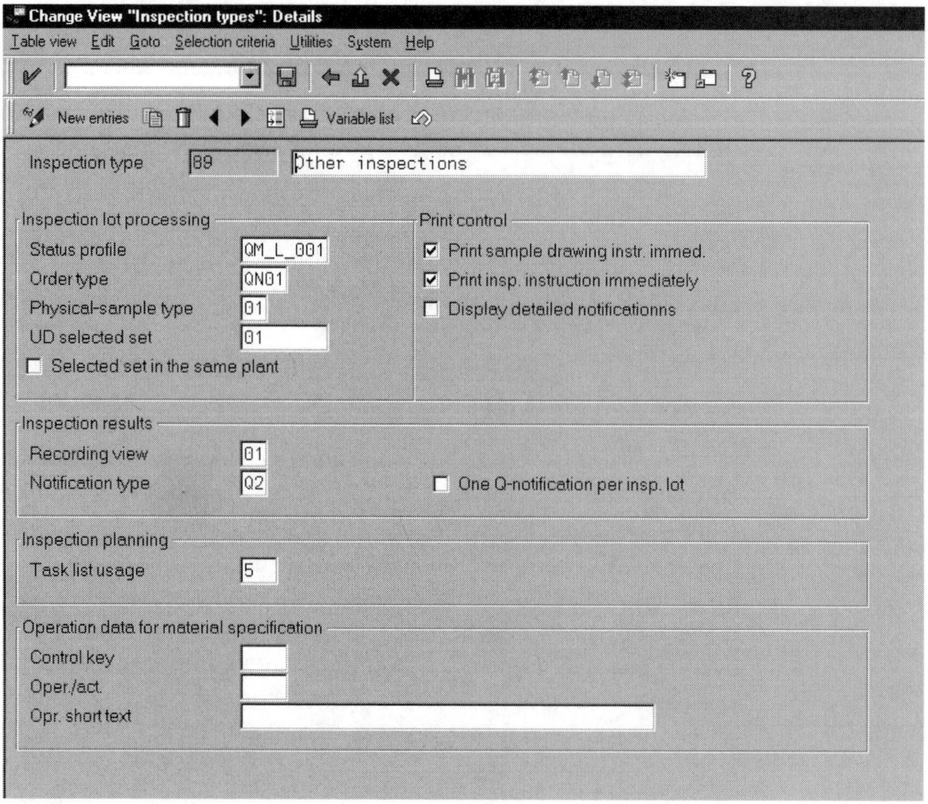

FIGURE 13.11 Changing inspection type in Customizing (© SAP AG)

In the Customizing transaction MAINTAIN INSPECTION TYPES, the short text is changed and the necessary control functions receive entries (Fig. 13.11).

We try to comply with the second criterion using the Customizing setting at DEFINE INSPECTIONS FOR GOODS MOVEMENTS, as can be seen in Figure 13.12. We thus achieve inspection lot creation with the inspection type 89 and inspection lot origin 89 – OTHER INSPECTIONS.

We select PROCESS MOVEMENT TYPES IN STOCK MANAGEMENT, and by marking MOVEMENT TYPE we enter the selection window for the movement types. With the entry 101 and RUN, the system selects all variations of the movement type 101. The window that now appears, DEFINITION OF NEW MOVEMENT TYPES, is closed immediately with BACK and we receive an overview of the maintenance functions of movement type 101. We continue by selecting to UPDATE CONTROL/WM MOVEMENT TYPES. You can see the window in Figure 13.13, CHANGE VIEW 'UPDATE CONTROL'.

To our consternation, we find out that there are a total of 77 variations of movement type 101 in the system. Fortunately, we can use various selection functions from the

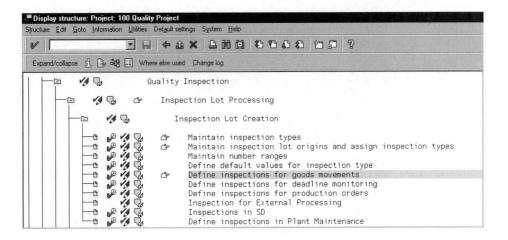

FIGURE 13.12   Navigation to INSPECTION FOR GOODS MOVEMENTS (© SAP AG)

menu bar to mark, maintain or exchange several entries at one time with our desired inspection lot origin.

For all entries, we replace INSPECTION LOT ORIGIN 01 GOODS RECEIPT with inspection lot origin 89 – OTHER. On saving the settings, the system issues a warning 'Caution with changes [entry belongs to SAP]', but it allows the intervention with a note from the online help 'Only for absolutely necessary changes'.

Further tests are run to temporarily confirm the success of our measures and the fulfilment of all requirements. In the next step, we release the settings for an integration test. In order to ensure that the settings do not produce any unwanted side-effects, a parallel query is sent to the SAP development department, asking them to check the matter. The reaction we receive is sobering. With the changes we have made, the possibility cannot be eliminated that error statuses could occur in stock management. At the same time, an acceptable proposal is made for an extension – for a charge – with our requirements. However, this procedure would have violated our fundamental project principle of only using original programs.

The new approach to a solution with manual inspection lot creation

The settings are reset to their original condition as shipped. At the moment, all that remains is to use inspection type 89 – OTHER INSPECTIONS, as this is not relevant to stock. This inspection type is used as a copy template for another inspection type 90 – PROTOTYPE INSPECTION. For each inspection type, we set a separate routing usage. This ensures that on inspection lot creation the suitable inspection plan is used.

For a later phase of the QM implementation, a simple supplementary program performs the inspection lot creation with posting to goods receipt.

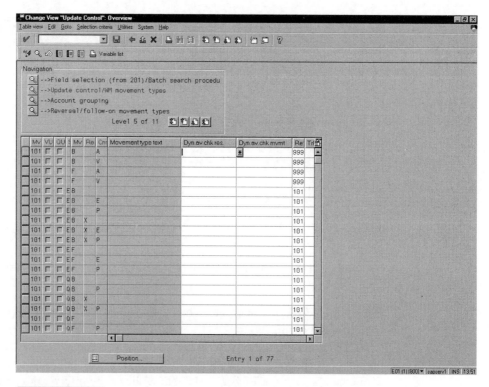

FIGURE 13.13 Change View 'Update Control' (© SAP AG)

This example is intended to show how tightly linked the Customizing areas are with the various business operations. In the case of difficult changes, it is absolutely necessary to hold integration meetings with the departments involved and also to contact the SAP development people.

13.5.1 Customizing 'maintain number ranges'

An important task in configuring the new system is the creation of the various number ranges. Among others, the following number ranges have special significance in the context of Quality Management:

- Material numbers.
- Inspection plan numbers.
- Routing numbers.
- Equipment numbers.
- PM task list numbers.
- Maintenance plan numbers.
- Quality notification numbers.

In general, a distinction is made between 'internal number assignment' and 'external number assignment'. Here, 'internal' means that the system itself assigns ascending numbers from a certain range (the reserved number range). In the case of 'external' number assignment, it is up to the user to assign a number, whereby the permitted range (number range) can be restricted by a default setting.

For clear and logical allocation as well as trouble-free transition from legacy systems to the new R/3 system, several matters must be cleared up first:

- Are there already defined number ranges in the legacy system?
- Should these numbers be continued?
- Should 'talking numbers' be used?
- Are there relationships between the various number categories?

In investigating the possible solutions, mixed forms can also be considered. In this way, it is possible to take over the numbering of the legacy system, but then to continue work with a system-internal number assignment.

An example of 'talking numbers' and mutual relationships of number categories was mentioned in Chapter 11, 'Test equipment management'. In that preset scenario, the number of the maintenance plan was set externally (i.e. by the user) in such a way that it was composed of a combination of the number of the material and the serial number.

A well thought-out and structured system of number ranges and skilful combination of internal and external number assignment greatly simplifies later work with the system and increases acceptance on the part of the employees.

CHAPTER 14

Migration concepts

BASIC PRINCIPLES

The implementation of SAP R/3 QM presents you with the task of transferring your existing data stock from the environment of Quality Planning into the R/3 system. The most important objects are inspection plans and possibly the quality level of the vendors. However, a requirement is that the structures of the transferred objects have a certain similarity. Check this point in advance with particular care. In most cases, the transfer of results from inspections is not really necessary and it is also very difficult.

Data import requires a well thought-out concept. The following sections should be regarded as 'tasks', which are to be performed, if possible, in the order given. Other aids include the 'Data Transfer Made Easy' CD available from SAP and the program 'IBIP' described further on in this chapter.

CREATE A DETAILED DEFINITION OF THE DATA TRANSFER

The purpose of this task is to obtain an overview of the data transfer. You specify which system replaces which and which data is to be copied.

Bear the following in mind:

- Data objects to be transferred.
- Transfer method, manual or automatic.
- Data quantity and quality in the legacy systems.
- Throughput and performance of the data transfer.
- Availability of standard R/3 data transfer programs.
- Approval of the detailed data transfer draft proposal.
- Procedure.

14.2.1 Sequence

Get an overview of the bigger picture

You have to perform three tasks in preparing for data transfer.

You must know your SAP system in order to decide which data is to be transferred (you need, for example, the material with the inspection data, but not open inspection orders). You must know the data of your legacy system.

If you want to use, for example, the quality level (dynamic modification level) of the SAP system, translate the last status and copy it into the R/3 system. When you check the database of your legacy system, find out whether this information is available. The knowledge as to what data is available can help you to decide how the data is to be transferred into the SAP system. If, for example, you have five vendors and 50,000 items in your material master data, enter the vendors manually and transfer the quality level automatically.

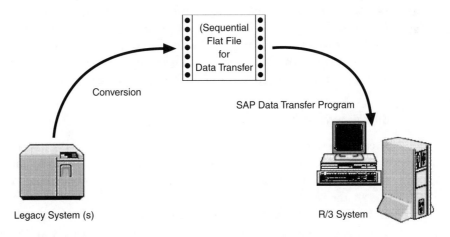

FIGURE 14.1   Conversion

This task describes the automatic data transfer, which is an effective method of transferring large quantities of data into your new system. This method ensures that the data is error-free when imported into the SAP R/3 system. Figure 14.1 shows the steps required for data transfer.

The data from your legacy system must be available in a format that can be read by the SAP R/3 system. The data must be saved in a flat text file.

SAP data transfer program

As soon as the data has been prepared, it can be imported automatically into the SAP system. An SAP data transfer program reads the prepared data and moves it into the SAP R/3 system.

Specify a data transfer method

Based on the conversion requirements, the transfer method must be specified for each business object.

You have the following options for business objects in data transfer:

- Using the SAP standard data transfer program.
- Manual data input with online transactions.
- Creation of Batch Input programs for data transfer.

Help with your decision in choosing a method can be found in the section *How To* in the R/3 system, Chapter 3 on the CD 'Data transfer made easy' (see Section 14.1). The method you choose for the data transfer determines the resources required (e.g. temporary staff for manual data input or programmers to write routines). The *How To* section provides an estimation of the required work overhead for each transfer method. You must know what data is on your legacy system, and you must be familiar with the SAP application assigned to the business objects to be transferred.

Specify data fields

Create a business object (e.g. an inspection plan) in the R/3 system to specify which data has to be transferred. Working on the system and the help documentation for the fields helps you to become familiar with the business object. This makes it easier to specify the fields.

While you are creating the object, you will find out which fields are absolutely essential (mandatory). Without input of data in these fields, you can neither save the data nor go to the next screen.

Specify the file structure

If you transfer data automatically with the SAP standard programs, you have to provide the data in a certain format and specify the target file structure. The format depends on the business object that you want to transfer.

Every SAP R/3 standard data transfer program requires a certain file format and a certain sequence of data records. Information can be found in the documentation of the program and in Chapter 2 of the *Initial Data Transfer Made Easy – Step by Step Guide to SAP Initial Data Transfer* (SAP, 1999).

Use the transaction SXDA (Betaversion with Release 3.1G) to specify the required data structure. You can create the corresponding file for each data transfer program, and use the flat file to check the completeness and consistency of the data.

You have two possibilities for the value of each field. You either specify a value or you make no entry. Entering nothing is not so easy. This is important when the data transfer program permits you to change a business object. There are two ways of entering nothing:

- Enter a RESET value to initialize or delete the value of a field.
- Enter a NODATA value to retain the original value of the field.

The SAP standard data transfer programs use '/' for the NODATA value and a blank for the RESET value.

Specify fields in flat files

When you specify the target file structure, you have to match up the required fields in each screen with the fields in the flat file. The flat file uses the same or similar field names as the online transaction.

Analyze the data of the legacy system

As there are many different types of legacy systems, SAP cannot provide expert knowledge for them all. This is why you have to specify which data is relevant and is available for your purposes. Your legacy system can contain functions or a Report Writer that allow you to retrieve data in the required flat file format.

The quality of the data on your legacy system is important. For example, if there are data fields that have not been maintained, errors occur when the data transfer program is running.

Pay attention to the number of data records. This influences the runtime of the data transfer program. The number of data records can be used as a basis for calculating the total runtime if you perform speed tests with a small number of data records.

Assign the data of the legacy system to R/3

If you know the data in both systems, you can assign the old data to the SAP fields. With this allocation, matching fields and field values to be changed are allocated: for example, you use 'lb' for 'pound' in the R/3 system instead of '1' in the legacy system.

If you make manual entries, do not assign the data to the flat file, but prepare the data in such a way that someone can enter it in the system.

Result

- Data transfer method.
- Detailed definition of the data fields to be transferred.
- Old data will be assigned to SAP R/3 data objects.
- Number of data records be transferred.
- Quality of the data.
- Detailed data transfer concept.

14.3 CREATE DATA TRANSFER PROGRAMS

Purpose

The purpose of this task is to develop the required programs for automatic transfer of data. Extract the data from your legacy system and make it available in the structure required by the transfer program of the R/3 system. The creation and testing of transfer programs can take up a lot of time.

Procedure

Decide how the data from the legacy system is to be extracted in order to transfer each business object automatically. If there is no standard data transfer program (see Appendix A of *Initial Data Transfer Made Easy Guidebook*, SAP 1999), you have to develop a Batch Input program to transfer the data into the R/3 system.

14.3.1 Sequence

You have the following possibilities:

Specify the programming language

You can use a programming language (ABAP/4, COBOL, etc.) to obtain the required format for the data. If you use ABAP4, you have to specify the corresponding structure in order to be able to insert the data in the ABAP Dictionary. Appendix B of the *Initial Data Transfer Made Easy Guidebook*, SAP 1999, contains an example (pseudo code9).

If you use C, COBOL, PL/1 or P_RPG, you can use the report RDDSRCG0 to define the required flat R/3 file structures in the necessary language format.

An ABAP/4 data transfer program consists of three steps:

▨ Reading the flat file on the legacy system. The flat file of the legacy system is created in text format or in an MS-Excel™ table.

▨ The data is saved in sequential data records with a fixed structure.

▨ The data is imported record by record by the ABAP/4 conversion program from a PC or UNIX directory into an internal R/3 table. The structure of the internal table is the same as the flat file structure and it enables direct access to individual fields of each data record.

Data conversion

▨ All data fields of a data record are assigned to the corresponding data fields in the R/3 system.

▨ During this operation, field formats can be changed and subprograms integrated to confirm the validity of the data or to convert the data values. You can use this, for example, to adapt units of measurement to the R/3 Customizing settings, thus ensuring that the Batch Input or Direct Input programs run correctly.

▨ The data format required by the Batch Input or Direct Input programs is described in the program documentation. You require an exact sequence of data records with various data structures. The various data record formats are specified by the R/3 tables (e.g. BGR00).

▨ Output of a flat file for Batch Input or Direct Input.

▨ The data records created by the conversion programs are saved in another flat file that is used by the SAP Batch Input or Direct Input programs.

The second chapter of the SAP *Initial Data Transfer Made Easy Guidebook* describes data structures for business objects. You can also use the transaction SXDA to create an example of a data record sequence. This helps you to recognize the required format and the sequence of data records to be created by the data transfer program. Appendix A of the SAP *Initial Data Transfer Made Easy Guidebook* contains an example of a data transfer program.

Use existing tools to provide data

If the legacy system has database tools that can be used to convert the data into the correct format, use them.

Use an allocation tool

Choose an external tool that meets your needs.

Create a data transfer program

If an automatic transfer is needed and there is no standard program, develop a Batch Input program.

Result

The result is that you obtain a data conversion program that corresponds to the definitions in the task *Create a Detailed Definition of the Data Transfer*.

TIP Ensure that each data field is converted correctly. Correct field formats are important, for example, to prevent field contents from being truncated.

14.4 PERFORM MANUAL DATA TRANSFER OPERATIONS

14.4.1 Purpose

The purpose of this task is to develop reliable methods of manual data transfer. Some of the old data must be transferred manually into your R/3 system. You must ensure the correctness and completeness of all manually transferred data.

14.4.2 Sequence

1. Create a list of data records for each business object that is to be entered manually in the R/3 system.

2. Use the R/3 transactions for data input. Sort the data list in the same order in which the data have to be entered in the R/3 system.

3. Ensure that all the required data is on the list.

4. Data records must have the format required by the R/3 transaction to prevent errors in the data input.

Result

Detailed, manual conversion methods are documented.

14.5 IBIP PROGRAM FOR DATA TRANSFER

The IBIP transaction is used to transfer master data in the PLANT MAINTENANCE and SERVICE components. In the area of QM, you can make your own changes to exploit the functions of the IBIP for the migration of test equipment, inspection plan data and quality notifications. The following description contains the most important information from the original SAP documentation.

Validity of the description

This description applies to the following transactions and/or functions:

- Transaction IBIP.
- Function module IBIP_BATCH_INPUT_RFC.
- IBIP_BATCH_INPUT.
- Transaction SA38 with ABAP RIIBIP00.

The above functions all offer the same possibilities, but they are started in different ways.

General operation of the transaction IBIP

1. Create source data. To do so, you have to use either external tools, such as Microsoft Access, or the data maintenance functions.

2. Specify the run mode. You have the following possibilities:
   - Call transaction' starts the application transaction immediately to run the data transfer.
   - 'BDC sess.' first creates a session. You then have to run this session with the transaction SM35 (see option 'Edit Folders') to run the data transfer.
   - 'Direct input' creates the desired object directly using function modules. In general, no dialog appears. Error-free data is written directly into the database by the function module.

3. Define the source and target file. This includes the path of your file as well as the origin of the data. If you want to save defective transactions, you have to specify a target file.

4. Run the transaction (see Fig. 14.2).

   To find out more, press F1 on the corresponding fields.

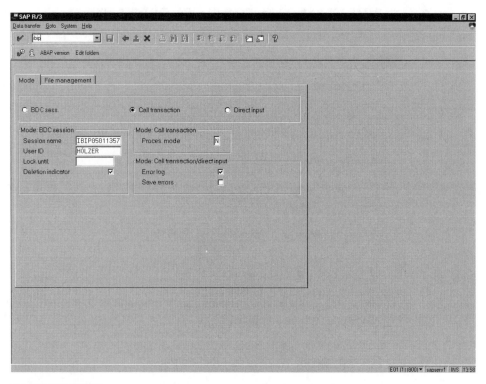

FIGURE 14.2 Data transfer using IBIP (© SAP AG)

Differences between transaction IBIP and ABAP Version RIIBIP00

The transaction IBIP provides testing tools and enables interactive processing of data. Defective input data can be corrected immediately. ABAP Version RIIBIP00 gives you the possibility to create a background job to run the data transfer regularly and with a constant setting.

Note on source file

Bear in mind that it neither makes sense nor is even possible to use the presentation server as source if you start RIIBIP00 as a batch job. In this case, no presentation server, and thus no dialog, is active. Files can then not be read directly from the presentation server. In the case of a batch job, you must select a source file from an application server (see Fig. 14.3).

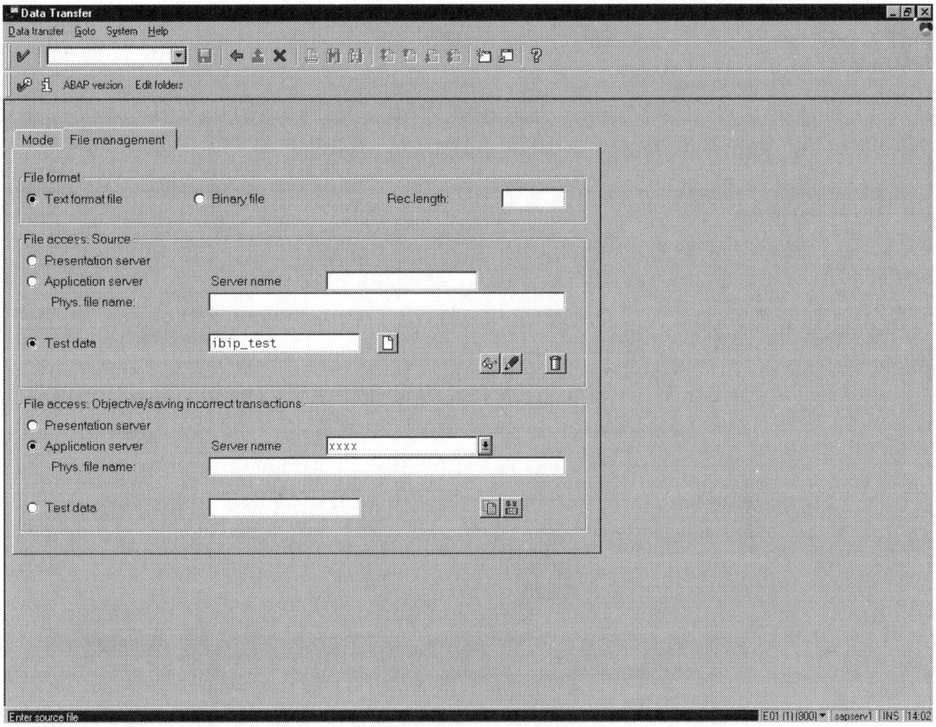

FIGURE 14.3 File management for test data (source file) (© SAP AG)

Batch input or direct input?

- Batch input

  RIIBIP00 is a general tool for data transfer, which is used to enter information in the SAP system using standard transactions and functional modules. You have to create an input file for one of the supported transactions in the corresponding structure

- Direct input

  You also have to specify the corresponding transactions in direct input mode. These abbreviations are used by the IBIP control to start the appropriate function module. They do not correspond to a concrete SAP transaction, but rather should be viewed as logical transactions

Requirements for successful data transfer

The source file must be accessible from the SAP system. The source file must have the required structure.

> **TIP**
>
> Selecting FILE MANAGEMENT | TEST DATA and double-clicking on the SHEET icon right beside the input field of the test data takes you to the next screen: DATA TRANSFER TEST DATA (see Fig. 14.4). The TCODE and RECORD NAME fields are to be filled with the corresponding catalog entries. EDIT RECORD opens an input mask with the fields from the selected record name – in this example, the TASK LIST HEADER. The record name IBIPTLST is already well suited as a template for transfer of inspection plan data, as the structures are very similar. See also the 'Customer Exit' section further on in this chapter.

RFC

If you use the function module IBIP_BATCH_INPUT_RFC by means of RFC, ensure that DIALOG is supported. DIALOG is frequently not possible. A requirement is a local SAP GUI. If DIALOG is not possible, you have to set the parameter IBIPPARMS-DARK equals X (see 'Interface to the function module'). In the case of RFC, there can be difficulties if the source file is not INT_TAB. This is why you should use the INT_TAB option.

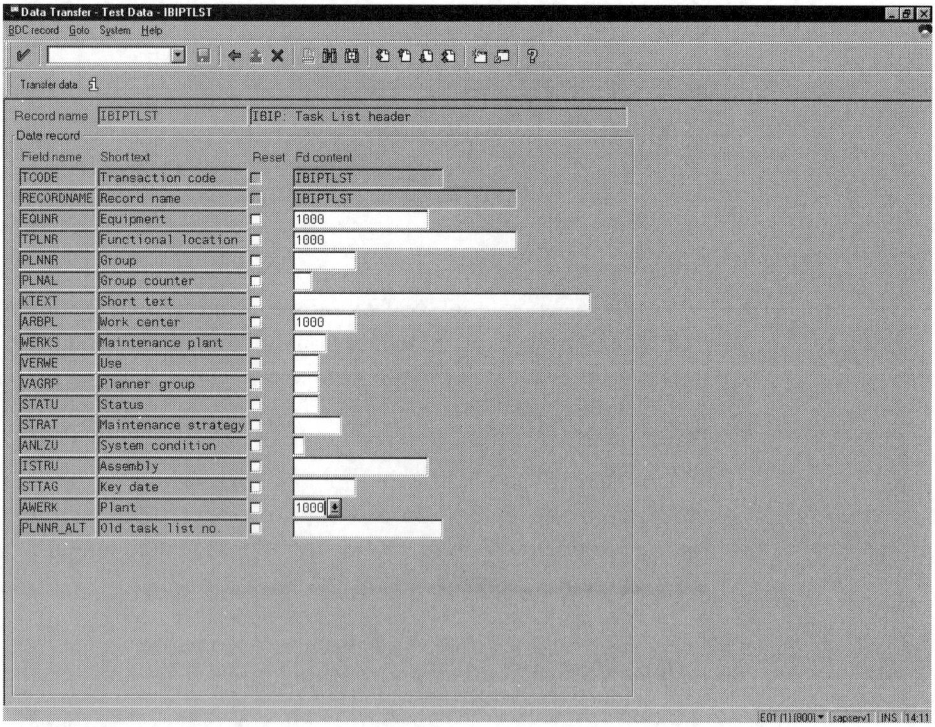

FIGURE 14.4   Structure of a test data record (© SAP AG)

Output

Either a Batch Input group with the associated name, a Call Transaction or Direct Input is output to save the records immediately.

Customer Exit

If you would like to have a transaction for data transfer which is not supported in IBIP, you can record the coding for this in the Customer Exit. To do so, read the documentation of the Customer Exit. You also have the possibility to use the Batch Input recording tool (TRANSACTION SHDB) to automatically create a program for data transfer. You can use this as the template for your coding in the Customer Exit.

Notes on the general structure

- Changes to field lengths

  Bear in mind that the field lengths have changed as of Release 4.0A. In particular, the TCODE and structure name have been extended. This means that you have to adapt files from earlier releases accordingly.

- Structure of the input records

  All input records should have the general structure of IBIPREC (see transaction SE12 in this connection). The first two fields are the same in all IBIP structures. You have to decide for each individual transaction in which fields you have to make entries and which you can leave blank.

- TCODE

  The TCODE (transaction code) can only be specified for the first record of the transaction.

- RECORDNAME

  The RECORDNAME must be specified for each record of the input file. The sequence of records in the input file is important. Ensure that you follow the hierarchical structures as specified further down under Direct Input and/or Batch Input and Call Transaction.

- Initial fields

  Initial fields in structures are generally not transported into the corresponding screen field. This means that blank fields are generally ignored. If you explicitly want to reset a field to the value '<blank>', you must mark the field in the Batch Input structure with the value '!'. This is the reset character. It means that a field is reset to its initial value. These rules also apply to option buttons and checkboxes.

▓ General name conventions

The structure of the individual transactions follows the general name convention IBIPxxxx for Direct Input IBIP_. As a rule, the change transactions use the same structure as the create transactions. xxxx is a general code and it represents the record type.

Date and time fields

Date fields must be specified in the Batch Input structures as YYYYMMDD. The date format defined for the logged-on user is checked (e.g. DD.MM.YYYY) and passed on to the screen. Time fields need the format HHMMSS and are also changed depending on the user-specific setting.

Size limits

If you want to transport several thousand records with this ABAP report, discuss with your system administration the available PAGING area of the machine on which you want to run the report. Each record requires 2 Kb. If the report aborts with size, paging or rolling area problems, try to load several small input files instead of one large one.

Lower/upper case

The transactions and record names must be written in upper case.

Key for the description of Direct Input, Batch Input and Call Transaction

▓ Means: '0 or more occurrences of an expected/permitted record'.

▓ Means: '0 or precisely 1 occurrences of an expected/permitted record'.

Direct input

Transaction NOTI_CREATE – create notification
    Structure – IBIP_NOTI_CREATE – single record, single notification
    IBIP_TEXT – long text for notification header
    IBIP_PART – partner for notification
    IBIP_NOTI_ACTIVITY – activities for notification header
    IBIP_TEXT – long text for activity
    IBIP_NOTI_TASK – tasks for notification header
    IBIP_TEXT – long text for task
    IBIP_NOTI_ITEM – items for notification
    IBIP_TEXT – long text for item
    IBIP_NOTI_CAUSE – cause for item

IBIP_TEXT – long text for cause

IBIP_NOTI_ACTIVITY – activities for item

IBIP_TEXT – long text for activity

IBIP_NOTI_TASK – tasks for item

IBIP_TEXT – long text for task

Comment on IBIP_TEXT: The field TEXT_MARK is not required here.

Transaction EQUI_CREATE – create equipment

Structure – IBIP_EQUI_CREATE – equipment record

Transaction ONF_CREATE – record confirmation of PM order

Structure – IBIP_CONF_CREATE

IBIP_CONF_CREATE

Within a transaction, you can make several confirmations, and this is why IBIP_CONF_CREATE can be used more than once.

Transaction CONF_CANCEL – cancel confirmation for PM order

Structure – IBIP_CONF_CANCEL

Transaction MEDO_CREATE – create measurement document

Structure – IBIP_MEDO_CREATE

NOTE If you want to transfer data using Direct Input, you have to prepare your data in the internal format (e.g. you must comply with leading zeros and lower/upper case). In the transaction IBIP, you have the possibility to start a conversion tool at *File management*. You can use this to have your data converted into the internal data format.

Batch Input and Call Transaction

Transaction IE01 – create equipment

Transaction IE02 – change equipment

Structure – IBIPEQUI – equipment record

IBIPNSTA – new status profile if required

IBIPSTAT – user status records

IBIPDOCU – document management system

IBIPPART – partner details (comment, see below)

IBIPTEXT (further information, see below)

for long text: TEXT_MARK = ' ' blank

for internal note: TEXT_MARK = '1'

IBIPCLAS – classification record (EqmtClass)

IBIPFEAT class features i.e. all versions for the class IBIPBDCD, see below (from Dynpro 102)

Transaction IL01 – create technical location

Transaction IL02 – change technical location

Structure – IBIPFLOC – technical location

IBIPNSTA – new status profile, if required

IBIPSTAT – user status records

IBIPDOCU – document management system

IBIPPART – partner details (comment, see below)

IBIPTEXT (further information, see below)

IBIPCLAS – classification record

IBIPFEAT class features i.e. all versions for the class

IBIPBDCD, see below (from Dynpro 'SAPMILO0' '2120')

Transaction IN04 – create object link (techn. locations)

Transaction IN05 – change object link (techn. locations)

Transaction IN07 – create object link (equipment)

Transaction IN08 – change object link (equipment)

Structure – IBIPOLNK – object link

IBIPNSTA – new status profile, if required

IBIPSTAT – user status records

IBIPDOCU – document management system

IBIPTEXT (further information, see below)

IBIPCLAS – classification record

IBIPFEAT class features i.e. all versions for the class

Transaction IP04 – create maintenance plan item

Structure – IBIPMPOS - maintenance plan item

IBIPTEXT (further information, see below)

IBIPOLST – object list

IBIPBDCD (from item data, see below)

Transaction IP01 – create maintenance plan

Structure – IBIPMPLA – maintenance plan

IBIPMPOS – maintenance plan item

IBIPTEXT (further information, see below)

IBIPOLST – object list

IBIPBDCD (from maintenance plan item, see below)

NB: If the field IBIPMPOS-WAPOS has been set, all other fields of the IBIPMPOS record are ignored. If the field IBIPMPOS-WAPOS is empty, the remaining fields of the IBIPMPOS record must be filled to describe the maintenance item.

TIP   Only maintenance plan types for which the call object is initial are supported (cf. Customizing maintenance plan types). The data for the data transfer must match the corresponding view of the reference object that was specified at the definition of the maintenance plan type. Changing the view of the reference objects is not possible with IBIP.

Transaction IP10 – schedule maintenance plan

 Structure – IBIPCALL – maintenance order (Standard IP30) or

 Structure – IBIPMPST – maintenance plan restart/start in the cycle

Transaction IA01 – create equipment plan

Transaction IA11 – create technical location plan

Transaction IA05 – create PM task list

 Structure – IBIPTLST – task list header

 IBIPTEXT (further information, see below)

 IBIPTLOP – operations

 IBIPTEXT (further information, see below)

 IBIPTMAT – material for an operation

 IBIPPRTS – production resources/tools (PRT)

 LONGTEXT (further information, see below)

 IBIPMPAC – maintenance packages/up to 32

 IBIPBDCD (comment, see below) of operation overview

Transaction IK01 – create measuring point

 Structure – IBIPMEAS measuring point details

 IBIPTEXT (further information, see below)

 IBIPBDCD (further information, see below)

Transaction IK11 – create measurement document

Structure – IBIPMVAL – measurement document

 IBIPTEXT (further information, see below)

 BIPBDCD (from Dynpro 'SAPLIMR0' '5210')

Transaction MB11 – goods movement

Structure – IBIPGISS – goods movement. The supported movement types are:

 221 Consumption for project from warehouse

 222 Consumption for project from warehouse – cancel

 261 Consumption for order from warehouse

 262 Consumption for order from warehouse – cancel

 281 Consumption for network plan from warehouse

 282 Consumption for network plan order from warehouse – cancel

 501 Receipt without purchase order in unrestricted use

 502 Receipt without purchase order in unrestricted use – cancel

 531 Receipt by-product in unrestricted use

 532 Receipt by-product in unrestricted use – cancel

 581 Receipt by-product in released, project from network plan

 582 Receipt by-product from network plan – cancel

Make sure that you always set the movement type, that you either transfer the reservation number or the material number and corresponding allocation (e.g. movement type 261 with an entry in the field for the order number (ORDNO)).

IBIPBDCD for Batch Input and Call Transaction

IBIPBDCD is used for the direct delivery of BDCDATA or the input of BDCDATA commands (IBIPFUNCT field for commands). If you want to use screens or functions that are not supported by the standard, you can enter the BDCDATA directly in the source file. The IBIPBDCD records are not processed, but rather are passed on unchanged as BDCDATA. This means you can extend the standard Batch Input processes without changing programs or writing new programs. The Batch Input sets up records with the structure BDCDATA. These records describe which Dynpros and which fields are to be sent. You can use IBIPBDCD to pass on prepared Dynpros directly.

Example

IBIPBDCD has the structure TCODE_SPAC, RECORDNAME, IBIPFUNCT plus BDCDATA.

To use IBIPBDCD records, proceed as follows:

1 Leave TCODE_SPAC blank.

2 Set RECORDNAME to IBIPBDCD.

3 Assign the DATA_AREA the structure of BDCDATA.

The field IBIPFUNCT can be left blank or filled with the commands specified below:

- " " (blank) = no function. This is the normal case. IBIPBDCD is interpreted as a pure BDCDATA and used unchanged as BDCDATA for Transaction Call. For further information, see Structure BDCDATA.

- *GOTO* = with function code in IBIPBDCD-FVAL go to Dynpro IBIPBDCD-PROGRAM IBIPBDCD-DYNPRO. That is, the function IBIPBDCD-FVAL is started. The next Dynpro is IBIPBDCD-PROGRAM IBIPBDCD-DYNPRO. If you do not set IBIPBDCD-PROGRAM or IBIPBDCD-DYNPRO, the current DYNPRO, for example PROGRAM, is taken. You can use *PUSH* and *POP* to mark and retrieve a Dynpro.

- *DYNP* = the next Dynpro is IBIPBDCD-PROGRAM IBIPBDCD-DYNPRO.

- *FUNC* = the function IBIPBDCD-FVAL is run.
  The next Dynpro is the current Dynpro.

- *FLD* = on the current Dynpro, the field
  or *FIELD* IPBDCD-FNAM is to be provided with the value IBIPBDCD-FVAL.

- *ENTR* = Data release on the current Dynpro. The next Dynpro is the current Dynpro.

- *PUSH* = Set current Dynpro on stack.

- *POP* = Retrieve current Dynpro from stack.

- *CURS* = Position cursor on field IBIPBDCD-FVAL.

Long text processing

You can use the structure IBIPTEXT and/or IBIP_TEXT to adopt the individual text lines of a long text.

NOTE The IBIPTEXT records (IBIP_TEXT records) must follow the associated object in the text file. A long text for a header record should immediately follow the header record, for example in the source file for the data transfer. If an additional comment TEXT_MARK is defined, it means that more than one long text is possible for a structure. This text identifier is used to distinguish the texts. The field TEXT_MARK must be set in this case. In all other cases, the field TEXT_MARK is ignored as only a long text is possible.

Partner details

If you also provide an IBIPPART record, all the existing partners are deleted. This means that you have to provide all the partners every time a partner (IBIPPART record) is included.

Classification: Classes and characteristics

The structure IBIPCLAS only enables allocation of a new class. If you want to change the characteristics of an existing class, you first have to use the record IBIPCDEL to delete the class and, in a second transaction, reallocate the class with IBIPCLAS and the characteristics with IBIPFEAT. Note regarding class type: within a transaction, you can only process classes of one class type; changing class types is not possible. Furthermore, you can use the corresponding data transfer programs of the classification to transfer the classification and characteristics. These are available to you in the transaction SXDA under the data transfer objects 0130, 0140 and 0150.

Test Help 1

The transaction IBIP (data transfer) provides the possibility to record test data. You can use this to test values in the input structures immediately and you then know which values belong in which fields. To do this, you can export the test data as a text file and then compare it with your data transfer file.

Test Help 2

The transaction IBIP provides the possibility to create test data. The report RIACCESS DDIC can be used to download structures into an MS-ACCESS database. You can then record simple test data and export this data (see menu option EXPORT table in MS-ACCESS). You have to use the format 'Specified Format' to receive the expected structure, i.e., your test file should have a structure matching the above example. The source file for Batch Input must not be formatted with " " or other 'delimiters'.

CHAPTER 15

ASAP (AcceleratedSAP)

ASAP – AcceleratedSAP – is the comprehensive solution for fast and uncomplicated implementation of R/3 projects. ASAP represents a method that attempts to switch from an intuitive to a structured implementation concept. The implementation method is continuously improved and updated by an international consulting team. Its basis is the feedback from customers already using ASAP. AcceleratedSAP optimizes the time invested, the quality and the efficient use of the resources available.

The tools include AcceleratedSAP-specific instruments to support project management, questionnaires for the business process consultants and a large number of technical manuals and checklists.

In principle, you cannot buy methods such as ASAP: a method must be used and lived. This is why the comprehensive tools of this method are also available to every user and consultant virtually free of charge.

What's new about this approach?

AcceleratedSAP was developed on the basis of proven business methods and implementation methods used by SAP customers all over the world. The main ingredient in the concept of AcceleratedSAP are the knowledge acquired with regard to accelerators and decelerators, i.e. accelerating and decelerating factors during the implementation process.

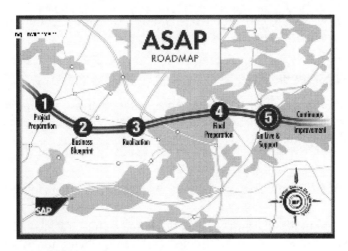

Can any customer use AcceleratedSAP?

Yes. Suitable components of AcceleratedSAP are used as accelerators for every kind of R/3 implementation in companies of all sizes. You have the possibility to use AcceleratedSAP in full or only those accelerators that support individual steps. ASAP has proven effective as the standard implementation method for SAP.

How does AcceleratedSAP affect the consulting partners of SAP?

SAP AG works with its consulting partners towards a joint objective: the timely provision of a cost-efficient, customer-specific R/3 system. They work together – not in competition – with the consulting partners to ensure successful implementation. AcceleratedSAP provides all those involved with a joint approach to the R/3 implementation. A certification program for AcceleratedSAP has been introduced worldwide.

How much does AcceleratedSAP cost?

The use of AcceleratedSAP does not generate any additional costs. AcceleratedSAP is part of the services provides by SAP and its partners. All the components of AcceleratedSAP are therefore supplied with the R/3 implementation and with upgrades. You can obtain additional material for a cover charge of 45 Euros.

Availability

As the contents and tools of AcceleratedSAP are created by an international team of experts, the English version is always available first. This is followed by the German version of AcceleratedSAP. AcceleratedSAP is also translated into other languages, including French, Spanish and Portuguese.

ASAP for upgrade projects

In addition to the 'roadmap' for the implementation and continuous optimization of the R/3 system, there is also a roadmap for upgrade projects. These roadmaps are supplied with a version of ASAP.

15.1 ROADMAP

Figure 15.1 illustrates the idea behind the roadmap. The ASAP method is a schedule for the implementation of SAP R/3 projects. The implementation is divided into five phases:

- Phase 1: Project preparation.
- Phase 2: Business blueprint.
- Phase 3: Realization.
- Phase 4: Production preparation.
- Phase 5: Go live and support.

In these phases, all the steps for carrying out a project are run through from the first meeting to the productive operation. In the following sections, you will receive a general overview of the procedure. The supporting tools will only be shown here as examples, as these need to be put together on an individual basis for each project.

15.1.1 Phase 1: Project preparation

Pool your resources. Appropriate planning and well-prepared organization are the secret of smooth implementation. As a matter of fact, planning with AcceleratedSAP is really simple (see Fig. 15.2). First of all, you have to make sure that the following requirements are met.

Acceptance

All decision-makers must be unanimously in favour of the project. From the outset, they should be in agreement that the R/3 system will support most areas of the company. Acceptance is the key to accelerating your R/3 implementation.

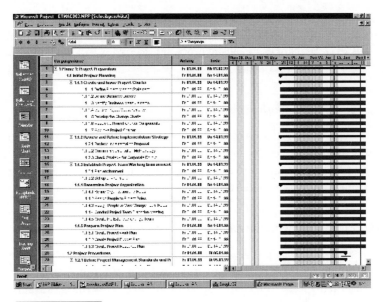

FIGURE 15.2　Prepared project plan (on ASAP CD)

Clear project objectives

- An efficient decision-making process.
- A company culture that permits change.

Now put together a team of employees from different areas of the company for the R/3 implementation, and then you can start.

Avoid nasty surprises

Your TeamSAP consultants help you to estimate your requirements and expectations. The Estimator project in AcceleratedSAP guides your team through a number of prepared questions and through interviews with the top managers and key operating managers of your company. This can be used to determine what they expect of the R/3 system and the speed of the R/3 implementation. The TeamSAP consultants evaluate the responses and estimate the overall scope of the project, including the required resources (time overhead, costs, personnel). This forms your starting point.

Learn as you go

Your internal team members begin with preliminary training, in which the necessary R/3 awareness for the product and processes is to be set up. Topics of the Level 1 training course are: the service and support structure of SAP, the framework of the implementation and SAP-specific terminology. The focal point of the R/3 curriculum is the important inter-modular business processes that simulate your real business processes. Your team uses realistic processes, scenarios and models to promote rapid and low-cost completion of the tasks.

Keep operation smooth by means of frequent inspections

While you are moving forward along the road towards R/3 implementation, you can ensure the quality of the process. An SAP specialist for quality assurance performs inspections at regular intervals. This special independent check ensures that your R/3 implementation can move straight ahead at full speed.

Start the journey with the blessing of the management team

With all systems at 'go', it's time for the executive kick-off. Your team presents the project plan and the central advantages of the R/3 implementation to the company management. You can take this opportunity to discuss the checkpoints for monitoring of targets, budgets and schedules. Finally, have your plan for R/3 implementation approved by the management team.

Your team is on the starting grid and the preparations have been completed. A trouble-free ride can be expected. The journey enters Phase 2: Business blueprint.

15.1.2 Phase 2: Business blueprint

Now it's time to document your R/3 implementation and various parameters. In management meetings, in group discussions and in one-to-one discussions, fill out a number of questionnaires. The answers help the TeamSAP consultants to get to know the central activities in your company and to document future business processes and requirements.

A blueprint for your company style

During the business blueprint phase, your TeamSAP consultants narrow down the range of functions of the R/3 systems in such a way that it fits in precisely with your industry-specific business processes. The project team uses the questionnaires and models of the R/3 implementation tools to document your business processes: the aim is to create a picture of the future appearance of your company (see Fig. 15.3). Industry profiles accelerate this process additionally by providing predefined, tried and tested business methods for different industries. At the end, you have a comprehensive blueprint of your company – your documentation for a successful R/3 implementation. AcceleratedSAP can be a great benefit in projects of all sizes. Projects that require re-engineering or operative improvements, however, are the not focal point.

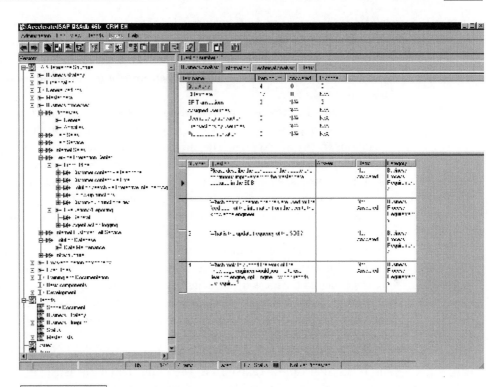

FIGURE 15.3   Sample questions from the Q & A database (on the ASAP CD) (© SAP AG)

Instead, the TeamSAP consultants help you to develop new business process methods and create the foundation for continuous improvements based on the R/3 system. The business blueprint is the design for the remainder of your R/3 implementation and also for future upgrades.

While your blueprint is being created, the members of your project team start Level 2 training in the integrated R/3 business system. They take part in basic training for all application modules, and learn the most important factors for the implementation of complete company solutions. Open the hood and use the opportunity to 'get your own hands dirty'. Level 2 training teaches you business process skills step by step. At the end of the training course, your team will be able to assemble your R/3 engine.

With the blueprint in your hand, you can now begin to configure your R/3 system. Off to Phase 3: Realization.

15.1.3 Phase 3: Realization

You have now reached cruising speed. On the basis of the business blueprint, you start the two-stage process of configuring your R/3 system. First of all, your TeamSAP consultant configures the baseline system (prototype). In a second step, the project team performs the fine tuning, where the R/3 system is adapted to your business process requirements. Let us take, for example, the area of customer orders and assume that the majority of orders for your business sector are placed by telephone. Your TeamSAP consultant configures the system for this standard case. Your baseline – or prototype – system will comprise approximately 80 percent of the transactions required for your day-to-day business.

As the initial configuration is based on the blueprint developed by your team, the baseline system provides you with an original view of the handling of your business operations in the R/3 system. The speed increases when the AcceleratedSAP process organizes your R/3 implementation with a view to the greatest possible efficiency in handling resources. Parallel activities are performed in tandem at an early stage of the process. The result is a considerable saving in time.

This is followed by Step 2, which completes the configuration and also includes the remaining 20 percent of the business operations. With the example of customer orders, settings are now made for exceptional cases: orders placed by fax and/or mail, etc. Together with your TeamSAP consultant, you divide your business processes into cycles of related business flows. These cycles are used as milestones on your project route and enable you to test certain elements of the business process with immediate feedback. This is where practical handling leads to thorough knowledge of your R/3 system.

When defining exception rules in your system, you should take a look at the 'tips and tricks' that can be called up in the Implementation Assistant. In this way, your company can profit from the broad wealth of experience of consultants from all branches of industry that have guided R/3 to productive starts all over the world. If you are in the Implementation Assistant, look for the detailed Test Guide. This will help you to group and configure business processes. You can use these simplification options to make the configuration process more efficient.

An automatic log book records your journey

During the realization phase, you can use other R/3 implementation tools, for example the Implementation Guide (IMG). If you link your newly defined project framework with the IMG, you obtain a guide that explains the configuration tasks for each process step by step. You can now use the full range of guidelines, work steps and configuration data of each R/3 component. You can also document your route to R/3 by creating notes in the IMG. You create a detailed travel diary, a log of every change or supplement you make to your R/3 system. This log book provides you with access to the latest configuration data at any time. Maybe you can imagine how this simplifies the creation of reports to your management team, and how it gets communication and support running at full throttle.

Develop your skills even further in Level 3 training

Level 3 training revs up the engine during the realization phase. In this advanced training, the project team develops the necessary skills for taking over the wheel of your R/3 system. During this training course, you can acquire specialized skills in advanced workshops that specifically take account of the special situation of your company. Your project team can also take part in industry-specific workshops, and has access to reference materials and training documents for self-directed learning. This ensures the continuous development of skills.

Future improvements are part of the plan. The system set up by your team in the realization phase forms a strong platform for continuous business change. Even when the R/3 implementation has been completed, the same processes and tools can be used to optimize business changes, expansions and system upgrades. For each change, extension or improvement, you can also create your own company-internal guidelines that facilitate a rollout to your subsidiaries.

Knowledge transfer puts you behind the steering wheel

Your project team is now firmly seated behind the wheel and is well prepared – ready to cover the rest of the journey. You reach an autonomous state effortlessly if your TeamSAP consultants pass on their R/3 know-how to the members of your project team. Now, as your R/3 baseline system is fully configured and ready for use, you continue with Phase 4: Production preparation.

15.1.4 Phase 4: Production preparation

Production preparation consists of a stringent check of your system and thorough training of the users. In this phase, your R/3 is fine-tuned before the Go Live. You make all the necessary settings to prepare your R/3 system and your company for the productive start. During the preparation for Go Live, you perform final system tests and carry out user training. The final step is to import your business data into the new system.

Test and tune for maximum performance

As you have been checking your R/3 system at regular intervals during the whole journey, the time involved for tests is now kept to a minimum. In the production preparation phase, you perform stress and throughput tests which are essential for the optimization of the capability of your system. On the basis of integration tests, in which the later conditions are simulated, the accuracy and usability of conversion and interface programs are checked.

The acceptance of the new system on the part of users is also checked, to ensure a smooth transition to the Go Live. You should also check a few preventive maintenance aspects to ensure that your R/3 system has maximum efficiency. The R/3 Going

Live Check is where SAP experts can log on to your R/3 from outside, analyse the system configuration, and offer valuable advice on optimizing the system.

Training for every single user

The key to success for your R/3 implementation is that your end users quickly become familiar with the new system. It is important that your employees feel comfortable in the R/3 system. The 'train-the-trainer' method generates a high level of acceptance, as users are trained by users – namely the experienced employees in your company. Your R/3 users are provided with the skills they need to use the R/3 system in the best possible way in their areas of work. Training is work centre-specific, so that all users know exactly how they use the R/3 system to perform their daily tasks.

Make preparations for the Go Live green light

Your project team prepares a strategy for the productive start. With your plan for gradual data conversion, you ensure that all the data from your legacy systems are transferred efficiently and accurately into the R/3–integrated information system. Preparation for the Go Live is at the same time a preparation for possible questions from users. These employees must be given the feeling at productive start that they are supported. They want to know who they can turn to with their questions. This task must be performed by your internal service. Finally, the project team sets up the first audit operations and a support structure as preparation for the home strait. When the production preparation is concluded, it is time to start the engine for Phase 5: Go Live & Support.

15.1.5 Phase 5: Go Live & Support

Going Live is more than simply a matter of turning the ignition key on your system. Until now, you have focused mainly on rapid implementation of the R/3 system with the aim of achieving long-term benefits for the company as quickly as possible.

In this phase, you have to introduce procedures and measurement methods that you can use from now on to check the benefits from your R/3 investment. The longer you are on the road with the R/3 system, the more familiar the handling of R/3 specialist know-how, product support and preventive maintenance measures will become.

The engine runs smoothly with support and services

SAP Support and SAP Services ensure that your R/3 system continues to run without disruption, cleanly and economically. Our support continues beyond setting you on the right road. SAP helps you in every phase of the R/3 life cycle. An extended network of SAP experts is available to you, whenever and wherever you need support. This means that you can access R/3 expertise, product support and maintenance services worldwide, 24 hours a day and 365 days a year. Flexible and fast-reacting Support Services can be reached by remote connections or at your local SAP branch office.

Take a look at the following services

The Online Service System (OSS) is a central communications network between you, SAP partners and SAP. With a remote connection, you can pass on questions or problems to SAP in electronic form and automatically trace the development of a solution. The Online Service System enables you access to the collection of solutions to problems experienced in the past by SAP customers.

Remote Consulting Services permit SAP consultants to log into your R/3 system directly by modem connection or by Personal Video Conferencing. During these sessions, you can transfer your requests to the remote consultant – technical questions, process- and application-specific problems, through to aspects of upgrade support.

After Go-Live, EarlyWatch&trade offers you active system diagnosis. SAP can use EarlyWatch&trade to detect potential problems at an early stage and provide immediate help. In this way, you can always rely on optimum availability and performance capability of the system. Our Support Services have been set up with your requirements in mind. You can rely on SAP accompanying you along the path to success, even if your requirements continue to develop.

With speed and skill we have overtaken the competition

You've made it: your R/3 system is productive. You have reached the finish in record time and have been economical with your resources. Now that your R/3 system is fully equipped, your company will start to exploit a *Return On Information* and *Return On Investment (ROI)* never achieved before.

It is now time to get back to what you do best: leading your company towards success. In the final analysis, this is what SAP R/3 is all about.

15.2   ADVANTAGES FOR THE IMPLEMENTATION PROJECT

AcceleratedSAP optimizes the time invested, quality and efficient deployment of all resources by coordinating all the activities needed for successful conclusion of your R/3 project.

The most important advantages are:

▨ *Faster R/3 implementation for faster profitability*

A target-oriented project management and a detailed project plan with predefined work steps and quality checks help to keep R/3 projects under control. 'The greatest danger is creeping growth of the project.'

'A fast implementation pays off in faster profitability.' These are some typical reactions from companies of all sizes and from all industries. AcceleratedSAP provides strategies that help you to separate what is important from what is not, and to perform a process-oriented implementation.

▨ *Worldwide standardized implementation process*

No matter whether you are implementing R/3 on a company-wide basis or working with other consulting firms abroad, all consultants have access to AcceleratedSAP and use it for your R/3 implementation.

▨ *Quality checks and know-how transfers*

A quality check is built into the close of every phase in AcceleratedSAP. SAP also offers evaluations to asses the project progress and indicate possible risk factors in an R/3 implementation. Furthermore, the SAP consultants make their know-how available to the R/3 team at the customer during the realization phase to ensure that the customer is independent after the implementation.

▨ *Efficient use of available resources*

It is a well-known fact that every project could do with more staff. Some have obligations elsewhere, others are deployed in different locations ... AcceleratedSAP takes account of these circumstances and recommends the background knowledge, experience and other knowledge the members of the project team should have.

▨ *Reusability for future implementations*

Documents such as the Business Blueprint can be used again for a company-wide implementation or a new R/3 phase or, where necessary, adapted and extended.

▨ *Everything in one location*

If you have already implemented an R/3 project, you probably have your own versions of many accelerators. However, ASAP provides you with all the components in one location from the outset. You don't have to reinvent the wheel with us.

▨ *Uniform documentation of the R/3 solution*

ASAP contains a uniform concept for all types of document typically created during the implementation process. Where possible, documents are reused. For example, parts of the Business Blueprint are integrated in the user documentation.

▨ *Nothing is forgotten*

AcceleratedSAP ensures that nothing is left out. In particular, it coordinates the interaction between business and technical tasks: our studies have shown that project managers normally need more support in these two areas – depending on their background.

▨ *Insight into the implementation process*

With the AcceleratedSAP Roadmap, it is easier than ever before to understand the implementation process, especially when there are people on the team who have never carried out an R/3 implementation. No one has difficulty understanding where they currently are, what is planned, what the components of each individual phase are, why they do this or that, and so on.

▨ *Concentration on early project stages*

AcceleratedSAP takes care of numerous operations that are easily underestimated and have often in the past been dealt with too late, for example the conversion of data, the configuration of interfaces or the assignment of access rights. The rule of thumb is that problems must be determined in the business blueprint phase, so that they can be tackled with one eye on the budget, the timeframe and the available resources. This applies in particular to possible functional gaps.

Glossary

ABAP/4   Abbreviation for Advanced Business Application Programming. SAP's own programming language which can be used to program applications for the R/3 system, system extensions and reports. The extension /4 means that it is a fourth-generation programming language (among other things, object-oriented).

ASAP (AcceleratedSAP)   A collection of methods and tools for accelerated implementation of SAP R/3.

Batch   Part quantity of a material kept separately from other part quantities of the same material in the stock.

Example: Different production lots (e.g. in the case of paints or drugs), delivery lots, quality levels of a material.

Batch input   Description of the interface for data transfer. Above all for the transfer of large quantities of data from the legacy system before the productive start, but also for large-scale data imports later on.

Batch master record   If a supplied material or a material from own production are subject to batch operation, a batch master record is created. The relevant data for the batch is stored in this master record.

Business process   A process/business process is a chain of business activities with determinable individual results.

Catalog   Catalogs are used for uniform description of defects, decisions, tasks and much more. In R/3, there are a great many catalogs in which the user can enter codes and written texts. In addition to the catalog types created by SAP in the standard version, other, user-specific catalogs can be added.

Client   A group or composition of legal, organizational, commercial and/or administrative units with one shared purpose (example: a corporate group).

Client   In the context of client–server configurations, the client is the workstation (or PC) on which the graphical user interface (SAPGUI) is installed.

Company code   Smallest organizational unit of external accounting for which full, autonomous accounting can be set up.

Completion, commercial   Function run for a maintenance order if no more cost postings are to be expected. The commercial completion of a maintenance order has the effect that the order is given the status 'completed' and that it is locked for all changes in processing. The commercial completion can only be made when the maintenance order has already been technically completed.

Completion, technical   Function run for a maintenance order if the planned work has been performed. The technical completion of a maintenance order has the effect that:

▧ Only certain changes can be made for the order.

▧ Data are fixed and can no longer be changed.

▧ Outstanding order requests, reservations, etc. are deleted.

▧ The Plant Maintenance notifications for the order are completed.

Confirmation   Function used to record the drawn materials, working hours used, additional materials required, travel costs incurred, technical findings and changes made.

Confirmation, technical   Recording of technical confirmation data. This data includes, e.g.:

▧ Cause of damage.

▧ Location of damage on object.

▧ Data on machine downtimes.

▧ Data on system availability.

▧ Actions performed and findings.

Cost accounting code   Organizational unit within a company for which full, autonomous cost accounting can be performed. A cost accounting code can comprise one or more company codes which use different currencies. The associated company codes must all use the same operational chart of accounts.

Cost centre   Organizational unit within a cost accounting code representing a clearly delineated location of cost generation.

Customer master record   This master record contains all the necessary information on a customer from the point of view of Sales and Distribution and Accounting. The customer appears in Accounting among accounts receivable.

Customizing   Setting the R/3 system to company-specific requirements.

Dynamic modification, dynamic modification rule   This permits changes to the inspection severity and sampling scope for an inspection.

Equipment   Individual, physical object which is to be maintained independently; it can be installed in a technical system or a subsystem. Each item of equipment is managed in a separate equipment master record. Equipment is used in Plant Maintenance and in the following areas:

▧ Production (production resources/tools).

▧ Quality assurance (test equipment and measuring devices).

- Materials Management (serialized materials).

- Sales and Distribution (customer devices).

Histogram   Display of quantitative measured values as a frequency distribution.

IDES   IDES is the sample company in the R/3 system, set up for the purposes of training and demonstration. IDES is the abbreviation for International Demonstration and Education System. Most of the screen dumps in this book were created using IDES.

Inspection instruction   Work paper specifying the inspection characteristics and test equipment for each inspection operation.

Inspection lot   Order to inspect a certain quantity of a material or equipment. Inspection lots can be created automatically or manually. The inspection lot contains important information (e.g. creation date, lot size, sample size, vendor, etc.). It summarizes the data involved in the inspection such as inspection specifications, inspection results, appraisal costs and usage decision.

Inspection plan   In this plan type, inspection planning records all the elements from the area of quality inspection. These include, for example, the inspection steps (operations and characteristics), sampling procedures, test equipment, equipping and inspection times, and inspection work centres.

Inspection severity   Generic term for the different scopes of the inspection depending on the quality level. A distinction is made between reduced, normal and increased inspections.

Logistics   The logistics chain stretches from raw materials production and procurement across a large number of processes, all the way to the sale of the final product – whether goods or services.

Maintenance plan   A method of describing the scope and schedule for the maintenance and inspection tasks to be performed on technical objects.

A distinction is made between three types of maintenance plan:

- Time-dependent maintenance plans.

- Output-dependent maintenance plans.

- Multiple counter plans.

A maintenance plan consists of:

- Maintenance schedule.

- Maintenance item(s).

Material   Goods that are the object of business activity. A material can be purchased, sold, produced, maintained, repaired or replaced.

Material number   Number that uniquely identifies a material in the R/3 system.

Material specification   The material specification can be used as an inspection specification instead of an inspection plan or as a supplement to an inspection plan.

Partner   Unit within or outside your own organization which is of interest from a business point of view and with which a relationship can be set up within the framework of a business activity. A partner can be a person or a legal entity.

Examples of partners:

- Partners within your own organization

  - Sales manager

  - Test equipment management clerk

  - Test equipment user.

▓ Partners outside your own organization

- Customers
- Prospective customers
- Contacts.

Plant   Organizational unit in Logistics, which structures the company. Materials are produced and/or goods and services are provided in a plant.

Plant maintenance task list   Standardized sequence of work operations for performance of certain maintenance work on equipment. The plant maintenance task list is not linked to a certain item of equipment. It contains all the operations, materials and operating resources required for a certain maintenance task.

Production resources/tools (PRT)   Production resources/tools are operating resources involved in shaping (e.g. tool, device) or that are used to check adherence to dimensions, properties and functional requirements (e.g. measurement and test equipment). Production resources/tools can also be information resources such as drawings or programs. Production resources/tools are assigned to operations in task lists or plant orders where they are required. They are abbreviated to PRT.

Profit centre   Organizational unit in Accounting, which divides the company with a management orientation, i.e. for the purpose of internal control.

Purchasing organization   Organizational unit within Logistics, which structures the company according to the needs of Purchasing. A purchasing organization procures materials and/or services; it negotiates purchasing terms with the vendors and is responsible for this business.

Quality level (Q level)   The quality level is a data record in which the inspection stage for the next inspection is stored. It creates a reference between the material, dynamification level and vendors, and contains information such as the number of inspections that were OK, and the number of inspections since the last stage change.

Quality score (QS)   A number calculated for the quality delivered by a vendor. It is determined from the code of the usage decision or from the proportion of defects. Typically, the score is between 1 and 100, whereby 100 represents a very good valuation.

Random sample inspection   Quality inspection based on a sampling instruction for evaluation of an inspection lot.

Report   ABAP/4 program that reads data from the database and usually prepares and outputs it in list form.

Report Writer   The Report Writer is a utility that can be used to create reports for various applications on an individual basis.

Routing   Work preparation uses this plan type to record all the elements from the area of work planning. These include, for example, the work steps (operations), the production resources/tools, equipping and working times, work centres.

Run chart   Display of the development of values as a curving graph.

SAA standard   Abbreviation for System Application Architecture. A standard created by IBM which, among other things, also standardizes the user interface and the arrangement of menu items.

Sample drawing instruction   Work paper with important information required for the drawing of random samples or physical samples from an inspection lot.

Sampling instruction   Instruction on the scope of the sample to be drawn.

Sampling procedure   Rule for calculation of the sampling scope.

Sampling scheme   Collection of sampling instructions according to higher-order factors resulting from the sampling system. For example, the acceptable quality limits and the inspection level are used as higher-order factors.

Sampling system   Collection of sampling schemes with rules for their application.

SAPscript   Page description language for structuring texts and forms.

Serial number   Number that is assigned to a single item of material in addition to the material number to enable a distinction between the individual item and all other items of this material. The combination of material number and serial number is unique.

Standard plan   The standard plan contains virtually all the objects of the task list and the inspection plan. It is used mainly as a plan profile for variations of a plan or as a general template.

Stock type   Three stock types are possible for a material:

- Released stock.

- Quality stock.

- Blocked stock.

Storage location   Organizational unit enabling a distinction between material stocks within a plant.

Test equipment and measuring devices   Facilities, objects, documents or substances required before or during the inspection. Test equipment can be fixed facilities of a work centre, portable devices, or objects.

In the inspection plan of the R/3 system, test equipment can be defined on different levels of detail:

- Group level (product group).

- Material level (material number, type).

- Single item (equipment).

Test equipment can be maintained using maintenance plans.

Transaction   Logically completed operation in the R/3 system. From the point of view of the user, a transaction is a completed application on application level (e.g. the creation of a list of inspection lots or inspection lot creation).

Variable check   Quality inspection based on quantitative characteristics.

Vendor   Business partner who supplies materials or services for payment. The vendor appears in Accounting among accounts payable.

Vendor master record   Data record containing all the information necessary for business activities with a vendor. This data includes e.g. address data and bank data.

Work centre   Organizational unit that specifies where and by whom an operation is to be performed. The work centre has a certain available capacity. The work performed at or by the work centre is valuated with clearing rates determined by the cost centres and activity types. The following units can be defined as work centres:

- Machines.

- People.

- Assembly lines.

- Teams.

Abbreviations

ABAP	Advanced Business Application Programming
ALE	Application Link Enabling Loose linking of distributed applications
AQAP	Allied Quality Assurance Publications
AQL	Acceptable Quality Level
ASAP	Accelerated SAP Accelerated implementation of R/3
BAPI	Business Application Programming Interface
BOR	Business Object Repository
CAQ	Computer Aided Quality Assurance
CATT	Computer Aided Test Tool Additional tool for testing individual software developments
CIP	Continuous Improvement Process
CSP	Complementary Software Program Program extensions from software partners
DRM	Distributor Reseller Management
EDP	Electronic Data Processing
EFQM	European Foundation for Quality Management
EIS	Executive Information System

EPC	Event-controlled Process Chain
ESD	Electro Static Discharge
PRT	Production Resources/Tools
FIS	Financial Information System
FMEA	Failure Mode and Effects Analysis
GMP	Good Manufacturing Practice Quality requirements of the processing industry
IAC	Internet Application Component SAP transactions for internet applications
IDES	International Demo and Education System Fully configured model company
IDI	Inspection Data Interface Interface for exchange of inspection data
IMG	Implementation Guide
OK	OK (no defects discovered)
ISO	International Standardization Organization
IT	Information technology e.g. EDP facilities
LAN	Local Area Network (company-internal network)
LDAP	Lightweight Directory Access Control
LIB	Logistics Information Library
LIMS	Laboratory Information and Management System
LIS	Logistics Information System
NOK	Not OK (defective)
OIW	SAP Open Information Warehouse
PDF	Portable Document Format File format for Adobe Acrobat
PIS	Personnel Information System
QS	Quality Score
QM	Quality Management
QMIS	Quality Management Information System
QCC	Quality Control Chart
RFC	Remote Function Call
SAA	System Application Architecture
SPC	Statistical Process Control
SQL	Structured Query Language Query language for relational databases
SSL	Secure Sockets Layer
STI	Statistical Data Interface Interface for exchange of statistical data

VDA	Verband der deutschen Automobilindustrie e.V. (Federation of German Automobile Industry)
UD	Usage Decision
WAN	Wide Area Network Cross-company networking
XML	Extensible Markup Language

Bibliography

Bernecker, K. (1990). *Anleitung zur Statistischen Prozeßlenkung.* DGQ Schrift Nr. 16–33, 1st edn. 1990.

DGQ (1987). *Rechnerunterstützung in der Qualitätssicherung.* DGQ Schrift Nr. 14–20, 1st edn.

DGQ (1987). *Begriffe im Bereich der Qualitätssicherung.* DGQ Schrift Nr. 11–04, 4th edn.

DIN, Deutsches Institut für Normung (German Standards Institute) (1993) *DIN ISO 2859–1. Annahmestichprobenprüfung anhand der Anzahl fehlerhafter Einheiten oder Fehler (Attributprüfung).* Beuth Verlag, Berlin.

DIN, Deutsches Institut für Normung (German Standards Institute) (1994). *DIN EN ISO 9000–1. Normen zum Qualitätsmanagement und zur Qualitätssicherung/QM-Darlegung, Part 1: Leitfaden zur Auswahl und Anwendung.* Beuth Verlag, Berlin.

DIN, Deutsches Institut für Normung (German Standards Institute) (1994). *DIN EN ISO 9001. Qualitätsmanagementsysteme. Modell zur Qualitätssicherung/QM-Darlegung in Design, Entwicklung, Produktion, Montage und Wartung.* Beuth Verlag, Berlin.

DIN, Deutsches Institut für Normung (German Standards Institute) (1994). *DIN EN ISO 9004–1. Qualitätsmanagement und Elemente eines Qualitätsmanagementsystems, Teil 1: Leitfaden.* Beuth Verlag, Berlin.

DIN, Deutsches Institut für Normung (German Standards Institute) (1995). *DIN EN ISO 8402. Quality Management. Terms.* Beuth Verlag, Berlin.

DIN, Deutsches Institut für Normung (German Standards Institute) (1996). *DIN EN ISO 14001. Umweltmanagementsysteme Spezifikation mit Anleitung zur Anwendung.* Beuth Verlag, Berlin.

DIN, Deutsches Institut für Normung (German Standards Institute) (1999). E DIN EN ISO 9001. 2000. Qualitätsmanagement – Systeme – Forderungen. Beuth Verlag, Berlin.

Fischer, P. (1999). *Computer- & Internet-Lexikon*. SmartBooks, CH-Kilchberg.

Ford/General Motors/Chrysler (1995). *QM System Requirements QS 9000*. Carwin Continous Ltd., Essex, England, 2nd edn.

Hake, D., Steil, H., Stowasser, M. (1999). Qualitätsoffensive in der Automobilindustrie. *QZ*, Jahrg. 44, p. 1244.

Kaltenbach, T. and Woerrlein, H. (1992). *Das große Computer Lexikon*. Markt & Technik, Munich, 3. Aufl.

Keller, G. (1999). *SAP R/3 prozeßorientiert anwenden*. Addison-Wesley, Munich, 3rd edn.

Kuba, W. (1987). *Computergestützte Projektorganisation*. Verlagsgesellschaft Rudolf Müller GmbH.

Masing, W. (ed.) (1988). *Handbuch der Qualitätssicherung*. Hanser Verlag, Munich, 2nd edn.

Meissner, G. (1997). SAP – die heimliche Software-Macht. Hoffmann und Campe, Hamburg.

Möhrlen, R. and Kokot, F. (1998). *SAP R/3–Kompendium*. Markt & Technik, Munich.

Perez, M. (1998). *Geschäftsprozesse im Internet mit SAP R/3*. Addison-Wesley, Munich.

SAP AG (ed.) (1999). *Initial Data Transfer Made Easy – Step by Step Guide to SAP Initial Data Transfer*. Walldorf.

SAP AG (ed.) (1999). *Functions in detail – Plant Maintenance*. Walldorf.

SAP AG (ed.) (1999). *Functions in detail – Quality, Management*. Walldorf.

SAP AG (ed.) (1999). *Functions in detail – Service Management*. Walldorf.

SAP AG (ed.) (1999) SAP R/3 Quality Management CD-ROM. Walldorf.

Sobotta, H.(1999). Auch die einfache Lösung führt zum Ziel. *QZ*, Jahrg. 44, p. 76.

Steinbach, W. and Masing, W. (1998). Manual of Quality Assurance. HanserVerlag, Munich, 2nd edn.

Taucher, F. (1999). Neues Denken in Prozessen. *QZ*, Jahrg. 44 , p. 1197.

VDA (1998). *Quality Management in the Automobile Industry. Sicherung der Qualität von Lieferungen*, vol. 2. Verband der Automobilindustrie eV, 3rd edn.

VDA (1995). *Sicherung der Qualität in der Automobilindustrie. Sicherung der Qualität vor Serieneinsatz*. Band 4, Teil 1+2. Verband der Automobilindustrie eV, 2nd edn.

VDA (1998). *Qualitätsmanagement in der Automobilindustrie. QM System Audit*. Band 4, Teil 1+2. Verband der Automobilindustrie eV, 4th edn.

VDA (1995). *Quality Management in the Automobile Industry. Grundlagen zum Austausch von Qualitätsdaten*, vol. 7. Verband der Automobilindustrie eV, 2nd edn.

VDI/VDE-Gesellschaft Meß- und Regelungstechnik (1985). *VDI/VDE/DGQ 2619 Prüfplanung*. Beuth Verlag, Berlin.

Index

ABAP/4 (language) 51, 440
    ABAP Query 337
    reports 337–8
Accelerated SAP *see* ASAP
accreditation 3
action log 318
activities, in quality notification 308–11
Advanced Business Application Programming
        see ABAP/4 (language)
Allied Quality Assurance Publications *see*
        AQAP
allocation values 166–7
analyses 333–5
application help in R/3 system 70–1
appraisal costs 155, 228–9, 281–2
approval of products for delivery 81
AQAP (Allied Quality Assurance Publications)
        2, 3
ASAP (Accelerated SAP) 428–39, 440
assemblies 295
    displaying 295, 297
attribute inspections 93
audit inspection 262

BAPIs (Business Application Programming
        Interfaces) 241
batch administration 83–4, 234, 249–50
batch input 83–4, 85, 440
batch logs 280–1
batch management *see* batch administration
batch master record 106–7, 440
window 107
batch tracing 86
batches 440
BC *see* SAP Basis Components (BC)
bill of materials *see* assemblies
Business Application Programming Interfaces
        see BAPIs

Business Directory 380
business processes 17, 440
    modelling 18
    use of reference models 19–20
Business Workflow 303–4, 315–16
buttons 58, 59

capability 92
CAQ *see* Computer Aided Quality Assurance
        (CAQ)
catalog structure 114–15
catalog types 112–14
catalogs 110–15, 440
certificate processing 195–9
certificate profiles 196–8
certificate receipt 249
certificates 8, 87, 190, 232
    creation over the internet 375–8
change master records 104–6, 146–8
change record 146
characteristics 94, 154–5, 157–67, 192
    attributive *see* characteristics, qualitative
    control indicators 157–61, 186
    defect codes 166
    dependent 163–4
    inspection plan structure 148
    leading 163–4
    qualitative 157, 162, 217–18
    quantitative 157, 162–3, 219–20
    recording results 214–25
    required 221
    test equipment assignment 155–6, 164–5
    unplanned 221
    updating allocation values 166–7
    valuation types 223
checkboxes 61
client concept 48–9
client-server architecture 33, 440

450